Patristic Essentials

Christianity in the First and Second Centuries: Essential Readings. Edited by Kevin Douglas Hill. Introduction by Paul Foster.

CHRISTIANITY IN THE FIRST AND SECOND CENTURIES

Christianity in the First and Second Centuries: Essential Readings

Edited by Kevin Douglas Hill

Introduction by Paul Foster

Fontes

Christianity in the First and Second Centuries: Essential Readings

Copyright © 2022 by Kevin Douglas Hill

ISBN-13: 978-1-948048-64-4 (paperback)

All rights reserved. No part of this publication may be reproduced, stored in a retrieval system, or transmitted in any form or by any means—electronic, mechanical, photocopy, recording, or any other—except for brief quotations in printed reviews, without the prior permission of the publisher.

Excerpts from the following books were reproduced by permission of the Licensor through PLSclear: Mary Beard, John North, and Simon Price, A Sourcebook. Vol. 2 of Religions of Rome (Cambridge University Press, 1998); James E. G. Zetzel, ed., Cicero: On the Commonwealth and On the Laws (Cambridge University Press, 1999); Delbert Burkett, An Introduction to the New Testament and the Origins of Christianity (Cambridge University Press, 2002) reproduced with permission of the Licensor through PLSclear.

Typesetting by Monolateral

FONTES PRESS
DALLAS, TX
www.fontespress.com

Contents

Series Preface xi

1. Introduction, by Paul Foster 1
    1.1. Christianity in the Second Century 1
    1.2. The Apostolic Fathers 2
        1.2.1. First Clement 4
        1.2.2. The Letters of Ignatius of Antioch 6
        1.2.3. Polycarp, *Letter to the Philippians* 8
        1.2.4. The Didache 9
        1.2.5. The Shepherd of Hermas 12
        1.2.6. Other Writings in the Apostolic Fathers Collection 14
    1.3. The Early Christian Apologists 22
    1.4. Conclusion 25

2. The First Epistle of Clement to the Corinthians 27

3. The Second Epistle of Clement 59

4. The Letters of Ignatius 69
    To the Ephesians 69
    To the Magnesians 76
    To the Trallians 77
    To the Romans 79
    To the Philadelphians 81
    To the Smyrnaeans 82
    To Polycarp 85

5. The Letter of Polycarp to the Philippians 89

6. The Martyrdom of Polycarp 95

7. Didache 105

8. The Epistle of Barnabas 113

9. The Shepherd of Hermas 127

10. The Epistle to Diognetus 161

11. The Apology of Quadratus 171

12. The Fragments of Papias 173

13. The Apology of Aristides 177

14. Justin Martyr: The First Apology 189

15. Justin Martyr: The Second Apology 219

16. Justin Martyr: The Dialogue with Trypho 227
17. Tatian the Syrian: Address to the Greeks 267
18. Athenagoras of Athens: Embassy for the Christians 275
19. Theophilus of Antioch: Apology to Autolycus 293
    Book 1 293
    Book 2 298

Appendix 1: Select Readings on Greco-Roman Religion
and the Imperial Cult 307

Appendix 2: Select Readings on Persecution and the Early
Church 311

Further Reading 323

Translations Used in this Volume 327

Scripture Index 329

Dedication

This volume is dedicated to all past and present translators of Scripture and ancient Christian literature.

Series Preface

Since the middle of the twentieth century, English readers have seen a resurgence in English translations and editions of early Christian texts, including writings from the Patristic era.[1] New translations and critical editions have been produced for both popular and lesser-known texts. Compilations dedicated to specific themes have also emerged, such as a series on Patristic interpretations of Scripture. In light of this resurgence, readers may ask, quite understandably, do we need another series?

This series was borne out of the conviction that, despite this welcome resurgence in Patristic resources, certain gaps remain. With the increasing number of Patristic works available, students and non-experts face greater difficulties determining which texts to focus on. Should one begin with the classics, such as those by Athanasius and Augustine, and then move out from there? Or is it best to work through early Christian literature chronologically? Regardless of one's chosen path, readers must still determine the specific works and editions to read. Older translations of many works are available online, but these translations are often in archaic English, and they do not benefit from the latest scholarship and critical editions. Modern translations and editions benefit from improved accuracy and readability, but at times they are difficult to access due to cost and availability.

The present series aims to partially solve these problems by providing expertly curated readings in accessible translations at an affordable cost. Each volume includes a helpful introduction written by a leading or emerging scholar. To reduce cost, existing translations have been revised to reflect contemporary English and improve accuracy in consultation with the original

---

[1] Loosely defined as the period from about the end of the first century AD to the Second Council of Nicaea (AD 787).

languages (using critical editions where possible). The editors and curators have also consulted newer translations of difficult passages (indicated in the footnotes). To make references and further research more accessible to a broad English audience, references have been generally restricted to a limited number of useful secondary sources available in English, and the names of Patristic texts and other ancient works have been given in English rather than Latin.

The specific writers and texts included in each volume have been carefully considered to provide selections that will represent the broader body of Patristic literature and will also be useful to readers as diverse as students, theologians, and church leaders. To facilitate this goal, selections focus on the following five categories, listed alphabetically.

1. **Biblical Interpretation.** Material that represents significant early Christian hermeneutics and exegesis, including early Christian uses of Scripture, interpretations of key Scriptures, and contributions to the formation of the canon of Scripture.
2. **Christian Spirituality and Practice.** Material that represents significant early Christian ethics, spiritual practices, and other perspectives on living in the world as followers of Christ.
3. **Church History and Context.** Material that represents historical contexts, including significant early Christian events, experiences, or practices.
4. **Reception History.** Material that is of considerable influence or significance in Christian thought or in the reception of ancient Christian literature.
5. **Theology.** Material that is representative of significant early Christian theological beliefs, perspectives, debates, or questions.

In sum, Patristic Essentials is designed to provide a curated collection of essential readings from early Christian literature for a broad audience, in an accessible and attractive format, with new introductions written by experts familiar with the latest scholarship.

Jacob N. Cerone
Michael A.G. Haykin
Kevin Douglas Hill
Todd A. Scacewater

Introduction

1.1. Christianity in the Second Century

The second century was a period of fundamental importance in the history of Christianity. By this period, the challenging teachings of Jesus of Nazareth and the deep theological reflections of Paul, among others, had begun to be collected in written form. These texts provided a basis for theological thought as second-century believers formed communities of faith and developed ecclesial structures that were underpinned by the foundational ideas of these figures. Yet even these texts left certain questions unanswered and contemporary challenges unresolved. Therefore, some of the leading figures of the second century continued the tradition of attempting to resolve their problems and explain their theological beliefs in written form. However, despite the importance of the second century for the development of Christianity, the sources remain relatively sparse and there is a paucity of information about the lives of believers and their communities during this period. Instead, we are left with localized information from specific moments during that century.

One of the key sources, especially for the first half of the second century, is the collection of texts known as the Apostolic Fathers. This artificial collection, which is largely a modern construct, brings together writings that span different decades, genres, and theological perspectives. Yet despite that difference, or maybe even because of it, one can see a creative diversity of perspectives, and alongside those differing ideas, perceive a developing process of standardization in respect to certain expressions of Christian belief and the normalization of structures of leadership.

In parallel with the texts that were to become known as the Apostolic Fathers, another genre of Christian writing emerged in the second century, the *apologia* or Apology. These writings sought, in literary form, to make an intellectually reasoned and philosophically consistent defense of the practice of Christianity, addressed typically to leading figures in the Roman Empire. Whether those imperial figures ever read a single word contained in any Christian Apology is debatable. Yet, regardless of that, such writings exhibit a greater degree of confidence in the rationality of Christian faith. At the same time, these texts seek to reassure detractors that such a belief system was in essence quietistic and of no threat to the Empire. Instead, they argued, the Christian faith benefited the empire because it resulted in believers living more ethical lives while behaving generously to those in wider society. In some ways, the early Apologies represent the first sustained attempt to tackle questions of the relationship between church and state, the interplay between Christianity and civil society, and most fundamentally, how Christians can live alongside those who do not share their faith-commitments in a constructive and beneficial manner.

Therefore, together the writings of the Apostolic Fathers and the Apologists encapsulate much of the vibrancy of the developing Christian movement in the second century. Admittedly, these writings do not tell the whole story of the movement in this period. However, the insights they provide are invaluable. It is due to the perspectives and details contained in these texts that one can see the growth—numerically, structurally, and intellectually—of Christianity during this period of rapid expansion and development.

1.2. The Apostolic Fathers

In antiquity, there is little surviving evidence that the texts now known as the Apostolic Fathers were collected or circulated together. The two small exceptions both occur in great biblical codices. At the end of Codex Sinaiticus, which dates from the fourth century, after the manuscript of Revelation (or the Apocalypse of John), two further texts are to be found. These are the Epistle of Barnabas and portions of the Shepherd of Hermas. Similarly, the fifth century Codex Alexandrinus also has two further texts after Revelation. These are the writings known as the First Epistle of Clement and the Second Epistle of Clement (1–2 Clement), although the second is neither an epistle nor does it appear to be written by the same person who wrote the initial letter to the church in Corinth.

It is not until the eleventh century with Codex Hierosolymitanus (H 54), dated to June 11, 1056 on the basis of a colophon, that one finds a manuscript that contains several of the texts later designated as the Apostolic Fathers.

This codex was discovered by Philotheos Bryennios, the Metropolitan of Nicomedia, in 1873 in the library of the Jerusalem Monastery of the Holy Sepulchre at Constantinople. Later the codex was moved for safekeeping to the library of the Greek Orthodox Monastery in Jerusalem, where it is still housed. Along with other texts that were to become known as the Apostolic Fathers was the Didache, which had not been previously discovered in any manuscript. In addition, the codex contained the Epistle of Barnabas, 1–2 Clement, and the long recension of a collection of twelve letters of Ignatius. Here there is something that partially resembles the collection of texts that would later become known as the writings of the Apostolic Fathers. The next step in the development of this collection occurred with printed editions of these texts. In 1672 Jean-Baptiste Cotelier published what can be recognized as the first printed edition of texts that were to become known as the Apostolic Fathers. His volume contains seven writings (taking the letters of Ignatius as a whole). These are the Epistle of Barnabas, 1–2 Clement, the Shepherd of Hermas, the epistles of Ignatius, the Epistle of Polycarp, and the Martyrdom of Polycarp. The book was published under a Latin title that translates as *The Writings of the Fathers who Flourished in the Apostolic Period.*[1] It was not until a couple of decades later when William Wake, a future Archbishop of Canterbury, published his English edition of the same texts, under the title of *The Genuine Epistles of the Apostolic Fathers* (1693), that the label Apostolic Fathers was used as a designation for these writings. Since then, with various additions, the corpus of writings has grown, but the collective name by which these second-century texts are known has become established as the Apostolic Fathers.

Now, following the practice of taking the seven authentic letters of Ignatius as a unity, a maximalist but fairly standard collection of eleven writings has emerged. These eleven texts constitute the corpus of writings that comprise the Apostolic Fathers. Following the ordering in the third edition of Michael Holmes' volume of original language texts with English translations, these eleven writings are: 1 Clement, 2 Clement, the letters of Ignatius, the Letter of Polycarp to the Philippians, the Martyrdom of Polycarp, the Didache, the Epistle of Barnabas, the Shepherd of Hermas, the Epistle to Diognetus, the fragment of the Apology of Quadratus, and the Fragments of Papias. These texts bring together writings of different genres, broadly written in the first half of the second century—although some may be slightly earlier and a few

---

1 Jean-Baptiste Coetelier, *Ss. Patrum, qui temporibus apostolicis floruerunt, Barnabae, Clementis, Hermae, Ignatii, Polycarpi Opera, edita et inedita, vera, & supposititia: Una cum Clementis, Ignatii, Polycarpi Actis atque Martyriis* (Paris, 1672).

could be somewhat later. A couple of the writers such as Ignatius and Polycarp had met one another. Presumably, however, the majority had not. Yet, despite the fact that their writings were not composed with the intention of forming a corpus or being read together, when they are brought together, the holistic impression they create is greater than the sum of their individual impact. Together, they speak of a diverse and thriving movement. They reflect the rich literary output of a movement spread throughout various sections of the Roman Empire. Collectively, they help readers to understand how a small band of followers of a Galilean teacher evolved from a marginal radical group within Judaism to emerge as the predominant religion of the late Roman Empire, and even to stretch its influence beyond the geographical frontiers of imperial geopolitics.

1.2.1. First Clement

This lengthy letter does not name any individual as author, but instead declares itself to have been sent from the church in Rome to the church in Corinth. Perhaps a group of leaders, maybe presbyters, in Rome commissioned the letter. However, the writing has a unified style which suggests its composition was the work of a single person writing on behalf of the leaders of the church in Rome. The letter is written in response to a situation in Corinth that had developed when the established leaders in that community were forced from office. The letter extols the virtues of peace and concord, and it rejects dissension and factionalism. However, alongside this central concern the letter is wide-ranging in the topics it covers. An uncharitable assessment might be that the author loses focus. That judgement would likely be incorrect. It appears that the range of topics addressed is intended for the purpose of building common-ground and establishing a shared core of theological beliefs. From this foundation, the author is then able to respond to the trickier topic of disputes over leadership in the Corinthian community. This approach is instructive in regard to the relationship between Christian communities around the beginning of the second century. The leaders of the church in Rome appear to have had a global view of the church. This meant they were concerned about the disunity and tensions in Corinth and thus they were willing to offer guidance. However, at the time the letter was written, there does not yet appear to be a formal structure or hierarchy in the church of Rome that authorized the proffering of advice to another group. That may account for the tactful, cautious, and lengthy preamble prior to addressing the main topic of concern more fully.

The letter falls broadly into two sections. The first section (1 Clement 1–38) describes the reason for writing as being "questions disputed among you" (1.1) and more specifically that "the worthless rose up against those who were in honor; those of no reputation rose up against the renowned, the foolish against the prudent, the young against the old" (3.2). However, in the remainder of the first section these problems are only addressed tangentially. The approach is to set out examples and general principles drawn from Scripture and other commonly known sources. For instance, immediately after having described the leadership dispute as the basis for writing, the letter discusses the examples of Cain and Abel and other biblical figures (4.1–13). The repeated refrain is that "jealousy" caused Cain to murder his brother, "jealousy" caused Joseph's brothers to sell him into slavery, and from the author's perspective "jealousy" was a factor in the stories of Moses and David. The discussion of this general theme continues with more recent examples—especially Peter and Paul being put to death due to jealousy, then the discussion continues by noting the call and opportunity for repentance (chs. 7–8). Thus, while in this section these themes are in general not explicitly related to the contemporary situation in Corinth, no doubt the first hearers of the letter as it was read in that city cannot have failed to perceive the purpose of laying out these examples.

After a brief transitional unit (ch. 39), the second section (chs. 40–65) then more directly applies the lessons outlined in the first section to the current situation of factions and dissension in Corinth. That the earlier material in the first part of the letter was presented as examples to be followed is apparent in the opening of the second part. The author states, "Since these things are apparent to us, and we have looked into the depths of the divine knowledge, we ought to do in order all things that the Master commanded us to perform at appointed times" (40.1). Greater clarity on the root cause of the dispute is provided when the letter states that the apostles knew "there would be strife for the title of bishop" (44.1). The letter claims that appointment to the office of bishop was to be permanent, and hence only when the officer-holder died was a replacement to be appointed (44.2). The letter concludes by drawing attention to the letter-carriers or envoys who were sent with the letter. It is stated that their purpose is to report back to the Roman community concerning a return to "peace and harmony" in Corinth when the community returns to "good order" (65.1).

This text, written toward the end of the first century or the beginning of the second century, reveals much about the problems that faced early Christian communities and the way these disparate groups were linked and in fact viewed themselves as part of a larger whole. It becomes apparent that such small groups could be susceptible to forceful individuals or subgroups wishing to take control. This suggests that clear lines of leadership succession were not in place, even despite the clear intentions that the letter attributes to the apostles. Notwithstanding this, such acts of usurping leadership were not immune from criticism for other Christ communities. Thus, it is possible to see a continued network of believing communities. This perhaps signals the initial stages of a wider ecclesial hierarchy that transcended strictly local leadership. At the very least the actions of a single group were to be held accountable by other Christian communities. Consequently, this lengthy letter provides key insights into early Christian theology and ecclesiology, and it reveals some of the structural developments that were required to transform individual communities dependent on charismatic and unstable leadership into a wider movement with a sense of global identity and a regularized form of leadership and succession.

1.2.2. The Letters of Ignatius of Antioch

Ignatius is perhaps the best-known figure among the Apostolic Fathers. The executed bishop of Antioch left behind an epistolary legacy that was written during a period of a few weeks while he was being transported to Rome. The concentrated and impassioned rhetoric of his letters is matched by a profound theological reflection on Christology, eucharistic beliefs, ecclesiology, and rejection of what he deems to be false beliefs. Today, his letters survive in three revised editions: the so-called short, middle, and long recensions. Scholars generally understand the seven letters of the middle recension to represent Ignatius' authentic writings. The significance of his ideas is perhaps attested by the degree of tampering the letter collection suffered in subsequent centuries. The longer recension developed in at least two stages. First, the original seven letters were interpolated and several addition letters written in Greek were added to the corpus. These modifications promote the views of the ultra-Arians in the second half of the fourth century. Later still, several Latin letters were added to the letter collection. These additional epistles portray a correspondence between Ignatius and the virgin Mary. These stem from a later period reflecting heightened devotion to Mary.

However, the seven original letters provide striking theological affirmations. They unambiguously declare Jesus to be God. Alongside this, they affirm the full humanity of Christ and the reality of his sufferings. This was in direct response to the views of those who have been called docetists. That is, those who claimed that Christ's humanity and sufferings were not real, but only in appearance (Gk: δοκέω = *dokeō*, "I appear"). Furthermore, Ignatius is the first Christian writer to clearly set out a pattern of threefold ministry comprising a single bishop in each location, supported by a council of presbyters or elders, with deacons carrying out many practical ministries for the wider community and supporting the bishop. Ignatius portrays those who oppose the legitimate local bishop as being enemies of God. Here it is possible to discern a move away from a more free-form style of Christian meetings and leadership to a structure that is regularized and hierarchical in nature. There is also a more developed understanding of the Eucharist that aligns with the christological beliefs of Ignatius. Hence, in response to false teachers with suspect views about the reality of Christ's humanity, he further asserts that "they abstain from Eucharist and prayer, because they do not confess that the Eucharist is the flesh of our Savior Jesus Christ" (Ignatius, *To the Smyrnaeans* 7.1). Furthermore, without hesitation or considering the statement to be controversial, Ignatius repeatedly describes Jesus Christ as being God or our God. Thus, in his opening salutation to the believers in Ephesus he tells them that they are "united and elect through true suffering by the will of the Father and Jesus Christ our God" (Ignatius, *To the Ephesians* salut.). Writing to the church in Smyrna he states "I give glory to Jesus Christ, the God who has given you wisdom" (Ignatius, *To the Smyrnaeans* 1.1). So albeit without the ontological language of later fourth century christological debates, Ignatius describes Christ as being both human and yet also God.

It would be a failing simply to read the letters of Ignatius in light of contested and controversial theological opinions. Fundamentally, he seeks to teach recipients of his letters about ethics and the practice of righteous living. The pairing of faith and love is repeated at several points in his letters, and these virtues are the cardinal characteristics that should exemplify Christian life (cf. Ignatius, *To the Ephesians* 14.1; *To the Smyrnaeans* 6.1). Like several of his near contemporaries, Ignatius' call for appropriate ethical behavior is motivated by eschatological considerations. Believers are to know that they are living in the last times, that there is a coming judgment, and that they are to be motivated to correct living both because of the grace they have received and because of the coming judgment (Ignatius, *To the Ephesians* 11.1).

It is striking that in these emotionally-charged letters, written under the duress of impending execution, Ignatius writes with such clarity while interlocking many fundamental ideas of theology and ecclesiology. It is unlikely that all these perspectives were conceived during the period of transportation to Rome. As such, writing at some point in the first quarter of the second century, Ignatius is illustrative of the developments and the mode of articulation of Christian faith and belief during that period.

1.2.3. Polycarp, *Letter to the Philippians*

It could be argued that Polycarp was the central figure of the Christian movement in the second century. This might appear to be an overblown claim given that scholars generally attribute to him only one relatively short surviving letter. However, what is written about him and to him reveals the esteem from other Christian leaders. This, coupled with his lengthy period as a Christian leader in Smyrna, means that his influence spans across much of the second century.

Polycarp's *Letter to the Philippians* is both a responsive and pastoral epistle. It was written to address issues that were raised in another letter sent to him by the Christian community at Philippi. The responsive letter states that at the invitation of the Philippians, Polycarp was addressing them on the topic of righteousness. However, the topic was not selected out of arcane or academic interest. As the letter unfolds there are repeated warnings against the temptation to become enamored with money. Yet, it is not until late in the letter that it becomes apparent that the issue of love of money is being discussed because of a misdemeanor that occurred in the community. Polycarp speaks directly about the case of Valens, a former presbyter, and his unnamed wife. The letter states that Polycarp is grieved by the case of Valens because "he so little understands the [office] that was given to him" (Polycarp, *To the Philippians* 11.1). Although Polycarp does not describe exactly what Valens had done (the Philippians already knew the details) his stinging denouncement of the love of money makes it clear that Valens had committed a financial misdemeanor. In exasperated tones Polycarp asks the rhetorical question, "How may he who cannot attain self-control in these matters enjoin it on another?" (11.2). Following on from this question Polycarp declares the love of money to be a form of idolatry, and he warns that those tempted by wealth will be subject to the judgment of the Lord. It is impossible to reconstruct the precise details of the offense, but assuming that it involved some form of embezzlement from the community's funds is probably close to the mark.

While Polycarp reveals his deep disappointment at what has happened, nonetheless he remains the consummate pastor. He tells the Philippians that he is "deeply sorry" for both Valens and his wife, and he prays that the Lord may offer him true repentance (11.4). To some that may seem to be little more than a carefully constructed set-piece. However, what follows suggests that Polycarp was genuinely concerned for the well-being and restoration of

Valens. He counsels the Philippians, despite what has happened, to be reasonable in this matter, and he states specifically in relation to Valens and his wife "do not regard such people as enemies, but call them back as fallible and straying members, that you may make whole the body of you all" (11.4). In this way, Polycarp is perhaps best understood as a pastoral theologian. That is, he was a leader who reflected on the Christian message and its core theological commitments in light of ecclesial needs and pressing pastoral concerns.

That assessment stands in contrast to others who have seen little theological value in this writing. In dismissive tones, Thomas Torrance damned it as being "a little disappointing to the student of historical theology."[2] A couple of decades earlier an even more negative assessment was made in German scholarship. Martin Dibelius impugned the writing as "a completely unoriginal, very insignificant but well-intended letter."[3] While it is the case that in no sense can Polycarp's letter be characterized as a work of systematic theology, such assessments appear to judge the theological values by the norms of a later period and do not adequately recognize the significant theological contribution the letter makes in a particular context addressing specific pastoral questions.

Polycarp may not have left the same literary output as contemporary figures such as Ignatius. His rhetoric might not be equally aflame with passion and anger. His theological affirmations might not be as daring and as innovative. Yet, in many ways he may be more representative, and hence more revealing of the nature of the Christ movement in the second or third decade of the second century. He occupies a central place in understanding the Jesus movement in this period, not just temporally but more importantly ecclesially and pastorally. He was a conciliatory figure, available to communities beyond Smyrna who recognized him as a leader of notable standing among Christian communities, and hence others consulted him for his pastoral leadership. As such the oft-maligned *Letter to the Philippians* may be one of the most important documents available to those who wish to understand the structures and the beliefs of the nascent Jesus movement in that period.

1.2.4. The Didache

The text known as the Didache or the Teaching of the Twelve Apostles was one of the most recent additions to the collection of the writings of the Apostolic

---

[2] Thomas F. Torrance, *The Doctrine of Grace in the Apostolic Fathers* (Oliver and Boyd, 1948), 91.

[3] Martin Dibelius, *Geschichte des urchristlichen Literarur* (de Gruyter, 1926), 119; trans. B. Dehandschutter, "Polycarp's Epistle to the Philippians: An Early Example of Reception," *Bibliotheca Ephemeridum Theologicarum Lovaniensium* 86 (1989): 275–291, here 275.

Fathers. However, since the discovery of this text in the late nineteenth century it has nearly without exception appeared as one of the writings included in printed editions of the Apostolic Fathers. The reasons are perhaps mainly twofold. First, the text claims a very close connection with the apostles. In fact, the title in the main Greek manuscript states that the document is the "Teaching of the Twelve Apostles." In this sense it is more apostolic than any of the other texts in the collection since unlike the other texts that seem to have emerged in the generation after the apostles, the Didache claims to have apostolic authorship. If that claim concerning authorship were true, then it is perhaps more apostolic than any other early Christian text since it states it was not written by a single apostle, but by all twelve. Presumably Judas was not one of those twelve. Whether Matthias was intended as an author, or if the term "the twelve" had simply become a standard designation is impossible to tell. The second reason for its inclusion probably relates to determinations about the relatively early date of the text. In reality it is an incredibly difficult text to date, and the problem is exacerbated by the fact that it shows some signs of being a composite or evolving text that gained extra layers with the passage of time. As a result the proposed period of composition has been suggested by some to be even earlier than AD 50, while others have dated it as late as the third century. For various reasons both of these extreme endpoints do not appear plausible. The text as it stands appears to know a range of gospel traditions, especially ideas and phrases drawn from the Gospel of Matthew. Equally, its contents appear to reflect fairly primitive church structures that might predate those described in the writings of Ignatius and Polycarp. For these reasons, a date somewhere in the region of 90–110 appears to align with the material contained in the text. However, certainty is far from possible.

The document comprises various elements. It commences with a so-called two-ways tractate, that places before readers a stark binary choice concerning the way they can choose to live their lives. Thus, the opening line of the text directly declares: "There are two ways, one of life and one of death, and there is much difference between the two ways" There is then a lengthy discussion and exploration of these two ways of life (Didache 1.1–6.2). The next major section of the text (6.3–10.7) is of particular interest since it provides insight into how at least one early Jesus group conducted its rituals and community practices. The section opens with a brief injunction to abstain from meat offered to idols. This statement reiterates Paul's instruction on the topic (1 Cor 8:1–13; 10:19–22), albeit in shorter and more focused form. More detail is provided concerning baptismal practice. The initiate is to be baptized in the threefold name of Father, Son and Holy Spirit, preferably in cold running water. However, adopting a pragmatic approach, the text states that if such a water supply is not available then it is acceptable to pour water on the head three times using the same threefold name. The person being baptized is to fast along with others in the community who are able to do so. Furthermore, the one who is to be baptized is to be instructed in the faith for one or two days beforehand (Didache 7.1–4). Thus, the Didache portrays a greater regulation and standardization of baptismal practice. The next two set of instructions concern fasting, which is to be observed on Wednesdays and Fridays, and prayer with a form of the Lord's Prayer included in the text along with the instruction to "pray like this three times a day" 8.3). The longest set of instructions pertain to the Eucharist. Here the text is particularly fulsome and includes the liturgical words to be used during the Eucharist (9.1–10.7).

The next topic addressed by the Didache is that of church order with particular focus on leadership or authority roles in the group. The text seeks to provide guidance on what may have been a tension between resident leaders and itinerant authority figures who visited the community. In this way the text potentially reflects a period of transition between a more charismatic structure with visiting apostles and that of a more settled and regularized hierarchy in established groups (11.1–13.7). The group is instructed to appoint bishops and deacons. The text makes the point that these appointed leaders are not to be despised "for they are those who are honored among you with the prophets and teachers" (15.2). Here again it is possible to discern a clash between the charismatic and itinerant figures who exercised a peripatetic ministry, and the emergent more settled and perhaps less dynamic leaders who were local group members who perhaps lacked honor in their own home towns.

The text concludes with an eschatological section which first exhorts those addressed to remain faithful and prepared, and to continue the practice of meeting together in the hope of the coming return of the Lord (16.1–2). The second and final part of the text is an apocalyptic description of the last times. Nearly every phrase has an antecedent drawn from the apocalyptic sections of the Gospels or Paul's letters. The text reflects a group still aflame with eschatological expectations and yet also one that quarried scriptural texts to give an account of the last events.

From beginning to end the Didache is a fascinating text. It provides a window into Christian beliefs and practices probably sometime around the beginning of the second century. However, it is necessary not to extrapolate too much from this document. Not only does it appear to be a composite of various traditions, more significantly it is not possible to tell the degree to which its perspectives were representative of the wider early Christian movement, or if this was an idiosyncratic and localized Jesus community. Notwithstanding such limitations, there is no other equally early text from within the ambit of early Christianity that provides so much insight into how that faith commitment may have been lived out in a local setting.

1.2.5. The Shepherd of Hermas

The longest text among the writings that comprise the Apostolic Fathers, the Shepherd of Hermas is not only a complex text, but also one whose contents perhaps seem most distant from modern readers. In large part this is due to the allegorical language it employs. This form of communication makes much of its message obscure for modern readers. Notwithstanding this, if the number of surviving copies is any guide, then this was one of the most read and appealing texts to ancient readers.

Contemporary analysis has tended to divide the text into three section based on the genre of the material. On this basis the text consists of five visions (Shepherd of Hermas 1–25), a series of twelve mandates or commandments (chs. 26–49), and ten similitudes or parables (chs. 50–114). However, manuscript and internal evidence may suggest that the text originated differently. Holmes notes that "[b]oth the important Michigan papyrus and the Sahidic Coptic version begins with Vision 5 (ch. 25)."[4] Moreover, in Visions 1–4 a female figure discloses revelatory knowledge to Hermas. This figure does not appear again in the rest of the work. By contrast, in the remainder of the work it is the shepherd who reveals heavenly truths to Hermas. This suggests that whole was not composed as a unity. This may mean that either more than one author was involved in writing various sections of what is now understood to be a single work, or that the text was composed by a single author but on multiple occasions over an extended period of time. Both the manuscript evidence and the apparent literary seams reveal a work with a complex compositional history, which may have been read in different forms in antiquity and not in the extended continuous version that is typically printed in modern editions.

The text opens in a manner that appears to portray Hermas as a slave: "the man who raised me up sold me to a woman named Rhoda, in Rome" (1.1). If this intended to portray real life-events, then Hermas was somehow sold to a

---

4 M. W. Holmes, ed., *The Apostolic Fathers: Greek Texts and English Translations*, 3rd ed. (Baker, 2007), 446.

Introduction   13

woman in Rome named Rhoda, lost contact with her, but met her again many years later and "began to love her as a sister." This may imply the two characters had become Christians. Hermas longs for Rhoda to be his wife due to her "beauty and character." Later, while away from Rome he receives a vision. The heavens are open to him. He sees the woman he desired—presumably Rhoda—who informs him that she has been taken into heaven "to accuse you of your sins before the Lord." After an exchange between the characters, Hermas is told to "pray to God, and he will heal the sins of you and of all your house and of all the saints" (1.9). Since the scope of this prayer and the forgiveness that will arise extends beyond Hermas himself, one is left with the impression that the encounter with Rhoda might be an allegorical representation of all failure to pursue righteous living, and a call for repentance that leads to purity of thought and pious conduct on the part of all believers.

In vision 5 a different revelatory figure appears, "a man with a glorious appearance, dressed like a shepherd" (25.1). At the end of this section readers are informed that the shepherd is "the angel of repentance" (25.7), and Hermas receives a command to write down the material that follows in the text. Immediately there follows the set of twelve commandments or mandates, which are a charter for virtuous and ethical Christian life. Having received this lengthy ethical teaching, Hermas is told that he is to "walk in them [the commandments] and exhort those who hear, that their repentance may be pure for the rest of the days of their life" (46.2). Again, repentance is a key theme of the work as a whole. However, the call for repentance is collective and not individual, and Hermas' role as a teacher of the community emerges. He is to "fulfill the ministry," which the Shepherd gives him. When Hermas protests the impossibility of keeping the morally-demanding commandments, the shepherd informs Hermas that as the angel of repentance he rules over the devil and that he will be with members of Hermas' community so that they might be able to withstand temptations. The text concludes with ten parables. In length the parables occupy more space than the previous two sections of the text combined. Most famous is the ninth parable, which continues the metaphor of the tower used earlier. This is a parable with an explanation, and here Hermas is told that the tower represents the church. Toward the end of the interpretation the angel of repentance reminds Hermas and the readers of his text not to trample on the mercy of God, even though God is patient with sins. Thus readers are exhorted yet again to "repent, therefore, in a way that is beneficial to you" (109.5 [Holmes]).

To modern readers the message of "repentance" in this text sounds belabored and perhaps overly shaped by idealized perspectives. The allegorical language is at times impenetrable. The length of the text certainly meant that it was not read in a single sitting to a group of hearers. So one is left with a perplexing text. Its message can appear overly pious, if not a little priggish. Its use of allegory appears to obscure the central message, and its length can make for tedious reading. However, that is a modern perspective. The Shepherd of Hermas was translated into multiple ancient languages and read widely in the early church. It is a reminder that the tastes of early believers and their forms of spirituality were not identical to those of contemporary readers.

1.2.6. Other Writings in the Apostolic Fathers Collection

The writing know as 2 Clement or more fully as the Second Letter of Clement "is not a letter, nor is it by Clement."[5] In fact the identity of the author and the place of composition are unknown. However, a scholarly consensus has emerged that dates the text to around the middle of the second century. The reason for its naming as 2 Clement appears to result from the surviving manuscript tradition. In the two Greek manuscripts, Codex Alexandrinus (5th century) and Codex Hierosolymitanus (AD 1056), as well as in the surviving translation in a Syriac manuscript (AD 1169–1170), the text is always immediately preceded by the First Letter of Clement. Thus, it appears that by association the text became attributed to Clement and identified as a second letter.

However, in terms of genre the text is neither a real or fictive letter. Most frequently it has been identified as some type of homily or sermon. Yet due to the range of different types of sermons, this designation might not be particularly helpful. It has also been seen as having a parenetic function. That is, it provides advice or instruction on correct moral behavior that arises from the presumed and shared Christian perspectives that underpin the text. Notably, it has a focus on Jesus, especially in his role as eschatological judge. Thus, the understanding of the final reckoning and exhortation to correct moral behavior are presented to readers as twin motivations and mechanisms by which salvation can be obtained. The author's presentation of ideas pertaining to the salvation of believers results in a tension between the belief that the saving work of Christ is established in the past (e.g., "he saved us when we were perishing," 2 Clement 1.4), and the idea that it is dependent on upright living and thus can only be known at the end of life (e.g., "let us then do righteousness, that we may be saved at the end," 19.3). Such a tension is not uncharacteristic of early Christian theology.

---

5 This neat formulation is drawn from Holmes, ed., *The Apostolic Fathers: Greek Texts and English Translations*, 132.

In essence, 2 Clement offers a call to a pattern of life that is commensurate with Christian values. As such this text provides insight into the type of exhortations teachers offered to their communities, as well as reflecting the understanding of the correct pattern of Christian living.

Another text that may have become included in the corpus by name association is the Martyrdom of Polycarp. However, in the manuscript tradition that survives from the tenth to thirteenth centuries, the Martyrdom of Polycarp circulated independently from the Epistle of Polycarp. The two texts were brought together in Cotelier's printed edition of 1672, and it has been included in the majority of printed editions of the Apostolic Fathers since then. Obviously, the date of the text of the Martyrdom of Polycarp is related to the date of Polycarp's death, which it recounts. That date is itself subject to debate. The first main option is an earlier date: AD 155 or 156 or even 157 dependent on the names of the proconsuls of Asia and other chronological indicators in Martyrdom of Polycarp 21. The second option is the date about a decade later in AD 167, which depends on Eusebius's statement that Polycarp was put to death in the seventh year of the reign of Marcus Aurelius (Eusebius, *Ecclesiastical History* 4.14.10–4.15.1). A third minority view that has garnered little support is that Eusebius miswrote seventh instead of seventeenth year of Marcus Aurelius, and hence Polycarp was killed in AD 176. The dating of the account of Polycarp's death has proved even more problematic.

The date of composition of the martyrdom account has been much debated. The earliest possible date suggested is typically AD 156, less than a year after the death of Polycarp, on the basis of an interpretation of Martyrdom of Polycarp 18.3 that understands the text to suggest that the first anniversary of the death of Polycarp has not yet been commemorated. What is apparent at the end of the text itself is that a series of transmission notes have been appended by later copyists (Martyrdom of Polycarp 21–22). This indicates that the entire text was not composed at a single moment in time. Yet, this leaves open the question of whether the bulk of the text (chs. 1–20) arose as a unified composition, or whether it went through multiple stages and gathered additional material in that process. This has resulted in a number of proposals for dating. It has been suggested that the surviving text may have been based on eyewitness accounts but reflects theological reflection on martyrdom. Thus, the text as a whole was written later in the third quarter of the second century. Others have seen evidence of multiple layers that became part of the present form of the text between the second to fourth centuries. It has also been suggested that the text is a stylized martyrdom account from the third century. From this perspective, while the text is a unified composition, it has little connection with historical events surrounding the death of Polycarp. The debates are convoluted and cannot be quickly discussed or easily resolved.

The value of the document is contained in the understanding of martyrdom that it espouses. The portrayal of Polycarp as one who undergoes a noble death rather than betray his faith is presented as being exemplary. Yet alongside this, as the Quintus story illustrates (ch. 4), Christians are not voluntarily to present themselves for martyrdom. While there is little direct citation of material drawn from gospel texts, it is apparent that the way in which the account of Polycarp's death is narrated is intended to evoke parallels or patterns based upon the death of Jesus. Within this text one can see the early beginnings of the practice of the veneration of martyrs. However, there is no awareness of the problems this would cause in relation to ecclesial structures and parallel authority within the third-century church.

Thus the Martyrdom of Polycarp, whether it was written nearly contemporaneously with the death of Polycarp or composed several decades later, remains an early example of Christian martyrological literature. It reveals the early stages of the veneration of martyrs, and it views their death as patterned on the passion of Christ. In this sense it provides a deeper understanding of the devotion that existed among early believers who lived with a perceived threat of persecution, albeit that such persecutions were sporadic, and typically limited in geographical scope. The message of the text was that fidelity even to death was in fact the highest example of faith and that such faithfulness in turn ensured eternal life with Jesus.

The Epistle of Barnabas takes the form of a letter. It commences with a greeting and a word of thanksgiving or rejoicing on behalf of the addressees. However, unlike a genuine letter, no specific recipients are named, the identity of the sender is not disclosed, and the destination of the letter is not stated. The letter closes with a "farewell" (Barnabas 21.9), which is a feature in the closing of many ancient letters. Despite this, the epistolary form is a literary fiction. The text is actually primarily an essay that discusses the relationship between emergent Christianity and its parent religion, Judaism (chs. 2–17). A particular emphasis is placed on the use of allegory and an understanding of prophecy as a vehicle to refashion the surface meaning of the Hebrew Scriptures. It is argued that these Scriptures instead of primarily speaking to the original hearers, were in fact futurist prophetic messages that pointed forwarded to Christ and proleptically announced the Christian message of salvation. Toward its conclusion the Epistle of Barnabas turns to the topic of ethical behavior. Here it adopts the "two ways" form (chs. 18–20), which presents two types of "teaching and power." The author states the following regarding the origin of these binary opposites: "one of light and the other of darkness, and there is a great difference between these two ways" (chs. 18.1). This form of instruction is remarkably similar to the two ways statement in the Didache. However, it is unlikely that there is any direct literary dependence between the two documents. Instead, they both seem to be developing an earlier Jewish form of ethical exhortation.

The reason for attaching the name "Barnabas" to this work as part of the title is not obvious. Barnabas is not named anywhere in the text. However, the earliest complete version of the text, found in the fourth century Codex Sinaiticus, contains the title Epistle of Barnabas. So, the name of Barnabas was associated with the text from a very early stage. The principal concern of the text, namely explaining the relationship between Christianity and Judaism with particular reference to understanding the place of the Jewish Scriptures, suggests that the text (or at least Barnabas 2–17) may have emerged in a context when this was still an unresolved issue. Chiefly on the basis of that observation, the text has been broadly dated to the period AD 70–150. It is virtually certain that the text was written after AD 70, since it refers to the destruction of the temple (ch. 16). Referring to the temple, the author states that "those who destroyed this temple will themselves build it" and furthermore "it was destroyed by the enemy; at present even the servants of the enemy will build it up again" (16.3–4 [Holmes]). If these statements reflect historical events, then it is possible that what is being described is the construction of a temple to Jupiter on the site of the destroyed second temple. The text speaks of this rebuilding as a future event. Following the visit of Hadrian around AD 129/130, the city of Jerusalem was renamed Aelia Capitolina and construction commenced on the temple to Jupiter. Its completion around AD 132 led to the Bar Kokhba revolt. This may suggest a specific date for the letter of between AD 130–132. However, several scholars have not been convinced that the description permits such a specific identification. Rather, seeing parallels with the theological concerns and forms of ethical teaching contained in the Didache and with the letters of Ignatius, such scholars prefer a date toward the end of the first century, perhaps AD 96–100. Whichever option is preferred, the text comfortably sits within the chronological period in which the majority of writings in the Apostolic Fathers corpus were composed.

The value of the Epistle of Barnabas stems from the insight it provides in relation to understanding early Christian interpretation of the Jewish Scriptures. In particular, it contains evidence of a certain type of supersessionist theology that viewed the message of the Hebrew Bible as being not primarily written to the first recipients, but rather functioning prophetically and allegorically for the benefit of Christian readers. In this vein, the author declares to his fellow believers in Christ, "understand, then, you children of gladness, that the good Lord has foretold all things to us, that we might know to whom we ought to give thanks and praise for everything" (7.1). Hence, the somewhat stark central claim of the Epistle of Barnabas is that the Jewish Scriptures were intended to speak to Christians and not primarily to the first recipients of those writings, and especially that they were not written for the benefit of Jews contemporary with the Epistle of Barnabas.

The so-called Epistle to Diognetus is even less a genuine letter than the Epistle of Barnabas. It is directed to a figure addressed as "most excellent Diognetus," but it does not have the typical features that are expected in either a letter opening or closing. Instead, the genre of the text belongs to the well-known type of the *apologia*, or Apology, which sought to make a reasoned defense of the Christian faith to a figure or group that had some political power in Greco-Roman world of the second and third centuries.

The Epistle to Diognetus is an enigma. Elsewhere it has been described in the following way: "No text and no context."[6] The text is not named by other surviving Christian writings from antiquity, nor is there any obvious citation of its contents. To make matters worse there is no surviving manuscript of this text. Apparently the only known manuscript of the Epistle to Diognetus was discovered in Constantinople in 1436 in a fishmonger's shop among a pile of wrapping papers. Hence, it came to light shortly before the fall of Constantinople. Copies were made in the late sixteenth century and then again in the nineteenth century. The original manuscript was housed in the library in Strasbourg. However, the library and the manuscript of the Epistle to Diognetus were destroyed in a fire in 1870 during the Franco-Prussian War. Thus, scholars now rely solely on a set of modern transcriptions to access the contents of the text.

The date of composition is difficult to determine. It is usually placed in the second half of the second century. Apparently, this is based on alignment with the dates of other examples of Christian apologetic literature. Whereas the material in chapters 1–10 is apologetic in style and with content being explicitly addressed to Diognetus using the singular "you," in the final two chapters (Epistle to Diognetus 11–12) the content changes to that of an exhortation to believers and at times the plural form of "you" is employed (e.g., 11.8). For many this has suggested a literary seam. Whether the two parts were written

---

6 Paul Foster, "The Epistle to Diognetus," in *The Writings of the Apostolic Fathers*, ed. Paul Foster (Continuum, 2007), 147–156, here 147.

by the same author, maybe at different times or by different people, is difficult to determine.

The text characterizes any form of worship apart from that practiced by Christians to be idolatry. In responding to pagan religion, the author exploits the traditional Jewish critique that worship of idols fashioned by humans is demonstrably a false piety directed toward an object rather than actual worship of the most high God. The superiority of Christian worship free from idols is asserted as self-evident: "Christians are not enslaved to such gods" (2.10). The innovative move on the part of the author is to accuse Jews of worshipping in a manner that is akin to idolatry. While the author concedes that Jews do not worship objects made by humans hands, it is asserted that the practice of offering sacrifices betrays the same mentality as pagans. Namely, Jews and pagans alike believe their practices show respect to the deity by presenting material objects. In opposition to this view the author simply observes that God is "him who is in need of nothing" (3.5). The author then presents the case that Christians are beneficial for civic society. He claims that "what the soul is to the body, that is what Christians are to the world" (6.1). The argument continues by asserting that even when Christians are punished or poorly treated even that is for the benefit of the world. It is stated that by their purity of life and by their imperishable souls they bring righteousness and knowledge of the immortal God.

The text, like others of the apologetic genre, reveals the expression of a more philosophical understanding and presentation of the Christian faith. Despite a sense of increased opposition to the Christian faith, the author of the Epistle to Diognetus does not resile from this perceived hostility. Instead, the writer engages in a forthright and robust attempt at an intellectual defense of the faith. In many ways this represented the first example of Hellenistic Christians seeking to employ the tools of rationality and philosophy to seek legitimization for their beliefs. In fact they went further. Such writers argued that their Christian belief or philosophy was not simply equivalent in rationality to Greek counterparts but was indeed superior to other forms of belief and reasoning. This was a bold claim, but one that reflected a desire on the part of certain second-century Christians to demonstrate that their faith could acquit itself in terms of rationality and logic even alongside the esteemed philosophical schools of thought.

The remaining two texts are different from the others that are typically included in collections of the writings of the Apostolic Fathers. Like the Epistle to Diognetus, there is no surviving manuscript of these two writings. However, unlike Diognetus, it is not the case that a more or less complete manuscript of these texts was destroyed in the modern period. For both the Apology of Quadratus and the text written by Papias entitled *Expositions of the Dominical Logia*, what is known of these texts is in the form of partial and often fleeting citations in the writings of other early Christian authors.

For the Apology of Quadratus, a single citation is preserved in Eusebius' *Ecclesiastical History* 4.3.1–2). Eusebius states that he has access to a complete copy of this work, and that it was addressed to the Emperor Hadrian. The sequence of events supplied in Eusebius' writings suggest that Quadratus' treatise was written around the beginning of Hadrian's reign, perhaps between AD 117–125. Due to its brevity, the citation that Eusebius preserves can be given in full. Quadratus states:

> *But our savior's works were always present, since they were true. Those who were healed, and those who were raised from the dead—they were seen not only when they were being healed and when they were raised, but were also always present, not only while the savior was sojourning but also after he departed. They existed for a sufficient time so that some of them made it to our time* (Eusebius, *Ecclesiastical History* 4.3.2).

This fragment presents a single argument. It seeks to establish the veracity of the miracles of Jesus by highlighting the testimony of the recipients of healing. It is claimed that some those who were healed, while perhaps no longer alive, had survived or "made it to our own time," however that is defined. Therefore, Quadratus claims that people among the current generation of Christians had direct testimony from those who claimed to have been healed by Jesus himself.

It is perhaps unsurprising that such an argument is not redeployed by later apologists. As time passed, the chain of connection to Jesus grew longer, and the link to first hand testimony became less compelling. Yet this fragment is significant for several reasons. First, it attests the early use of the form of the *apologia* as a defense of the nascent Christian religion. Regardless of whether or not Hadrian ever read the work, it also reveals that some believers also wished their faith to be better known by imperial figures. The hope was that the authorities would perceive Christianity to be rational and non-threatening to the empire as a whole.

Writing sometime broadly around the period when Quadratus penned his apology, Papias the bishop of Hierapolis composed his five-volume work, *Expositions of the Dominical Logia*. The work was different from the other writings among the Apostolic Fathers since, as its title suggests, it was some type of interpretative or exegetical work. The focus is on the interpretation of sayings of Jesus found in written Gospels and perhaps some that had been transmitted to Papias through oral tradition. There is also a focus on some of the eschatological teachings of Jesus.

The fragments themselves are a hodgepodge of different types of material, culled from various authors and spanning several centuries. It is no longer possible to reconstruct with any certainty the shape and contents of the entire five-volume work, although that has not stopped some from trying to do so. Those attempts are speculative and have not generated any consensus, apart from the view that such a task is impossible.

In his edition of the Apostolic Fathers in the section dealing with Papias, Holmes presents twenty-eight fragments that are related to Papias, along with a further five entitled "traditions of the elders" preserved in the writings of Irenaeus. Following Lightfoot, Holmes notes that "reasons have been advanced, however, for thinking that these 'traditions of the elders' were mediated to Irenaeus through Papias."[7] It may be best to set these five additional citations aside and to focus on the twenty-eight that have stronger claim to have originated with Papias. Yet even here there is a difference. Some of these examples are not citations of statements written by Papias, but are comments about Papias written by later authors. Those comments identify Papias as bishop of Hierapolis. They communicate a connection between Papias and Polycarp who were both leaders in their respective communities. The time in office of these two figures appears to have overlapped and the geographical location of their churches was relatively proximate.

For those interested in early views on the composition of the Gospels, some of the material Eusebius attributes to Papias provides fascinating although at times problematic information. Papias is stated to have preserved the tradition that Mark was the interpreter of Peter and wrote his gospel on the basis of recording Peter's recollections of the ministry of Jesus. Furthermore, as a clarification it is stated that the events in the Gospel of Mark are not presented in chronological order since Mark was dependent on Peter "who adapted his teaching to the needs of his hearers, but with no intention of giving a connected account of the Lord's sayings." More puzzling still is the statement attributed to Papias in regard to Matthew of whom he says, "Matthew wrote the oracles in the Hebrew language, and everyone interpreted them as he was able" (Eusebius, *Ecclesiastical History* 3.31.3). The difficulty is that the Gospel of Matthew strongly appears to have been composed in Greek and not Hebrew. It is dependent on the Gospel of Mark for much of

---

7 Holmes, ed., *The Apostolic Fathers: Greek Texts and English Translations*, 727.

its material, which is also a text written in Greek. So the question arises how one is to account for the statement that Matthew composed the oracles in the Hebrew dialect. Perhaps there are two options. First, Papias was referring to a different work and not to the Gospel of Matthew. Alternatively, maybe he was just wrong, and on the basis of Matthew's citation of Jewish Scriptures and interest in the Law he made the erroneous assumption that the Gospel of Matthew was originally composed in Hebrew.

Many of the other fragments are equally fascinating, and they raise further questions, several of which cannot be resolved. However, for all the uncertainty that this collection of citations of fragments of Papias' work occasions, it reveals that from the early second century Christians were striving to interpret and to better understand the sayings of Jesus. Moreover, it is clear that the words of Jesus were considered the bedrock of the faith that Christian believers held.

1.3. The Early Christian Apologists

The so-called Christian apologists form a group somewhat separate from the Apostolic Fathers. Due to the length of their individual writings these texts are not printed in full in a single volume. However, the writings of the early Christian apologists do overlap to some extent with the Apostolic Fathers. It must be admitted that there is really no good reason why two of the apologetic texts among the writings of the Apostolic Fathers (the Epistle to Diognetus and the fragment of the Apology of Quadratus) are included in that corpus. Perhaps some will say these two texts are included with the Apostolic Fathers because of their early date. That is partially true, especially for the Apology of Quadratus, but perhaps not for the Epistle to Diognetus. Moreover, in the same section of Eusebius' *Ecclesiastical History* where he mentions Quadratus, he also mentions a second writer of an apology writing in the same period. Eusebius states, "Aristides too, a man of faith and devoted to our religion, has, like Quadratus, left behind a defense of the faith addressed to Hadrian. His writing, too, is still preserved by many" (Eusebius, *Ecclesiastical History* 4.3.2 [Lake]). Not only does Eusebius locate the composition of the Apology of Aristides during the reign of Hadrian, but in his next section he comments that "in the third year of the same reign Alexander, the bishop of the Romans, died" (4.4.1 [Lake]). Given that the events narrated by Eusebius are arranged broadly in chronological sequence, it would appear on this basis that both Quadratus and Aristides composed their apologies during the early part of Hadrian's reign, namely AD 117–120. This would indeed make both Quadratus and Aristides the earliest known Christian apologists. Yet for no apparent reason Quadratus is most frequently included with the Apostolic Fathers, and Aristides treated separately as an early Christian apologist. Hence his work has not been included in collections of the Apostolic Fathers. One can only observe that the reasons for inclusion in one collection or another are not strictly logical, nor entirely consistent.

Notwithstanding the issues of taxonomic arrangement, it is the case that Christian apologists came to prominence in the second half of the second century. Justin Martyr wrote his *First Apology* sometime shortly after the middle of the second century. His central purpose was to provide a rational explanation of the Christian faith in order to persuade Roman authorities that it was unnecessary to execute believers who refused to renounce their faith in Christ rather than to swear allegiance to Caesar.[8] Justin adopts a lengthy and somewhat flowery form of address, revealing that one had to approach imperial figures with a mixture of deference and flattery. He writes, "To the emperor Titus Aelius Hadrianus Antoninus Pius Augustus Caesar, and to his son Verissimus, the philosopher, and to Lucius, the natural son of Caesar and the adopted son of Pius, a lover of learning." The imperial practice of incorporating names of predecessors can make identification confusion. The addressee is, however, the emperor Antoninus Pius (138–161). Verissimus was the nickname given to Marcus Aurelius the learned and philosophical successor of Antonius Pius. It is no coincidence that Justin refers to Verissimus as a philosopher. Justin seeks to write an intellectual defense of the Christian faith, and hence writes philosopher to philosopher, in the hope that his argument will be weighed on the basis of its rationality and reason.

In form, Justin's *Apologies* would have been recognizable at least in part to the Roman authorities. It conforms to the style and format of a *libellous*, that is, a petition addressed to a government official seeking intervention to rectify a perceived injustice. Many examples of non-Christian *libelli* or petitions survive from antiquity. Justin seeks to defend Christianity using the legal tools of the Roman empire and by deploying arguments based upon Greek philosophy and rational thought. If Justin's writing was familiar to its addressees in terms of its legal format and philosophical style, it was unusual in other ways. First, its length makes it abnormal in comparison with typical petitions. Second, its content is unique to the case he presents. Both these factors may have been detrimental to it being read and receiving a positive outcome. The length of Justin's apologetic writings makes it difficult to summarize the

---

8 For a fuller discussion, see Denis Minns and Paul Parvis, eds., *Justin, Philosopher and Martyr: Apologies*, Oxford Early Christian Texts (Oxford University Press, 2009), 44–46.

content. However, some of the key points may be listed. Justin's request is that the charges against Christians be re-examined and considered fairly in light of rational thinking (Justin Martyr, *First Apology* 3.1). He then spends considerable time rebutting the charge that Christians reject the gods. His defense is that Christians worship the true God (6.1–12.8). Justin then provides his own summary of the teachings of Jesus with specific emphasis on adherence to paying taxes and honoring the emperor (12.11–23.2). In the next section he strives to establish the veracity of Christianity by showing the way in which it fulfilled prophecy. Moreover, he claims Moses as a proto-Christian to establish the antiquity of the supposedly new faith. According to Justin, Christianity cannot thus be rejected as a recent innovation. Furthermore, he asserts that Plato borrowed ideas from Moses, thereby seeking to demonstrate the rationality of the Christian faith. The closing section provides an account of Christian worship—especially its central rites of baptism and Eucharist (61.1–63.8). The purpose is to portray Christianity as a quietistic and non-threatening belief system. The apology concludes by restating the case for a just and fair treatment and understanding of Christians.

The type of literary work that Justin and his predecessors formulated resulted in a flowering of apologetic writings. The apologists are typically thought of as being active in the second half of the second century. The reality is that the apologetic form reaches well into the third century during the period while Christianity continued to be subject to what was admittedly sporadic and localized acts of violence. Justin's pupil Tatian wrote his *Oratio ad Graecos* (*Address to the Greeks*) to provide a defense for Christianity and an argument in favor of its superiority. He also makes the case that Christianity, through the prophets and Moses, was an ancient faith. This line of argument reveals the prevailing suspicion against innovation in beliefs, and hence why the nascent Christian faith received such a negative response in certain quarters. Other notable figures of the second century who penned apologies include Melito of Sardis, *Apology to Marcus Aurelius* (AD 169–170), Athenagoras, *Embassy for the Christians* addressed to Marcus Aurelius and his son Commodus (AD 176–177), Theophilus of Antioch, *Apology to Autolycus* (AD 180–192), and Tertullian who wrote the first known example of an apologetical work in Latin, *Apologeticus* (ca. AD 197). Yet in many ways the fullest expression of the *apologia* genre is to be found in a work written around the middle of the third century. Origen of Alexandria was pressed to write a rebuttal of Celsus's anti-Christian work, *The True Word*. This work had been in circulation for well over half a century prior to the composition of Origen's response. Bringing his immense philosophical learning and exegetical skill to bear, Origen systematically sought to dismantle the arguments of his literary interlocutor in his own work known by the Latin title *Contra Celsum* (*Against Celsus*). To this day, this remains one of the most impressive works of sustained defense of the Christian faith.

What the apologetic tradition reveals from early figures such as Quadratus and Aristides, and from Justin and down to Origen, is the existence of an intellectually robust and socially engaged form of Christianity. This was a form of faith that would not be hidden under a bushel, but instead demanded a place alongside philosophers and fellow intellectuals. In the face of sporadic periods of persecution instead of cowering retreat, these writers went on the offensive. Through reason and argument they employed existing legal channels and philosophical reasoning to present Christianity as a force that was beneficial to the Roman Empire and as a belief system which was based on a logic that was at least the equal of contemporary Platonizing thought. This was a Christianity that sought to engage with intellectual argument, that declared itself to have a key contribution to civil society, and in the face of both real and perceived hostility, declared itself to be the friend rather than the foe of those in power. While many of the arguments in the surviving apologetic works from the second and third centuries may appear foreign if not bizarre to modern readers, it is the model of reasoned engagement with intellectual learning and civil society that remains the lasting contribution of these writers to subsequent generations of Christian thought.

1.4. Conclusion

Together with the Apostolic Fathers, the early Christian Apologists map out much of the territory for later generations of Christianity in terms of its understanding of core beliefs, the development of ecclesial structures and practices, dialogue with those outside the community of faith, and engagement with wider society. The second century was perhaps the most formative period of Christianity. It bequeathed to later Christians a form of the faith that was self-confident and willing to engage openly with those beyond its faith boundaries. This is a legacy that it is still important to remember.

Paul Foster
School of Divinity, University of Edinburgh
Feast of Polycarp, Bishop of Smyrna, 23 February 2021

2

The First Epistle of Clement to the Corinthians

Context
Author: Possibly Clement of Rome
Provenance: Rome
Date: c. AD 70–96[1]

Opening

The church of God that sojourns in Rome to the church of God that sojourns in Corinth, to those who are called and sanctified by the will of God through our Lord Jesus Christ. Grace and peace from God Almighty be multiplied to you through Jesus Christ.

Problems Caused by Jealousy

1

1. Due to the sudden and repeated misfortunes and calamities that have befallen us, we acknowledge that our attention has been somewhat delayed in turning to the questions disputed among you, beloved, and especially the abominable and unholy sedition, alien and foreign to the elect of God, which a few rash and self-willed persons have made blaze up to such a frenzy that your name, venerable and famous, and worthy as it is of all men's love, has been much slandered. 2. For who has stayed with you without approving of the virtue and steadfastness of your faith? Who has not admired the sobriety

---

[1] See Andrew Gregory, "1 Clement: An Introduction," in *The Writings of the Apostolic Fathers*, ed. Paul Foster (T&T Clark, 2007), 28–29.

and gentleness of your faith in Christ? Who has not reported your character so magnificent in its hospitality? And who has not blessed your perfect and secure knowledge? 3. For you did all things without prejudice, and walked in the laws of God, obedient to your rulers, and paying all fitting honor to the older among you. To the young, you prescribed temperate and respectable thoughts, and to the women you gave instruction that they should do all things with a blameless and respectable and pure conscience, yielding a dutiful affection to their husbands. And you taught them to remain in the rule of obedience and to manage their households in a manner worthy of respect and moderation.

2

1. And you were all humble-minded and in no way arrogant, yielding subjection rather than demanding it, "giving more gladly than receiving" (cf. Acts 20:35).[2] Satisfied with the provision of Christ, and paying attention to his words, you stored them up carefully in your hearts and kept his sufferings before your eyes. 2. Thus a profound and rich peace was given to all, and you had an insatiable desire to do good, and the Holy Spirit was poured out in abundance on you all. 3. You were full of holy plans, and with pious confidence you stretched out your hands to Almighty God in a spirit of goodness, asking him to be merciful toward any unwilling sin. 4. Day and night you strove on behalf of the whole family of believers that the number of his elect should be saved with mercy and compassion. 5. You were sincere and innocent, and you bore no malice to one another. 6. All sedition and all schism was abominable to you. You mourned over the transgressions of your neighbors; you judged their shortcomings as your own. 7. You did not withhold any act of kindness, and you were "ready for every good work" (Titus 3:1). 8. You were adorned by your virtuous and honorable citizenship and did all things in the fear of God. The commandments and ordinances of the Lord were "written on the tables of your heart" (Prov 7:3).

3

1. All glory and growth were given to you, and what was written was fulfilled: "My beloved ate and drank, and he grew wide and fat and kicked" (Deut 32:15). 2. From this arose jealousy and envy, strife and sedition, persecution and disorder, war and captivity. 3. And so the "worthless" rose up "against those who were in

---

2 The Apostolic Fathers and Greek Apologists quote from Greek versions of the Scriptures. However, unless specified otherwise, the Scripture citations added by the editor follow the Hebrew and English versification for the reader's advantage in looking up the passages.

honor" (Isa 3:5); those of no reputation rose up against the renowned, the foolish against the prudent, the "young against the old" (Isa 3:5). 4. Because of this, righteousness and peace are removed when a person abandons the fear of God and the eye of faith in each grows dim. People neither follow the ordinances of his commandments nor use their citizenship worthily of Christ. Instead, each goes after the lusts of their wicked hearts, and each has revived the unrighteousness and impious "envy by which death came into the world" (Wis 2:24).

4

1. For it is written, "And it came to pass after certain days that Cain offered to God a sacrifice of the fruits of the earth, and Abel himself also offered of the first-born of the sheep and of their fat. 2 And God looked on Abel and his gifts, but he had no respect to Cain and his sacrifices. 3. And Cain was greatly grieved, and his face fell. 4. And God said to Cain, 'Why are you grieved, and why has your face fallen? If you offered rightly, but did not divide rightly, did you not sin? 5. Be still: he will turn to you, and you will rule over him.' 6. And Cain said to Abel his brother, 'Let us go to the plain.' And it came to pass that, while they were in the plain, Cain rose against his brother Abel and killed him" (Gen 4:3–8). 7. You see, brothers and sisters, that jealousy and envy produced fratricide. 8. Because of jealousy our father Jacob ran from the face of Esau his brother. 9. Jealousy caused Joseph to be persecuted to death and to come into slavery. 10. Jealousy forced Moses to fly from the face of Pharaoh, King of Egypt, when his fellow countryman said to him, "Who made you a judge or a ruler over us? Would you kill me as you killed the Egyptian yesterday?" (Exod 2:14). 11. Because of jealousy Aaron and Miriam were lodged outside the camp. 12. Jealousy brought down Dathan and Abiram alive into Hades, because they rebelled against Moses the servant of God. 13. Because of jealousy David incurred envy not only from strangers, but suffered persecution even from Saul, King of Israel.

5

1. But, to cease from the examples from the olden days, let us come to those who contended in the days closest to us. Let us take the noble examples of our own generation. 2. Because of jealousy and envy the greatest and most righteous pillars of the church were persecuted and contended to death. 3. Let us set before our eyes the good apostles: 4. Peter, who because of unrighteous jealousy suffered not one or two but many trials; then, having given

his testimony, went to the glorious place that was his due. 5. Because of jealousy and strife Paul showed the way to the prize of endurance; 6. seven times he was in bonds, he was exiled, he was stoned, he was a herald both in the east and in the west, he gained the noble fame of his faith, 7. he taught righteousness to all the world, and when he had reached the limits of the west he gave his testimony before the rulers, and he thus passed from the world and was taken up into the holy place—the greatest example of endurance.

6

1. To these men with their holy lives was added a great number of the chosen, who were the victims of jealousy and who set a noble example for us in their endurance under many indignities and tortures. 2. Because of jealousy women were persecuted as Danaids and Dircae,[3] suffering terrible and unholy indignities. They steadfastly finished the course of faith, and they received a noble reward, weak in the body though they were. 3. Jealousy has estranged wives from husbands and made of no effect the saying of our father Adam, "This is now bone of my bone and flesh of my flesh" (Gen 2:23). 4. Jealousy and strife have overthrown great cities and rooted up mighty nations.

On Repentance

7

1. We are not only writing these things to you, beloved, for your admonition, but also to remind ourselves. We are in the same arena, and the same struggle is before us. 2. Therefore, let us put aside empty and vain cares; and let us come to the glorious and venerable rule of our tradition; 3. and let us see what is good and pleasing and acceptable in the sight of our Maker. 4. Let us fix our gaze on the blood of Christ and know that it is precious to his Father because it was poured out for our salvation and brought the gift of repentance to the entire world. 5. Let us review all the generations; and let us learn that in generation after generation the Master has given an opportunity for repentance to those who will turn to him. 6. Noah preached repentance and those who obeyed were saved. 7. Jonah foretold destruction to the men of Nineveh, but when they repented, they received forgiveness of their sins from God in answer to their prayer and gained salvation, though they were aliens to God.

---

3 This is a possible reference to Greek mythology. The meaning of this phrase is highly contested, but it may refer to the persecution of Christian women for their faith.

8

1. Ministers of the grace of God spoke through the Holy Spirit about repentance, 2. and even the Master of the universe himself spoke with an oath about repentance: "For as I live," said the Lord, "I do not desire the death of the sinner so much as his repentance" (Ezek 33:11), and he added a gracious declaration: 3. "Repent, O house of Israel, from your iniquity. Say to the sons of my people, 'If your sins reach from the earth to heaven, and if they are redder than scarlet, and blacker than sackcloth, and you turn to me with all your hearts and say "Father," I will listen to you as a holy people'" (cf. Ezek 33). 4. And in another place he speaks in this way: "Wash and make yourselves clean, put away your wickedness from your souls before my eyes, cease from your wickedness, learn to do good, seek out justice, rescue the wronged, give judgement for the orphan, do justice to the widow, and come and let us reason together, says the Lord. If your sins are red as crimson, I will make them white as snow, and if they are red as scarlet, I will make them white as wool, and if you are willing and call out to me, you will eat the good things of the land, but if you are not willing, and you do not call out to me, a sword will devour you, for the mouth of the Lord has spoken these things" (Isa 1:16–20). 5. Thus desiring to give to all his beloved a share in repentance, he established it by his almighty will.

On Faith and Obedience

9

1. Therefore let us obey his excellent and glorious will. Let us fall before him as suppliants of his mercy and goodness; let us turn to his pity and abandon the vain toil and strife and jealousy that leads to death. 2. Let us fix our gaze on those who have rendered perfect service to his excellent glory. 3. Let us take Enoch, who was found righteous in obedience and was transported rather than dying. 4. Noah was found faithful in his service, in foretelling a new beginning to the world, and through him the Master saved the living creatures that entered in harmony into the ark.

10

1. Abraham, who was called "the friend" (Isa 41:8; Jas 2:23), was found faithful in his obedience to the words of God. 2. In obedience he left his country and

his kindred and his father's house, that by leaving behind a little country and a feeble people and a small house he might inherit the promises of God. For God said to him, 3. "Depart from your land and from your people and from your father's house to the land that I will show you, and I will make you a great nation, and I will bless you, and I will magnify your name, and you will be blessed; and I will bless those that bless you, and I will curse those that curse you, and all the tribes of the earth will be blessed in you" (Gen 12:1–3). 4. And again, when he was separated from Lot, God said to him, "Lift up your eyes and look from the place where you are now, to the north and to the south and to the east and to the west; for all the land that you see, to you will I give it and your offspring forever. 5. And I will make your offspring like the dust of the earth. If someone can count the dust of the earth, your offspring will also be able to be counted" (Gen 13:14–16). 6. And again he says, "God led forth Abraham, and said to him, 'Look up to the heaven and count the stars, if you can count them; so will your offspring be.' And Abraham believed God, and it was credited to him as righteousness" (Gen 15:5–6; Rom 4:3). 7. Because of his faith and hospitality, a son was given to him in his old age, and in his obedience, he offered him as a sacrifice to God on the mountain that God showed him.

11

1. For his hospitality and devotion, Lot was saved out of Sodom when the whole countryside was judged by fire and brimstone, and the Master made clear that he does not forsake those who hope in him but delivers to punishment and torture those who turn aside to others. 2. For a sign of this was given when his wife went with him but changed her mind and did not remain in agreement with him; she became a pillar of salt even to this day. This was to make known to all that those who are double-minded and have doubts about the power of God incur judgment and become a warning to all generations.

12

1. For her faith and hospitality Rahab, who was called a harlot, was saved. 2. For when the spies were sent to Jericho by Joshua the son of Nun, the king of the land knew that they had come to spy out his country, and he sent men to seize them, that they might be captured and put to death. 3. So the hospitable Rahab took them in and hid them in the upper room under the stalks of flax. 4. And when the king's men came and said, "Those spying on our land came

to you; bring them out, for this is what the king commands," she answered, "The men whom you seek did indeed come to me, but they went away and are proceeding on their journey," and she pointed in the wrong direction. 5. And she said to the men, "I know assuredly that the Lord God is delivering to you this land; for the fear and dread of you has fallen on those who dwell in it. When therefore it will come to pass, that you take it, save me and my father's house." 6. And they said to her, "It will be as you have said. When, therefore, you know that we are at hand, gather all your family under your roof, and they will be safe; for all those found outside the house will perish." 7. And they proceeded to give her a sign, that she should hang a scarlet thread outside her house, which foreshadowed that all who believe and hope on God will have redemption through the blood of the Lord. 8. You see, beloved, that the woman is an instance not only of faith but also of prophecy.

13

1. Therefore, brothers and sisters, let us be humble, putting aside all arrogance and conceit and foolishness and anger, and let us do what is written, for the Holy Spirit says, "Do not let the wise man boast in his wisdom, nor the strong man in his strength, nor the rich man in his riches, but he that boasts, let him boast in the Lord, to seek him out and to do what is just and righteous" (Jer 9:23–24), remembering especially the words that the Lord Jesus spoke when he was teaching gentleness and patience. 2. For he said: "Be merciful, that you may obtain mercy. Forgive, that you may be forgiven. As you do, so will it be done unto you. As you give, so will it be given unto you. As you judge, so will you be judged. As you are kind, so will kindness be shown to you. With the measure you use, it will be measured to you" (cf. Matt 5:7; 6:14–15; 7:1–2, 12). 3. With this commandment and with these injunctions let us strengthen ourselves to walk in obedience to his hallowed words and let us be humble-minded, for the holy word says, 4. "On whom will I look, but on the meek and gentle and him who trembles at my sayings" (Isa 66:2).

14

1. Therefore, my brothers and sisters, it is right and holy to obey God rather than to follow those who in pride and unruliness are the instigators of an abominable jealousy. 2. For we will incur no common harm, but great danger, if we rashly yield ourselves to the purposes of men who rush into strife and sedition to estrange us from what is right. 3. Let us be kind to one another

according to the compassion and sweetness of our Maker. 4. For it is written, "The kind will inhabit the land, and the guiltless will be left on it, but they who transgress will be destroyed from it" (Prov 2:21–22; Ps 37:9, 38). 5. Again, he says: "I saw the ungodly lifted high and exalted as the cedars of Lebanon. And I went by, and behold he was no more; and I sought his place, but could not find it. Protect the innocent and behold the upright; for there is a remnant for the man of peace" (Ps 37:35–37).

15

1. Moreover, let us cling to those whose peacefulness is based on piety and not to those whose wish for peace is hypocritical. 2. For it says in one place: "This people honors me with their lips, but their heart is far from me" (Isa 29:13). 3. And again, "They blessed with their mouth but cursed in their hearts" (Ps 62:4). 4. And again it says, "They loved him with their mouth, and they lied to him with their tongue, and their heart was not right with him, nor were they faithful in his covenant" (Ps 78:36–37). 5. Therefore, "Let the deceitful lips be dumb that speak iniquity against the righteous" (Ps 31:18). And again, "May the Lord destroy all the deceitful lips, a tongue that speaks great things, those who say, 'Let us magnify our tongue, our lips are our own, who is lord over us?' 6. For the misery of the poor and groaning of the needy, now will I arise, says the Lord, I will place him in safety, 7. I will deal boldly with him" (Ps 12:3–6).

16

1. For Christ is with those who are humble, not with those who exalt themselves over his flock. 2. Despite all his power, the scepter of the greatness of God, the Lord Jesus Christ, came not with the pomp of pride or of arrogance but with humility, as the Holy Spirit spoke about him. For it says, 3. "Lord, who has believed our report, and to whom was the arm of the Lord revealed? We declared him before the Lord as a child, as a root in thirsty ground; there is no form in him, nor glory, and we saw him, and he had neither the form [of beauty] nor glory, but his form was without honor, less than the form of man, a man living among stripes and toil, and acquainted with the endurance of weakness; for his face was turned away, he was dishonored and not esteemed. 4. He is the one who bears our sins and suffers for us, and we regarded him as subject to pain and stripes and affliction, 5. but he was wounded for our sins and he has suffered for our iniquities. The chastisement for our peace was upon him; with his bruises we were healed. 6. All of us, like sheep, went

astray—each man went astray in his path; 7. and the Lord delivered him up for our sins, and he did not open his mouth because of his affliction. As a sheep he was brought to the slaughter, and as a lamb quiet before its shearer, so he did not open his mouth. In his humiliation, justice was taken away. 8. Who will declare his generation? For his life is taken away from the earth. 9. For the iniquities of my people he came to death. 10. And I will give the wicked for his burial, and the rich for his death; for he committed no iniquity, nor was guile found in his mouth. And the Lord's will is to purify him from stripes. 11. If you make an offering for sin, your soul will see long-lived offspring. 12. And it is the Lord's will to take of the toil of his soul, to show him light and to form him with understanding, to justify a righteous man who serves many well. And he himself will bear their sins. 13. For this reason he will inherit many, and he will share the spoils of the strong; because his soul was delivered to death, and he was counted among the transgressors. 14. And he bore the sins of many, and for their sins he was delivered up" (Isa 53:1–12). 15. And again he says, "But I am a worm and no man, an object of reproach among men, and despised by the people. 16. All who saw me, mocked me; they spoke with their lips, they shook their heads; he hoped on the Lord, let him deliver him, let him save him, for he has pleasure in him" (Ps 22:6–8). 17. You see, beloved, the example that is given to us; for if the Lord was humble in this way, what should we do, who through him have come under the yoke of his grace?

17

1. Let us also be imitators of those who went about "in the skins of goats and sheep" (Heb 11:37), heralding the coming of Christ. We mean Elijah and Elisha, and moreover Ezekiel, the prophets, and in addition to them the famous men of old. 2. Great fame was given to Abraham, and he was called the Friend of God, and he, fixing his gaze in humility on the Glory of God, says "But I am dust and ashes" (Gen 18:27). 3. Moreover, it is also written about Job: "Now Job was righteous, blameless, and true, a worshipper of God, who kept himself from all evil" (Job 1:1). 4. But he accuses himself, saying, "No man is clean from defilement, not even if he only lives a single day" (Job 14:4–5 LXX). 5. Moses was called "Faithful with all his house" (Num 12:7), and through his ministry God judged Egypt with their scourges and torments; but Moses, though he was given great glory, did not use great words. Instead, when an oracle was given to him from the bush, he said: "Who am I that you should send me? I am a man of feeble speech, and a slow tongue" (Exod 3:11; 4:10). 6. And again he says, "But I am just like smoke from a pot."

18

1. But what will we say of the famous David? God said about him, "I have found a man after my own heart, David the son of Jesse. I have anointed him with eternal mercy" (1 Sam 13:14). 2. But David also says to God, "Have mercy upon me, O God, according to your great mercy, and according to the multitude of your compassions, blot out my transgression. 3. Wash me yet more from my iniquity, and cleanse me from my sin; for I know my iniquity, and my sin is ever before me. 4. Against you only did I sin and did evil before you, so you might be justified in your words, and might prevail when you are judged. 5. For I was conceived in iniquity, and in sin did my mother bear me. 6. For, behold, you have loved truth, you have made plain to me the secret and hidden things of your wisdom. 7. You shall sprinkle me with hyssop, and I will be cleansed; you shall wash me, and I will be whiter than snow, 8. you shall make me hear joy and gladness; the bones that have been humbled will rejoice. 9. Turn your face from my sins and blot out all my iniquities. 10. Create a clean heart in me, O God, and renew a right spirit in my inmost parts. 11. Do not cast me away from your presence nor take your Holy Spirit from me. 12. Give me back the joy of your salvation, strengthen me with your governing spirit. 13. I will teach the wicked your ways, and the ungodly will be converted to you. 14. Deliver me from blood-guiltiness, O God, the God of my salvation. 15. My tongue will rejoice in your righteousness. O Lord, you shall open my mouth, and my lips will tell of your praise. 16. For if you had desired sacrifice, I would have given it; in whole burnt offerings you will not delight. 17. The sacrifice to God is a broken spirit; a broken and a humbled heart God will not despise" (Ps 51:1–17).

19

1. The humility and obedient submission of so many men of such great fame have rendered better not only us but also the generations before us, who received his sayings in fear and truth. 2. Seeing then that we have received a share in many great and glorious deeds, let us hasten on to the goal of peace, which was given to us from the beginning, and let us fix our gaze on the Father and Creator of the whole world and cling to his splendid and excellent gifts of peace and to his good deeds done to us. 3. Let us contemplate him with our mind, let us gaze with the eyes of our soul on his long-suffering purpose, let us consider how free from wrath he is toward all his creatures.

20

1. The heavens, which move at his appointment, are peacefully subject to him. 2. Day and night follow the course allotted by him without hindering each other. 3. Sun and moon and the companies of the stars roll on according to his direction, in harmony, in their appointed courses, and they do not swerve from them at all. 4. The earth teems according to his will at its proper seasons, and it puts forth food in full abundance for people and beasts and all the living things that are on it, without objection and without changing any of his decrees. 5. The unsearchable places of the abysses and the unfathomable realms of the lower world are controlled by the same ordinances. 6. The hollow of the boundless sea is gathered by him working it into its allotted places, and it does not pass the barriers placed around it, but does as he has ordered it; 7. for he said, "You may come this far, and your waves will be broken within you" (Job 38:11). 8. The ocean, which men cannot pass, and the worlds beyond it, are ruled by the same injunctions of the Master. 9. The seasons of spring, summer, fall, and winter give turns to one another in peace. 10. The stations of the winds fulfill their service without hindrance at the proper time. The everlasting wellsprings, created for enjoyment and health, supply sustenance for the life of man without fail; and the smallest of animals meet together in harmony and peace. 11. All these things the great Creator and Master of the universe ordained to be in peace and harmony, and he does good to all things, and more especially to us who have fled to his mercies for refuge through our Lord Jesus Christ, 12. to whom be the glory and the majesty forever and ever. Amen.

21

1. Take heed, beloved, lest his many good works toward us become a judgment on us, if we do not do good and virtuous deeds before him in harmony, and are not citizens worthy of him. 2. For he says in one place, "The Spirit of the Lord is a lamp searching the inward parts" (cf. Prov 20:27). 3. Let us observe how near he is, and that nothing escapes him—neither our thoughts nor the plans that we make. 4. It is right, therefore, that we should not be deserters from his will. 5. Let us offend foolish and thoughtless men, who are exalted and boast in the pride of their words, rather than God. 6. Let us revere the Lord Jesus Christ, whose blood was given for us, let us respect those who rule us, let us honor the aged, let us instruct the young in the fear of God, let us lead our wives to that which is good. 7. Let them exhibit the lovely habit of

purity; let them show forth the innocent will of meekness; let them make the gentleness of their tongue manifest by their silence; let them not give their affection by factious preference but in holiness to all equally who fear God. 8. Let our children share in the instruction that is in Christ; let them learn the strength of humility before God, the power of pure love before God, how beautiful and great is his fear and how it gives salvation to all who live in holiness with a pure mind. 9. For he is a searcher of thoughts and desires; his breath is in us, and when he decides, he will take it away.

22

1. Now the faith that is in Christ guarantees all these things, for he himself through his Holy Spirit calls us in this way: "Come, children, call out to me; I will teach you the fear of the Lord. 2. Who is the man that desires life, that loves to see good days? 3. Make your tongue cease from evil, and your lips cease from guile. 4. Depart from evil and do good. 5. Seek peace and pursue it. 6. The eyes of the Lord are upon the righteous, and his ears are open to their petition; but the face of the Lord is against those who do evil, to destroy the memory of them from the earth. 7. The righteous cried, and the Lord heard him and delivered him out of all his afflictions" (Ps 34:11–19). 8. Many are the scourges of the sinner, but mercy will surround those that hope on the Lord" (Ps 32:10).

On the Resurrection

23

1. The all-merciful and beneficent Father has compassion on those who fear him, and he kindly and lovingly bestows his favors on those that draw near to him with a simple mind. 2. Therefore, let us not be double-minded, nor let our soul be fanciful about his excellent and glorious gifts. 3. Let this Scripture be far from us, in which he says, "Wretched are the double-minded, who doubt in their soul and say 'We have heard these things even in the days of our fathers, and behold we have grown old, and none of these things has happened to us.' 4. Oh, foolish men, compare yourself to a tree. Take a vine; first it sheds its leaves, then there comes a bud, then a leaf, then a flower, and after this the unripe grape, then the full bunch."[4] See how in a little time the fruit of the tree comes to ripeness. 5. Truly his will shall be quickly and suddenly

---

4 Source unknown.

accomplished, as the Scripture also bears witness that "he will come quickly and will not tarry; and the Lord will suddenly come to his temple, and the Holy One for whom you look" (Isa 13:22 LXX).

24

1. Let us consider, beloved, how the Master eventually proves to us that there will be a future resurrection, of which he has made the first fruits by raising the Lord Jesus Christ from the dead. 2. Let us look, beloved, at the resurrection that is taking place at its proper season. 3. Day and night show us a resurrection. The night sleeps, the day arises; the day departs, night comes. 4. Let us take the crops, how and in what way the sowing takes place. 5. The sower went forth and cast each of the seeds into the ground, and they fall onto the ground, parched and bare, and suffer decay; then from their decay the greatness of the providence of the Master raises them up, and from one grain more grow and bring forth fruit.

25

1. Let us consider the strange sign that takes place in the east, that is in the districts near Arabia. 2. There is a bird that is called the Phoenix. It is the only one of its kind, and it lives five hundred years, and when the time of its dissolution in death is at hand, it makes itself a sepulcher of frankincense and myrrh and other spices, and when the time is fulfilled, it enters into it and dies. 3. Now, from the corruption of its flesh there springs a worm, which is nourished by the juices of the dead bird, and it grows wings. Then, when it has become strong, it takes up that sepulcher, in which are the bones of its predecessor, and it carries them from the country of Arabia as far as Egypt until it reaches the city called Heliopolis. 4. In the daylight in the sight of all, it flies to the altar of the sun, places them there, and then starts back to its former home. 5. Then the priests inspect the registers of dates, and they find that it has come at the fulfilment of the five hundredth year.

26

1. Do we then consider it a great and wonderful thing that the Creator of the universe will bring about the resurrection of those who served him in holiness, in the confidence of a good faith, when he shows us the greatness of his promise even through a bird? 2. For he says in one place "And you will raise

me up, and I will praise you," and "I laid down and slept; I rose up, for you are with me" (Ps 3:5). 3. And again Job says, "And you will raise up this flesh of mine that has endured all these things" (Job 19:26).

27

1. In this hope then let our souls be bound to him who is faithful in his promises and righteous in his judgments. 2. He who has commanded us not to lie—he will much more not be a liar himself; for nothing is impossible with God except to lie. 3. Therefore, let faith in him be kindled again in us, and let us consider that all things are close to him. 4. By the word of his majesty he established all things, and by his word can he destroy them. 5. "Who will say to him, 'what have you done?' Or who will resist the might of his strength?" (Wis 12:12). When he wills, and as he wills—that is how he will do all things, and none of his decrees will pass away. 6. Everything is in his sight, and nothing has escaped from his counsel, 7. since "the heavens declare the glory of God, and the skies tell of his handiwork, day utters speech to day, and night tells knowledge to night. And there are neither words nor speeches, and their voices are not heard" (Ps 19:1–3).

28

1. Since all things are seen and heard by him, let us fear him and avoid foul desires of evil deeds, that we may be sheltered by his mercy from the judgments to come. 2. For where can any of us flee from his mighty hand, and what world will receive those who seek to desert him? 3. For the Scripture says in one place: "Where will I go, and where will I hide from your presence? If I ascend into heaven, you are there. If I depart to the ends of the earth, there is your right hand. If I make my bed in the abyss, there is your spirit" (Ps 139:7–8). 4. Therefore, where can a person depart or where will a person escape from him who embraces all things?

Exhortation to Obedience and Faith

29

1. Therefore, let us approach him in holiness of soul, raising pure and undefiled hands to him, loving our gracious and merciful Father, who has made us the portion of his choice for himself. 2. For it is written: "When the most

high divided the nations, when he scattered the sons of Adam, he established the bounds of the nations according to the number of the angels of God. His people, Jacob, became the portion of the Lord; Israel was the lot of his inheritance" (Deut 32:8–9). 3. And in another place he says, "Behold the Lord takes to himself a nation from the midst of nations, as a man takes the first fruit of his threshing floor, and the Holy of Holies will come forth from that nation."

30

1. Seeing, then, that we are the portion of one who is holy, let us do all the deeds of sanctification, fleeing from evil speech and abominable and impure embraces, drunkenness and youthful lusts, and abominable passion, detestable adultery, and abominable pride. 2. "For God," he says, "resists the proud but gives grace to the humble" (Prov 3:34). 3. Let us then join ourselves to those who are given grace from God; let us put on harmony in meekness of spirit and self-control, keeping ourselves far from all gossip and evil speaking, and be justified by deeds, not by words. 4. For he says "He that speaks much must also listen much; or does he that is a good speaker think that he is righteous? 5. Blessed is he that is born of woman and has a short life. Do not be profuse in speech" (Job 11:2–3 LXX). 6. Let our praise be with God and not from ourselves, for God hates those who praise themselves 7. Let testimony to our good deeds be given by others, as it was given to our fathers, the righteous ones. 8. Impudence and arrogance and boldness belong to those that are accursed by God; gentleness and humility and meekness are with those who are blessed by God.

31

1. Let us cling, then, to his blessing and let us consider what are the paths of blessing. Let us observe the deeds of old. 2 Why was our father Abraham blessed? Was it not because he worked righteousness and truth through faith? 3. Isaac in confident knowledge of the future was gladly led as a sacrifice. 4. Jacob departed from his country in meekness because of his brother and went to Laban and served him, and to him was given the scepter of the twelve tribes of Israel.

32

1. And if anyone will candidly consider this in detail, he will recognize the

greatness of the gifts given by him. 2. For from him come the priests and all the Levites, who serve the altar of God. From him comes the Lord Jesus according to the flesh. From him come the kings and rulers and governors in the succession of Judah, and the other scepters of his tribes are in no small renown seeing that God promised that "your seed will be as the stars of heaven" (Gen 26:4). 3. All of them therefore were renowned and magnified, not through themselves or their own works or the righteous actions that they had committed, but through his will. 4. And so we, who by his will have been called in Christ Jesus, are not made righteous by ourselves or by our wisdom or understanding or reverence or the deeds we have done with a pious heart, but through faith, by which Almighty God has justified all men from the beginning of the world. To him be glory forever and ever. Amen.

33

1. What will we do, then, brothers and sisters? Will we be slothful in doing good and cease from love? May the Master forbid that this should happen, at least to us, but let us be zealous to accomplish every good deed with energy and readiness. 2. For the Creator and Master of the universe himself rejoices in his works. 3. For by his infinitely great might he established the heavens, and by his incomprehensible understanding he ordered them; and he separated the earth from the water that surrounds it and fixed it upon the secure foundation by his own will; and the animals that move in it, he commanded them to exist by his own decree; the sea and the living things in it, he made ready, and enclosed by his own power. 4. Above all, human beings, the most excellent and exceedingly great work of his intelligence, with his sacred and faultless hands he formed humans in the likeness of his own image. 5. For God said: "Let us make human beings according to our image and likeness; and God made human beings, male and female he made them" (Gen 1:28). 6. So when he had finished all these things, he praised them and blessed them and said, "Increase and multiply" (Gen 1:28). 7. Let us observe that all the righteous have been adorned with good works; and the Lord himself adorned himself with good works and rejoiced. 8. Having therefore this pattern, let us follow his will without delay; let us do the work of righteousness with all our strength.

34

1. The good workman receives the bread of his labor with confidence; the

lazy and careless cannot look his employer in the face. 2. Therefore we must be prompt in doing good, since all things are from him. 3. For he warns us: "Behold the Lord comes, and the reward he offers is before him, to pay to each according to his work" (cf. Isa 40:10; Rev 22:12). 4. He exhorts us, therefore, if we believe in him with our whole heart, not to be lazy or careless in every good work. 5. Let our glorying and confidence be in him; let us be subject to his will; let us consider the whole multitude of his angels, how they stand ready and minister to his will. 6. For the Scripture says, "Ten thousand times ten thousand stood by him, and thousands upon thousands ministered to him, and they cried 'Holy, Holy, Holy is the Lord Sabaoth, the whole creation is full of his glory'" (cf. Dan 7:10; Isa 6:3). 7. Therefore, we too must gather together with harmony of conscience and cry earnestly to him, as if it were with one mouth, that we may share in his great and glorious promises, 8. for he says, "Eye has not seen, and ear has not heard, and it has not entered into the heart of man, what things the Lord has prepared for those that wait for him" (1 Cor 2:9).

35

1. How blessed and wonderful, beloved, are the gifts of God! 2. Life in immortality, splendor in righteousness, truth in boldness, faith in confidence, self-control in holiness; and all these things are accessible to our understanding. 3. What, then, are the things that are being prepared for those who wait for him? The Creator and Father of the ages, the All-Holy One, himself knows their greatness and beauty. 4. Let us then strive to be found among the number of those who wait, that we may receive a share of the promised gifts. 5. But how will this be, beloved? If our understanding is fixed faithfully on God; if we seek the things that are well-pleasing and acceptable to him; if we fulfill the things which are in harmony with his faultless will, and follow the way of truth, casting away from ourselves all iniquity and wickedness, covetousness, strife, malice and fraud, gossip and evil speaking, hatred of God, pride and arrogance, vainglory and inhospitality. 6. For those who do these things are hateful to God, and "not only those who do them, but also those who take pleasure in them" (Rom 1:32). 7. For the Scripture says: "But God said to the sinner: Why do you declare my ordinances, and take my covenant in your mouth? 8. You have hated instruction and cast my words behind you. When you saw a thief, you ran with him, and you made your portion with the adulterers. Your mouth has multiplied iniquity, and your tongue weaved deceit. You sat to speak evil against your brother, and you put a stumbling block in

the way of your mother's son. 9. You have done these things and I kept silent; you supposed, O wicked one, that I will be like you. 10. I will reprove you and set myself before your face. 11. Understand then these things, you who forget God, lest, like a lion, he seizes you, and there be no one to deliver. 12. A sacrifice of praise will glorify me, and therein is the way that I will show him the salvation of God" (Ps 50:16–23).

36

1. This is the way, beloved, in which we found our salvation—Jesus Christ, the high priest of our offerings, the defender and helper of our weakness. 2. Through him we fix our gaze on the heights of heaven; through him we see the reflection of his faultless and lofty countenance; through him the eyes of our hearts were opened; through him our foolish and darkened understanding blossoms toward the light; through him the Master willed that we should taste the immortal knowledge; who, being the brightness of his majesty is as much greater than angels since he has inherited a more excellent name. 3. For it is written: "He makes his angels spirits, and his ministers a flame of fire" (Heb 1:7). 4. And about his Son, the Master said: "You are my son; today I have begotten you. Ask of me, and I will give you the Gentiles for your inheritance, and the ends of the earth for your possession" (Heb 1:5; Ps 2:7–8). 5. And again, he says to him: "Sit at my right hand until I make your enemies a footstool for your feet" (Heb 1:13; Ps 110:1). 6. Who then are the enemies? Those who are wicked and oppose his will.

Exhortation to Mutual Service and Order within the Church

37

1. Let us then serve as soldiers, brothers and sisters, with all earnestness, following his faultless commands. 2. Let us consider those who serve our general; consider with what good order, habitual readiness, and submissiveness they perform their commands. 3. Not all are prefects, nor tribunes, nor centurions, nor in charge of fifty men or the like, but each carries out in his own rank the commands of the king and of the generals. 4. The great cannot exist without the small, nor the small without the great; there is a certain mixture among all, and herein lies the advantage. 5. Let us take our body; the head is nothing without the feet; likewise, the feet are nothing without the head. The smallest members of our body are necessary and valuable to the whole body,

and all work together and are united in a common subjection to preserve the whole body.

38

1. Therefore, let our whole body be preserved in Christ Jesus, and let each be subject to his neighbor, according to the position granted to him. 2. Let the strong care for the weak and let the weak reverence the strong. Let the rich man bestow help on the poor and let the poor give thanks to God, that he gave him one to supply his needs; let the wise manifest his wisdom not in words but in good deeds; let him who is humble-minded not testify to his own humility, but let him leave it to others to bear him witness; let him who is pure in the flesh not be boastful, knowing that it is another who bestows on him his self-control. 3. Let us consider, then, brothers and sisters, of what matter we were formed, who we are, and with what nature we came into the world, and how he who formed and created us brought us into his world from the darkness of a grave and prepared his benefits for us before we were born. 4. Since, therefore, we have everything from him, we ought to give him thanks in everything, to whom be glory forever and ever. Amen.

39

1. Foolish, imprudent, silly, and uninstructed men mock and deride us, wishing to exalt themselves in their own conceits. 2. For what can mortal man do, or what is the strength of him who is a child of earth? 3. For it is written "There was no shape before my eyes, but I heard a sound and a voice. 4. What then? Shall a mortal be pure before the Lord? Or will a man be blameless in his deeds, seeing that he does not trust his servants, and has noted crookedness in his angels? 5. Yes, the heaven is not pure before him. Away then, you who inhabit houses of clay, of which, even of the same clay, we ourselves were made. He struck them like a moth, and so from morning until evening they ceased to exist; they perished, without being able to help themselves. 6. He breathed on them and they died because they had no wisdom. 7. But call now, if any will answer you, or if you shall see any of the holy angels; for wrath destroys the foolish, and envy puts to death him that is in error. 8. I have seen the foolish taking root, but at once their sustenance was consumed. 9. Let their sons be far from safety; let them be mocked in the gates of their inferiors, with no one to deliver them: for what was prepared for them the righteous will eat, and they themselves will not be delivered from evil" (Job 4:16–5:5).

40

1. Since these things are apparent to us, and we have looked into the depths of the divine knowledge, we ought to do in order all things that the Master commanded us to perform at appointed times. 2. He commanded us to celebrate sacrifices and services, and that this should be done neither carelessly nor randomly but at fixed times and hours. 3. He has himself fixed by his supreme will the places and persons whom he desires for these celebrations, in order that all things may be done devoutly according to his good pleasure and be acceptable to his will. 4. So then those who offer their oblations at the appointed seasons are acceptable and blessed, for they follow the laws of the Master and do no sin. 5. For to the High Priest his proper ministrations are allotted, and to the priests the proper place has been appointed, and on Levites their proper services have been imposed. The layman is bound by the ordinances for the laity.

41

1. Brothers and sisters, let each one of us be well pleasing to God in our own position, and have a good conscience, not transgressing the appointed rules of his ministry, with all reverence. 2. My brothers and sisters, not in every place are the daily sacrifices offered or the free-will offerings, or the sin-offerings and trespass-offerings, but only in Jerusalem; and there also the offering is not made in every place, but before the shrine, at the altar, and the offering is first inspected by the high priest and the ministers already mentioned. 3. Those therefore who do anything contrary to that which is agreeable to his will suffer the penalty of death. 4. You see, brothers and sisters, that the more knowledge we have been entrusted with, the greater risk we incur.

42

1. The apostles received the gospel for us from the Lord Jesus Christ, and Jesus the Christ was sent from God. 2. Therefore, Christ is from God and the Apostles from Christ. In both ways, then, they were in accordance with the appointed order of God's will. 3. Having therefore received their commands and being fully assured by the resurrection of our Lord Jesus Christ, and with faith confirmed by the word of God, they went forth in the assurance of the Holy Spirit preaching the good news that the Kingdom of God is coming. 4. They

preached from district to district, and from city to city, and they appointed their first converts, testing them by the Spirit, to be bishops and deacons of the future believers. 5. And this was no new method, for bishops and deacons had been written of many years before, for the Scripture says the following in one place: "I will establish their bishops in righteousness, and their deacons in faith" (Isa 60:17 LXX).[5]

43

1. And what wonder is it if those who were in Christ, and were entrusted by God with such a duty, established those who have been mentioned? Since the blessed Moses also, being "a faithful servant in all his house" (Num 12:7), noted down in the sacred books all the injunctions that were given to him; and the other prophets followed him, bearing witness with him to the laws that he had given. 2. And when jealousy arose over the priesthood, and the tribes were quarrelling as to which of them was adorned with that glorious title, Moses himself commanded the rulers of the twelve tribes to bring him rods with the name of a tribe written on each; and he took them, and bound them, and sealed them with the rings of the rulers of the tribes, and he put them away in the Tabernacle of Testimony on the table of God. 3. And he shut the Tabernacle and sealed the keys, as he had done with the rods, 4. and he said to them, "Brothers, of whichever tribe the rod will bud, this God has chosen for his priesthood and ministry (cf. Num 17). 5. And when it was daylight, he called together all of Israel, six hundred thousand men, and showed the seals to the rulers of the tribes, and opened the Tabernacle of Testimony, and took forth the rods, and the rod of Aaron was found not only to have budded, but also to be bearing fruit. 6. What do you think, beloved? That Moses did not know beforehand that this was going to happen? Assuredly he knew, but he acted in this way so that there should be no disorder in Israel, to glorify the name of the true and only God, to whom be the glory forever and ever. Amen.

Exhortation to Reinstate those Ousted from Leadership in Corinth

44

1. Our apostles also knew through our Lord Jesus Christ that there would be strife for the title of bishop. 2. For this reason, therefore, since they had received perfect foreknowledge, they appointed those who have been already

---

5 The Greek uses ἐπίσκοπος ("bishop") and διάκονος ("deacon").

mentioned, and afterward they added that if they should fall asleep, other approved men should succeed to their ministry. 3. Therefore, we consider that it is not right to remove from their ministry those who were appointed by them, or later on by other eminent men, with the consultation of the whole church, and have ministered to the flock of Christ without blame, humbly, gently, and generously, and for many years have received a universally favorable testimony. 4. For our sin is not small, if we eject from the episcopate those who have blamelessly and devoutly offered its sacrifices. 5. Blessed are those presbyters who finished their course before now and have obtained a fruitful and perfect release in the ripeness of completed work, for they have now no fear that any will remove them from the place appointed to them. 6. For we see that despite their good service you have removed some from the ministry which they fulfilled blamelessly.

45

1. You are competitive, brothers and sisters, and zealous for the things that lead to salvation. 2. You have studied the Holy Scriptures, which are true and given by the Holy Spirit. 3. You know that nothing unjust or counterfeit is written in them. You will not find that the righteous have been cast out by holy men. 4. The righteous were persecuted; but it was by the wicked. They were put in prison; but it was by the unholy. They were stoned by law-breakers; they were killed by men who had conceived foul and unrighteous envy. 5. They suffered these things and gained glory by their endurance. 6. For what will we say, brothers and sisters? Was Daniel cast into the lions' den by those who feared God? 7. Or were Ananias, Azarias, and Misael shut up in the fiery furnace by those who ministered to the great and glorious worship of the Most High? God forbid that this be so. Who then did these things? Hateful men, full of all iniquity, were roused to such a pitch of fury, that they inflicted torture on those who served God with a holy and faultless purpose, not knowing that the Most High is the defender and protector of those who serve his excellent name with a pure conscience, to whom be glory forever and ever. Amen. But they who endured in confidence obtained the inheritance of glory and honor; they were exalted and were enrolled by God in their memorial forever and ever. Amen.

46

1. We also, brothers and sisters, must therefore cling to such examples. 2. For

it is written, "Cling to the holy, for they who cling to them will be made holy."[6] 3. And again in another place it says, "With the innocent man you will be innocent, and with the elect man you will be elect, and with the perverse man you will do perversely" (Ps 18:25–26). 4. Let us then cling to the innocent and righteous, for these are God's elect. 5. Why are there strife and passion and divisions and schisms and war among you? 6. Or do we not have one God and one Christ and one Spirit of grace poured out upon us? And is there not one calling in Christ? 7. Why do we divide and tear asunder the members of Christ, and raise up strife against our own body, and reach such a pitch of madness as to forget that we are members one of another? Remember the words of the Lord Jesus, 8. for he said: "Woe to that man! It would have been better for him if he had not been born than that he should offend one of my elect; it would have been better for him that a millstone be hung around his neck and he be cast into the sea, than that he should turn aside one of my elect" (cf. Matt 26:24; Luke 17:2). 9. Your schism has turned aside many, has cast many into discouragement, many to doubt, and all of us into grief—and your sedition continues.

47

1. Take up the epistle of the blessed Apostle Paul. 2. What did he first write to you at the beginning of his preaching? 3. With true inspiration he charged you concerning himself and Cephas and Apollos, because even then you had made yourselves partisans. 4. But that partisanship entailed less guilt on you; for you were partisans of apostles of high reputation, and of a man approved by them. 5. But now consider who they are who have perverted you and have lessened the respect due to your famous love for the brothers and sisters. 6. It is a shameful report, beloved, extremely shameful, and unworthy of your training in Christ, that on account of one or two persons the steadfast and ancient church of the Corinthians is being disloyal to the presbyters. 7. And this report has not only reached us but also those who dissent from us, so that you bring blasphemy on the name of the Lord through your folly and are moreover creating danger for yourselves.

48

1. Let us then quickly put an end to this, and let us fall down before the Master and pray to him with tears that he may have mercy upon us and be reconciled

---

6 Source unknown.

to us and restore us to our holy and undefiled practice of love for the brothers and sisters. 2. For this is the open gate of righteousness that leads to life, as it is written: "Open to me the gates of righteousness, that I may enter into them and praise the Lord; 3. this is the gate of the Lord, the righteous will enter through it" (Ps 118:19–20). 4. So then of the many gates that open, the gate that opens to righteousness is the one in Christ, in which are blessed all who enter and make straight their way in holiness and righteousness, accomplishing all things without disorder. 5. Let a man be faithful, let him have power to declare knowledge, let him be wise in the discernment of arguments, let him be pure in his deeds; 6. for the more he seems to be great, the more he ought to be humble and to seek the common good of all and not his own benefit.

49

1. Let the one who has love in Christ perform the commandments of Christ. 2. Who can explain the bond of the love of God? 3. Who is sufficient to tell the greatness of its beauty? 4. The height to which love lifts us cannot be expressed. 5. Love unites us to God. Love covers a multitude of sins. Love bears all things, is long-suffering in all things. There is nothing vulgar, nothing arrogant in love; love admits no schism, love makes no sedition, love does all things in harmony. In love all the elect of God were made perfect. Without love nothing is pleasing to God. 6. In love the Master received us; it was for the sake of the love that he had toward us that Jesus Christ our Lord gave his blood by the will of God for us, and his flesh for our flesh, and his soul for our souls.

50

1. See, beloved, how great and wonderful love is, and that there is no way to express its perfection. 2. Who can be found in it except for those to whom God grants it? Let us then beg and pray on account of his mercy that we may be found in love, without human partisanship, free from blame. 3. All the generations from Adam until this day have passed away; but those who were perfected in love by the grace of God have a place among the pious, who will be made manifest at the coming of the kingdom of Christ. 4. For it is written: "Enter into my chambers for a very little while, until my wrath and fury pass away, and I will remember a good day, and will raise you up out of your graves" (Isa 26:20; Ezek 37:12). 5. Blessed are we, beloved, if we keep the commandments of God in the harmony of love, that through love our sins may be

forgiven. 6. For it is written "Blessed are those whose iniquities are forgiven, and whose sins are covered; blessed is the man whose sin the Lord will not reckon, and in whose mouth is no deceit" (Ps 32:1–2). 7. This blessing was given to those who have been chosen by God through Jesus Christ our Lord, to whom be the glory forever and ever. Amen.

51

1. Let us then pray that forgiveness may be granted to us for our transgressions and for what we have done through any attacks of the adversary. And those also who were the leaders of sedition and disagreement should consider the common hope. 2. For those who live in fear and love would prefer that they themselves should fall into suffering rather than their neighbors; and they pronounce condemnation against themselves rather than against the harmony that has been handed down to us nobly and righteously. 3. For it is better for a man to confess his transgressions than to harden his heart, just as the heart of those who rebelled against God's servant Moses was hardened, and their condemnation was made clear, 4. for, "they went down into Hades alive" (Num 16:33) and "death will be their shepherd" (Ps 49:14). 5. Pharaoh and his army and all the rulers of Egypt, the chariots and their riders, were sunk in the Red Sea and perished for no other reason than because their foolish hearts were hardened after the signs and wonders that had been done in the land of Egypt by God's servant Moses.

52

1. The Master, brothers and sisters, needs nothing. He asks nothing of anyone, except that we confess to him. 2. For David, the chosen, says: "I will confess to the Lord, and it will please him more than a young calf that grows horns and hoofs; let the poor see this and be glad" (Ps 69:30–32). 3. And again he says: "Sacrifice to God a sacrifice of praise and pay to the Highest your vows; and call upon me in the day of your affliction, and I will deliver you and you will glorify me. 4. For the sacrifice of God is a broken spirit" (Ps 50:14–15; 51:17).

53

1. For you understand, and understand well, the sacred Scriptures, beloved, and you have studied the sayings of God. Therefore, we write these things to remind you. 2. For when Moses went up the mountain and spent forty days

and forty nights in fasting and humiliation, God said to him: "Go down quickly, for your people, whom you brought out of the land of Egypt, have committed iniquity; they have quickly abandoned the way you commanded them; they have made themselves molten idols" (Deut 9:12). 3. And the Lord said to him: "I have spoken to you once and twice, saying, 'I have seen this people, and behold it is stiff-necked; let me destroy them, and I will wipe out their name from under heaven, and I will make you into a nation great and wonderful and much more than this'" (Deut 9:13–14). 4. And Moses said: "May this not be, Lord; pardon the sin of this people, or else blot me out of the book of the living also" (Exod 32:32). 5. O great love! O unsurpassable perfection! The servant is bold with the Lord—he asks forgiveness for the people or begs that he himself may be blotted out together with them.

54

1. Who then among you is noble? Who is compassionate? Who is filled with love? 2. Let him say: "sedition and strife and divisions have arisen on my account; I will depart; I will go away wherever you wish, and I will obey the commands of the people; only let the flock of Christ have peace with the presbyters set over it." 3. He who does this will win for himself great glory in Christ, and every place will receive him, for "the earth is the Lord's, and the fullness thereof" (Ps 24:1). 4. This has been in the past and will be in the future, the conduct of those who live without regrets as citizens in the city of God.

55

1. Let us also bring forward examples from the Gentiles. Many kings and rulers, when a time of pestilence has set in, have followed the counsel of oracles, and given themselves up to death, that they might rescue their subjects through their own blood. Many have gone away from their own cities, that sedition might have an end. 2. We know that many among ourselves have given themselves to bondage that they might ransom others. Many have delivered themselves to slavery and provided food for others with the price they received for themselves. 3. Many women have received power through the grace of God and have performed many deeds of manly valor. 4. The blessed Judith, when her city was besieged, asked the elders to let her to go out into the camp of the strangers. 5. So she gave herself up to danger and went forth out of love for her country and her people in their siege, and the Lord

delivered over Holofernes by the hand of a woman. 6. Not less also did Esther, who was perfect in faith, endanger herself, that she might rescue the nation of Israel from the destruction that awaited it; for with fasting and humiliation she prayed to the all-seeing Master of the Ages, and he saw the humility of her soul, and rescued the people for whose sake she had faced peril.

56

1. So let us also intercede for those who have fallen into any transgression, that goodness and humility may be given to them, that they may submit not to us but to the will of God; for in this way they will have fruitful and perfect remembrance before God and the saints, and they will find compassion. 2. Let us receive correction, which none should be upset about, beloved. The admonition that we make, one to another, is good and immeasurably helpful, for it unites us to the will of God. 3. For the holy word says: "The Lord disciplined me, but he did not deliver me over to death; the Lord disciplines the ones he loves and every son that he receives" (Prov 3:12; Heb 12:6). 5. For, "the righteous one will discipline me with mercy and reprove me, but do not let the oil of sinners anoint my head" (Ps 141:5). 6. And again he says: "Blessed is one whom the Lord reproved; and do not reject the admonition of the Almighty, for he causes pain and restores again; 7. he wounded, and his hands healed. 8. He will deliver you from trouble six times, and the seventh time evil will not touch you. 9. In famine he will rescue you from death, and in war he will free you from the hand of the sword. 10. And he will hide you from the scourge of the tongue, and you will not fear when evils approach. 11. You will laugh at the unrighteous and wicked, and you will not be afraid of wild beasts; 12. for wild beasts will be at peace with you. 13. Then you will know that your house will have peace, and the tabernacle you inhabit will not fail. 14. And you will know that your offspring will be many and your children like the grass of the field. 15. And you will come to the grace like ripened corn that is harvested in its due season, or like a heap on the threshing-floor, which is gathered together at the appointed time" (Job 5:17–26). 16. You see, beloved, how great is the protection given to those that are disciplined by the Master, for he is a good Father and disciplines us so that we may obtain mercy through his holy discipline.

57

1. You, therefore, who laid the foundation of the sedition, submit to the

presbyters, and receive the correction of repentance, bending the knees of your hearts. 2. Learn to be submissive, putting aside the boastful and the haughty self-confidence of your tongue, for it is better for you to be found small but honorable in the flock of Christ, than to be pre-eminent in reputation but to be cast out from his hope. 3. For the excellent wisdom says the following: "Behold, I will bring forth to you the words of my spirit, 4. and I will teach you my speech, since I called and you did not obey, and I put forth my words and you did not attend, but made my counsels of no effect and disobeyed my reproofs; therefore will I also laugh at your ruin, and I will rejoice when destruction comes upon you, and when sudden confusion overtakes you, and catastrophe comes as a storm, or when persecution or siege comes upon you. 5. For it will come to pass that when you call upon me, I will not hear you. The evil will seek me, and they will not find me. For they hated wisdom and they rejected the fear of the Lord; nor would they attend to my counsels but mocked my reproofs. 6. Therefore they will eat the fruits of their own way and will be filled with their own wickedness; 7. for because they wronged the innocent, they will be put to death, and inquisition will destroy the wicked. But he who hears me will dwell with confidence in his hope, and he will be at rest, with no fear of any evil" (Prov 1:23–33).

58

1. Let us then be obedient to his most holy and glorious name and let us escape the threats that have been spoken by wisdom beforehand to the disobedient, that we may dwell in confidence on the most sacred name of his majesty. 2. If you receive our counsel, there will be nothing for you to regret, for as God lives and as the Lord Jesus Christ lives and the Holy Spirit—the faith and hope of the elect—if anyone has performed the decrees and commandments given by God without backsliding but with humility of mind and eager gentleness, this one will be enrolled and chosen in the number of those who are saved through Jesus Christ, through whom be the glory forever and ever. Amen.

59

1. But if some are disobedient to the words that have been spoken by him through us, let them know that they will entangle themselves in transgression and no little danger. 2. We, however, will be innocent of this sin, and we will pray with eager requests and supplication that the Creator of the Universe

may guard unharmed the number of his elect that has been numbered in all the world through his beloved child Jesus Christ, through whom he called us from darkness to light, from ignorance to the full knowledge of the glory of his name.

Closing Prayer

3. [Grant us] to hope on your name, the source of all creation. Open the eyes of our heart to know you, that you alone are the highest in the highest and remain holy among the holy. You humble the pride of the arrogant; you destroy the reasonings of nations; you raise up the humble and lower the lofty; you make rich and make poor; you kill and make alive; you alone are the benefactor of spirits and are God of all flesh; you look on the abysses; you see into the works of human beings; you are the helper of those in danger, the savior of those in despair, the creator and watcher over every spirit; you multiply nations upon earth and have chosen from them all those that love you through Jesus Christ your beloved child, and through him you have taught us, made us holy, and brought us to honor. 4. We ask you, Master, to be our helper and protector. Save those of us who are in affliction; have mercy on the lowly; raise the fallen; show yourself to those in need; heal the sick; return the wanderers of your people; feed the hungry; ransom our prisoners; raise up the weak; comfort the faint-hearted; let all nations know you, that you are God alone, and that Jesus Christ is your child, and that we are your people and the sheep of your pasture.

60

1. For you, through your operations, make clear the eternal structure of the world; you, Lord, created the earth. You, who are faithful in all generations, righteous in judgment, wonderful in strength and majesty, wise in your creation, and prudent in establishing your works, good in the things that are seen, and gracious among those that trust in you, O Merciful and Compassionate One, forgive us our iniquities, and unrighteousness, and transgressions, and shortcomings. 2. Do not take into account every sin of your servants and handmaids, but cleanse us with the cleansing of your truth, and guide our steps to walk in holiness of heart, to do the things that are good and pleasing before you and before our rulers. 3. Yes, Lord, let your face shine upon us in peace for our good, so that we may be sheltered by your mighty hand, and delivered from all sin by your uplifted arm, and deliver us from

those who hate us wrongfully. 4. Give harmony and peace to us and to all that dwell on the earth, as you gave it to our fathers who called on you in holiness with faith and truth, and grant that we may be obedient to your almighty and glorious name, and to our rulers and governors upon the earth.

61

1. You, Master, have given the power of sovereignty to them through your excellent and inexpressible might, that we may know the glory and honor given to them by you, and be subject to them, resisting your will in nothing. And to them, Lord, grant health, peace, harmony, and stability, that they may administer the government that you have given them without offence. 2. For you, heavenly Master, King of eternity, have given to the sons of men glory and honor and power over the things that are on the earth; O Lord, direct their deliberations according to that which is good and pleasing before you, that they may administer with piety in peace and gentleness the power given to them by you, and that they may find mercy in your eyes. 3. O you who alone are able to do these things and far better things for us, we praise you through Jesus Christ, the high priest and guardian of our souls, through whom be glory and majesty to you, both now and for all generations and forever and ever. Amen.

Closing

62

1. We have now written to you, brothers and sisters, sufficiently touching on the things that pertain to our worship and are most helpful for a virtuous life for those who wish to guide their steps in devotion and righteousness. 2. For we have touched on every aspect of faith and repentance and true love and self-control and sobriety and patience, and we have reminded you that you are bound to please almighty God with holiness in righteousness and truth and long-suffering, and to live in harmony, bearing no malice, in love and peace with eager gentleness, even as our fathers, whose example we quoted, were well-pleasing in their humility toward God, the Father and Creator, and toward all men. 3. And our pleasure in reminding you of this was all the greater because we knew quite well that we were writing to persons who were faithful and distinguished and had studied the sayings of the teaching of God.

63

1. It is therefore right that we should respect so many and such great examples, and bow our necks, and take up the position of obedience, so that ceasing from vain sedition we may gain without any fault the goal set before us in truth. 2. For you will give us joy and gladness, if you are obedient to the things that we have written through the Holy Spirit, and if you root out the wicked passion of your jealousy according to the request for peace and harmony that we have made in this letter. 3. And we have sent faithful and prudent men, who have lived among us without blame from youth to old age, and they will be witnesses between you and us. 4. We have done this so that you may know that our whole care has been and is directed to your speedy attainment of peace.

64

1. Now may God—the All-Seeing One, the Master of spirits, and the Lord of all flesh, who chose the Lord Jesus Christ, and us through him to be his special people—give to every soul that has called on his glorious and holy name, faith, fear, peace, patience and long-suffering, self-control, purity, and sobriety, that they may be well-pleasing to his name through our high priest and guardian, Jesus Christ, through whom be to him glory and majesty, might, and honor, both now and to all eternity. Amen.

65

1. Send back to us quickly our messengers Claudius Ephebus and Valerius Bito, with Fortunatus, in peace with gladness, in order that they may report all the sooner the peace and harmony that we pray for and desire, that we may also all the more quickly rejoice in your good order. 2. The grace of our Lord Jesus Christ be with you and with everyone everywhere that has been called by God through him, through whom be to him glory, honor, power and greatness and eternal dominion, from eternity to eternity. Amen.

3

The Second Epistle of Clement

Context
Author: Unknown
Provenance: Possibly Corinth[1]
Date: c. AD 150

Exhortation to Obedience in Response to God's Mercy

1

1. Brothers and sisters, we must think of Jesus Christ as of God, as the judge of the living and the dead, and we must not think little of our salvation, 2. for if we think little of him, we also hope to obtain little. And those who listen as though it were a little matter, they are sinning; and we also are sinning, if we do not know from what place, and by whom, and to what place we were called, and how great the sufferings were that Jesus Christ endured for our sake. 3. What in return, then, shall we give to him, or what fruit shall we offer that is worthy of what he has given us? And how great is the debt of holiness that we owe him? 4. For he gave us the light, he called us "son," as a Father, he saved us when we were perishing. 5. What praise, then, or what reward shall we give him in return for what we received? 6. We were blind in our understanding, worshipping stone, and wood, and gold, and silver, and copper, the works of men, and our whole life was nothing else than death. We were covered with darkness, and our eyes were full of fog; but we have received

---

1 On provenance and date, see Paul Parvis, "2 Clement and the Meaning of the Christian Homily," in *The Writings of the Apostolic Fathers*, 34–37.

our sight, and by his will we have cast off the cloud that covered us. 7. For he had pity on us and saved us in his mercy, and he perceived the great error and destruction that was in us, and the hopelessness of our salvation without him; 8. for he called us when we did not exist, and it was his will that out of nothing we should come into being.

2

1. "Rejoice, you who are barren and bear no children; break forth and cry, you who do not have labor; for the deserted woman has many more children than the woman with a husband" (Isa 54:1). In saying, "Rejoice, you who are barren and bear no children," he meant us, for our church was barren before children were given to her. 2. And in saying, "Cry, you who do not have labor," he means that we should offer our prayers in sincerity to God and not grow weary as women who give birth. 3. And in saying, "For the deserted woman has many more children than the woman with a husband," he meant that although our people seemed to be deserted by God, now we who have believed have become many more than those who seemed to have God. 4. And another Scripture also says, "I did not come to call the righteous but sinners" (Mark 2:17).[2] 5. He means that those who are perishing must be saved, 6. for it is great and wonderful to give strength, not to the things that are standing, but to those that are falling. 7. So Christ also willed to save the perishing, and he saved many, coming and calling us who were already perishing.

3

1. Therefore, since he has shown such great mercy toward us, see above all that we who are alive do not sacrifice to the dead gods and do not worship them, but through him know the Father of truth. What is the true knowledge about him except that we should not deny the one through whom we knew him? 2. And he himself also says, "Whoever confesses me before men, I will confess him before my Father" (Matt 10:32); 3. this then is our reward, if we confess him through whom we were saved. 4. But how do we confess him? By doing what he says, and not disregarding his commandments, and honoring him not only with our lips, but with all our heart and all of our mind. 5. And he says also in Isaiah, "This people honors me with their lips, but their heart is far from me" (Isa 29:13).

---

2 Holmes, *The Apostolic Fathers*, 141 notes "this appears to be the earliest instance of a NT passage being quoted as *scripture*."

4

1. Let us, then, not merely call him Lord, for this will not save us. 2. For he says, "Not everyone that says to me 'Lord, Lord,' will be saved, but only the one that does righteousness" (cf. Matt 7:21). 3. So then, brothers and sisters, let us confess him in our deeds, by loving one another, by not committing adultery, by not speaking against another, by not being jealous, but by being self-controlled, merciful, good; and we ought to sympathize with each other, and not be lovers of money. By these deeds we confess him, and not by the opposite kind. 4. And we must not fear men instead of God. 5. For this reason, if you do these things, the Lord said, "If you are gathered together with me in my bosom, and do not do my commandments, I will cast you out, and I will say to you, 'Depart from me, I do not know where you are from, you workers of iniquity.'"[3]

Exhortation to Live for the World to Come

5

1. Therefore, brothers and sisters, let us forsake our sojourning in this world, and do the will of him who called us, and let us not fear to go forth from this world, 2. for the Lord said, "You shall be as lambs in the midst of wolves" (Matt 10:16), 3. and Peter answered and said to him, "What if the wolves tear apart the lambs?" 4. Jesus said to Peter, "Let the lambs have no fear of the wolves after their death; and you have no fear of those that kill you but can do nothing more to you; instead, fear him who after your death has power over body and soul, to cast them into the flames of hell" (cf. Matt 10:28; Luke 12:4–5). 5. And be well assured, brothers and sisters, that our sojourning in this world in the flesh is a little thing and lasts a short time, but the promise of Christ is great and wonderful, and brings us rest, in the kingdom that is to come and in everlasting life. 6. What then shall we do to attain these things except lead a holy and righteous life, and regard the things of this world as not our own, and not desire them? 7. For by desiring to obtain these things we fall from the way of righteousness.

6

1. And the Lord says: "No servant can serve two masters" (Matt 6:24). If we

---

3 Source unknown; Holmes, *The Apostolic Fathers*, 143 notes it may be from the *Gospel of the Egyptians*.

desire to serve both God and money, it is unprofitable to us, 2. "For what does it benefit a man if he gains the whole world but loses his soul?" (Matt 16:24). 3. Now the world that is, and the world to come are two enemies. 4. This world speaks of adultery, and corruption, and love of money, and deceit, but that world bids these things farewell. 5. We cannot then be the friends of both; but we must bid farewell to this world, to consort with that which is to come. 6. We reckon that it is better to hate the things that are here, for they are little, and short-lived, and corruptible, but to love the things that are there, the good things that are incorruptible. 7. For if we do the will of Christ, we will gain rest; but if not, nothing will rescue us from eternal punishment if we neglect his commandments. 8. And the Scripture also says in Ezekiel that, "even if Noah and Job and Daniel arise, they shall not rescue their children in the captivity" (Ezek 14:14). 9. But if even such righteous men as these cannot save their children by their own righteousness, with what confidence will we enter the kingdom of God, if we do not keep our baptism pure and undefiled? Or who will be our advocate if we are not found to have devout and righteous works?

7

1. So then, my brothers and sisters, let us contend, knowing that the contest is close at hand, and that many make voyages for corruptible prizes, but not all are crowned, except for those who have toiled much and contended well. 2. Let us then contend so that we may all be crowned. 3. Let us run the straight course, the immortal contest, and let many of us sail to it and contend, that we may also receive the crown, and if we cannot all receive the crown, let us at least come near to it. 4. We must remember that if someone who takes part in a contest for a corruptible prize is found to be cheating, this person is flogged, picked up, and thrown out of the racecourse. 5. What do you think? What will one suffer who cheats in the contest for that which is incorruptible? 6. About those who have not kept the seal of baptism he says: "Their worm shall not die, and their fire shall not be quenched, and they shall be a spectacle for all flesh" (Isa 66:24).

8

1. So then, while we are on earth, we should repent. 2. For we are clay in the hand of the craftsman. For in the manner of a potter, if he makes a vessel, but it twists or breaks in his hands, he molds it again, but if he has already put it

into the fire of the kiln, he can no longer mend it. So, we also, as long as we are in this world, should repent with all our heart of the wicked deeds that we have done in the flesh, that we may be saved by the Lord, while we still have time for repentance. 3. For after we have departed from this world, we can no longer make confession or repent any more in that place. 4. So then, brothers and sisters, if we do the will of the Father, if we keep the flesh pure, and if we observe the commandments of the Lord, we will obtain eternal life. 5. For the Lord says in the Gospel, "If you did not guard that which is small, who shall give you that which is great? For I tell you that he who is faithful in that which is least, is faithful also in that which is much" (Luke 16:10–12). 6. He means this: Keep the flesh pure, and the seal of baptism undefiled, that we may obtain eternal life.

9

1. And let none of you say that this flesh is not judged and does not rise again. 2. Understand this: in what state did you receive salvation, in what state did you receive your sight, except in this flesh? 3. We must therefore guard the flesh as a temple of God, 4. for as you were called in the flesh, you will also come in the flesh. 5. If Christ, the Lord who saved us, though he was originally spirit, became flesh and so called us, so also, we will receive our reward in this flesh. 6. Let us then love one another, that we may all attain to the kingdom of God. 7. While we have opportunity to be healed let us give ourselves to God, who heals us, giving him what is due. 8. What is due? Repentance from a sincere heart. 9. For he has knowledge of all things beforehand, and he knows the things in our hearts. 10. Let us then give him praise, not only with our mouth, but also from our heart, that he may receive us as sons. 11. For the Lord said, "My brothers and sisters are these who do the will of my Father" (Matt 12:50).

10

1. Therefore, my brothers and sisters, let us do the will of the Father who called us, that we may live, and pursue virtue and abandon vice, which is the forerunner of our sins, and let us flee from ungodliness lest evil overtake us. 2. For, if we are zealous to do good, peace will pursue us. 3. For this reason it is not possible for people to find peace: they bring forward human fears and prefer the pleasures of the present to the promises of the future. 4. For they do not know how great torment the pleasures of the present entail, and what

is the joy of the promised future. 5. And if they did these things by themselves, it could be endured; but, as it is, they are continuing in teaching evil to innocent souls, and they do not know that they will incur a double judgment, both themselves and their hearers.

11

1. Let us then serve God with a pure heart, and we shall be righteous, but if we do not serve him, because we do not believe the promise of God, we shall be miserable. 2. For the prophetic word also says: "Miserable are the double-minded that doubt in their heart, who say, 'These things we heard long ago and in the time of our fathers, but we have waited day after day, and we have seen none of them.' 3. Foolish men! Compare yourselves to a tree. Take a vine: first it sheds its leaves, then there comes a bud, after this the unripe grape, then the full bunch. 4. So also my people have had tumults and afflictions; afterwards it shall receive the good things."[4] 5. Therefore, my brothers and sisters, let us not be double-minded, but let us be patient in hope, that we may also receive the reward. 6. For he, who promised to pay each person what they are owed for their deeds, is faithful. 7. If then we do righteousness before God, we will enter his kingdom and receive the promises that "no ear has heard, nor eye has seen, nor has entered the human heart" (1 Cor 2:9).

12

1. Let us then wait for the kingdom of God, from hour to hour, in love and righteousness, seeing that we do not know the day when God will appear. 2. For when the Lord himself was asked by someone when his kingdom would come, he said: "When the two shall be one, and the outside as the inside, and the male with the female neither male nor female."[5] 3. Now "the two are one" when we speak with one another in truth, and there is but one soul in two bodies without dissimulation. 4. And by "the outside as the inside" he means this: that the inside is the soul, and the outside is the body. Therefore, just as your body is visible, so let your soul be apparent in your good works. 5. And by "the male with the female neither male nor female" he means this: that when a brother sees a sister, he should have no thought of her as female, nor she of him as male. 6. When you do this, he says, the kingdom of my Father will come.

---

4 Source unknown.
5 Cf. *Gospel of Thomas* 22; Clement of Alexandria, *Miscellanies* 3.13.

13

1. Therefore, brothers and sisters, let us at last repent without delay, and be sober for our good, for we are full of much folly and wickedness; let us wipe off from ourselves our former sins, and let us gain salvation by repenting with all our souls. Let us not be people pleasers and let us wish to please by our righteousness not ourselves alone but also those who are outside, that the name may not be blasphemed on our account. 2. For the Lord says, "My name is blasphemed in every way among all the nations" (Isa 52:5), and again, "Woe to the one on whose account my name is blasphemed." 2 How is it blasphemed? 3. In that you do not do what I desire. For when the nations hear from our mouth the sayings of God, they wonder at their beauty and greatness; afterward, when they find out that our deeds are unworthy of the words that we speak, they turn from their wonder to blasphemy, saying that it is a myth and delusion. 4. For when they hear from us that God says: "It is no credit to you, if you love them that love you, but it is a credit to you, if you love your enemies and those that hate you" (Luke 6:32, 35)—when they hear this they marvel at this extraordinary goodness; but when they see that we not only do not love those that hate us, but not even those who love us, they laugh at us, and the name is blasphemed.

14

1. So then, brothers and sisters, if we do the will of our Father, God, we will belong to the first church, the spiritual one that was created before the sun and moon; but if we do not do the will of the Lord, we will fall under the Scripture that says, "My house became a den of robbers" (Matt 21:13). Therefore, let us choose to belong to the church of life, that we may win salvation. 2. Now I imagine that you are not ignorant that the living church is the body of Christ. For the Scripture says: "God made man male and female" (Gen 1:27); the male is Christ, the female is the church. And moreover, the books and the apostles declare that the church belongs not to the present but has existed from the beginning; for she was spiritual, as was also our Jesus, but he was made manifest in the last days that he might save us; 3. and the church, which is spiritual, was made manifest in the flesh of Christ, showing us that if any of us guard her in the flesh without corruption, we will receive her back again in the Holy Spirit. For this flesh is an antitype of the Spirit; no one who has corrupted the antitype will receive the reality. So then, he means this, brothers and sisters: guard the flesh, that you may receive the Spirit. 4. Now if we say that the flesh

is the church, and the Spirit is Christ, of course he who has abused the flesh, has abused the church. Such a one therefore will not receive the Spirit, which is Christ. 5. The flesh has the power to receive such a great a gift of life and immortality if the Holy Spirit is joined to it; no one can express or speak of the things that the Lord has prepared for his elect.

15

1. Now I think that I have not given poor advice about self-control, and if anyone follows it, he will have no regret but will save both himself and me, his counsellor; for it is no small reward to turn to salvation a soul that is wandering and perishing. 2. For this is what we can pay back to God, who created us, if he who speaks and hears both speaks and hears with faith and love. 3. Let us then remain righteous and holy in our faith, that we may pray with confidence to God, who says, "While you are speaking, I will say, 'Behold here am I'" (Isa 58:9). 4. For this saying is the sign of a great promise; for the Lord says that he is more ready to give than we to ask. 5. Let us then accept such great goodness, and not begrudge others for gaining such benefits, for as great joy as these words offer to those who do them, so severe a condemnation do they threaten to the disobedient.

A Final Exhortation to Repentance

16

1. Seeing therefore, brothers and sisters, that we have received no small opportunity for repentance, let us, now that we have time, turn to the God who calls us, while we still have one who awaits us. 2. For if we bid farewell to these enjoyments and conquer our soul by giving up its wicked lusts, we will share in the mercy of Jesus. 3. But you know that the day of judgment is already approaching as a burning oven, and some of the heavens will melt, and the whole earth will be like lead melting in the fire, and then the secret and open deeds of men will be made clear. 4. Almsgiving is therefore good even as penitence for sin; fasting is better than prayer, but the giving of alms is better than both; and love covers a multitude of sins, but prayer from a good conscience rescues from death. Blessed is everyone who is found full of these things; for almsgiving lightens sin.

17

1. Let us then repent with our whole heart, that none of us perish along the way. For if we have commandments to tear men away from idols and to instruct them, how much more is it our duty to save a soul from perishing that already knows God? 2. Let us then help one another, and bring back those that are weak in goodness, that we may all be saved, and convert and exhort one another. 3. And let us not merely seem to believe and pay attention now, while we are being exhorted by the elders, but also when we have gone home let us remember the commandments of the Lord, and let us not be dragged aside by worldly lusts, but let us try to come here more frequently, and to make progress in the commands of the Lord; that we may all have the same mind and be gathered together unto life. 4. For the Lord said: "I come to gather together all the nations, tribes, and languages" (Isa 66:18). Now by this he means the day of his appearing, when he will come and ransom each of us according to his works. 5. And the unbelievers will see his glory and might, and they will be amazed when they see the sovereignty of the world given to Jesus and will say: "Woe to us, that it was you, and we knew it not, and did not believe, and were not obedient to the elders when they told us of our salvation." And "their worm will not die, and their fire will not be quenched, and they will be a spectacle to all flesh" (Isa 66:24). 6. He means that day of judgment, when they will see those who were ungodly among us and perverted the commandments of Jesus Christ. 7. But the righteous, who have done good and have endured torture and have hated the indulgences of the soul, when they see how those who have done wrong and denied Jesus by word or deed are punished with terrible torture in unquenchable fire, the righteous will give glory to their God, saying: "There will be hope for him who has served God with all his heart."

18

1. And so, let us belong to those who give thanks and who have served God, and not to the ungodly who are judged. 2. For I myself too am altogether sinful, and I have not yet escaped temptation, but I am still in the midst of the devices of the devil, yet I am striving to pursue righteousness, that I may have the strength at least to draw near to it, in fear of the judgment to come.

Closing[6]

19

1. Therefore, brothers and sisters, following the God of truth, I am reading you an exhortation to pay attention to that which is written, that you may both save yourselves and the one who is the reader among you. For as a reward, I beg of you that you repent with all your heart and give to yourselves salvation and life. For if we do this, we will set an example for all who are younger, who wish to devote themselves to piety and the goodness of God. 2. And let us not be displeased or vexed in our foolishness when anyone admonishes us and turns us from unrighteousness to righteousness. For sometimes when we do evil, we do not know it because of the double-mindedness and unbelief that is in our breasts, and we are darkened in our understanding by vain desires. 3. Let us then do righteousness, that we may be saved at the end. Blessed are they who obey these instructions—though they suffer for a short time in this world, they shall gather the immortal fruit of the resurrection. 4. Therefore, the godly should not be grieved if they are miserable in the present times, for a blessed time awaits them. They will live again in heaven with our fathers and will have rejoicing throughout a sorrowless eternity.

20

1. Also, do not let your mind be grieved when we see the unrighteous enjoying wealth, and the servants of God oppressed. 2. Let us have faith, brothers and sisters. We are contending in the contest of the living God, and we are being trained by the present life, that we may gain the crown that is to come. 3. None of the righteous has attained a reward quickly but waits for it; 4. for if God should pay the recompense of the righteous quickly, we would be training ourselves in commerce and not in godliness; for we should seem to be righteous when we were pursuing not piety but gain. For this reason, divine judgment punishes a spirit that is not righteous and loads it with chains. 5. To the only invisible God, the Father of truth, who sent forth to us the Savior and prince of immortality, through whom he also revealed to us truth and the life of heaven, to him be the glory forever and ever. Amen.

---

6 Starting in the 20th century, the unity of 2 Clement was questioned, with some scholars arguing that 19.1 up to the doxology in 20.4 was an addition to the text. See the summary in Christopher Tuckett, *2 Clement: Introduction, Text, and Commentary* (Oxford University Press, 2012), 27–33, who notes that "in the end, not a lot may depend on the issue."

4

The Letters of Ignatius

Context
Author: Ignatius of Antioch
Provenance: Asia Minor[1]
Date: c. AD 125–150

To the Ephesians

Opening Greeting

Ignatius, who is also called Theophorus,[2] to the church, worthy of all praise, that is at Ephesus in Asia—blessed with greatness by the fullness of God the Father, predestined from eternity for abiding and unchangeable glory, united and elect through true suffering by the will of the Father and Jesus Christ our God—abundant greetings in Jesus Christ and in blameless joy.

1

1. I became acquainted through God with your much beloved name, which you have obtained by your righteous nature, according to faith and love in Christ Jesus our Savior. You are imitators of God, and, having rekindled, by the blood of God, your brotherly work, you completed it perfectly. 2. For when you heard that I had been sent as a prisoner from Syria for the sake of our

---

[1] Ignatius wrote his letters after he had been arrested and was on his way to be martyred in Rome. On the date and provenance, see Paul Foster, "The Epistles of Ignatius of Antioch," in *The Writings of the Apostolic Fathers*, 84–89.

[2] Literally "the God-Bearer."

common name and hope, in the hope of obtaining by your prayers the privilege of fighting with beasts at Rome, that by so doing I might be enabled to be a true disciple, you hastened to see me. 3. Seeing then that I received in the name of God your whole congregation in the person of Onesimus, a man of inexpressible love and your bishop, I beg you by Jesus Christ to love him, and for all to resemble him. Blessed is he who granted you to be worthy to have such a bishop.

2

1. Now concerning my fellow servant, Burrhus, your deacon by the will of God, who is blessed in all things, I beg that he may stay longer, for your honor and for that of the bishop. And Crocus also, who is worthy of God and of you, whom I received as an example of your love, has relieved me in every way—may the Father of Jesus Christ refresh him in like manner—together with Onesimus and Burrhus and Euplus and Fronto, in whose persons I have seen you all in love. 2. May I always have joy in you if I be but worthy. It is, therefore, right in every way to glorify Jesus Christ, who has glorified you, that you may be joined together in one subjection, subject to the bishop and to the presbytery, and may in all things be sanctified.

3

1. I do not give you commands as if I were someone great, for though I am a prisoner for the name, I am not yet perfect in Jesus Christ; for only now I am beginning to be a disciple, and I speak to you as to my fellow learners. For I needed to be prepared by you in faith, exhortation, endurance, and long-suffering. 2. But since love does not let me be silent concerning you, for this reason I have taken it upon myself to exhort you, that you live in harmony with the will of God. For Jesus Christ, our inseparable life, is the will of the Father, even as the bishops are, who have been appointed throughout the world, by the will of Jesus Christ.

Exhortation to Live in Harmony with the Will of the Bishop

4

1. Therefore, it is fitting that you should live in harmony with the will of the bishop, as indeed you do. For your honorable presbytery, which is worthy of

God, is attuned to the bishop as the strings to a harp. By your concord and harmonious love, Jesus Christ is being sung. 2. Now, each of you are to join in this choir, so that being harmoniously in concord, you may receive the key note[3] of God in unison and sing with one voice through Jesus Christ to the Father, that he may both hear you and may recognize, through your good works, that you are members of his Son. It is therefore profitable for you to be in blameless unity, in order that you may always commune with God.

5

1. For if I, in a short time, gained such fellowship with your bishop, which was not human but spiritual, how much more do I count you blessed who are so united with him as the church is with Jesus Christ, and as Jesus Christ is with the Father, that all things may sound together in unison! 2. Let no one be deceived: unless someone is within the sanctuary he lacks the bread of God, for if the prayer of one or two has such power, how much more comes from the prayers of the bishop and the whole church? 3. So then the man who does not join in the common assembly is already arrogant and has separated himself. For it is written "God resists the proud" (Prov 3:34). So then, let us be careful not to oppose the bishop, that we may be subject to God.

6

1. And the more anyone sees that the bishop is silent, the more that person should fear him. For everyone whom the master of the house sends to do business, we should receive as we would the one who sent him. Therefore, it is clear that we must regard the bishop as the Lord himself. 2. Indeed Onesimus himself gives great praise to your good order in God, for you all live according to truth, and no heresy dwells among you; indeed, you do not even listen to anyone unless the person speaks concerning Jesus Christ in truth.

Warning against Immoral and False Teachers

7

1. For there are some who make a practice of carrying about the name with

---

3 Following J. B. Lightfoot, *The Apostolic Fathers*. Edited and completed by J. R. Harmer (Macmillan and Co., 1891). Gk. χρῶμα; cf. the chromatic musical scale.

wicked guile and do other things unworthy of God. You must shun them as wild beasts, for they are ravenous dogs, who bite secretly, and you must be on your guard against them, for they are unlikely to be healed. 2. There is one physician, who is both flesh and spirit, born and yet not born, who is God in man, true life in death, both of Mary and of God, first passible and then impassible, Jesus Christ our Lord.

8

1. Therefore, let no one deceive you, and indeed you have not been deceived, but belong wholly to God. For since no strife is present among you, which might torture you, you do indeed live according to God. I am dedicated and devoted to you Ephesians, and your church, which is famous to eternity. 2. Those who are fleshly cannot do spiritual things, neither can they who are spiritual do carnal things, just as faith is incapable of the deeds of infidelity, and infidelity of the deeds of faith. But even what you do according to the flesh is spiritual, for you do all things in Jesus Christ.

9

1. I have learnt, however, that some from elsewhere have stayed with you, who have evil doctrine; but you did not let them sow it among you, and stopped your ears, so that you might not receive what they sow, seeing that you are as stones of the temple of the Father, made ready for the building of God our Father, carried up to the heights by the engine of Jesus Christ, that is the cross, and using as a rope the Holy Spirit. And your faith is your crane, and love is the path that leads up to God. 2. You are then all fellow travelers, and carry with you God, and the temple, and Christ, and holiness, and are in every way adorned by the commandments of Jesus Christ. And I share in this joy, for it has been granted to me to speak to you through my writing, and to rejoice with you, that you love nothing, according to human life, but God alone.

Further Exhortations

10

1. Now pray unceasingly for others, for there is in them a hope of repentance, that they may find God. Let them become your disciples, at least through your deeds. 2. Be yourselves gentle in answer to their wrath; be humble minded in

answer to their proud speaking; offer prayer for their blasphemy; be steadfast in the faith for their error; be gentle for their cruelty, and do not seek to retaliate. 3. Let us be proved to be their brothers by our gentleness and let us hasten to be imitators of the Lord (who was more mistreated? who was more destitute? who was more condemned?), in order that no weed of the devil be found in you but that you may remain in all purity and sobriety in Jesus Christ, both in the flesh and in the Spirit.

11

1. These are the last times. Therefore, let us be modest, let us fear the long-suffering of God, that it may not become our judgment. For let us either fear the wrath to come or love the grace that is present—one of the two. Only let us be found in Christ Jesus for true life. 2. Without him let nothing seem good to you, for in him I carry about my chains, the spiritual pearls in which may it be granted for me to rise again through your prayers, which I beg that I may ever share in, that I be found in the lot of the Christians of Ephesus, who also were always of one mind with the apostles in the power of Jesus Christ.

12

1. I know who I am and to whom I write. I am condemned, you have obtained mercy; I am in danger, you are established in safety; 2. you are the passageway for those who are being slain for the sake of God, fellow-initiates with Paul, who was sanctified, who gained a good report, who was rightly blessed, in whose footsteps may I be found when I shall attain to God, who in every epistle makes mention of you in Christ Jesus.

13

1. Seek, then, to come together more frequently to give thanks and glory to God. For when you gather together frequently, the powers of Satan are destroyed, and his mischief is brought to nothing, by the concord of your faith. 2. There is nothing better than peace, by which every war in heaven and on earth is abolished.

14

1. None of these things are unknown to you if you possess perfect faith toward

Jesus Christ, and love, which are the beginning and end of life; for the beginning is faith and the end is love, and when the two are joined together in unity it is God, and all other noble things follow after them. 2. No man who professes faith sins, nor does the one who has obtained love hate. The tree is known by its fruit; so, they who profess to be of Christ will be seen by their deeds. For the deed is not a profession in the present but is shown by the power of faith if a man continues to the end.

Another Warning against Immoral and False Teachers

15

1. It is better to be silent and be real, than to talk and to be unreal. Teaching is good if the teacher does what he says. There is then one teacher who spoke, and it came to pass, and what he has done even in silence is worthy of the Father. 2. He who has the word of Jesus for a true possession can also hear his silence, that he may be perfect, that he may act through his speech, and be understood through his silence. 3. Nothing is hidden from the Lord, but even our secret things are near him. Let us therefore do all things as though he were dwelling in us, that we may be his temples, and that he may be our God in us. This indeed is so and will become clear to us by the love which we justly have for him.

16

1. Do not err, my brothers and sisters; they who corrupt families will not inherit the kingdom of God. 2. If then those who do this according to the flesh suffer death, how much more if a man corrupts by false teaching the faith of God for the sake of which Jesus Christ was crucified? Such a one shall go in his foulness to the unquenchable fire, as also will he who listens to him.

17

1. This is the reason the Lord received ointment on his head: that he might breathe immortality on the church. Do not be anointed with the evil odor of the doctrine of the prince of this world, lest he leads you away captive from the life that is set before you. 2. But why are we not all prudent, seeing that we have received knowledge of God, that is, Jesus Christ? Why are we perishing in our folly, ignoring the gift that the Lord has truly sent?

On Salvation through the Mysteries of Christ's Life and Death

18

1. My spirit is devoted to the cross, which is an offence to unbelievers, but to us is salvation and eternal life. "Where is the wise? Where is the debater?" (1 Cor 1:20). Where is the boasting of those who are called prudent? 2. For our God, Jesus the Christ, was conceived by Mary by the plan of God, as well "of the seed of David" (Rom 1:3) and of the Holy Spirit; he was born, and was baptized, that by himself submitting he might purify the water.

19

1. And the virginity of Mary, and her giving birth were hidden from the prince of this world, as was also the death of the Lord—three mysteries to be proclaimed aloud that were accomplished in the stillness of God. 2. How then was he manifested to the world? A star shone in heaven beyond all the stars, and its light was unspeakable, and its newness caused astonishment, and all the other stars, with the sun and moon, gathered in chorus around this star, and it far exceeded them all in its light; and there was perplexity about where this new thing came from, which was so unlike them. 3. By this all magic was dissolved and every bond of wickedness vanished away, ignorance was removed, and the old kingdom was destroyed, for God was manifest as man for the newness of eternal life, and that which had been prepared by God received its beginning. Hence all things were disturbed because the abolition of death was being planned.

Closing

20

1. If Jesus Christ permits me through your prayers, and it be his will, in the second book, which I propose to write to you, I will teach you about the divine plan regarding the new man Jesus Christ, which I have begun to discuss, dealing with his faith and his love, his suffering and his resurrection; 2. especially if the Lord reveals to me that you all join together in the common meeting, in grace from his name, in one faith, and in Jesus Christ, who was of the family of David according to the flesh, the Son of Man and the Son of God, so that you obey the bishop and the presbytery

with an undisturbed mind, breaking one bread, which is the medicine of immortality, the antidote that makes us not die but live forever in Jesus Christ.

21

1. May my soul be given for yours, and for those whom you sent in the honor of God to Smyrna, where I also write to you, thanking the Lord and loving Polycarp as I do also you. Remember me as Jesus Christ also remembers you. 2. Pray for the church in Syria, where I am led as a prisoner to Rome, being the least of the faithful who are there, even as I was thought worthy to show the honor of God. Farewell in God our Father and in Jesus Christ, our common hope.

To the Magnesians

Prohibition against Living "according to Judaism"

8

1. Do not be led astray by strange doctrines or by old fables that are profitless. For if we are living until now according to Judaism, we confess that we have not received grace. 2. For the divine prophets lived according to Jesus Christ. Therefore, they were also persecuted, being inspired by his grace, to convince the disobedient that there is one God, who manifested himself through Jesus Christ his Son, who is his Word proceeding from silence, who in all respects was well-pleasing to him that sent him.

9

1. If then they who walked in ancient customs came to a new hope, no longer living for the Sabbath, but for the Lord's Day, on which also our life sprang up through him and his death—though some deny him—and by this mystery we received faith, and for this reason we also suffer, that we may be found disciples of Jesus Christ our only teacher; 2. if these things are so, then how shall we be able to live without him, of whom even the prophets were disciples in the Spirit and to whom they looked forward as their teacher? And for this

reason, he, the one whom they waited for in righteousness, when he came raised them from the dead.

10

1. Let us then not be insensible to his goodness, for if he should imitate us in our actions we are lost. For this reason, let us be his disciples, and let us learn to lead Christian lives. For whoever is called by any name other than this is not of God. 2. Put aside then the evil leaven, which has grown old and sour, and turn to the new leaven, which is Jesus Christ. Be salted in him, that none among you may be corrupted, since by your odor you shall be tested. 3. It is monstrous to talk of Jesus Christ and to practice Judaism. For Christianity did not base its faith on Judaism, but Judaism on Christianity, and every tongue believing in God was brought together in it.

11

1. Now I say this, beloved, not because I know that there are any of you that are thus, but because I wish to warn you, though I am less than you, not to fall into the snare of vain doctrine, but to be convinced of the birth and suffering and resurrection which took place at the time of the procuratorship of Pontius Pilate; for these things were truly and certainly done by Jesus Christ, our hope, from which may God grant that none of you be turned aside.

[...]

To the Trallians

On Ignatius' Self-Restraint concerning his Teachings

4

1. I have many thoughts in God, but I restrain myself, lest I should perish through boasting, for at present it is far better for me to be timid, and not to give heed to them who puff me up. For they who speak in this way are a scourge to me. 2. For I desire to suffer, but I do not know if I am worthy, for the jealousy of the devil to many is not obvious, but against me it fights the more. I have need therefore of meekness, by which the prince of this world is brought to nothing.

5

1. Am I not able to write to you about heavenly things? Yes, but I am afraid that I should do you harm, "seeing you are babes" (cf. 1 Cor 3:1–2). Pardon me, for I refrain lest you be choked by what you cannot receive. 2. For I myself am not yet a disciple, even though I am in bonds and can understand heavenly things, and the places of the angels and the gatherings of principalities, and things seen and unseen, for much is lacking to us, that we may not lack God.

Warning against False Teachings

6

1. I ask you, therefore—yet not I but the love of Jesus Christ—live only on Christian fare, and refrain from strange food, which is heresy. 2. For these men mingle Jesus Christ with themselves in specious honesty, which is like mixing a deadly poison with honeyed wine, which the ignorant person gladly takes in his baneful pleasure—and it is his death.

7

1. Therefore, beware of such men; and this will be possible for you, if you are not puffed up, and are inseparable from God, from Jesus Christ, and from the bishop, and the ordinances of the apostles. 2. The one who is inside the sanctuary is pure, but the one who is outside the sanctuary is not pure; that is to say whoever does anything apart from the bishop and the presbytery and the deacons is not pure in conscience.

8

1. It is not that I know that there is anything of this kind among you, but I warn you because you are dear to me, and I foresee the snares of the devil. Therefore, adopt meekness and be renewed in faith, which is the flesh of the Lord, and in love, which is the blood of Jesus Christ. 2. Let none of you have a grudge against your neighbor. Give no occasion to the heathen, in order that the congregation of God may not be blasphemed because of a few foolish persons. For, "Woe to the one through whom my name is vainly blasphemed among any" (Isa 52:5).

On the Reality of Christ's Sufferings

9

1. Be deaf therefore when anyone speaks to you apart from Jesus Christ, who was of the family of David, and of Mary, who was truly born, both ate and drank, was truly persecuted under Pontius Pilate, was truly crucified and died in the sight of those in heaven and on earth and under the earth; 2. who also was truly raised from the dead, when his Father raised him up, as in the same manner his Father shall raise up in Christ Jesus us, we who believe in him, without whom we have no true life.

10

1. But if, as some who are without God—that is, are unbelievers—affirm, his suffering was only an appearance (but it is they who are merely an appearance),[4] why am I a prisoner, and why do I even long to fight with the beasts? In that case I am dying in vain and indeed lying concerning the Lord.

11

1. Flee from these wicked offshoots, which bear deadly fruit, which if a man eats, he presently dies. For these are not the plantings of the Father. 2. For if they were, they would appear as branches of the cross (and their fruit would be incorruptible), by which, through his passion, he calls you who are his members. The head therefore cannot be borne without limbs, since God promises union, that is himself.

[...]

To the Romans

On His Martyrdom

4

1. I am writing to all the churches, and I give injunctions to all men, that I am

---

4 "Appearance" is from Greek δοκέω, from which the name "Docetism" was derived. Docetism refers to the heterodox teaching that Christ only appeared to become human and suffer.

dying willingly for God's sake, if you do not hinder it. I beg you, do not be unseasonably kind to me. Allow me to be eaten by the beasts, through which I can attain to God. I am God's wheat, and I am ground by the teeth of wild beasts that I may be found as the pure bread of Christ. 2. Rather, entice the wild beasts that they may become my tomb and leave no trace of my body, that when I fall asleep, I may not be burdensome to anyone. Then, when the world will not even see my body, I will truly be a disciple of Jesus Christ. Pray to Christ on my behalf, that I may be found a sacrifice through these instruments. 3. I do not order you as did Peter and Paul; they were apostles, I am a convict; they were free, I am even until now a slave. But if I suffer, I will be Jesus Christ's freedman, and in him I shall rise free. Now in my bonds I am learning to give up all desires.

5

1. From Syria to Rome I am fighting with wild beasts, by land and sea, by night and day, bound to ten "leopards" (that is, a company of soldiers), and they become worse when treated kindly. Now I become more of a disciple because of their ill deeds, but I am not justified by this. 2. I long for the beasts that are prepared for me; and I pray that they may be found ready for me; I will even entice them to devour me promptly; not as has happened to some whom they have not touched from fear; even if they are unwilling on their own, I will force them to do it. 3. Grant me this favor. I know what is expedient for me; now I am beginning to be a disciple. May nothing of things seen or unseen envy me, that I may attain to Jesus Christ. Let there come on me fire, and cross, and struggles with wild beasts, cutting, and tearing asunder, wrenching of bones, mangling of limbs, crushing of my whole body, cruel tortures of the devil—may I but attain to Jesus Christ!

6

1. The ends of the earth and the kingdoms of this world shall profit me nothing. It is better for me to die in Christ Jesus than to be king over the ends of the earth. I seek him who died for our sake. I desire him who rose for us. The pains of birth are upon me. 2. Allow me, my brothers and sisters; do not hinder me from living; do not wish me to die. Do not give to the world one who desires to belong to God, nor deceive him with material things. Allow me to receive the pure light; when I have come there, I will become a man. 3. Allow me to follow the example of the Passion of my God. If anyone has him within himself, let

him understand what I wish, and let him sympathize with me, knowing the things that constrain me.

7

1. The prince of this world wishes to tear me to pieces, and to corrupt my mind toward God. Let none of you who are present help him. Rather, be on my side, that is on God's. Do not speak of Jesus Christ and yet desire the world. 2. Let no envy dwell among you. Even if when I come I beg you myself, do not be persuaded by me, but rather obey this, which I write to you: for in the midst of life I write to you desiring death. My lust has been crucified, and there is in me no fire of love for material things; but only water living and speaking in me, and saying to me from within, "Come to the Father." 3. I have no pleasure in the food of corruption or in the delights of this life. I desire the bread of God, which is the flesh of Jesus Christ, who was of the seed of David, and for drink I desire his blood, which is incorruptible love.

[...]

To the Philadelphians

On False Teachings and One Eucharist

3

1. Abstain from evil growths, which Jesus Christ does not tend, because they are not the planting of the Father. Not that I have found division among you but a filter [against these growths]. 2. For as many as belong to God and Jesus Christ—these are with the bishop. And as many as repent and come to the unity of the church—these also shall be of God, to be living according to Jesus Christ. 3. Do not be deceived, my brothers and sisters: if anyone follows a maker of schism, he does not inherit the kingdom of God; if anyone follows strange doctrine, he has no part in the Passion.

4

1. Be careful therefore to use one Eucharist (for there is one flesh of our Lord

Jesus Christ, and one cup for union with his blood, one altar, as there is one bishop with the presbytery and the deacons, my fellow servants), in order that whatever you do you may do it according to God.

[...]

To the Smyrnaeans

Ignatius, who is also called Theophorus, to the church of God the Father and the beloved Jesus Christ, which has obtained mercy in every gift, and is filled with faith and love, and falls behind in no gift, most worthy of God, and gifted with holiness—the church that is in Smyrna in Asia: abundant greetings to you in a blameless spirit and in the Word of God.

On Those Who Deny the Reality of Christ's Incarnation

1

1. I give glory to Jesus Christ, the God who has given you wisdom; for I have observed that you are established in immoveable faith, as if nailed to the cross of the Lord Jesus Christ, both in flesh and spirit, and confirmed in love by the blood of Christ, being fully persuaded as touching our Lord, that he is in truth of the family of David according to the flesh; God's son by the will and power of God; truly born of a Virgin, baptized by John that all righteousness might be fulfilled by him; 2. truly nailed to a tree in the flesh for our sakes under Pontius Pilate and Herod the Tetrarch (and we are from the fruit of his divinely blessed Passion) that he might set up a sign for all ages through his resurrection, for his saints and believers, whether among the Jews, or among the Gentiles, in the one body of his church.

2

1. For he suffered all these things for us that we might attain salvation, and he truly suffered even as he also truly raised himself, not as some unbelievers say, that his suffering was merely in appearance, but it is they who are merely in appearance, and even according to their opinions it shall happen to them, and they shall be without bodies and phantom-like.

3

1. For I know and believe that he was in the flesh even after the resurrection. 2. And when he came to those with Peter, he said to them: "Take, touch me, and see that I am not a phantom without a body" (cf. John 20:27). And they immediately touched him and believed, being mingled both with his flesh and spirit. Therefore, they despised even death, and were proved to be above death. 3. And after his resurrection, he ate and drank with them as a being of flesh, although he was united in spirit to the Father.

4

1. Now I warn you of these things, beloved, knowing that you also are so minded. But I guard you in advance against beasts in the form of men, whom you must not only not receive, but if it is possible not even meet, but only pray for them, if perchance they may repent, difficult though that be—but Jesus Christ, who is our true life, has the power over this. 2. For if it is merely in appearance that these things were done by our Lord, I am also a prisoner in appearance. And why have I given myself up to death, to fire, to the sword, to wild beasts? Because near the sword is near to God, with the wild beasts is with God; in the name of Jesus Christ alone am I enduring all things, that I may suffer with him, and the perfect man himself gives me strength.

5

1. There are some who ignorantly deny him, or rather were denied by him, being advocates of death rather than of the truth. These are they whom neither the prophecies nor the law of Moses persuaded, nor the gospel even until now, nor our own individual sufferings. 2. For they have the same opinion concerning us. For what does anyone profit me if he praises me but blasphemes my Lord and does not confess that he was clothed in flesh? But he who says this has denied him absolutely and is clothed with a corpse. 3. Now I have not thought it right to put into writing their unbelieving names; but I wish that I might not even remember them, until they repent concerning the Passion, which is our resurrection.

6

1. Let no one be deceived; even things in heaven and the glory of the angels,

and the rulers visible and invisible—even for them there is a judgment if they do not believe on the blood of Christ. Let the one who receives it, truly receive it. Let no high office puff up anyone, for faith and love is everything, and nothing has been preferred to them. 2. But mark those who have strange opinions concerning the grace of Jesus Christ, which has come to us, and see how contrary they are to the mind of God. For they have no care for love; none for the widow; none for the orphan; none for the distressed; none for the afflicted; none for the prisoner or for him released from prison; none for the hungry or thirsty.

7

1. They abstain from Eucharist and prayer, because they do not confess that the Eucharist is the flesh of our Savior Jesus Christ, who suffered for our sins, whom the Father raised up by his goodness. These who deny the gift of God are perishing in their disputes; but it would be better for them to have love, that they also may attain to the resurrection. 2. It is right to refrain from such men and not even to speak about them in private or in public, but to give heed to the prophets and especially to the Gospel, in which the Passion has been revealed to us and the resurrection has been accomplished. But flee from divisions as the beginning of evils.

8

1. See that you all follow the bishop, as Jesus Christ follows the Father, and the presbytery as if it were the apostles. And revere the deacons as the command of God. Let no one do anything that pertains to the church without the bishop. Let that be considered a valid Eucharist which is celebrated by the bishop or by one whom he appoints. 2. Wherever the bishop appears, let the congregation be present; just as wherever Jesus Christ is, there is the Catholic church. It is not lawful either to baptize or to hold an "agape" without the bishop;[5] but whatever he approves, this is also pleasing to God, that everything which you do may be secure and valid.

9

1. Moreover, it is reasonable for us to return to soberness, while we still have time to repent toward God. It is good to know God and the bishop. He who

---

5 "Agape" refers to a communal meal shared among members of the church.

honors the bishop has been honored by God; he who does anything without the knowledge of the bishop is serving the devil. 2. Let all things then abound to you in grace, for you are worthy. In all respects you have refreshed me, and may Jesus Christ give refreshment to you. You have loved me in my absence, and in my presence. God is your reward, and if for his sake you endure all things, you will attain to him.

[...]

To Polycarp

Ignatius, who is also called Theophorus, to Polycarp, who is bishop of the church of the Smyrnaeans, or rather has for his bishop God the Father and the Lord Jesus Christ, abundant greetings.

Various Exhortations

1

1. Welcoming your godly mind, which is fixed as if on immovable rock, I glory exceedingly that it was granted to me to see your blameless face; may I forever enjoy it in God! 2. I exhort you to press forward on your course, in the grace which you are endued, and to exhort all people to gain salvation. Vindicate your office with all diligence, both in the flesh and spirit. Care for unity, for there is nothing better. Help all people, as the Lord also helps you; patiently endure all people in love, as you indeed do. 3. Be diligent with unceasing prayer. Ask for wisdom greater than you have; be watchful and keep the spirit from slumbering. Speak to each individually after the manner of God. Bear the sicknesses of all as a perfect athlete. Where the toil is greatest, the gain is great.

2

1. If you love good disciples, it is no credit to you; rather bring to subjection by your gentleness the more troublesome. Not all wounds are healed by the same plaster. Relieve convulsions by gentle applications. 2. Be prudent as the serpent in all things and pure as the dove forever. For this reason, you consist of flesh and spirit, that you may deal tenderly with the things that appear visibly; but pray that the invisible things may be revealed to you, that you

may lack nothing and abound in every gift. 3. The time calls on you to attain to God, just as pilots require wind, and the storm-tossed sailor seeks a harbor. Be sober as God's athlete. The prize is immortality and eternal life, of which you have been persuaded. In all things I am devoted to you—I and my bonds, which you cherished.[6]

3

1. Do not let those that appear to be plausible, but teach strange doctrine, overthrow you. Stand firm as an anvil that is struck. The task of great athletes is to suffer punishment and yet conquer. But we especially must endure all things for the sake of God, that he also may endure us. 2. Be more diligent than you are. Mark the seasons. Wait for him who is above seasons, timeless, invisible, who for our sakes became visible, who cannot be touched, who cannot suffer, who for our sakes accepted suffering, who in every way endured for our sakes.

4

1. Do not let the widows be neglected. Be yourself their protector after the Lord. Let nothing be done without your approval, and do nothing yourself without God, as has been your practice; stand fast. 2. Let the meetings be more numerous. Seek all by their name. 3. Do not be haughty to slaves, either men or women; do not let them be puffed up either, but rather let them endure slavery to the glory of God, that they may obtain a better freedom from God. Let them not desire to be set free at the church's expense, that they be not found the slaves of lust.

5

1. Flee from evil arts; preach against them instead. Speak to my sisters that they should love the Lord and be content with their husbands in flesh and in spirit. In the same way instruct my brothers in the name of Jesus Christ "to love their wives as the Lord loved the church" (cf. Eph 5:25). 2. If any man can remain in self-control to the honor of the flesh of the Lord, let him do so without boasting. If he boasts, he is lost, and if it be made known except to the bishop, he is polluted. But it is right for men and women who marry

---

6 Following Lightfoot, *The Apostolic Fathers*.

to be united with the consent of the bishop, that the marriage be according to the Lord and not according to lust. Let all things be done to the honor of God.

6

1. Give heed to the bishop, that God may also give heed to you. I am devoted to those who are subject to the bishop, presbyters, and deacons; and may it be mine to have my lot with them in God. Labor with one another, struggle together, run together, suffer together, rest together, rise up together as God's stewards and assessors and servants. 2. Be pleasing to him in whose ranks you serve, from whom you receive your pay—let none of you be found a deserter. Let your baptism remain as your arms, your faith as a helmet, your love as a spear, your endurance as your panoply, let your works be your deposits that you may receive the back-pay due to you. Be therefore long-suffering with one another in gentleness, as God is with you. May I have joy in you always.

Closing

7

1. Since the church in Antioch has peace through your prayers, as it has been reported to me, I was myself the more encouraged in the freedom from care given by God, if I may but attain to God through my sufferings, that I may be found your disciple at the resurrection. 2. You ought, O Polycarp, most blessed of God, to summon a godly council, and elect someone who is very dear to you and is zealous, who can be called God's courier; appoint him to go to Syria to glorify your zealous love to the glory of God. 3. A Christian has no power over himself but gives his time to God. This is the work of God and of yourselves, when you complete it. For I believe in the grace of God, that you are ready to do the good deeds that are proper for God. I exhort you by no more than these few lines, for I recognize your fervor for the truth.

8

1. Since I could not write to all the churches because of my sudden sailing from Troas to Neapolis as the will of God directs, you shall write as one possessing the mind of God to the churches on the road in front of me, that they also shall treat me in the same way (let those who can, send messengers, and

the others send letters through those whom you send, that you may be glorified by a memorable deed), as is worthy of you. 2. I greet all by name, and the wife of Epitropus with the whole house of herself and her children. I greet my beloved Attalus. I greet him who shall be appointed to go to Syria. Grace will be with him through all, and with Polycarp, who sends him. 3. I bid you farewell always in our God, Jesus Christ; may you remain in him in the unity and care of God. I greet Alce, a name very dear to me. Farewell in the Lord.

5

The Letter of Polycarp to the Philippians

Context
Author: Polycarp
Provenance: Possibly Smyrna
Date: c. AD 135–150[1]

Opening

Polycarp and the elders with him to the church of God sojourning in Philippi; mercy and peace from God Almighty and Jesus Christ our Savior be multiplied to you.

1

I rejoice greatly with you in our Lord Jesus Christ that you have followed the pattern of true love, and have helped on their way, as opportunity was given you, those who were bound in chains, which fits the saints, and are the diadems of those who have been truly chosen by God and our Lord. 2. I rejoice also that your firmly rooted faith, which was famous in past years, still flourishes and bears fruit to our Lord Jesus Christ, who endured for our sins, even to the suffering of death, whom God raised up, having loosed the pangs of Hades, 3. in whom, though you did not see him, you believed in unspeakable and glorified joy—into which joy many desire to come, knowing that by grace you are saved, not by works but by the will of God through Jesus Christ.

---

[1] See Paul Foster, "The Epistles of Ignatius of Antioch," in *The Writings of the Apostolic Fathers*, 89.

Exhortation to Serve God in Fear and Truth

2

1. Therefore, preparing yourselves, serve God in fear and truth, putting aside empty vanity and vulgar error, believing on him who raised up our Lord Jesus Christ from the dead and gave him glory and a throne at his right hand, to whom are subject all things in heaven and earth, whom all breath serves, who is coming as the Judge of the living and of the dead, whose blood God will require from those who disobey him. 2. Now he who raised him from the dead will also raise us up if we do his will, and walk in his commandments, and love the things which he loved, refraining from all unrighteousness, covetousness, love of money, evil-speaking, false witness, rendering not evil for evil, or insult for insult or blow for blow, or curse for curse, 3. but remembering what the Lord taught when he said, "Judge not, that you might not be judged; forgive and it shall be forgiven you; be merciful that you may obtain mercy, with the measure you measure, it will be measured back to you" (Matt 7:1–2), and, "Blessed are the poor, and they who are persecuted for the sake of righteousness, for theirs is the Kingdom of God" (Luke 6:20).

3

1. These things, brothers and sisters, I write to you about righteousness, not at my own instance, but because you first invited me. 2. For neither am I, nor is any other like me, able to follow the wisdom of the blessed and glorious Paul, who when he was among you in the presence of the men of that time taught accurately and steadfastly the word of truth, and also when he was absent wrote letters to you, from the study of which you will be able to build yourselves up into the faith given you; 3. which is the mother of us all when hope follows, and love of God and Christ and neighbor goes before. For if one be in this company, he has fulfilled the command of righteousness, for he who has love is far from all sin.

On the Conduct of Husbands, Wives, and Widows

4

1. But the love of money is the beginning of all evils. Knowing therefore that we brought nothing into the world and we can take nothing out of it, let us

arm ourselves with the armor of righteousness, and let us first of all teach ourselves to walk in the commandment of the Lord; 2. next teach our wives to remain in the faith given to them, and in love and purity, tenderly loving their husbands in all truth, and loving all others equally in all chastity, and to educate their children in the fear of God. 3. Let us teach the widows to be discreet in the faith of the Lord, praying ceaselessly for all people, being far from all slander, evil-speaking, false witness, love of money, and all evil, knowing that they are an altar of God, and that all offerings are tested, and that nothing escapes him, including reasonings or thoughts or the secret things of the heart.

On the Conduct of Deacons, Younger Men, and Virgins

5

1. Knowing then that God is not mocked, we ought to walk worthily of his commandment and glory. 2. Likewise, the deacons must be blameless before his righteousness, as the servants of God and Christ and not of man, not slanderers, not double-tongued, not lovers of money, temperate in all things, compassionate, careful, walking according to the truth of the Lord, who was the servant of all. For if we please him in this present world, we will receive from him that which is to come; even as he promised us to raise us from the dead, and that if we are worthy citizens of his community, we will also reign with him, if we have but faith. 3. Likewise also, let the younger men be blameless in all things; caring above all for purity, and curbing themselves from all evil; for it is good to be cut off from the lust of the things in the world, because every lust wars against the Spirit, and neither the sexually immoral nor effeminate nor men who have sex with men will inherit the Kingdom of God, nor they who do iniquitous things. Therefore, it is necessary to refrain from all these things, and to be subject to the presbyters and deacons as to God and Christ. The virgins must walk with a blameless and pure conscience.

On the Conduct of Presbyters

6

1. And let the presbyters also be compassionate, merciful to all, bringing back those that have wandered, caring for all the weak, neglecting neither widow, nor orphan, nor poor, but ever providing for that which is good before God and man, refraining from all wrath, bias, unjust judgment, being far from all

love of money, not quickly believing evil of any, not hasty in judgment, knowing that we all owe the debt of sin.

Additional Exhortations

2. If then we ask the Lord to forgive us, we also ought to forgive, for we stand before the eyes of the Lord and of God, and we must all appear before the judgment seat of Christ, and each must give an account of himself. 3. So then let us serve him with fear and all reverence, as he himself commanded us, and as did the apostles, who brought us the gospel, and the prophets who foretold the coming of our Lord. Let us be zealous for good, refraining from offence and from the false brothers and sisters and from those who bear the name of the Lord in hypocrisy, who deceive empty-minded men.

7

1. For everyone who does not confess that Jesus Christ has come in the flesh is an anti-Christ; and whoever does not confess the testimony of the cross is of the devil; and whoever perverts the sayings of the Lord for his own lusts and says that there is neither resurrection nor judgment—this man is the first-born of Satan. 2. Therefore, leaving the foolishness of the crowd, and their false teaching, let us turn back to the word which was delivered to us in the beginning, alert to prayer and persevering in fasting, asking the all-seeing God in our supplications to lead us not into temptation, even as the Lord said, "The spirit is willing, but the flesh is weak" (Matt 26:41).

8

1. Let us then persevere unceasingly in our hope and in the pledge of our righteousness that is in Christ Jesus, who bore our sins in his own body on the tree, who did no sin, neither was deceit found in his mouth, but for our sakes, that we might live in him, he endured all things. 2. Let us then be imitators of his endurance, and if we suffer for his name's sake let us glorify him. For this is the example which he gave us in himself, and this is what we have believed.

9

1. Now I ask you all to obey the word of righteousness, and to endure with all the endurance which you also saw before your eyes, not only in the blessed

Ignatius, and Zosimus, and Rufus, but also in others among yourselves, and in Paul himself, and in the other apostles; 2. being persuaded that all of these ran not in vain but in faith and righteousness, and that they are with the Lord in the place which is their due, with whom they also suffered. For they did not love this present world but him who died on our behalf and was raised by God for our sakes.

10

1. Therefore, stand fast in these things and follow the example of the Lord, firm and unchangeable in faith, loving the brotherhood, affectionate to one another, joined together in the truth, forestalling one another in the gentleness of the Lord, despising no man. 2. When you can do good do not delay it, for almsgiving frees from death; be subject one to the other, having your conversation blameless among the gentiles, that you may receive praise for your good works and that the Lord may not be not blasphemed in you. 3. But woe to him through whom the name of the Lord is blasphemed. Therefore, teach sobriety to all and show it forth in your own lives.

On Valens, a Strayed Presbyter

11

1. I am deeply grieved for Valens, who was once made a presbyter among you, because he so poorly understands the office that was given to him. I advise, therefore, that you keep from evil, and be pure and truthful. Keep yourselves from all evil. 2. For how can one who cannot attain self-control in these matters prescribe it on another? If any man does not abstain from evil, he will be defiled by idolatry and shall be judged as if he were among the gentiles, who do not know the judgment of God. Or do we not know, as Paul teaches, that the saints will judge the world? 3. But I have neither perceived nor heard any such thing among you, among whom the blessed Paul labored, who are praised in the beginning of his epistle. For about you he boasts in all the churches who then alone had known the Lord, for we had not yet known him. 4. Therefore, brothers and sisters, I am deeply grieved for Valens and for his wife, and may the Lord grant them true repentance. Therefore, be yourselves also moderate in this matter, and do not regard such people as enemies, but call them back as fallible and straying members, that you may make whole the body of you all. For in doing this you edify yourselves.

12

1. For I am confident that you are well versed in the Scriptures, and from you nothing is hid; but to me this is not granted. Only, as it is said in these Scriptures, "Be angry and do not sin," and "Do not let the sun set on your anger (Eph 4:26). Blessed is the man who remembers this, and I believe that it is so with you. 2. Now may God and the Father of our Lord Jesus Christ, and the eternal Priest himself, Jesus Christ, the Son of God, build you up in faith and truth, and in all gentleness, and without anger and in patience, and in long-suffering, and endurance, and purity, and may he give you a share and part with his saints, and to us with you, and to all under heaven who shall believe in our Lord and God Jesus Christ and in his Father, who raised him from the dead. 3. Pray for all the saints. Pray also for the emperors, and for rulers, and princes, and for those who persecute you and hate you, and for the enemies of the Cross, that your fruit may be manifested among all men, that you may be perfected in him.

Closing

13

1. Both you and Ignatius wrote to me that if anyone was going to Syria, he should also take your letters. I will do this if I have a convenient opportunity, either myself or the man whom I am sending as a representative for you and me. 2. We send you, as you asked, the letters of Ignatius, which were sent to us by him, and others which we had with us. These are attached to this letter, and you will be able to benefit greatly from them. For they contain faith, patience, and all the edification that pertains to our Lord. Let us know anything further that you have heard about Ignatius himself and those who are with him.

14

1. I have written this to you by Crescens, whom I commended to you when I was present, and now commend again. For he has behaved blamelessly among us, and I believe that he will do the same with you. His sister will be commended to you when she comes to you. Farewell in the Lord Jesus Christ in grace, with all who are yours. Amen.

6

The Martyrdom of Polycarp

Context
Author: The church of Smyrna
Provenance: Smyrna
Date: c. AD 156 or 157[1]

Opening

The church of God which sojourns at Smyrna, to the church of God sojourning in Philomelium, and to all the congregations of the holy and catholic church in every place: mercy, peace, and love from God the Father and our Lord Jesus Christ, be multiplied.

1

We have written to you, brothers and sisters, about the martyrs and especially about the blessed Polycarp, who put an end to the persecution, having, as it were, set a seal upon it by his martyrdom. For almost all the events that happened previously, took place so that the Lord might show us from above a martyrdom in accordance with the gospel. For Polycarp waited to be delivered up, even as the Lord had done, so that we also might become his followers, while we look not merely at what concerns ourselves but have regard also for our neighbors. A true and well-founded love not only wishes for one's self to be saved but for all one's brothers and sisters to be saved as well.

---

[1] See Sara Parvis, "The Martyrdom of Polycarp," in *The Writings of the Apostolic Fathers*, 127–132.

2

All the martyrdoms that took place according to the will of God were blessed and noble. For it is fitting for us who profess greater devotion than others to attribute the authority over all things to God. And truly, who can fail to admire the martyrs' nobleness of mind, and their patience, with that love toward their Lord which they displayed? Who, when they were so torn with scourges that the frame of their bodies was laid open, even to the very inward veins and arteries, still patiently endured, while even those that stood by pitied and bewailed them? But they reached such a height of nobility that not one of them let out a sigh or a groan. In this way, they proved to us that those holy martyrs of Christ, at the very time when they suffered such torments, were absent from the body—or rather, that the Lord then stood by them and communed with them. And, looking to the grace of Christ, they despised all the torments of this world, redeeming themselves from eternal punishment in a single hour. For this reason, the fire of their savage executioners appeared cool to them. For they focused on escaping from the eternal fire that will never be quenched, and they looked forward with the eyes of their heart to those good things that are laid up for those who endure; things "which no ear has heard, nor eye seen, and which have not entered into the heart of man" (1 Cor 2:9). These things were revealed by the Lord to them, since they were no longer men but had already become angels. And, in like manner, those who were condemned to the wild beasts endured dreadful tortures, being stretched out upon beds full of spikes, and subjected to various other kinds of torments, in order that, if it were possible, the tyrant might, by their lingering tortures, lead them to a denial [of Christ].

On Germanicus and Quintus

3

For the devil did indeed invent many things against them; but thanks be to God since he could not prevail over all. For the most noble Germanicus strengthened the timidity of others by his own patience, and he fought heroically with the wild beasts. For, when the proconsul tried to persuade him and urged him to take pity upon his age, he called the wild beast toward himself, and provoked them, desiring to quickly escape from an unrighteous and impious world. Upon seeing this, the whole multitude, marveling at the nobility of mind displayed by the devout and godly race of Christians, cried out, "Away with the atheists; let Polycarp be sought out!"

4

Now one named Quintus, a Phrygian who had recently come from Phrygia, became afraid when he saw the wild beasts. This was the man who forced himself and some others to turn themselves in. After many attempts, the proconsul persuaded him to make the oath and to offer a sacrifice. Because of this, brothers and sisters, we do not commend those who turn themselves in, seeing the gospel does not teach us to do so.

The Arrest of Polycarp

5

But the most admirable Polycarp, when he first heard [that he was sought for], was not disturbed but resolved to remain in the city. However, in deference to the wishes of many, he was persuaded to leave the city. He departed to a house in the country, not far from the city. There he stayed with a few others, engaged in nothing else night and day than praying for all men, and for the churches throughout the world, according to his usual custom. And while he was praying, he received a vision three days before he was taken. [In the vision] the pillow under his head seemed to be on fire. Upon this, turning to those that were with him, he said to them prophetically, "I must be burnt alive."

6

And when those who sought him were close at hand, he departed to another dwelling, where his pursuers immediately came after him. But when they did not find him there, they seized two youths, one of whom, being subjected to torture, confessed. It was therefore impossible that Polycarp should continue to hide, since those that betrayed him were of his own household. The chief of police then, who was called by the same name, Herod, hastened to bring him into the stadium. [This all happened] so that Polycarp might fulfil his special lot in life, being made a partaker of Christ, and so that those who betrayed him might undergo the punishment of Judas himself.

7

His pursuers then, along with horsemen, and taking the youth with them, went forth at supper-time on the day of the preparation,[2] carrying their usual weapons, as if going after a robber. And around evening time, they found him lying down in the upper room of a certain little house, from which he might have escaped into another place; but he refused, saying, "The will of God be done" (cf. Acts 21:14). So, when he heard that they were there, he went down and spoke with them. Those that were present marveled at his age and constancy, and some of them said, "Why was so much effort made to capture such a venerable man?" Then he immediately ordered that something to eat and drink should be set before them, as much indeed as they cared for, while he asked them to allow him an hour to pray without disturbance. And after they gave him leave, he stood and prayed, being full of the grace of God, so that he could not cease for two full hours, to the astonishment of those that heard him, and many began to repent that they had arisen against so godly and venerable an old man.

8

Polycarp prayed for everyone who had at any time met him, both small and great, both illustrious and obscure, as well as the whole catholic church throughout the world. After he had finished praying, and the time of his departure had arrived, they set him upon a donkey and led him into the city, the day being that of the great Sabbath. And the chief of police, Herod, accompanied by his father Nicetes, met Polycarp. Taking him up into their carriage, they sat beside him and attempted to persuade him, saying, "What harm is there in saying, 'Caesar is Lord' and in sacrificing with the other ceremonies observed on such occasions, and so ensure your safety?" At first, he gave them no answer; but when they continued to urge him, he said, "I will not do as you advise me." So they, having no hope of persuading him, began to speak terrible words against him, and then they violently threw him out of the carriage, causing him to dislocate his leg. But without being disturbed, and as if suffering nothing, he eagerly continued forward with all haste, and he was led to the stadium, where the uproar was so great that there was no possibility of being heard.

---

2 That is, on Friday.

Polycarp's Martyrdom

9

Now, as Polycarp was entering the stadium, a voice from heaven came to him, saying, "Be strong, and show yourself a man, Polycarp!" No one saw who it was that spoke to him, but those of our brothers and sisters who were present heard the voice. And as he was brought forward, the uproar became great when they heard that Polycarp was taken. And when he came near, the proconsul asked him whether he was Polycarp. On his confessing that he was, [the proconsul] tried to persuade him to deny [Christ], saying, "Have respect for your old age," and other similar things, according to their custom, [such as], "Swear by the fortune of Caesar; repent and say, 'Away with the atheists.'" But Polycarp, sternly gazing at the crowd of wicked heathen in the stadium, and waving his hand toward them, and groaning, looked up to heaven and said, "Away with the atheists." Then, the proconsul urged him, saying, "Swear an oath, and I will set you free; reproach Christ"; Polycarp declared, "For eighty-six years I have served him, and he never did me any wrong. How can I blaspheme my King and my Savior?"

10

And when the proconsul pressed him again, saying, "Swear by the fortune of Caesar," Polycarp answered, "Since you vainly insist that, as you say, I should swear by the fortune of Caesar and pretend not to know who and what I am, let me make this clear to you: I am a Christian. And if you wish to learn what the doctrines of Christianity are, pick a day, and I will tell you them." The proconsul replied, "Persuade the people." But Polycarp said, "I have considered it right to offer an account of my faith to you, for we are taught to give all due honor (which entails no injury upon ourselves) to the powers and authorities that are ordained of God. But as for these others, I do not consider them worthy of receiving an account from me."

11

The proconsul then said to him, "I have wild beasts at hand. I will throw you to them unless you repent." But Polycarp answered, "Call them then, for we are not accustomed to repent of what is good in order to adopt what is evil, and it is good for me to be changed from what is evil to what is righteous."

But again the proconsul said to him, "I will cause you to be consumed by fire, seeing as you despise the wild beasts, if you will not repent." But Polycarp said, "You threaten me with fire that burns for an hour and after a little is extinguished, but you are ignorant of the fire of the coming judgment and of eternal punishment, reserved for the ungodly. But why do you delay? Bring forth what you will."

12

While Polycarp spoke these and many other similar things, he was filled with confidence and joy, and his face was full of grace, so that not only did Polycarp not become troubled and fall to the ground from the things said to him, but on the contrary, the proconsul was astonished and sent his herald to proclaim in the midst of the stadium three times, "Polycarp has confessed that he is a Christian." After this proclamation was made by the herald, the whole crowd both of the heathen and Jews, who dwelt at Smyrna, cried out with uncontrollable fury and in a loud voice, "This is the teacher of Asia, the father of the Christians, and the overthrower of our gods, the one who has been teaching many not to sacrifice or to worship the gods." Speaking thus, they cried out and besought Philip, the Asiarch, to let loose a lion upon Polycarp. But Philip answered that it was not lawful for him to do so, seeing the shows of wild beasts were already finished. Then it seemed good to them to cry out unanimously that Polycarp should be burnt alive. This fulfilled the vision that had been revealed to Polycarp about his pillow, when, seeing it on fire as he was praying, he turned around and said prophetically to the faithful that were with him, "I must be burnt alive."

13

This, then, was carried out with greater speed than it was spoken. The multitudes immediately gathered wood and kindling from the shops and baths, and the Jews especially, according to custom, eagerly assisted them in it. And when the funeral pyre was ready, Polycarp, laying aside all his garments, and loosening his belt, sought also to take off his sandals—a thing he was not accustomed to do, since every one of the faithful was always eager to do it for him and to touch his skin. For, on account of his holy life, he was, even before his martyrdom, honored in every good way. Immediately they surrounded him with the materials that had been prepared for the funeral pyre. But when they were about to fasten him with nails, he said, "Leave me as I am, for he that gives me strength to endure the fire will also enable me, without you securing me by nails, to remain without moving in the pyre."

14

They did not nail him then, but simply bound him. And Polycarp, placing his hands behind himself, and being bound like a distinguished ram taken from a great flock for sacrifice, and prepared to be an acceptable burnt-offering to God, looked up to heaven and said, "O Lord God Almighty, the Father of your beloved and blessed Son Jesus Christ, by whom we have received the knowledge of you, the God of angels and powers, and of every creature, and of the whole race of the righteous who live before you, I give you thanks that you have counted me worthy of this day and this hour, that I should be counted among your martyrs, in the cup of your Christ, to the resurrection of eternal life, both of soul and body, through the incorruption of the Holy Spirit. May I be accepted among them this day before you as a rich and acceptable sacrifice, just as you, the ever-truthful God, foreordained and revealed beforehand to me, and now have fulfilled. Therefore I also praise you for all things; I bless you; I glorify you, along with the everlasting and heavenly Jesus Christ, your beloved Son, with whom, to you and the Holy Spirit, be glory both now and in all coming ages. Amen."

15

When he had said this "amen," and so finished his prayer, those who were appointed for the purpose kindled the fire. And as the flame blazed forth in great fury, we, who were granted to be witnesses to it, beheld a great miracle. And we have been preserved that we might report to others what took place. For the fire, taking the shape of an arch, like the sail of a ship when filled with the wind, circled the body of the martyr. And he appeared within it, not like flesh that is burnt, but like bread that is baked, or as gold and silver glowing in a furnace. Moreover, we perceived such a sweet smell, as if frankincense or some other precious spices had been smoking there.

16

After quite some time, when those wicked men perceived that Polycarp's body could not be consumed by the fire, they commanded an executioner to approach and pierce him with a dagger. And when the executioner did this, a dove came out, along with a great quantity of blood, so that the fire was extinguished. And all the people marveled that there should be such a difference between the unbelievers and the elect, of whom this most admirable Polycarp was one, having in our own times been an apostolic and prophetic teacher, and bishop of the catholic church in Smyrna. For every word that went out of his mouth either has been or will yet be accomplished.

17

But when the adversary of the race of the righteous, the envious, malicious, and wicked one, perceived the impressive nature of Polycarp's martyrdom and the blameless life he had led from the beginning, and how he was now crowned with the wreath of immortality, having beyond dispute received his reward, the adversary did his utmost to ensure that not even the smaller memorial of Polycarp could be taken away by us, although many desired to do this and to become possessors of his holy flesh. It was for this reason that the adversary suggested to Nicetes, the father of Herod and brother of Alce, that Nicetes go and ask the governor not to give up Polycarp's body to be buried, "lest," he said, "forsaking him that was crucified, they begin to worship this one." This he said at the suggestion and urgent persuasion of the Jews, who also watched us as we sought to take Polycarp out of the fire. They did not know that it is impossible for us ever to forsake Christ, who suffered for the salvation of those who will be saved throughout the whole world (the blameless one for sinners), or to worship any other. For he, being the Son of God, is the one we worship; but the martyrs, as disciples and followers of the Lord, we worthily love on account of their extraordinary affection toward their own King and Master. With them, may we also be made fellow-partakers and fellow-disciples!

18

The centurion then, seeing the strife excited by the Jews, placed the body in the fire, which consumed it. After, we collected his bones, treating them as though more precious than the most exquisite jewels and more purified than gold. We deposited them in a fitting place, where, gathering as opportunity allows us, with joy and rejoicing, the Lord shall grant us to celebrate the anniversary of his martyrdom.[3] We celebrate both in memory of those who have

---

[3] This verse may indicate that the letter was written less than a year after Polycarp's martyrdom.

already finished their course, and for the exercising and preparation of those yet to walk in their steps.

19

This, then, is the account of the blessed Polycarp, who, although the twelfth martyr in Smyrna (considering also those of Philadelphia), occupies a place of his own in the memory of all people, for he is spoken about everywhere, even by the heathen. He was not merely an illustrious teacher but also a preeminent martyr, whose martyrdom all desire to imitate, as having been altogether consistent with the gospel of Christ. For, having through patience overcome the unjust governor, and thus acquired the crown of immortality, he now, with the apostles and all the righteous, rejoicingly glorifies God, even the Father, and blesses our Lord Jesus Christ, the Savior of our souls, the Governor of our bodies, and the Shepherd of the catholic church throughout the world.

Closing

20

Since you asked us to make you well acquainted with what really took place, we have presently sent you this summary account through our brother Marcus. After you have learned from it, please send it to the brothers and sisters who are further away, so that they also may glorify the Lord, who chooses [some for martyrdom] from among his servants. To him who is able to bring all of us by his grace and goodness into his everlasting kingdom, through his only-begotten Son Jesus Christ, to him be glory, and honor, and power, and majesty, forever. Amen. Greet all the saints. Those that are with us greet you, and Evarestus, who wrote this letter, with all his house.

Coda [4]

21

Now, the blessed Polycarp suffered martyrdom on the second day of the month of Xanthicus,[5] February 23, on the great Sabbath, at two o'clock in

---

4 What follows appears to be later additions to the manuscript.
5 Xanthicus is the sixth month in the Macedonian calendar.

the afternoon. He was arrested by Herod, when Philip the Trallian was the high priest and Statius Quadratus was the proconsul, but Jesus Christ is King forever, to whom be glory, honor, majesty, and an everlasting throne, from generation to generation. Amen.

22

We wish you, brothers and sisters, all happiness, while you walk by the word of Jesus Christ according to the gospel; with him be glory to God the Father and the Holy Spirit, for the salvation of his holy elect, after whose example the blessed Polycarp suffered, following in whose steps may we too be found in the kingdom of Jesus Christ!

These things Gaius transcribed from the copy of Irenaeus (who was a disciple of Polycarp), having himself been close with Irenaeus.

And I Socrates transcribed them at Corinth from the copy of Gaius. Grace be with you all.

And I again, Pionius, wrote them from the previously written copy, having carefully searched into them, and the blessed Polycarp having manifested them to me through a revelation, even as I shall show in what follows. I have collected these things, when they had almost faded away through the lapse of time, that the Lord Jesus Christ may also gather me along with his elect into his heavenly kingdom, to whom, with the Father and the Holy Spirit, be glory forever and ever. Amen.

7

Didache

Context[1]
Author: Possibly a Jewish-Christian community[2]
Provenance: Possibly Syria
Date: AD 90–110

The Teaching of the Lord through the Twelve Apostles to the Nations

The Two Ways

1

There are two ways, one of life and one of death, and there is much difference between the two ways. Therefore, the way of life is this: first, love the Lord who made you. Second, love your neighbor as yourself, and whatever you desire not to happen to you, you also do not do to another. Now, the teaching of these words is this: Bless those who curse you and pray for your enemies, but fast for those who persecute you. For what grace is there if you love those who love you? Do not the gentiles do the same thing? But you, love those who hate you and you will not have an enemy. Abstain from fleshly and corporeal desires. If anyone gives to you a blow on your right cheek, turn to him also the other and you will be complete. If anyone compels you one mile, go with him

---

1 Also titled the *Teaching of the Twelve Apostles*.
2 So Jonathan A. Draper, "The Didache," in *The Writings of the Apostolic Fathers*, ed. Paul Foster (T&T Clark, 2007), 15.

two. If anyone takes your garment, give to him also your tunic. If someone takes from you what is yours, do not demand it back, for you cannot. Give to all who ask you, and do not ask for anything back, for the Father desires to give to all from his own gifts. The one who gives according to the commandment is blessed, for he is innocent. Woe to the one who takes. For if someone takes because he has a need, he will be innocent. But the one who does not have a need will yield judgment. Why did he take and for what reason? Then, when he is imprisoned, he will be examined concerning the things he did, and he will not leave there until he repays the last penny. But also concerning this, it is said, "Let your alms sweat in your hands until you know to whom you should give."

2

Now the second commandment of the teaching: You shall not murder. You shall not commit adultery. You shall not sodomize children. You shall not commit fornication. You shall not steal. You shall not practice magic. You shall not make potions. You shall not murder a child by abortion nor shall you kill a child after it has been born. You shall not desire that which belongs to your neighbor. You shall not swear falsely. You shall not bear false witness. You shall not revile. You shall not bear a grudge. You shall not be double-minded nor double-tongued, for being double-tongued is a snare leading to death. Your word shall not be false or vain but filled with action. You shall not be covetous or ravenous or hypocritical or malicious or arrogant. You shall not take up evil plans against your neighbor. You shall not hate any man, but you shall reprove some; pray for others, and love others more than your own life.

3

My child, flee from all evil and from all that resembles it. Do not become quick-tempered, for wrath leads to murder, nor become zealous nor quarrelsome nor hot-tempered, for murders are bred from all these. My child, do not become lustful, for lust leads to fornication, nor become foul-mouthed nor lustful in the eyes, for from all these is bred adultery. My child, do not be a soothsayer, since it leads to idolatry, nor an enchanter, nor an astrologer, nor a magician, nor desire to see these things, for from all these is bred idolatry. My child, do not be a liar, since lying leads to theft, nor be a lover of money, nor be conceited, for from all these are bred thefts. My child, do not be a grumbler, since it leads to blasphemy, nor arrogant nor evil minded, for from all these are bred blasphemies. Rather, be meek since the meek will inherit the earth. Be patient and merciful and innocent and tranquil and upright and always trembling at the words you heard. You shall not exalt yourself, nor be overly confident in yourself. You shall not join yourself with the haughty, but you shall live with the righteous and humble. You shall receive the experiences that come upon you as good, because you know that nothing happens without God.

4

My child, the one who speaks to you the word of God you shall remember night and day, and you shall honor him as the Lord. For, wherever the lordship is spoken, there is the Lord. Now, you shall not seek out daily the presence of the saints, in order that you may rely on their words. You shall not make division, but you shall bring peace to those who quarrel. You shall judge righteously. You shall not show favoritism in order to convict someone on the basis of sins. You shall not be uncertain whether something shall be or not. Do not be one who stretches out the hands to receive but withdraws them from giving. If you obtain through your own hands, you shall give a ransom for your sins. You shall not hesitate to give, nor shall you grumble while giving. For you will know who is the good paymaster of the reward. You shall not turn away the needy one, but you shall share everything with your brother, and you shall not claim anything to be your own. For if there are partners in the imperishable, how much more in perishable things. You shall not withdraw your hand from your son or from your daughter, but from youth you shall teach the fear of God. You shall not command your male servant or maidservant—those who are hoping in the same God—while you are angry, lest they not fear the God who is over you both. For he is not coming to call by favoritism, but to call upon those the Spirit prepared. But you slaves, be submissive to your masters, as a symbol of God, modestly and fearfully. You shall hate all hypocrisy and everything that does not please the Lord. You shall not abandon the commandments of the Lord, but you shall keep that which you have received, neither adding nor taking away. You shall confess your sins in church, and you shall not come to your prayer with an evil conscience. This is the way of life.

5

Now, the way of death is this: First of all, it is evil and filled with a curse. Murders, adulteries, lusts, fornications, thefts, idolatries, divinations, sorceries, robberies, false testimonies, hypocrisies, duplicities, guile, arrogance, malice, pride, covetousness, obscene speech, jealousy, overconfidence, high-mindedness, pretension, persecutors of good, haters of truth, lovers of falsehood, not knowing the reward for righteousness, not clinging to good or righteous judgment, who care not for the good, but for evil, who are far from humility and patience, lovers of worthless things, pursuers of rewards, not having mercy on the poor, nor laboring for the oppressed, not knowing the one who made them, murderers of children, corrupters of what God has molded, who turn away those who are in need, inflictors of the oppressed, advocates of the rich, lawless judges of the poor, altogether sinful! May you be delivered, children, from all these.

6

See that no one leads you astray from this way of the teaching, because he teaches you apart from God. For if you are able to bear the whole yoke of the Lord, you will be perfect. But if you are not able, do what you can. Now, concerning food, bear what you are able. But keep yourself intently from food sacrificed to idols, for it is worship of dead gods.

On Baptism

7

Now concerning baptism, baptize in this way: after you have already said these things, baptize in the name of the Father and of the Son and of the Holy Spirit in living water. But if you do not have living water, baptize in other water. And if you are not able to baptize in cold water, baptize in warm water. But if you have neither, pour water on the head three times in the name of the Father and Son and Holy Spirit. Now, before baptism, let the one baptizing and the one being baptized fast, and any others who are able. And command the one being baptized to fast for one or two days beforehand.

On Fasting and Prayer

8

But do not let your fasts be with the hypocrites, for they fast on the second and fifth day of the week, but you fast on the fourth and sixth day. Neither pray like the hypocrites, but, as the Lord commanded in his Gospel, pray like this: "Our Father in heaven, let your name be made holy. Let your kingdom come, let your will be done, as in heaven so also on earth. Give us today our daily bread and forgive us our debts, as we forgive our debtors. And do not lead us into temptation, but deliver us from the evil one. For yours is the power and the glory forever" (Matt 6:9–13).

Pray like this three times a day.

On the Eucharist

9

Now concerning the Eucharist, give thanks thus: first, concerning the cup: "We give thanks to you, our Father, because of the holy vine of your servant David, which you made known to us through Jesus, your Son. To you be glory forever."

Now, concerning the broken bread: "We thank you, our Father, because of the life and knowledge that you made known to us through Jesus your Son. To you be glory forever. Just as this broken bread was scattered over the mountains and gathered together and became one, thus let your church be gathered together from the ends of the earth into your kingdom, because yours is the glory and the power through Jesus Christ forever."

But let no one eat or drink from your Eucharist except those who have been baptized into the name of the Lord, for even concerning this the Lord said, "Do not give what is holy to the dogs."

10

Now, after being satisfied, give thanks thus: "We thank you, Holy Father, because of your holy name, which you caused to dwell in our hearts, and because of the knowledge and faith and immortality that you made known to us through Jesus, your Son. To you be glory forever."

"You, almighty Master, created all things for the sake of your name, and food and drink you gave to mankind for enjoyment, in order that we might give thanks to you. But to us you graciously gave spiritual food and drink, and eternal life through your servant. Above all, we give thanks to you because you are mighty. To you be glory forever."

"Remember, Lord, your church, to deliver her from all evil and to complete her through your love. And gather from the four winds her who has been sanctified into your kingdom that you prepared for her, because yours is the power and the glory forever. Let grace come and let this world pass away. Hosanna to the God of David. If anyone is holy, let him come. If anyone is not, let him repent. Maranatha! Amen."

But permit the prophets to give thanks however they desire.

On Visiting Teachers

11

Therefore, if anyone comes and teaches you all these things just spoken of, receive him. But if the teacher himself, after straying, teaches another teaching leading to destruction, do not listen to him. But if his teaching adds righteousness and knowledge of the Lord, receive him as the Lord.

Now, concerning the apostles and prophets, according to the standard of the gospel do thus: Every apostle who comes to you, receive him as the Lord. But he shall not stay except one day, unless there is a need, and then one more day. But if he stays three days, he is a false prophet. Now when the apostle leaves, let him take nothing except bread, until he lodges, and if he asks for money, he is a false prophet. And every prophet who speaks by the Spirit, do not test or judge him, for every sin will be forgiven, but this sin will not be forgiven. But, not every person who speaks by the Spirit is a prophet, only if he has the conduct of the Lord. Therefore, the false prophet and the prophet will be known by their conduct. And every prophet who orders a meal in the Spirit shall not eat from it, unless he is indeed a false prophet. And every prophet who teaches the truth, if he does not do what he teaches, is a false prophet. But every prophet proven to be genuine who works for the earthly mystery of the church, but is not teaching to do whatever he does, shall not be judged by you, for he has his judgment with God. For the ancient prophets did likewise. But whoever says in the Spirit, "Give me money," or something else, do not listen to him. But if he says to give to others who are in need, let no one judge him.

12

Let everyone who comes in the name of the Lord be welcomed. But then, after examining him, you will know, for you will have insight, true and false. If one who comes is travelling through, assist him as much as you are able. But he shall not stay with you more than two or three days, if there is a need. But if he desires to dwell with you, in order that he might be a craftsman, let him work and eat. But if he does not have a skill, according to your insight consider how he may live with you as a Christian without being idle. But if he does not desire to do so, he is cashing in on Christ. Give heed to these.

13

Now every true prophet who desires to stay with you is worthy of his food. Likewise, a true teacher is himself also worthy, like the worker, of his food. Therefore, every first-fruit of the production of the wine press and threshing floor, of oxen and sheep, you shall take and give this first-fruit to the prophets, for they are your high priests. But if you do not have a prophet, give to the poor. If you make bread, take and give the first-fruit according to the commandment. Likewise, when you open a jar of wine or oil, take and give the first-fruit to the prophets. And of money and clothing and every possession, take the first-fruit, as it seems good to you, and give according to the commandment.

On Gathering

14

Each Lord's Day, when you gather together, break bread and give thanks after you have confessed your trespasses, in order that your sacrifices may be pure. But let no one who has a quarrel with his friend gather together with you until they are reconciled, in order that your sacrifice may not be defiled. For this is that which was spoken by the Lord: In every place and time, offer to me a pure sacrifice, because I am a great king, says the Lord, and my name is wonderful among the nations.

On Deacons and Elders

15

Therefore, appoint for yourselves elders and deacons worthy of the Lord, men who are humble and do not love money and are true and have been proven among you, for they themselves also carry out the ministry of the prophets and teachers. Therefore, do not despise them, for they are those who are honored among you with the prophets and teachers.

Now, reprove one another not angrily, but peacefully, as you have in the Gospel, and do not let anyone who has wronged another speak anything, nor let him hear from you until he repents. Now, your prayers and your almsgiving and all your deeds, do them as you have in the Gospel of our Lord.

Warning about the Coming of the Lord

16

Stay alert over your life. Do not let your lamps be put out, and do not let your loins grow weary, but be prepared. For you do not know the hour in which our Lord will come. But you shall gather together frequently in order to seek what is fitting for your souls. For the entire time of your faith will not profit you, unless you are made perfect in the last time.

For in the last days false prophets and corrupters will multiply, and the sheep will be turned into wolves, and love will be turned into hate. For while lawlessness increases, they will hate and persecute and betray one another. And then the deceiver of the world will be revealed as a son of God and will perform signs and wonders, and the earth will be given over into his hands, and he will do disgusting things which have never happened from eternity. Then the creation of mankind will have come into the fiery test, and many will fall away and perish, but those who endure in their faith will be saved by him who is accursed. And then the true signs will be revealed. First, a sign of an opening in heaven. Then, a sign of the sound of a trumpet. And third, the resurrection of the dead. Yet not of everyone, but as it has been said, "The Lord will come, and all his saints with him" (cf. Zech 14:5).

8

The Epistle of Barnabas

Context
Author: Unknown
Provenance: Possibly Egypt[1]
Date: c. AD 96–100 or 130–132

Opening

1

Greetings, sons and daughters, in the name of our Lord Jesus Christ, who loved us in peace.

Seeing that the divine fruits of righteousness abound among you, I rejoice exceedingly and above measure in your happy and honored spirits, because you have with such effect received the engrafted spiritual gift. Therefore, I also inwardly rejoice all the more, hoping to be saved, because I truly perceive in you the Spirit poured forth from the riches of the fount of the Lord. Your greatly desired appearance has thus filled me with amazement over you. I am therefore persuaded of this and fully convinced in my own mind, that since I began to speak among you, I understand many things because the Lord has accompanied me in the way of righteousness. I am also on this account bound by the strictest obligation to love you above my own soul because great faith and love dwell in you while you hope for the life which he has promised. Considering this, therefore—that if I should take the trouble

---

[1] See James Carleton Paget, "The Epistle of Barnabas," in *The Writings of the Apostolic Fathers*, 73–75.

to communicate to you some portion of what I have myself received, it will prove to me a sufficient reward that I minister to such spirits—I have hastened briefly to write to you, in order that, along with your faith, you might have perfect knowledge. There are then three doctrines of the Lord: "the hope of life" is the beginning and end of our faith; and righteousness is the beginning and end of judgment; love of joy and of gladness is the testimony of the works of righteousness.[2] For the Lord has made known to us by the prophets both the things that are past and present, giving us also the first-fruits of the knowledge of things to come. As we see these things accomplished one by one, we ought with the greater richness of faith and elevation of spirit to draw near to him with reverence. I then, not as your teacher, but as one of yourselves, will set forth a few things by which in present circumstances you may be rendered more joyful.

On True Sacrifices

2

Since, therefore, the days are evil, and Satan possesses the power of this world, we ought to give heed to ourselves, and diligently inquire into the ordinances of the Lord. Fear and patience, then, are helpers of our faith; and long-suffering and self-control are things which fight on our side. While these things remain pure in what respects the Lord, wisdom, understanding, insight, and knowledge rejoice along with them. For he has revealed to us by all the prophets that he needs neither sacrifices, nor burnt offerings, nor oblations, saying, "What is the multitude of your sacrifices to me, says the Lord? I am full of burnt offerings, and do not desire the fat of lambs, and the blood of bulls and goats, not when you come to appear before me: for who has required these things at your hands? Tread no more on my courts; if you bring with you fine flour, it is in vain. Incense is an abomination to me, and I cannot endure your new moons and Sabbaths" (Isa 1:11–14 LXX). He has therefore abolished these things so that the new law of our Lord Jesus Christ, which is without the yoke of necessity, might have its offering not made by human hands. And again, he says to them, "Did I command your fathers, when they went out from the land of Egypt, to offer to me burnt offerings and sacrifices? But this rather I commanded them: Let no one of you hold any evil in his heart against his neighbor, and do not love a false oath (Jer 7:22–23 LXX; Zech 8:17 LXX). We

---

2 Following Kirsopp Lake, *The Apostolic Fathers*, 2 vols. Loeb Classical Library 24–25 (Harvard University Press, 1912–1913).

ought therefore, being possessed of understanding, to perceive the gracious intention of our Father, for he speaks to us, desiring that we, not going astray like them, should ask how we may approach him. To us, then, he declares, "A sacrifice to God is a broken spirit; a smell of sweet savor to the Lord is a heart that glorifies him that made it" (Ps 51:19). We ought therefore, brothers and sisters, to carefully inquire concerning our salvation, lest the wicked one, having made his entrance by deceit, should hurl us away from our [true] life.

[...]

On the Old and New Covenants and the Work of Christ

4

It is therefore appropriate for us, who greatly inquire about events at hand, to search diligently into those things which can save us. Let us then utterly flee from all the works of iniquity, lest these should take hold of us; and let us hate the error of the present time, that we may set our love on the world to come; let us not give loose reins to our soul, that it should have power to run with sinners and the wicked, lest we become like them. The final stumbling-block approaches, concerning which it is written, as Enoch says.[3] For this reason the Lord has cut short the times and the days, that his beloved may hasten; and he will come to the inheritance. And the prophet also speaks thus: "Ten kingdoms shall reign upon the earth, and a little king shall rise up after them, who shall subdue under one three of the kings" (Dan 7:24). In like manner Daniel says concerning the same, "And I beheld the fourth beast, wicked and powerful, and more savage than all the beasts of the earth, and how from it sprang up ten horns, and out of them a little budding horn, and how it subdued three of the great horns under one" (Dan 7:7–8). You ought therefore to understand. And this also I further beg of you, as being one of you, and loving you both individually and collectively more than my own soul, to take heed now to yourselves, and not to be like some, adding largely to your sins, and saying, "The covenant is both theirs and ours." But they thus finally lost it, after Moses had already received it. For the Scripture says, "And Moses was fasting in the mount forty days and forty nights, and received the covenant from the Lord, tables of stone written with the finger of the hand of the Lord" (Exod 34:28; 31:18); but turning away to idols, they lost it. For the Lord speaks thus to Moses: "Moses go down quickly; for the people whom you have brought out of the land of Egypt have transgressed" (Exod 32:7). And Moses

---

3 Reference unknown.

understood and cast the two tables out of his hands; and their covenant was broken, in order that the covenant of the beloved Jesus might be sealed upon our heart, in the hope which flows from believing in him. Now, desiring to write many things to you, not as your teacher, but as one who loves you, I have taken care not to fail to write to you from what I myself possess, with a view to your purification. We take earnest heed in these last days; for the whole [past] time of your faith will profit you nothing, unless now in this wicked time we also withstand coming sources of danger, as becomes the sons of God. That the Black One may find no means of entrance, let us flee from every vanity, let us utterly hate the works of the way of wickedness. Do not, by retiring apart, live a solitary life, as if you were already [fully] justified; but coming together in one place, make common inquiry concerning what tends to your general welfare. For the Scripture says, "Woe to them who are wise to themselves, and prudent in their own sight!" (Isa 5:21 LXX). Let us be spiritually minded; let us be a perfect temple to God. As much as we are able, let us meditate upon the fear of God, and let us keep his commandments, that we may rejoice in his ordinances. The Lord will judge the world without respect of persons. Each will receive as he has done: if he is righteous, his righteousness will precede him; if he is wicked, the reward of wickedness is before him. Take heed, lest resting at our ease, as those who are the called [of God], we should fall asleep in our sins, and the wicked prince, acquiring power over us, should thrust us away from the kingdom of the Lord. And all the more attend to this, my brothers and sisters, when you reflect and behold, that after such great signs and wonders were done in Israel, they were thus [at length] abandoned. Let us beware lest we be found [fulfilling that saying], as it is written, "Many are called, but few are chosen" (Matt 22:14).

5

It was for this reason that the Lord endured to deliver up his flesh to corruption, that we might be sanctified through the remission of sins, which is effected by the sprinkling of his blood. For it is written concerning him, partly with reference to Israel, and partly to us; and [the Scripture] says: "He was wounded for our transgressions and bruised for our iniquities; with his stripes we are healed. He was brought as a sheep to the slaughter, and as a lamb that is dumb before its shearer" (Isa 53:5, 7). Therefore, we ought to be deeply grateful to the Lord because he has made known to us things that are past, and he has given us wisdom concerning things present, and he has not left us without understanding in regard to things which are to come. Now,

The Epistle of Barnabas

the Scripture says, "Not unjustly are nets spread out for birds" (Prov 1:17). This means that the man perishes justly, who, having a knowledge of the way of righteousness, rushes off into the way of darkness. And further, my brothers and sisters, if the Lord endured to suffer for our soul, he being Lord of all the world, to whom God said at the foundation of the world, "Let us make man after our image, and after our likeness" (Gen 1:26), understand how it was that he endured to suffer at the hand of men. The prophets, having obtained grace from him, prophesied concerning him. And he (since it behooved him to appear in flesh), that he might abolish death, and reveal the resurrection from the dead, endured in order that he might fulfill the promise made to the fathers, and by preparing a new people for himself, might show, while he lived on earth, that he, when he has raised mankind, will also judge them. Moreover, teaching Israel, and doing such great miracles and signs, he preached to them, and greatly loved them. But when he chose his own apostles who were to preach his gospel, [he chose from among those] who were sinners above all sin, that he might show he came "not to call the righteous, but sinners to repentance" (Mark 2:17). Then he revealed himself to be the Son of God. For if he had not come in the flesh, how could men have been saved by beholding him? Their eyes cannot even bear to look upon the rays of the sun (and then sun is merely a work of his hands and will cease to exist). The Son of God therefore came in the flesh with this aim: that he might bring to a head the sum of their sins who had persecuted his prophets to the death. For this purpose, then, he endured. For God says, "The stroke of his flesh is from them," and "when I shall strike down the shepherd, then the sheep of the flock will be scattered" (Zech 13:7). He himself desired to suffer in this way, for it was necessary that he should suffer on the tree. For the prophet says regarding him, "Spare my soul from the sword, fasten my flesh with nails; for the assemblies of the wicked have risen up against me" (Ps 22:20; Ps 119:20; Ps 22:16). And again, he says, "Behold, I have given my back to scourges, and my cheeks to strokes, and I have set my countenance as a firm rock" (Isa 50:6–7).

6

When, therefore, he had fulfilled the commandment, what did he say? "Who will contend with me? Let him oppose me. Or who will enter into judgment with me? Let him draw near to the servant of the Lord" (Isa 50:6–7 LXX). "Woe to you, for you shall all become old, like a garment, and the moth shall eat you up" (Isa 51:8). And again, the prophet says, "Since as a mighty stone he is laid for crushing, behold I cast down for the foundations of Zion a stone, precious, elect, a cornerstone, honorable" (Isa 28:16). Next, what did he say? "And he who shall trust in it shall live forever" (cf. Isa 28:16). Is our hope, then, upon a stone? Far from it. But [the language is used] since he laid his flesh [as a foundation] with power; for he says, "And he placed me as a firm rock" (Isa 50:7). And the prophet says again, "The stone which the builders rejected, the same has become the head of the corner" (Ps 118:22). And again, he says, "This is the great and wonderful day which the Lord has made" (Ps 118:24). I write the more simply to you, that you may understand. I am devoted to your love. What, then, again says the prophet? "The assembly of the wicked surrounded me; they encompassed me as bees do a honeycomb" (Ps 22:16), and "upon my garment they cast lots" (Ps 22:18). Since, therefore, he was about to be manifested and to suffer in the flesh, his suffering was foretold. For the prophet speaks against Israel, "Woe to their soul, because they have counselled an evil counsel against themselves, saying, 'Let us bind the just one, because he is displeasing to us'" (Isa 3:9–10). And Moses also says to them, "Behold these things, says the Lord God: Enter into the good land which the Lord promised to Abraham, and Isaac, and Jacob, and inherit it, a land flowing with milk and honey" (Exod 33:1, 3). What, then, says knowledge? Learn: "Trust," she says, "in him who is to be manifested to you in the flesh—that is, Jesus." For man is earth in a suffering state, for the formation of Adam was from the face of the earth. What, then, does this mean: "into the good land, a land flowing with milk and honey"? Blessed be our Lord, who has placed in us wisdom and understanding of secret things. For the prophet says, "Who shall understand the parable of the Lord, except him who is wise and prudent, and who loves his Lord?" Since, therefore, having renewed us by the remission of our sins, he has made us after another pattern, [it is his purpose] that we should possess the soul of children, since he has created us anew by his Spirit. For the Scripture says concerning us, while he speaks to the Son, "Let us make man after our image, and after our likeness; and let them have dominion over the beasts of the earth, and the birds of the sky, and the fish of the sea" (Gen 1:26). And the Lord said, on beholding the fair creature man, "Increase, and multiply, and replenish the earth" (Gen 1:28). These things [were spoken] to the Son. Again, I will show you how, in respect to us, he has accomplished a second fashioning in these last days. The Lord says, "Behold, I will make the last like the first."[4] In reference to this, then, the prophet proclaimed, "Enter into the land flowing with milk and honey, and have dominion over it" (Exod 33:3). Behold, therefore, we have been refashioned, as again he says in another prophet, "Behold, says the Lord, I will take away from these, that is, from those whom the Spirit

---

4 Source unknown.

The Epistle of Barnabas

of the Lord foresaw, their stony hearts, and I will put hearts of flesh within them" (Ezek 11:19), because he was to be manifested in flesh and to sojourn among us. For, my brothers and sisters, the habitation of our heart is a holy temple to the Lord. For again says the Lord, "And where shall I appear before the Lord my God and be glorified?" (Ps 42:2). He says, "I will confess to you in the congregation in the midst of my brothers and sisters; and I will praise you in the midst of the assembly of the saints" (Ps 22:22). We, then, are they whom he has led into the good land. What, then, does milk and honey mean? This: that as the infant is kept alive first by honey, and then by milk, so also we, being quickened and kept alive by the faith of the promise and by the word, shall live ruling over the earth. But he said above, "Let them increase, and rule over the fishes." Who then can govern the beasts, or the fishes, or the birds of the sky? For we ought to perceive that to govern implies authority, so that one should command and rule. If, therefore, this does not exist at present, yet still he has promised it to us. When? When we ourselves also have been made perfect [so as] to become heirs of the covenant of the Lord.

7

Understand, then, you children of gladness, that the good Lord has foretold all things to us, that we might know to whom we ought to give thanks and praise for everything. If therefore the Son of God, who is Lord and who will judge the living and the dead, suffered, that his wounding might give us life, let us believe that the Son of God could not have suffered except for our sakes. Moreover, when crucified, he was given vinegar and gall. Listen to how the priests of the people gave previous indications of this. His commandment having been written, the Lord spoke that whosoever did not keep the fast should be put to death because he was to offer in sacrifice for our sins the vessel of the Spirit, in order that the type established in Isaac when he was offered upon the altar might be fully accomplished. What, then, does he say through the prophet? "And let them eat of the goat that is offered with fasting for all their sins."[5] Attend carefully: "And let all the priests alone eat the inwards, unwashed with vinegar."[6] Why? Because to me, who am to offer my flesh for the sins of my new people, you are to give gall with vinegar to drink: you alone, eat, while the people fast and mourn in sackcloth and ashes. [These things were done] that he might show that it was necessary for him to suffer for them. What, then was the commandment? Give your attention.

---

5 Source unknown.
6 Source unknown.

Take two goats, good and alike, and offer them. And let the priest take one as a burnt offering for sins. And what should they do with the other? "Accursed," he says, "is the one" (cf. Lev 16:8). Notice how the type of Jesus now comes out. "And all of you spit upon it, and pierce it, and encircle its head with scarlet wool, and thus let it be driven into the wilderness."[7] And when all this has been done, he who bears the goat brings it into the desert, takes the wool off from it, and places that upon a shrub called "rachia," of which also we are accustomed to eat the fruits when we find them in the field. From this kind of shrub alone the fruits are sweet. Why then, again, is this? Pay attention. [You see] "one upon the altar, and the other accursed"; and why [do you behold] the one that is accursed is crowned? Because they shall see him then in that day having a scarlet robe about his body down to his feet; and they shall say, "Is not this he whom we once despised, and pierced, and mocked, and crucified?" Truly this is he who declared himself to be the Son of God. For how alike is he to him! With a view to this, [he required] the goats to be of good condition, and similar, that, when they see him then coming, they may be amazed by the likeness of the goat. Behold, then, the type of Jesus who was to suffer. But why is it that they place the wool amid thorns? It is a type of Jesus set before the view of the church. [They place the wool among thorns] so that anyone who wishes to bear it away may find it necessary to suffer much (because the thorn is formidable) and thus obtain it only as the result of suffering. Thus also, he says, "Those who wish to behold me, and lay hold of my kingdom, must obtain me through tribulation and suffering."

[...]

On Circumcision

9

He speaks moreover concerning our ears, how he has circumcised both them and our heart. The Lord says in the prophet, "Hearing with their ears, they obeyed me" (Ps 18:44). And again, he says, "Those who are far away shall hear clearly; they shall know what I have done" (Isa 33:13). And, "Be circumcised in your hearts, says the Lord" (Jer 4:4). And again, he says, "Hear, O Israel, for the Lord your God says these things" (Jer 7:2–3). And once more the Spirit of the Lord proclaims, "Who is he that wishes to live forever? By hearing let him hear the voice of my servant" (Ps 34:12). And again, he says, "Hear, O heaven, and give ear, O earth, for God has spoken these things for a testimony"

---

7 Source unknown.

(Isa 1:2). And again, he says, "Hear the word of the Lord, you rulers of this people" (Isa 1:10). And again, he says, "Hear, you children, the voice of one crying in the wilderness" (Isa 40:3). Therefore, he has circumcised our ears, that we might hear his word and believe, for the circumcision in which they trusted is abolished. For he declared that circumcision was not of the flesh, but they transgressed because an evil angel deluded them. He says to them, "These things says the Lord your God" (Jer 4:3–4)—(here I find a new commandment)—"Do not sow among thorns, but circumcise yourselves to the Lord." And why does he speak in this way: "Circumcise the stubbornness of your heart, and do not harden your neck"? (Deut 10:6). And again: "Behold, says the Lord, all the nations are uncircumcised in the flesh, but this people are uncircumcised in heart" (Jer 9:26). But you will say, "Truly, the people are circumcised as a seal." But so also is every Syrian and Arab, and all the priests of idols: are these then also within the bond of his covenant? Yes, the Egyptians also practice circumcision. Learn then, my children, concerning all things, that Abraham, the first who prescribed circumcision, looking forward in Spirit to Jesus, practiced that rite, having received the mysteries of the three letters. For [the Scripture] says, "And Abraham circumcised ten, and eight, and three hundred men of his household" (Gen 14:14). What, then, was the knowledge given to him in this? Learn the eighteen first, and then the three hundred. The ten and the eight are thus denoted: Ten by I, and Eight by H. You have [the initials of the name of] Jesus. And because the cross was to express the grace [of our redemption] by the letter T, he says also, "Three Hundred." He signifies, therefore, Jesus by two letters, and the cross by one.[8] He knows this, who has put within us the engrafted gift of his doctrine. No one has received from me a more excellent piece of knowledge than this, but I know that you are worthy.

[...]

On the Covenant

13

But let us see if this people or the former people is the heir, and if the covenant belongs to us or to them. Hear what the Scripture says concerning the people. Isaac prayed for Rebecca his wife because she was barren, and she

---

8 In the author's day, *iota* (I) and *eta* (H) were the tenth and eight letters of the Greek alphabet, respectively. *Iota* and *eta* are also the first two letters of the name Jesus (ΙΗΣΟΥΣ). *Tau* (T) is the symbol for the number three hundred, which the author notes also looks like the shape of the cross.

conceived. Furthermore also, Rebecca went forth to inquire of the Lord, and the Lord said to her, "Two nations are in your womb, and two peoples in your belly; and the one people shall surpass the other, and the older shall serve the younger" (Gen 25:21–23). You ought to understand who was Isaac and who was Rebecca, and concerning what persons he declared that this people should be greater than that.

And in another prophecy Jacob speaks more clearly to his son Joseph, saying, "Behold, the Lord has not deprived me of your presence; bring your sons to me, that I may bless them" (Gen 48:11, 9). And he brought Manasseh and Ephraim, desiring that Manasseh should be blessed because he was the elder. With this view, Joseph led him to the right hand of his father Jacob. But Jacob saw in Spirit the type of the people that would come afterwards. And what does Scripture say? Jacob changed the direction of his hands and laid his right hand upon the head of Ephraim (the second and younger), and Jacob blessed him. And Joseph said to Jacob, "Move your right hand to the head of Manasseh, for he is my first-born son." And Jacob said, "I know it, my son, I know it; but the elder shall serve the younger; yet he also shall be blessed" (Gen 48:14, 18). You see on whom he laid his hands, that this people should be first and heir of the covenant. If, still further, the same thing was revealed through Abraham, then we reach the perfection of our knowledge. What, then, does he say to Abraham? "Because you have believed, it is imputed to you as righteousness; behold, I have made you the father of those nations who believe in the Lord while in uncircumcision" (Gen 15:6, 17:5; Rom 4:11, 17).

14

Yes, but let us inquire if the Lord has really given that covenant which he swore to the fathers that he would give to the people. He did give it; but they were not worthy to receive it on account of their sins. For the prophet declares, "And Moses was fasting forty days and forty nights on Mount Sinai, that he might receive the covenant of the Lord for the people" (Exod 24:18; 31:18). And he received from the Lord two tablets, written in the Spirit by the finger of the hand of the Lord. And Moses having received them, carried them down to give to the people. And the Lord said to Moses, "Moses, go down quickly; for your people has sinned, whom you brought out of the land of Egypt" (Exod 32:7–9, 19). And Moses understood that they had again made graven images; and he threw the tablets out of his hands, and the tablets of the covenant of the Lord were broken. Moses then received it, but they proved themselves unworthy.

Now learn how we have received it. Moses, as a servant, received it; but the Lord himself, having suffered on our behalf, has given it to us, that we should be the people of inheritance. But he was manifested in order that they might be perfected in their iniquities, and that we, being constituted heirs through him, might receive the covenant of the Lord Jesus, who was prepared for this end, that by his personal manifestation, redeeming our hearts (which were already wasted by death, and given over to the iniquity of error) from darkness, he might by his word enter into a covenant with us. For it is written how the Father, about to redeem us from darkness, commanded him to prepare a holy people for himself. The prophet therefore declares, "I, the Lord your God, have called you in righteousness, and will hold your hand, and will strengthen you; and I have given you for a covenant to the people, for a light to the nations, to open the eyes of the blind, and to bring forth from chains them that are bound, and to free from prison those that sit in darkness" (Isa 42:6–7). You see, then, from what we have been redeemed. And again, the prophet says, "Behold, I have appointed you as a light to the nations, that you might be for salvation even to the ends of the earth, says the Lord God who redeems you" (Isa 49:6–7). And again, the prophet says, "The Spirit of the Lord is upon me; because he has anointed me to preach the gospel to the humble: he has sent me to heal the broken-hearted, to proclaim deliverance to the captives, and recovery of sight to the blind; to announce the acceptable year of the Lord, and the day of recompense; to comfort all that mourn" (Isa 61:1–2).

[…]

On the Temple

16

I will also speak with you about the temple and show how the wretched men erred by putting their hope on the building and not on the God who made them and is the true house of God. For they consecrated him in the temple almost like the heathen. But learn how the Lord speaks about abolishing it: "Who has measured the heaven with a span, or the earth with his outstretched hand? Have not I? says the Lord. Heaven is my throne, and the earth is my footstool, what house will you build for me, or what is the place of my rest?" (Isa 40:12; 66:1). You know that their hope was vain. Furthermore, he says again, "Behold, those who destroyed this temple will themselves build it" (cf. Isa 49:17). That is happening now. For owing to the war, it was destroyed by the enemy; at present even the servants of the enemy will build it up again. Again, it was made manifest that the city and the temple and the people of Israel were to be delivered up. For the Scripture says, "And it will come to pass in the last days that the Lord will deliver the sheep of his pasture, and the sheepfold, and their tower to destruction" (cf. 1 Enoch 89:56). And it took place according to what the Lord said. But let us inquire if a temple of God exists. Yes, it exists, where he himself said that he makes and perfects it. For it is written, "And it will come to pass when the week is ended that a temple of God will be built gloriously in the name of the Lord." I find then that a temple exists. Learn then how it will be built in the name of the Lord. Before we believed in God the habitation of our heart was corrupt and weak, like a temple really built with hands, because it was full of idolatry and was the house of demons through doing things which were contrary to God. "But it will be built in the name of the Lord."[9] Now give heed, in order that the temple of the Lord may be built gloriously. Learn in what way. When we received the remission of sins, and put our hope on the name, we became new, being created again from the beginning; therefore, God truly dwells in us, in the habitation which we are. How? His word of faith, the calling of his promise, the wisdom of the ordinances, the commands of the teaching, himself prophesying in us, himself dwelling in us, by opening the door of the temple (that is the mouth) to us, giving repentance to us, and thus he leads us, who have been enslaved to death into the incorruptible temple. For he who desires to be saved looks not at the man but at him who dwells and speaks in him, and is amazed at him, for he has never either heard him speak such words with his mouth nor has he himself ever desired to hear them. This is a spiritual temple being built for the Lord.

[...]

The Two Ways

18

But let us now pass to another sort of knowledge and doctrine. There are two ways of teaching and power: one of light and the other of darkness, and there is a great difference between these two ways. For over one are stationed the light-bringing angels of God, but over the other are stationed the angels of

---

9 Source unknown.

Satan. And God is Lord forever and ever, but Satan is prince of the time of iniquity.

19

The way of light, then, is as follows. If anyone desires to travel to the appointed place, he must be zealous in his works. The knowledge, therefore, which is given to us for the purpose of walking in this way is the following: You shall love the one who created you; you shall glorify the one who redeemed you from death. You shall be simple in heart, and rich in spirit. You shall not join yourself to those who walk in the way of death. You shall hate doing what is unpleasing to God; you shall hate all hypocrisy. You shall not forsake the commandments of the Lord. You shall not exalt yourself but shall be of a lowly mind. You shall not take glory for yourself. You shall not take evil counsel against your neighbor. You shall not allow arrogance to enter into your soul. You shall not commit fornication; you shall not commit adultery; you shall not be a corrupter of youth. You shall not let the word of God issue from your lips with any kind of impurity. You shall not be biased when you reprove someone for transgression. You shall be meek; you shall be peaceable. You shall tremble at the words which you hear. You shall not be mindful of evil against your brother. You shall not be of doubtful mind as to whether a thing shall be or not. You shall not take the name of the Lord in vain. You shall love your neighbor more than your own soul. You shall not kill a child in abortion; nor shall you do away with one after it is born.[10] You shall not withdraw your hand from your son or from your daughter, but from their infancy you shall teach them the fear of the Lord. You shall not covet what is your neighbor's, nor shall you be greedy. You shall not be joined in soul with the arrogant, but you shall be associated with the righteous and lowly. Receive the trials that come upon you as good things. You shall not be of double mind or of double tongue, for a double tongue is a snare of death. You shall be subject to the Lord, and to masters as the image of God, with modesty and fear. You shall not issue orders with bitterness to your slaves and maidservants, who trust in the same [God], lest you should not revere that God, who is above both; for he came to call people not according to their outward appearance but as the Spirit had prepared them. You shall share in all things with your neighbor; you shall not call things your own; for if you are sharers of common of things that are incorruptible, how much more [should you be sharers] of those things which are corruptible! You shall not be hasty with your tongue,

---

10 Gk. Οὐ φονεύσεις τέκνον ἐν φθορᾷ, οὐδὲ πάλιν γεννηθὲν ἀνελεῖς.

for the mouth is a snare of death. As far as possible, you shall be pure in your soul. Do not be ready to stretch forth your hands to take, while you contract them to give. You shall love, as the apple of your eye, everyone that speaks to you the word of the Lord. You shall remember the day of judgment, night and day. You shall seek out daily the company of the saints, either by word examining them, and going to exhort them, and meditating how to save a soul by the word, or by your hands you shall labor for the redemption of your sins. You shall not hesitate to give, nor murmur when you give. "Give to everyone that asks you," and you shall know who is the good giver of the reward. You shall preserve what you have received, neither adding to it nor taking from it. Until the end, you shall hate the wicked. You shall judge righteously. You shall not make a schism, but you shall pacify those that contend by bringing them together. You shall confess your sins. You shall not go to prayer with an evil conscience. This is the way of light.

20

But the way of darkness[11] is crooked, and full of cursing; for it is the way of eternal death with punishment, this way includes the things that destroy the soul: idolatry, arrogance, the abuse of power,[12] hypocrisy, double-heartedness, adultery, murder, robbery,[13] arrogance, transgression, deceit, malice, stubbornness, poisoning,[14] magic, greediness, and lack of the fear of God. It includes those who persecute the good, those who hate truth, those who love falsehood, those who do not know the reward of righteousness, those who do not cling to that which is good, those who do not give a just judgment to the widow and orphan, those who do not remain alert because of the fear of God, those who incline to wickedness, those from whom meekness and patience are far off; [these are] persons who love vanity, chase rewards, do not pity the needy, do not help those who are overcome with toil, who are prone to evil-speaking, who do not know the one who made them, who are murderers of children and destroyers of the workmanship of God, who turn away the one who is in need, who oppress the afflicted, who are advocates of the rich, who are unjust judges of the poor, and who are in every respect completely sinful.

[...]

---

11 Or the way of the Black One.
12 Or the arrogance of power or hunger for power.
13 Or rape.
14 Or witchcraft.

9

The Shepherd of Hermas

Context
Author: "Hermas" or possibly multiple authors/editors
Provenance: Rome
Date: Possibly completed c. AD 150 [1]

Vision 1

1 [Vision 1.1] [2]

1. The man who raised me sold me to a woman named Rhoda, in Rome. After many years I made her acquaintance again, and I began to love her as a sister. 2. After some time I saw her bathing in the river Tiber, and I gave her my hand and helped her out of the river. When I saw her beauty, I thought in my heart and said to myself, "I would be blessed if I had a wife of such beauty and character." This was my only deliberation, and no other—no, not one. 3. After some time, while I was going to Cumae,[3] and glorifying the creation of God for its greatness and splendor and might, as I walked along I became sleepy. And a spirit seized me and took me away through a certain area that had no paths, and through which it was impossible to walk, because the ground was

---

1 For a discussion of date and authorship, see Mark Grundeken, *Community Building in the Shepherd of Hermas: A Critical Study of Some Key Aspects* (Brill, 2015), 2–16.

2 There are two common chapter numbering formats; for the benefit of the reader, both have been included in this edition. The editor has chosen not to add his own descriptive section headings because the established headings (Visions, Commandments, Similitudes) already provide sufficient labels.

3 Cumae was a coastal Roman colony located about 130 miles (210 kilometers) south of Rome.

steep and eroded by streams of water. I crossed the river and came to the level ground, where I knelt down and began to pray to the Lord and to confess my sins. 4. While I was praying, the heavens opened, and I saw that woman whom I had desired. She greeted me from the heavens, saying, "Greetings, Hermas." 5. And I looked at her and said to her, "Lady, what are you doing here?" She answered, "I was taken up to accuse you of your sins before the Lord." 6. I said to her, "Are you now accusing me?" "No," she said, "but listen to the words that I am going to say to you. The God who dwells in heaven and created that which is out of that which is not, and who increased and multiplied it for the sake of his holy church—he is angry with you because you sinned against me." 7. I answered and said to her, "Did I sin against you? In what place, or when did I speak an evil word to you? Did I not always look on you as a goddess? Did I not always respect you as a sister? Why do you charge me falsely, Lady, with these wicked and impure things?" 8. She laughed and said to me, "The desire of wickedness came up in your heart. Or do you not think that it is an evil deed for a righteous man if an evil desire comes up in his heart? Yes, it is a sin," said she, "and a great one. For the righteous man has righteous deliberations. So long then as his deliberations are righteous his reputation remains in good standing in heaven, and he finds the Lord ready to assist him in all his doings. But those who have evil deliberations in their hearts bring upon themselves death and captivity, especially those who obtain this world for themselves, and pride themselves in their wealth, and do not lay hold of the good things that are to come. 9. Their hearts will repent, but they have no hope, for they have abandoned themselves and their life. But pray to God, and he will heal the sins of you and of all your house and of all the saints."

2 [Vision 1.2]

1. After she had spoken these words the heavens were shut, and I was shuddering and grieved. I began to say to myself, "If this sin is recorded against me, how will I be saved? Or how will I propitiate God for my past sins? Or with what words will I ask the Lord to forgive me?" 2. While I was deliberating and doubting these things in my heart, I saw before me a white chair of great size made of snow-white wool; and there came a woman, old and clothed in shining garments with a book in her hand, and she sat down alone and greeted me. "Greetings, Hermas!" And I, in my grief and weeping, said, "Greetings, Lady!" 3. And she said to me, "Why are you sad, Hermas? You who are patient and good-tempered, who are always laughing, why are

you so downcast in appearance and not merry?" And I said to her, "Because of a most excellent lady, who says that I sinned against her." 4. And she said, "By no means let this thing happen to the servant of God; but that [deliberation] about her did enter your heart. A deliberation such as that brings sin on the servants of God. For a deliberation such as this, to desire to do an evil deed against a revered spirit and one who has already been approved, is evil and terrible—especially if it comes from Hermas the temperate, who abstains from every evil desire and is full of all simplicity and great innocence.

3 [Vision 1.3]

1. "But it is not for this reason that God is angry with you, but in order that you should convert your family, which has sinned against the Lord, and against you, their parents. You are indulgent and do not correct your family; you have allowed them to become corrupt. For this reason, the Lord is angry with you, but he will heal all the past evils in your family. It is because of their sins and wickedness that you have been corrupted by the things of daily life. 2. But the great mercy of the Lord has had pity on you and on your family, and he will make you strong and will establish you in his glory—only do not be neglectful but have courage and strengthen your family. For as the blacksmith, by hammering his work, overcomes the task that he desires, so also the daily righteous word overcomes all wickedness. Do not cease, then, correcting your children, for I know that if they repent with all their heart, they will be written in the books of life with the saints." 3. After she had finished these words, she said to me, "Would you like to hear me read aloud?" I said, "I would like it, Lady." She said to me, "Listen then, and hear the glory of God." I heard great and wonderful things that I cannot remember; for all the words were frightful, such as a man cannot bear. But I remembered these last words, for they were profitable for us and gentle. 4. "Behold, the God of the powers, whom I love, by his mighty power, and by his great wisdom created the world, and by his glorious counsel surrounded his creation with beauty, and by his mighty word fixed the heavens and founded the earth upon the waters, and by his own wisdom and forethought created his holy church, which he also blessed. Behold, he changes the heavens, the mountains, the hills, and the seas, making all things straight for his chosen ones, to give them the promise that he made with great glory and joy, if they keep the commandments of God, which they received in great faith."

4 [Vision 1.4]

1. So, when she had finished reading and rose from the chair, four young men came along, and they took the chair and went away toward the east. 2. And she called me and touched my chest and said to me, "Did my reading please you?" And I said to her, "Lady, this last part pleases me, but the first part was hard and difficult." And she said to me, "This last part is for the righteous, but the first part was for the heathen and the apostates." 3. While she was speaking with me, two men appeared, and they took her by the arm, and they went away toward the east, where the chair had gone. But she went away cheerfully, and as she went said to me, "Be courageous, Hermas."[4]

Vision 2

5 [Vision 2.1]

1. About a year later, while I was going to Cumae, as I walked, I remembered the vision from the previous year, and the spirit seized me again and took me away to the same place where I had been the previous year. 2. So when I came to that place, I knelt and began to pray to the Lord and to glorify his name because he had thought me worthy and had shown me my former sins. 3. But after I rose from prayer, I saw before me the ancient lady, whom I had seen the year before, walking and reading from a little book. And she said to me, "Can you take this message to God's elect ones?" I said to her, "Lady, I cannot remember that much, but let me make a copy of the little book." "Take it," she said, "but give it back to me." 4. I took it and went away to a certain place in the country, and I copied it all, letter for letter, because I could not distinguish the syllables. When I had finished the letters of the little book, it was suddenly taken out of my hand—but I did not see who took it.

6 [Vision 2.2]

1. But after fifteen days, when I had fasted and prayed greatly to the Lord, the meaning of the writing was revealed to me. And this is what was written: 2. "Your children, Hermas, have rejected God, and have blasphemed the Lord, and have betrayed their parents in great wickedness, and they are called the betrayers of parents, and their betrayal has not profited them, but they have added to their sins evil deeds and piled up wickedness, and so their crimes have been made complete. 3. But make these words known to all your

---

4 Gk. Ἀνδρίζου, lit. "be manly."

children and to your wife, who will in the future be to you as a sister. For she also does not control her tongue, by which she sins. But when she has heard these words, she will control it and will obtain mercy. 4. After you have made known these words to them, which the Master commanded me to reveal to you, all the sins that they have previously committed will be forgiven, and all the saints will have their past sins forgiven up to this day, if they repent with their whole heart, and remove double-mindedness from their heart. 5. For the Master has sworn to his elect by his glory that if, after this day has been fixed, sin continues, they will find no salvation; for repentance for the just has an end. The days of repentance have been fulfilled for all the saints; but for the heathen repentance is open until the last day. 6. You will say, then, to the leaders of the church, that they must reform their ways in righteousness, so they may receive in full the promises with great glory. 7. You, therefore, who work righteousness must remain steadfast and do not be double-minded, so that your passing may be with the holy angels. Blessed are those who endure the great persecution that is coming and will not deny their life. 8. For the Lord has sworn by his Son that those who have denied their Christ have been rejected from their life, that is, those who will deny him in the days to come. But those who previously denied him have obtained forgiveness through his great mercy.

7 [Vision 2.3]

1. "But, Hermas, do not bear a grudge against your children any longer, nor neglect your sister, so that they may be cleansed from their former sins. For they will be corrected with righteous correction if you bear no grudge against them. Holding grudges produces death. But you, Hermas, had great troubles of your own because of the transgressions of your family, because you did not pay attention to them. You neglected them and became entangled in their evil deeds. 2. But you are saved by not having broken away from the living God, and by your simplicity and great temperance. These things have saved you, if you remain in them, and they save all whose deeds are such, and who walk in innocence and simplicity. These will overcome all wickedness and remain steadfast to eternal life. 3. Blessed are all they who do righteousness; they will not perish forever. 4. But say to Maximus, 'Behold, persecution is coming, if it seems good to you, deny the faith again.' 'The Lord is near those that turn to him,' as it is written in the Book of Eldad and Modat,[5] who prophesied to the people in the wilderness."

---

5 The apocryphal Book of Eldad and Modat has been lost; however, Dale C. Allison argues that James and 1 and 2 Clement preserve a few lines from it ("Eldad and Modad," *Journal for the Study of the Pseudepigrapha* 21, no. 2 [December 2011]: 99–131).

8 [Vision 2.4]

1. And a revelation was made to me, brothers and sisters, while I slept. It was made by a very handsome young man, who said to me, "Who do you think the ancient lady was, who gave you the little book?" I said, "The Sibyl." "You are wrong," he said, "she is not." "Who is she, then?" I said. "The church," he said. I said to him, "Why then is she old?" "Because," he said, "she was created the first of all things. This is the reason she is old; and it was for her sake that the world established." 2. And afterwards I saw a vision in my house. The ancient lady came and asked me if I had already given the book to the elders. I said that I had not given it. "You have done well," she said, "for I have words to add. When, therefore, I have finished all the words, you are to make them known to all the elect. 3. You shall therefore write two little books and send one to Clement and one to Grapte. Clement shall then send it to the cities abroad, for that is his duty; and Grapte shall exhort the widows and orphans; but in this city you shall read it yourself with the elders in charge of the church."

Vision 3

9 [Vision 3.1]

1. The third vision that I saw, brothers and sisters, was as follows. 2. I had fasted for a long time, and I asked the Lord to explain to me the revelation that he had promised to show me through that ancient lady. In the same night, the ancient lady appeared to me and said to me, "Since you are so persistent and zealous to know everything, come into the country, where you are farming, and at the fifth hour I will appear to you and show you what you must see." 3. I asked her, saying, "Lady, to what part of the field?" "Wherever you like," she said. I chose a beautiful, secluded spot; but before I spoke to her and mentioned the place, she said to me, "I will be there, where you wish." 4. I went, therefore, brothers and sisters, to the country, and I counted the hours, and I came to the spot where I had arranged for her to come, and I saw a couch of ivory placed there, and on the couch, there lay a linen pillow, and over it a covering of fine linen was spread out. 5. When I saw these things lying there, and no one in the place, I was greatly amazed, and I began to tremble and my hair stood on end, and I began to panic because I was alone. After I collected myself and remembered the glory of God and took courage, I knelt down and confessed my sins again to the Lord, as I had also done before. 6. And she

came with the six young men whom I had also seen on the previous occasion, and she stood by me and listened to me praying and confessing my sins to the Lord. She touched me and said, "Hermas! Stop asking all these questions about your sins; ask about righteousness, so that you may take some part of it to your family." 7. And she raised me up by the hand and took me to the couch and said to the young men, "Go and build." 8. And after the young men had gone away and we were alone, she said to me, "Sit here." I said to her, "Lady, let the elders sit first." She said, "Do what I tell you, and sit down." 9. Yet when I wished to sit on the right-hand side, she would not let me, but signaled to me with her hand to sit on the left. When therefore I thought about this and was grieved because she did not let me sit on the right hand, she said to me, "Are you disappointed, Hermas? The seat on the right is for others, who have already been found well-pleasing to God and have suffered for the Name. But you fall far short of sitting with them. But remain in your simplicity as you are doing, and you will sit with them, and so will all who do their deeds and bear what they also bore."

10 [Vision 3.2]

1. "What," I said, "did they bear?" "Listen," she said. Scourgings, imprisonments, great afflictions, crucifixions, wild beasts, for the sake of the Name." Therefore, it is given to them to be on the right hand of the holiness, and to everyone who shall suffer for the Name; but for the rest there is the left side. But both, whether they sit on the right or the left, have the same gifts, and the same promises, only the former sit on the right and have a certain glory. 2. And you desire to sit on the right side with them, but your failings are many. But you will be cleansed from your failings, and all who are not double-minded will be cleansed from all sins, up to this day." 3. When she had said this, she wished to go away, but I fell at her feet and begged her by the Lord to show me the vision that she had promised. 4. And she again took me by the hand and lifted me up, and she made me sit on the couch on the left and she sat on the right. And she lifted a certain glittering rod, and she said to me, "Do you see a great thing?" I said to her, "Lady, I see nothing." She said to me, "Behold, do you not see before you a great tower being built on the water with shining square stones?" 5. Now a tower was being built in a square by the six young men who had come with her; but tens of thousands of other men were bringing stones, some from the deep sea, and some from the land, and they were giving them to the six young men, and these men kept taking them and building. 6. The stones which had been dragged from the deep sea, they

placed without exception as they were into the building, for they had all been shaped and fitted into the joints with the other stones. And they fastened one to the other so that their joints could not be seen. But the building of the tower appeared as if it had been built of a single stone. 7. Of the other stones, which were being brought from the dry ground, they threw some away, and some they put into the building, and others they broke up and threw far from the tower. 8. And many other stones were lying around the tower, but the men did not use them for the building, for some of the stones were rotten, and others had cracks, and others were too short, and others were white and round and did not fit into the building. 9. And I saw other stones being thrown far from the tower and rolling onto the road. They did not stay on the road but rolled off the road and onto the rough ground. And others were falling into the fire and were being burnt. And others were falling near the water but could not be rolled into the water, although men wished them to be rolled into the water.

11 [Vision 3.3]

1. After she had showed me these things, she wished to leave. I said to her, "Lady, what does it benefit me to have seen these things if I do not know what they mean?" She answered me and said, "You are a persistent man, wanting to know about the tower." "Yes," I said, "Lady, in order that I may report to my brothers and sisters, and that they may be made more joyful, and when they hear these things may know the Lord in great glory." 2. And she said, "Many indeed will hear, but some of them will rejoice when they hear, and some will mourn. But these also, if they hear and repent, even they will rejoice. Hear then, the parables of the tower, for I will reveal everything to you. And no longer trouble me about revelation, for these revelations are finished, for they have been fulfilled. Yet you will not cease asking for revelations, for you are shameless. 3. The tower which you see being built is me, the church, who has appeared to you both now and previously. Ask, therefore, what you will about the tower, and I will reveal it to you, that you may rejoice with the saints." 4. I said to her, "Lady, since you have once thought me worthy to reveal everything to me, proceed with the revelation." And she said to me, "What is permitted to be revealed to you will be revealed; only let your heart be turned toward God and do not be double-minded as to what you see." 5. I asked her, "Why has the tower been built on the water, Lady?" "As I told you before, you are seeking diligently," said she, "and so by seeking you are finding out the truth. Hear, then, why the tower has been built upon the water: because your

life was saved and will be saved through water, and the tower has been founded by the utterance of the almighty and glorious Name, and it is maintained by the unseen power of the Master."

12 [Vision 3.4]

1. I answered and said to her, "Lady, this is great and wonderful. But, Lady, who are the six young men who are building?" "These are the holy angels of God, who were first created. The Lord delivered all creation to them, to make it increase and to build it up, and to rule the whole creation. Through them, therefore, the building of the tower will be completed." 2. "But who are the others, who are bringing the stones?" "They are also holy angels of God, but these six are greater than them. Therefore, the building of the tower will be completed, and all will rejoice together around the tower, and will glorify God because the building of the tower has been completed." 3. I asked her, saying, "Lady, I would like to know the purpose of the stones and what kind of significance they have." She answered me and said, "It is not because you are more worthy than all others that a revelation should be given to you, for there were others before you and better than you, to whom these visions ought to have been revealed. But in order that the name of God might be glorified, they have been, and will be, revealed to you because of the double-minded who dispute in their heart whether these things are so or not. Tell them that all these things are true, and that there is nothing beyond the truth, but that all things are strong and certain and well-founded.

13 [Vision 3.5]

1. "Listen then concerning the stones that go into the building. The stones which are square, white, and fit into their joints—they are the apostles and bishops and teachers and deacons, who walked according to the majesty of God and served the elect of God in holiness and reverence as bishops and teachers and deacons; some of them have fallen asleep and some are still alive. They always agreed among themselves, and had peace among themselves, and listened to one another, which is why their joints fit together in the building of the tower." 2. "But who are they who have been brought out of the deep sea and added onto the building, and whose joints fit in with the other stones that have already been built?" "These are they who have suffered for the name of the Lord." 3. "But I should like to know, Lady, who are the

other stones that are being brought from the dry land?" She said, "Those that go into the building without being cut are those whom the Lord approved because they walked in the uprightness of the Lord and preserved his commandments." 4. "And who are they who are being brought and placed in the building?" "They are young in the faith and faithful; but they are being exhorted by the angels to good deeds, because wickedness has been found in them." 5. "And who are they whom the builders were rejecting and throwing away?" "These are they who have sinned and wish to repent; for this reason they have not been cast far away from the tower, because they will be valuable for the building if they repent. Those, then, who are going to repent, if they do so, will be strong in the faith if they repent now, while the tower is being built; but if the building is finished, they will no longer have a place, but will be cast away. But they have only this—that they lie beside the tower."

14 [Vision 3.6]

1. "Do you wish to know who are those that are being broken up and cast far from the tower? Those are the sons of wickedness; and their faith was hypocrisy, and no wickedness departed from them. For this reason, they had no salvation, for because of their wickedness they are not useful for the building. Therefore, they were broken up and cast far away because of the anger of the Lord, for they had provoked his anger. 2. But the others that you saw, which were left lying, and were not going into the building, and are rotten, these are those that have known the truth but are not remaining in it." 3. "And who are they that have cracks?" "Those are the ones that bear malice in their hearts against one another, and who are not at peace among themselves. They maintain the appearance of peace, yet when they depart from one another, their wickedness remains in their hearts. That is the cracks that the stones have. 4. And the stones that are too short, they are the ones that have believed and that for the most part live in righteousness but also have some measure of wickedness. Therefore, they are short and not perfect." 5. "But who, Lady, are the white and round ones that do not fit into the building?" She answered and said to me, "How long will you be stupid and foolish, and ask everything and understand nothing? They are the ones that have faith but also have the riches of this world. When persecution comes, because of their wealth and because of business, they deny their Lord." 6. And I answered and said to her, "Lady, but then when will they be useful for the building?" "When," she said, "their wealth, which leads their souls astray, will be cut off from them, then they will be useful to God. For just as the round stone cannot become square

unless something is cut off and taken away from it, so too they who have riches in this world cannot be useful to the Lord unless their wealth is cut away from them. 7. Understand it first from your own case; when you were rich, you were useless, but now you are useful and helpful in life. Be useful to God, for you yourself are taken from the same stones."

15 [Vision 3.7]

1. "But as for the other stones that you saw being thrown far from the tower, and falling on to the road, and rolling from the road onto the rough ground—these are the ones who have believed but, because of their double-mindedness, leave their true road. They think that it is possible to find a better road, and they err and wander miserably in the rough ground. 2. And the stones that are falling into the fire and are being burnt, these are the ones who finally apostatize from the living God. It no longer enters their hearts to repent because of their licentious lusts and the crimes that they have committed. 3. But do you wish to know who are the others that are falling near the water and cannot be rolled into the water? These are the ones who have heard the word and wish to be baptized in the name of the Lord. Then, when [the cost of] true purity is remembered, they change their minds and turn back to their evil lusts. 4. So she ended the explanation of the tower. 5. I was still unabashed and asked her about all those stones that had been thrown away and do not fit into the building of the tower. I asked her if repentance is open to them and if they have a place in this tower. "Repentance," she said, "they have, but they cannot fit into this tower. 6. But they will fit into another place much less honorable, and even this only after they have been tormented and fulfilled the days of their sins, and for this reason they will be removed, because they shared in the righteous word. And then it will befall them to be removed from their torments, which were inflicted on them because of the wickedness of the deeds that they committed. But if repentance does not come into their hearts, they have no salvation, because of the hardness of their hearts."

16 [Vision 3.8]

1. When I ceased asking her all these things, she said to me, "Would you like to see something else?" I was anxious to see it and rejoiced greatly at the prospect. 2. She looked at me, smiled, and said, "Do you see seven women around the tower?" "Yes," I said, "I see them." "This tower is being supported by them according to the commandment of the Lord. 3. Hear now their qualities. The

first of them who is clasping her hands is called Faith. Through her the chosen of God are saved. 4. The second, who is girded and looks like a man, is called Self-Control; she is the daughter of Faith. Whoever follows her becomes blessed in his life, because he will abstain from all evil deeds, believing that if he refrains from every evil lust, he will inherit eternal life." 5. "But who are the others, Lady?" "They are daughters, one of the other, and their names are Simplicity, Knowledge, Innocence, Reverence, and Love. When therefore you perform all the deeds of their mother, you can live." 6. "I would like, Lady," I said, "to know what their powers are." "Listen," she said, "to the powers which they have. 7. Their powers are supported one by the other, and they follow one another according to their birth. From Faith is born Self-Control, from Self-Control Simplicity, from Simplicity Innocence, from Innocence Reverence, from Reverence Knowledge, from Knowledge Love. Their works therefore are pure and reverent and godly. 8. Whoever then serves them and has the strength to take hold of their works, will have his dwelling in the tower with the saints of God." 9. And I began to ask her about the times—if now is the end. But she cried out with a loud voice saying, "Foolish man, do you not see that the tower is still being built? When the building of the tower has been finished, the end comes. But the tower will be built quickly. Ask me nothing more. This reminder and the renewal of your spirits is sufficient for you and for the saints. 10. But the revelation was not for you alone, but for you to explain to them all, 11. after three days, for you must understand it first. But I charge you first, Hermas, with these words, which I am going to say to you. Speak all these words into the ears of the saints, so that they may hear them and do them and be cleansed from their wickedness, and you with them.

17 [Vision 3.9]

1. "Listen to me, children. I brought you up in great simplicity and innocence and reverence by the mercy of God, who instilled righteousness into you that you should be justified and sanctified from all wickedness and all crookedness. But you do not wish to cease from your wickedness. 2. Now, therefore, listen to me and be at peace among yourselves, and care for one another, and help one another, and do not take an excessive share of God's creations for yourselves, but give part of what you have to those who are in need. 3. For some are making their flesh sick by eating too much and are injuring their flesh. And the flesh of the others, who have nothing to eat, is being injured because they do not have sufficient food, and their body is being destroyed. 4. So this lack of sharing is harmful to you who are rich and do not share with

the poor. 5. Consider the judgment that is coming. Therefore, let those who have excess seek out those who are hungry, so long as the tower is not yet finished; for when the tower has been finished you will wish to do good but will have no opportunity. 6. See to it then, you who rejoice in your wealth, that the destitute may not groan, and their groans go up to the Lord, and you with your goods become locked out, outside the door of the tower. 7. Therefore I speak now to the leaders of the church and to those who take the chief seats. Do not be like the sorcerers, for sorcerers carry their charms in boxes, but you carry your charms and poison in your hearts. 8. You are hardened and will not cleanse your hearts and mix your wisdom together in a pure heart, so that you may find mercy by the great King. 9. See to it, therefore, children, that these disagreements do not rob you of your life. 10. How will you correct the chosen of the Lord if you yourselves suffer no correction? Therefore, correct one another and be at peace among yourselves, so that I may also stand joyfully before the Father, and give an account of all of you to the Lord."

[...]

Vision 4

22 [Vision 4.1]

1. The fourth vision which I saw, brothers and sisters, twenty days after the previous vision, was a type of the persecution which is to come. 2. I was going into the country by the Via Campana. The place is just over a mile from the public road,[6] and is easily reached. 3. As I walked by myself, I asked the Lord to complete the revelations and visions that he had shown me by his holy church, to make me strong and give repentance to his servants who had been offended, to glorify his great and glorious name because he had thought me worthy to show me his wonders. 4. And while I was glorifying him and giving him thanks, an answer came to me as an echo of my voice, "Do not be double-minded, Hermas." I began to reason in myself and to say, "In what ways can I be double-minded after being given such a foundation by the Lord and having seen his glorious deeds?" 5. And I approached a little further, brothers and sisters, and behold, I saw dust reaching to the sky, and I began to say to myself, "Are cattle coming and stirring up the dust?" And it was about a tenth of a mile away from me.[7] 6. When the dust grew greater and greater, I sup-

---

6 The distance is literally "ten stadia." A stadia is approximately 606 feet.
7 Lit. "one stadia."

posed that it was a sign. The sun shone out a little, and behold! I saw a great beast like a sea monster, and fiery locusts were coming out of his mouth. The beast was about a hundred feet long, and its head was like a piece of pottery. 7. And I began to weep and to pray for the Lord to rescue me from it, and I remembered the word that I had heard, "Do not be double-minded, Hermas." 8. Thus, brothers and sisters, being clothed in the faith of the Lord and remembering the great things that he had taught me, I took courage and faced the beast. And the beast came on with a rush that could destroy a city. 9. And I came near to it; and the sea monster, despite all its size, stretched itself out on the ground, and put forth nothing except its tongue, and it did not move at all until I had passed it by. 10. And the beast had on its head four colors: black, then the color of flame and blood, then gold, then white.

23 [Vision 4.2]

1. After I had passed by the beast and had gone about thirty feet further, behold! A maiden met me, adorned as if coming from the bridal chamber, all in white and with white sandals, veiled to the forehead, and a turban for a headdress, but her hair was white. 2. I recognized from the former visions that it was the church, and I rejoiced the more. She greeted me saying, "Greetings, O man," and I greeted her in return, "Greetings, Lady." 3. She answered me and said, "Did nothing meet you?" I said to her, "Yes, Lady, such a beast as could destroy nations, but by the power of the Lord, and by his great mercy, I escaped it." 4. "You did well to escape it," she said, "because you cast your care upon God, and you opened your heart to the Lord, believing that salvation can be found through nothing except through the great and glorious Name. Therefore, the Lord sent his angel, whose name is Thegri, who is over the beast, and shut his mouth that he should not hurt you. You have escaped great tribulation through your faith and because you were not double-minded when you saw so great a beast. 5. Go then and tell the Lord's elect ones of his great deeds; and tell them that this beast is a type of the great persecution that is to come. If then you are prepared beforehand, and repent with all your hearts toward the Lord, you will be able to escape it, if your heart is made pure and blameless, and you serve the Lord blamelessly for the rest of the days of your life. Cast your cares upon the Lord and he will make them straight. 6. Believe on the Lord, you who are double-minded, that he can do all things, and turns his wrath away from you, and sends scourges on you who are double-minded. Woe to those who hear these words and disobey; it would have been better for them not to have been born."

24 [Vision 4.3]

1. I asked her concerning the four colors that the sea monster had on its head. She answered and said to me, "Are you again curious about such matters?" "Yes," I said, "Lady, let me know what they are." 2. "Listen," she said, "the black is this world, in which you are living; 3. the color of fire and blood means that this world must be destroyed by blood and fire. 4. The golden part is you, who have fled from this world, for even as gold is tried in the fire and becomes valuable, so also you who live among them are being tried. Those then who remain and pass through the flames will be purified by them. Even as the gold puts away its dross, so also you will put away all sorrow and tribulation, and you will be made pure and become useful for the building of the tower. 5. But the white part is the world to come, in which the elect of God will dwell, for those who have been chosen by God for eternal life will be without spot and pure. 6. Therefore do not cease to speak to the ears of the saints. You also have the type of the great persecution to come, but if you are willing, it shall be nothing. Remember what was written before. 7. When she had said this she went away, and I did not see to what place she departed, for there was a cloud, and I turned backward in fear, thinking that the beast was coming.

Vision 5

25

1. While I was praying at home and sitting on my bed, there entered a man with a glorious appearance, dressed like a shepherd, covered with a white goatskin, with a bag on his shoulders and a staff in his hand. And he greeted me, and I greeted him back. 2. And at once he sat down by me and said to me, "I have been sent by the most revered angel to dwell with you the rest of the days of your life." 3. I thought he had come to tempt me, and I said to him, "Yes, but who are you? For I know to whom I was handed over." He said to me, "Do you not recognize me?" "No," I said. He said, "I am the shepherd to whom you were handed over."[8] 4. While he was still speaking, his appearance changed, and I recognized him, that it was he to whom I was handed over; and at once I was confounded, and fear seized me, and I was quite overcome with sorrow that I had answered him so rudely and foolishly. 5. But he answered me and said, "Do not be confounded, but be strong in my

---

8 This is the first time the shepherd is mentioned in the text.

commandments, by which I am going to command you. For I was sent," he said, "to show you again all the things that you saw before, for they are the main points that are helpful to you. First of all write my commandments and the parables; but the rest you are to write as I will show you. This is the reason," he said, "that I command you to write first the commandments and parables, that you may read them out at once and be able to keep them." 6. So, I wrote the commandments and parables as he commanded me. 7. If then you hear and keep them, and walk in them, and do them with a pure heart, you will receive from the Lord all that he promised you, but if you hear them and do not repent but continue to add to your sins, you will receive the contrary from the Lord. All these things the shepherd commanded me to write thus, for he was the angel of repentance.

Commandment 1[9]

26

1. First of all believe that God is one, who made all things and perfected them, and made all things to be out of that which was not, and contains all things, and is himself alone uncontained. 2. Believe then in him, and fear him, and in your fear be self-controlled. Keep these things, and you will cast away from yourself all wickedness, and will put on every virtue of righteousness, and will live to God, if you keep this commandment.

Commandment 2

27

1. He said to me, "Have simplicity and be innocent, and you will be like the children who do not know the wickedness that destroys the life of men. 2. In the first place, do not slander anyone, and do not gladly listen when someone speaks slander. Otherwise, by listening, you will also share in the sin of the person who slanders, if you believe the slander that is spoken. For by believing, you will also have something against your brother, and you will therefore share the sin of the one speaking slander. Slander is wicked. It is a restless devil, never making peace, but always living in strife. Refrain from it then, and you will have well-being at all times with all men. 4. And put on reverence, in which there is no evil stumbling-block, but all is smooth and joyful.

---

9 Traditionally these have been translated as "mandates." Gk. Ἐντολὴ.

Do good, even throughout all the toil which God gives you; give in simplicity to all who are in need, not doubting to whom you will give and to whom you will not; give to all, for to all God wishes gifts to be made of his own bounties. 5. Those then who receive will render an account to God why they received it and for what. For those who accepted through distress will not be punished, but those who accepted in hypocrisy will pay the penalty. 6. He therefore who gives is innocent; for as he received from the Lord the fulfilment of this ministry, he fulfilled it in simplicity, not doubting to whom he should give or not give. Therefore, this ministry fulfilled in simplicity was honorable before God. He therefore who serves in simplicity will live to God. 7. Keep therefore this commandment as I have told you, that your repentance and that of your family may be found to be in simplicity, and that your innocence may be pure and without stain.

Commandment 3

28

1. Again he said to me, "Love truth, and let all truth proceed from your mouth, that the spirit which God has made to dwell in this flesh may be found true by all men, and the Lord who dwells in you will thus be glorified, for the Lord is true in every word and with him there is no lie. 2. They therefore who lie reject the Lord and become defrauders of the Lord, not restoring to him the deposit which they received. For they received from him a spirit free from lies. If they return this as a lying spirit, they have defiled the commandment of the Lord and have robbed him." 3. When I heard this, I wept much, and when he saw me weeping, he said, "Why do you weep?" "Because, sir," I said, "I do not know if I can be saved." "Why?" "Because, sir," I said, "I have never yet in my life spoken a true word, but I have spoken deceitfully with all men, and indicated to everyone that my life was the truth, and no one ever contradicted me but believed my word. How then, sir," I said, "can I live after having done this?" 4. "Your thought," he said, "is good and true; for you ought to have walked in truth as God's servant, and an evil conscience ought not to dwell with the spirit of truth, nor ought grief to come on a spirit which is holy and true." "Never, sir," I said, "have I accurately understood such words." 5. "Now then," he said, "you do understand them. Keep them so that your former lies in your business may themselves become trustworthy now that these have been found true. For it is possible for those also to become trustworthy. If you keep these things and going forward keep the whole truth, you can obtain life

for yourself; and whoever will hear this commandment and abstain from the sin of lying shall live to God."

Commandment 4

29 [Commandment 4.1]

1. "I command you," he said, "to preserve purity and to not let any thought come into your heart about another man's wife, or about fornication or any such wicked things; for by doing this you do great sin. But if you always remember your own wife you will never sin. 2. For if this desire enters your heart, you will sin; and if you do similar wicked things, you commit sin. For this desire is a great sin for the servant of God. And if any man commits this wicked deed, he works death for himself. 3. See to it then that you abstain from this desire, for where holiness lives, lawlessness ought not to enter the heart of a righteous man." 4. I said to him, "Sir, allow me to ask you a few questions." "Go on," he said. "Sir, if a man has a wife faithful in the Lord, and he finds that she committed adultery, does the husband sin if he lives with her?" 5. He replied, "So long as he is ignorant, he does not sin, but if the husband knows her sin, and the wife does not repent, but remains in her fornication, and the husband goes on living with her, he becomes a partaker of her sin and shares in her adultery." 6. I said, "What then, sir, shall the husband do if the wife remains in this disposition?" "Let him divorce her," he said, "and let the husband remain by himself. But if he divorces his wife and marries another, he also commits adultery himself." 7. I said, "If then, sir, after the wife is divorced, she repents and wishes to return to her husband, should the husband take her back?" 8. "Yes," he said, "if the husband does not take her, he sins and covers himself with great sin; but it is necessary to receive the sinner who repents, but not often, for the servants of God have but one repentance. Therefore, for the sake of [the wife's possible] repentance, the husband ought not to marry. This is the course of action for wife and husband. Not only is it adultery if a man defiles his flesh, but whoever acts as the heathen do is also guilty of adultery, so that if anyone continues in such practices and does not repent, you should depart from him and do not live with him, otherwise you are also a sharer in his sin. 10. For this reason you were told to live by yourselves, whether husband or wife, for in such cases repentance is possible. 11. I, therefore," he said, "am not giving an opportunity to let this affair end in this way, but in order that he who has sinned shall sin no more, and for his former sin there is one who can give healing, for this one has the power over all things.

30 [Commandment 4.2]

1. And I asked him again, saying, "If the Lord has thought me worthy of having you always live with me, put up with a few more of my questions, since I have no understanding and my heart has been hardened by my past deeds. Give me understanding, for I am very foolish and have absolutely no understanding." 2. He answered me and said, "I am set over repentance, and I give understanding to all those who repent. Or do you not think," he said, "that this very repentance is itself understanding? To repent" he said, "is great understanding. For the sinner understands that he has done wickedness before the Lord, and the deed which he committed comes into his heart, and he repents and no longer does wicked things, but does good abundantly, and humbles his soul and punishes it because he sinned. You see, therefore, that repentance is great understanding." 3. For this reason, then, sir," I said, "I [wish to] know accurately from you about all things. First, because I am a sinner, that I may know what I must do to live, because my sins are many and manifold." 4. "You will live," he said, "if you keep my commandments and walk in them, and whoever will hear and keep these commandments will live to God."

31 [Commandment 4.3]

1. "I will," I said, "yet, sir, I continue to ask." "Go on," he said. "I have heard, sir," I said, "from some teachers that there is no second repentance beyond the one given when we went down into the water and received forgiveness of our past sins." 2. He said to me, "You have heard correctly, for that is so. For he who has received forgiveness of sin ought never to sin again, but to live in purity. 3. But since you ask accurately concerning all things, I will explain this also to you without giving an excuse to those who in the future will believe those who have already believed on the Lord. For those who have recently believed or will believe in the future have no repentance of sins, but have forgiveness of their past sins. 4. For those, then, who were called before these days, the Lord appointed for repentance, for the Lord knows the heart, and knowing all things beforehand he knew the weakness of man and the subtlety of the devil, that he will do some evil to the servants of God, and act wickedly towards them. 5. The Lord, therefore, being merciful, had mercy on his creation, and established this repentance, and to me was the control of this repentance given. 6. But I tell you," he said, "after that great and holy calling, if a man is tempted by the devil and sins, he has one repentance, but if he sins and repents repeatedly, it is of no use for such a man, for he will scarcely live." 7. I

said to him, "I attained life when I heard these things from you, for I know that if I do not again add to my sins I shall be saved." "You shall be saved," he said, "and all who do these things."

32 [Commandment 4.4]

1. I asked him again, saying, "Sir, explain this also to me." "Go on," he said. "If, sir," I said, "a wife, or on the other hand a husband, dies, and the survivor marries, does the one who marries commit sin?" 2. "He does not sin" he said, "but if he remains single, he gains for himself more exceeding honor and great glory with the Lord, but even if he marries, he does not sin. 3. Preserve therefore purity and holiness, and you will live to God. Going forward, from the day on which you were handed over to me, keep these things which I tell you and shall tell you, and I will dwell in your house. 4. And for your former transgression there will be forgiveness if you keep my commandments, and all men will obtain forgiveness, if they keep these commandments of mine and walk in this purity."

[...]

37

Commandment 7

1. "Fear the Lord," he said, "and keep his commandments. By keeping the commandments of God, you will be strong in every act, and your conduct will be beyond compare. For by fearing the Lord you will do all things well, for this is the fear you must have to be saved. 2. But do not fear the devil, for by fearing the Lord you have power over the devil because there is no might in him. But where there is no might, neither is there fear. But where there is glorious might, there is also fear. For everyone who has might gains fear. But he who does not have might is despised by all. 3. But fear the works of the devil, because they are evil. If therefore, you fear the Lord, you will not do them but depart from them. 4. There are therefore two sorts of fear. For if you wish to do that which is evil, fear the Lord and you will not do it. But, on the other hand, if you wish to do that which is good, fear the Lord, and you will do it. So that the fear of the Lord is mighty and great and glorious. Therefore, fear the Lord and you will live in him. And whoever fears him and keeps his commandment, will live to God." 5. "Why, sir," I said, "did you say of those who keep his commandments, 'they will live to God'?" "Because," he said,

"the whole creation fears the Lord, but it does not keep his commandments. Those, therefore, who fear him and observe his commandments, it is they who have life with God. But as for those who do not observe his commandments, they do not have life in him."

38

Commandment 8

1. "I told you," he said, "that the creatures of God are two-fold, and temperance is also two-fold. For from some things, we must refrain and from some things, not." 2. "Let me know, sir," I said, "from what we must refrain and from what not." "Listen," he said. "Refrain from evil, and do not do it, but do not refrain from good, but do it. For if you refrain from doing good, you do great sin; but if you refrain from doing evil, you do great righteousness. Therefore, refrain from all evil, and do good." 3. "What, sir," I said, "are the wicked things that we must refrain from?" "Listen," he said. "From adultery and fornication, from the lawlessness of drunkenness, from evil luxury, from much eating, and extravagance of wealth, and boastfulness and haughtiness and pride, and from lying and evil speech and hypocrisy, malice and all blasphemy. 4. These deeds are the wickedest of all in the life of men. The servant of God must therefore refrain from these deeds. For he who does not refrain from these cannot live to God. Hear therefore what follows on these things." 5. "But, sir" I said, "are there still other evil deeds?" "Yes," he said, "there are many from which the servant of God must refrain. Theft, lying, robbery, false witness, covetousness, evil desire, deceit, vain-glory, pride, and whatever is like to these. 6. Do you not think that these are wicked?" "Yes, very wicked," I said, "for the servants of God." "He who is serving God must refrain from all of these. Refrain, therefore, from all these, that you may live to God and be included with those who refrain from them. These then are the things from which you must refrain. 7. But now hear the things from which you must not refrain but must do," he said. "Do not refrain from that which is good but do it." 8. "And explain to me, sir," I said, "the power of the good things, so that I may walk in them and serve them, that by doing them I may be saved." "Listen, then," he said, "to the deeds of goodness, which you must do and not refrain from them. 9. First of all, faith, fear of God, love and harmony, words of righteousness, truth, patience; there is nothing better in the life of man than these. If any man keeps these things and does not refrain from them, he becomes blessed in his life. 10. Next hear the things which follow: to minister to widows, to look after orphans

and the destitute, to redeem from distress the servants of God, to be hospitable, for in hospitality may be found the practice of good, to resist none, to be gentle, to be poorer than all men, to revere the aged, to practice justice, to preserve brotherhood, to submit to insult, to be brave, to bear no malice, to comfort those who are oppressed in spirit, not to cast aside those who are offended in the faith, but to convert them and give them courage, to reprove sinners, not to oppress poor debtors, and whatever is like these things. 11. Do you not think," he said, "that these things are good?" "Yes, sir," I said, "for what is better than these things?" "Walk then in them," he said, "and do not refrain from them, and you will live to God. 12. Keep therefore this commandment. If you do good, and do not refrain from it, you will live to God, and all who act so shall live to God. And again, if you do not do that which is wicked, but refrain from it, you will live to God, and all will live to God who keep these commandments and walk in them."

[...]

Commandment 11

43

1. He showed me men sitting on a bench, and another man sitting on a chair, and he said to me, "Do you see the men sitting on the bench?" "Yes, sir," I said, "I see them." He said, "they are faithful, and the one who is sitting on the chair is a false prophet, who is corrupting the understanding of the servants of God. He corrupts the understanding of the double-minded, not of the faithful. 2. Therefore, these double-minded men come to him as to a seer, and they ask him about their future; and that false prophet, having no power of the divine spirit in himself, speaks with them according to their requests and according to the desires of their wickedness, and he fills their souls, as they themselves wish. 3. For he is empty and makes empty answers to empty men; for whatever question is asked, he answers according to the emptiness of the man. But he also speaks some true words, for the devil fills him with his spirit, to see if he can break any of the righteous. 4. Therefore, as many as are strong in the faith of the Lord, and have put on the truth, they do not join themselves to such spirits but refrain from them. But as many as are double-minded and constantly repent, they practice soothsaying, like the heathen, and bring greater shame upon themselves by their idolatry. For he who asks a false prophet concerning any act is an idolater and is devoid of the truth and is foolish. 5. For every spirit that is given from God does not

need to be [prompted with] questions but has the divine power and speaks all things on its own initiative, because it is from above, from the power of the divine spirit. 6. But the spirit which is [prompted and] questioned and speaks according to the lusts of man is earthly and light, and it has no power, and it does not speak at all unless it is questioned." 7. "How, then, sir," I said, "will a man know which of them is a true prophet and which a false prophet?" "Listen," he said, "concerning both the prophets, and as I will tell you, so you will judge the true prophet and the false prophet. Test the man who has the divine spirit by his life. 8. In the first place, he who has the spirit which is from above is meek and gentle, and lowly-minded, and refrains from all wickedness and evil desires of this world, and makes himself poorer than all men, and gives no answers to anyone when he is consulted, nor does he speak by himself (for the Holy Spirit does not speak when a man wishes to speak), but he speaks at that time when God wishes him to speak. 9. Therefore, when the man who has the divine spirit comes into a meeting of righteous men who have the faith of the divine spirit, and intercession is made to God from the assembly of those men, then the angel of the prophetic spirit rests on him and fills the man, and the man, being filled with the Holy Spirit, speaks to the congregation as the Lord wills. 10. Thus, then, the divine spirit will be apparent. Such, then, is the power of the Lord concerning the divine spirit. 11. Listen, now," he said, "concerning the spirit that is earthly, and empty, and has no power, but is foolish. 12. In the first place, that man who seems to have a spirit exalts himself and wishes to have the first place, and he is instantly impudent and shameless and talkative, and lives in great luxury and in many other deceits, and accepts rewards for his prophecy, and if he does not receive them, he does not prophesy. Is it then possible for a divine spirit to accept rewards and prophesy? It is not possible for a prophet of God to do this, but the spirit of such prophets is of the earth. 13. Next, on no account does he come near to an assembly of righteous men but shuns them. But he clings to the double-minded and empty, and prophesies to them in a corner, and deceives them by empty speech about everything according to their lusts, for he is also answering the empty. For an empty vessel that is put with others that are empty is not broken, but they match one another. 14. But when he comes into a meeting full of righteous men who have the divine spirit, and intercession is made by them, that man is made empty, and the earthly spirit flees from him in fear, and that man is made dumb and is altogether broken up, being able to say nothing. 15. For if you stack wine or oil in a cellar, and put among them an empty jar, and again wish to unstack the cellar, the jar which you put in empty you will find still empty. So also, the prophets who are empty, when they come to the spirits of just men, are found out to be such as when they came. 16. You have the life of both the prophets. Test, then, from his life and deeds, the man who says that he is inspired. 17. But believe yourself in the Spirit that comes from God and has power; but have no faith in the spirit that is from the earth and empty, because there is no power in it, for it comes from the devil. 18. Hear, then, the parable which I will tell you.

Take a stone and throw it up to heaven and see if you can touch it; or take a watering pump and spray it toward the sky and see if you can make a hole in the heavens." 19. "How, sir," I said, "can these things be? For both these things which you have spoken of are impossible." "Just as these are unable to be done," he said, "so also are the earthly spirits feeble and unable [to prophecy]. 20. Take now the power that comes from above. Hail is a very small pellet [of ice], and when it falls on man's head, how it hurts! Or, again, take a drop which falls on the ground from the roof, and makes a hole in stone. 21. You see, then, that the smallest things that come from above and fall on the earth have great power; so also the divine spirit that comes from above is powerful. Have faith, then, in this spirit, but refrain from the other."

Commandment 12

44 [Commandment 12.1]

1. He said to me, "Put away from yourself every evil desire, but put on the desire that is good and holy; for by putting on this desire you will hate the wicked desire, and you will curb it as you will. 2. For the wicked desire is cruel and hard to tame, for it is fearful, and destroys men greatly in its cruelty, but especially if a servant of God falls into it, and is not prudent, he is terribly destroyed by it. But it destroys those who do not have the good desire as a covering but are mixed with this world; these then it delivers to death." 3. "What, sir," I said, "are the deeds of the wicked desire, which delivers men to death? Let me know that I may refrain from them." "Listen," he said, "by what deeds the evil desire brings to death the servants of God.

45 [Commandment 12.2]

1. "Before all is desire for the wife or husband of another, and of extravagance of wealth, and much needless food and drink, and many other foolish luxuries. For all luxury is foolish and vain for the servants of God. 2. These desires then are wicked and bring the servants of God to death, for this desire is the

wicked daughter of the devil. It is necessary therefore, to refrain from the wicked desires, that by refraining you may live to God. 3. But as many as are overcome by them and do not resist them shall perish finally, for these desires are deadly. 4. But put on the desire of righteousness, and resist them, being armed with the fear of the Lord. For the fear of God dwells in the desire that is good. If the evil desire sees you armed with the fear of God, and resisting it, it will flee far from you and will no longer be seen by you, for fear of your weapons. 5. Therefore, when you have conquered it and triumph over it, come to the desire of righteousness, and giving it the victory which you have won, and serve it as it wishes. If you serve the good desire, and submit to it, you will be able to overcome the wicked desire, and subdue it as you wish."

46 [Commandment 12.3]

1. "I would like, sir," I said, "to know in what way I must serve the good desire." "Listen," he said, "Practice righteousness and virtue, and fear of the Lord, faith and meekness, and whatever good things are like to these. For by practicing these, you will be a well-pleasing servant of God and will live to him, and whoever will serve the good desire will live to God." 2. So he finished the twelve commandments and said to me, "You have these commandments; walk in them and exhort those who hear, that their repentance may be pure for the rest of the days of their life. 3. Carefully fulfill this ministry which I give you, and work greatly at it, for you will find favor with those who are about to repent, and they will obey your words, for I will be with you and will force them to be persuaded by you." 4. I said to him, "Sir, these commandments are great and beautiful and glorious, and able to make glad the heart of man if he be able to keep them. But I do not know if these commandments can be kept by man, because they are very hard." 5. He answered and said to me, "If you set it before yourself that they can be kept you will easily keep them, and they will not be difficult; but if it already comes into your heart that they cannot be kept by man, you will not keep them. 6. But now I say to you, if you do not keep them, but neglect them, you will not have salvation, nor your children, nor your house, because you have already judged for yourself that these commandments cannot be kept by man."

47 [Commandment 12.4]

1. And he spoke these things to me very angrily, so that I was confounded, and greatly afraid of him, for his appearance had changed so that a man could

not endure his wrath. 2. But when he saw me quite disturbed and confused he began to speak to me more gently and cheerfully, and said, "Foolish one without understanding and double-minded, do you not understand the glory of God, how great and mighty and wonderful it is, because he created the world for man's sake, and subdued all his creation to man, and gave him all power, to master all things under heaven? 3. If, then," he said, "man is the lord of all the creatures of God, and masters them, is it not possible to master these commandments also? The man," he said, "who has the Lord in his heart, can master all things and all these commandments. 4. But those who have the Lord on their lips, and yet their heart is hardened, are far from the Lord. For them, these commandments are hard and difficult to walk in. 5. Therefore, those of you who are empty and light in the faith, put the Lord into your heart, and you will know that nothing is easier or sweeter or more gentle than these commandments. 6. Be converted, those of you who walk in the commandments of the devil, which are difficult and bitter and cruel and foul, and do not fear the devil, for there is no power in him against you. 7. For I, the angel of repentance who masters him, will be with you. The devil can only cause fear, but fear of him has no force. Therefore, do not fear him and he will flee from you."

[...]

Parable 2

51

1. While I was walking in the country I noticed an elm and a vine, and I was thinking about them and their fruits, when the shepherd appeared to me and said, "What are you thinking to yourself about the elm and vine?" "I am thinking, sir," I said, "that they are very well suited to one another." 2. "These two trees," he said "are put as a type for the servants of God." "I should like," I said, "to know the type of the trees of which you speak." "You see," he said, "the vine and the elm?" "Yes, sir," I said, "I see them." 3. "This vine," he said, "bears fruit, but the elm is a sterile tree. But this vine, if it does not grow upon the elm, cannot bear much fruit, because it is spread on the ground, and the fruit that it bears when it is not hanging on the elm is rotten. When, therefore, the vine is attached to the elm, it bears fruit from itself and from the elm. 4. You see then that the elm gives much fruit, not less than the vine, but rather more." "How, sir," I said, "does it bear more?" "Because," he said, "the vine, when it hangs on the elm, gives much beautiful fruit, but when it is lying on the ground, it bears

but little fruit, which is rotten. This parable, therefore, applies to the servants of God, to the poor and the rich." 5. "How, sir?' I said, "let me know." "Listen," he said. "The rich man has much wealth, but he is poor toward the Lord, being busied about his riches, and his intercession and confession towards the Lord is very small, and that which he has is weak and small, and has no other power. But when the rich man rests upon the poor, and gives him what he needs, the rich man believes that what he does to the poor man can find a reward with God, because the poor is rich in intercession and confession, and his intercession has great power with God. The rich man, therefore, helps the poor in all things without doubting. 6. But the poor man, being helped by the rich, makes intercession to God, giving him thanks for him who gave to him, and the rich man is still zealous for the poor man, that he fails not in his life, for he knows that the intercession of the poor is acceptable and rich toward the Lord. 7. Therefore the two together complete the work, for the poor works in the intercession in which he is rich, which he received from the Lord; this he pays to the Lord who helps him. And the rich man likewise provides to the poor, without hesitating, with the wealth that he received from the Lord; and this work is great and acceptable with God, because he has understanding in his wealth, and has given to the poor man from the gifts of the Lord, and fulfilled his ministry rightly. 8. Among men, therefore, the elm appears as if it bore no fruit, and they do not know nor understand that if there is drought the elm which has water nourishes the vine, and the vine, having water continuously, gives double fruit, both for itself and for the elm. So also, the poor, interceding with the Lord for the rich, complement their wealth, and again, the rich helping the poor with their necessities complement their prayers. 9. Both, therefore, share in the righteous work. Therefore, he who does these things will not be deserted by God but will be inscribed in the books of the living. 10. Blessed are they who are wealthy and understand that their riches are from the Lord, for he who understands this will also be able to do some good service.

[...]

Parable 5

54 [Parable 5.1]

1. While I was fasting, and sitting on a certain mountain, and thanking the Lord for all that he had done with me, I saw the shepherd sitting by me. He said, "Why have you come here so early?" "Because, sir" I said, "I have a

station." 2. "What," he said, "is a station?" "I am fasting, sir," I said. "But," he said, "what is this fast, which you are fasting?" "I am fasting, sir," I said, "as I have been accustomed." 3. "You do not know," he said, "how to fast to the Lord, and this useless fast which you are fasting to him is not a fast." "Why, sir," I said, "do you say this?" "I tell you," he said, "that this fast which you think to fast is nothing, but I will teach you what is a fast, acceptable and complete to the Lord. Listen," he said, 4. "God does not wish for such a vain fast. For if you fast to God thus, you do nothing for righteousness. But fast to God in this way: 5. do nothing evil in your life, but serve the Lord with a pure heart; keep his commandments and walk in his ordinances, and let no evil desire arise in your heart, but believe in God, that if you do these things and fear him, and refrain from every wicked act, you will live to God; and if you do this you will fulfill a great fast and one acceptable to God."

55 [Parable 5.2]

1. "Listen to the parable that I am going to tell you about fasting. 2. A certain man had a field and many servants, and on part of the field he planted a vineyard. And he chose a certain servant, who was faithful, in good esteem and honor with him, and he called him and said to him, 'Take this vineyard which I have planted and fence it until I come, and do nothing more to the vineyard. And follow this order of mine, and you will have your freedom from me.' And the master of the servant went abroad. 3. Now when he had gone, the servant took and fenced the vineyard. When he had finished the fencing of the vineyard, he saw that the vineyard was full of weeds. 4. Therefore, he thought to himself, 'I have finished this order of the lord; I will next dig this vineyard, and it will be better when it is dug, and having no weeds will yield more fruit, not being choked by the weeds.' He took and dug the vineyard, and he pulled out all the weeds that were in the vineyard. And that vineyard became very beautiful and fertile with no weeds to choke it. 5. After a time, the master of the servant and the field returned, and he entered into the vineyard, and seeing the vineyard beautifully fenced, and moreover dug, and all the weeds pulled up and vines fertile, he was greatly pleased at the acts of the servant. 6. So he called his beloved son, whom he had as heir, and his friends whom he had as counselors, and told them what he had ordered his servant and what he had found accomplished. And they congratulated the servant for the character which the master gave him. 7. And he said to them, I promised this servant his freedom if he kept the orders which I gave him. Now he has kept my orders, and he has added good work in the vineyard and greatly pleased me. So, in

reward for this work that he has done, I wish to make him joint heir with my son because when he had a good thought, he did not ignore it but carried it out. 8. The son of the master agreed with this plan, that the servant should be joint heir with the son. 9. After a few days he made a feast and sent to the servant much food from the feast. But the servant took the food, which was sent to him by the master, kept what was sufficient for himself, and distributed the rest to his fellow servants. 10. And his fellow-servants were glad when they received the food, and they began to pray for him, that he might find greater favor with his master because he had treated them thus. 11. His master heard all these events and again rejoiced greatly at his conduct. The master again assembled his friends and his son and reported to them what the servant had done with the food that he had received, and they were still more pleased that the servant should be made joint heir with his son."

56 [Parable 5.3]

1. I said, "Sir, I do not know these parables and I cannot understand them if you do not explain them to me." 2. "I will explain everything to you," he said, "and everything that I talk with you. 3. I will show you his commandments, and if you do anything good, beyond the commandment of God, you will gain for yourself greater glory, and you will be more honorable with God than you were destined to be. If then, you keep the commandments of God, and add these services also, you will rejoice, if you keep them according to my commandment." 4. I said to him, "Sir, I will keep whatever you command me, for I know that you are with me." "I will be with you," he said, "because you have such zeal for doing good, and I will be with all, he said, who have this zeal. 5. This fast," he said, "if the commandments of the Lord are kept, is very good. You shall therefore keep this fast, which you are going to observe in this way: 6. First of all, stay away from every evil word and from every evil desire, and purify your heart from all the vanities of this world. If you keep these things, this fast will be perfect for you. 7. And you shall do the following: After completing what has been written, on the day you are fasting, do not eat anything except bread and water; take the money you would have spent that day on the food you would have eaten, and give that money to a widow or an orphan or to someone destitute; and be humble, so that through your humility the person who receives this money may fill his or her soul and pray to the Lord for you. 8. If you fulfill the fast as I commanded you, your sacrifice will be acceptable to God, and this fast will be written down to your credit, and your service is good and joyful and acceptable to the Lord. 9. You shall therefore

keep these things in this manner with your children and all your house, and if you keep them, you will be blessed, and all who hear them and keep them will be blessed and will obtain from the Lord whatever they ask."

57 [Parable 5.4]

1. I asked him much to explain to me the parable of the field and the master and the vineyard and the servant who fenced the vineyard, and the fences, and the weeds which were pulled up from the servant vineyard, and the son, and the friends the counselors, for I understood that all these things were a parable. 2. He answered and said to me, "You are very persistent with asking. You ought not," he said, "to ask at all, for if it is necessary for it to be explained to you, it will be explained." I said to him, "Sir, whatever you show me and do not explain I will have seen in vain and not understand what it is. So likewise, if you speak parables to me and do not interpret them for me, I will have heard something from you in vain." 3. He answered and said to me again, "Whoever," he said, "is God's servant and has his Lord in his heart seeks understanding from him and receives it, and he interprets every parable, and the sayings of the Lord which were spoken through parables are made known to him. But as many as are weak and idle in prayer, those hesitate to ask from the Lord. 4. But the Lord is very merciful and gives unceasingly to all who ask from him. But you, since you have been given power by the holy angel and received from him such intercession and are not idle, therefore do you not seek understanding from the Lord and receive it from him?" 5. I said to him, "Sir, when I have you with me, I must ask you and enquire of you, for you show me all things and speak with me, but if I had seen or heard them without you, I should have asked the Lord that it might be explained to me."

58 [Parable 5.5]

1. "I told you," he said, "just now, that you are obstinate and persistent in asking for the explanations of the parable. But since you are so persistent, I will explain to you the parable of the field and all the other implications of it, that you may make them known to everyone. Listen, now," he said, "and understand it. 2. The field is this world, and the Lord of the field is he who created everything and perfected it and gave it strength. And the servant is the Son of God, and the vines are this people that he planted. 3. And the fences are the holy angels of the Lord who support his people. And the weeds which are pulled up out of the vineyard are iniquities of the servants of God. And the

food which he sent to him from the supper is the commandments which he gave to his people through his Son, and the friends and counselors are the holy angels who were first created. And the absence of the master is the time which remains before his coming." 4. I said to him, "Sir, all of this is great and wonderful and glorious. How then," I said, "could I understand it? Nor is there any other man, however understanding he may be, who can understand it. Moreover, sir," I said, "explain to me what I am going to ask you." 5. "Say," he said, "what you wish." "Why," I said, "sir, is the Son of God in the parable given the form of a servant?"

59 [Parable 5.6]

1. "Listen,' he said, "The Son of God is not given the form of a servant but is given great power and lordship." "How, sir?" I said, "I do not understand." 2. "Because God planted the vineyard," he said, "that is, he created the people, and gave it over to his Son. And the Son appointed the angels over them to keep them. And he himself cleansed their sins, laboring greatly and undergoing much toil. For no vineyard can be dug without toil or labor. 3. When, therefore, he had cleansed the sins of the people, he showed them the ways of life and gave them the law that he received from his Father. 4. But listen why the Lord took his Son and the glorious angels as counselors concerning the inheritance of the servant. 5. God caused the Holy Spirit, who preexisted and created all creation, to dwell in the flesh that he willed. Therefore, this flesh, in which the Holy Spirit dwelt, served the Spirit well, walking in holiness and purity, and did not in any way defile the Spirit. 6. When, therefore, it had lived nobly and purely, and had labored with the Spirit, and worked with it in every deed, behaving with power and bravery, he chose it as a companion with the Holy Spirit, for the conduct of this flesh pleased him because it was not defiled while it was bearing the Holy Spirit on earth. 7. Therefore, he took the Son and the glorious angels as counselors, that this flesh also, having served the Spirit blamelessly, should have its own abode and not seem to have lost the reward of its service. For all flesh in which the Holy Spirit has dwelt will receive a reward if it is found undefiled and spotless. 8. You have the explanation of this parable also."

60 [Parable 5.7]

1. "I am glad, sir," I said, "to hear this explanation." "Listen, now," he said. "Guard this flesh of yours, pure and undefiled, that the spirit which dwells

in it may give a good report about it, and your flesh may be justified. 2. See to it, lest the idea enter your heart that this flesh of yours is mortal, and you abuse it in some defilement. For if you defile your flesh, you defile also the Holy Spirit, and if you defile the flesh, you will not live." 3. "But, sir," I said, "if anyone was ignorant before these words were heard, how can the man who defiled his flesh be saved?" "For the previous ignorance," he said, "it is possible for God alone to give healing, for he has all power. 4. That is if, in the future, you defile neither the flesh nor the spirit; for both are in communion, and neither can be defiled without the other. Keep, therefore, both pure, and you will live to God."

[...]

Parable 10 [10]

111 [Parable 10.1]

1. After I had written this book, the angel who had handed me over to the shepherd came to the house I was in, and he sat on the couch, and the shepherd stood at his right hand. Then he called me and said to me, 2. "I have handed you over," he said, "and your house to this shepherd, that you may be protected by him." "Yes, sir," I said. "If then," he said, "you wish to be protected from all vexation and all cruelty, and to have success in every good work and word and in every virtue of righteousness, walk in his commandments that he gave you, and you will be able to overcome all wickedness. 3. For, if you keep his commandments, all the lusts and delights of this world will be conquered for you, and success in every good undertaking will follow you. Take his perfection and moderation upon you, and say to all that he holds great honor and dignity with the Lord, and that he is set in great power and is powerful in his office. To him alone throughout all the world is given the power of repentance. Does he not seem to you to be powerful? But you despise his perfection and the modesty which he has toward you."

112 [Parable 10.2]

1. I said to him, "Ask him himself, sir, if since he has been in my house, I have done anything against his command to offend against him?" 2. "I know myself," he said, "that you have done nothing and will do nothing against his

---

10 The Greek has been lost from the middle of chapter 107 to the end. This follows the Latin.

command, and therefore I am speaking thus with you, that you may persevere; for he has given me a good account of you. But you shall tell these words to others, that they also who have repented, or shall repent, may have the same mind as you, and that he may give a good account to me of them, and I to the Lord." 3. "I myself, sir," I said, "tell the mighty acts of the Lord to all men, but I hope that all who have sinned before, if they hear this, will willingly repent and recover life." 4. "Remain then," he said, "in this ministry and carry it out. Whoever performs his commandments will have life, and such a one has great honor with the Lord. But those who do not keep his commands flee from their own life, and they are against him. They do not keep his commandments but are delivering themselves to death, and each one of them is guilty of his own blood. But I tell you, keep these commandments, and you will have a remedy for your sins."

[…]

The Epistle to Diognetus

Context
Author: Uncertain
Provenance: Uncertain
Date: Chapters 1–10: c. AD 150–200; 11–12: c. AD 200–250[1]

Opening

1

Since I perceive, most excellent Diognetus, that you are exceedingly zealous to learn the religion of the Christians and are asking very clear and careful questions concerning them, both who is the God in whom they believe and how they worship him, so that all disregard the world and despise death, and do not reckon as Gods those who are considered to be so by the Greeks, nor keep the superstition of the Jews, and what is the love that they have for one another, and why this new race or practice has come to life at this time, and not formerly. I indeed welcome this zeal in you, and I ask from God who bestows on us the power both of speaking and of hearing, that it may be granted to me to speak so that you may benefit as much as possible by your hearing, and to you to hear that I may not be made sorry for my speech.

---

[1] See Paul Foster, "The Epistle to Diognetus," in *The Writings of the Apostolic Fathers*, 156.

Refutation against Idols

2

1. Come then, clear yourself of all the prejudice that occupies your mind, and throw aside the custom that deceives you, and become as it were a new man from the beginning, as one, as you yourself also admitted, who is about to listen to a new story. Look, not only with your eyes, but also with your intelligence, what substance or form they chance to have whom you call gods and regard as such. 2. Is not one a stone, like that on which we walk, another bronze, no better than the vessels which have been forged for our use, another wood already rotten, another silver, needing a man to guard it against theft, another iron, eaten by rust, another earthenware, not a bit better than that which is supplied for the most ordinary service? 3. Are not all these of perishable material? Were they not forged by iron and fire? Did the wood-carver not make one, the brass-founder another, the silversmith another, the potter another? Before they were molded by their arts, into the shapes which they have, was it not possible and does it not still remain possible, for each of them to have been given a different shape? Could not vessels made out of the same material, if they met with the same artificers, be still made similar to such as they? 4. Again, would it not be possible for these, which are now worshipped by you, to be made by men into vessels like any others? Are they not all dumb? Are they not blind? Are they not without souls? Are they not without feeling? Are they not without movement? Are not they all rotting? Are they not all decaying? 5. Do you call these things gods? Are these what you serve? Are these what you worship and in the end you become like them? 6. Is this the reason why you hate the Christians, that they do not think that these are gods? 7. For is it not you, who, though you think and believe that you are praising the gods, are much more despising them? Are you not much rather mocking and insulting them, when you worship those of stone and earthenware without guarding them; but lock up at night and in the daytime place guards over those of silver and gold, so that they will not be stolen? 8. And, if they have powers of perception, by the honors which you think to pay them, you are rather punishing them, and, if they are without perception, you are refuting them by worshipping them with blood and burnt fat. 9. Let one of you suffer these things, let him endure that it should be done to him. Why, there is not a single man who would willingly endure this punishment, for he has perception and reason. But the stone endures, for it has no perception. Do you not then refute its

perception? 10. I could say much more about this, that Christians are not enslaved to such gods, but if anyone finds these arguments insufficient, I think it useless to say more.

Why Christians Do Not Worship as the Jews

3

1. In the next place I think that you are especially anxious to hear why the Christians do not worship in the same way as the Jews. 2. The Jews indeed, by abstaining from the religion already discussed, may rightly claim that they worship the one God of the Universe, and regard him as master, but in offering service to him in like manner to those already dealt with they are quite wrong. 3. For just as the Greeks give a proof of foolishness by making offerings to senseless and deaf images, so the Jews ought rather to consider that they are showing foolishness, not reverence, by regarding God as in need of these things. 4. For He who made heaven and earth and all that is in them, and who bestows on all of us that which we need, would not himself have need of any of these things which he himself supplies to those who think that they are giving them. 5. For after all, those who think that they are consecrating sacrifices to him by blood and burnt fat, and whole burnt offerings, and that they are revering him by these honors, seem to me to be in no way better than those who show the same respect to deaf images. For it seems that the one offers to those who cannot partake of the honor, the others to him who is in need of nothing.

4

1. Moreover, I do not suppose that you need to learn from me that, after all, their scruples about food and superstition about the Sabbath, and their pride in circumcision and the sham of their fasting and feast of the new moon, are ridiculous and unworthy of any argument. 2. For how can it be anything but unlawful to receive some of the things created by God for the use of man as if well created, and to reject others as if useless and superfluous? 3. And what can it be but impious falsely to accuse God of forbidding that a good deed should be done on the Sabbath day? 4. And what does it deserve but ridicule to be proud of the mutilation of the flesh as a proof of election, as if they were, for this reason, especially beloved by God? 5. And their attention to the stars and moon, for the observance of months and days, and for

their arbitrary distinctions between the changing seasons ordained by God, making some into feasts, and others into occasions of mourning; who would regard this as a proof of piety and not much more of foolishness? 6. So then, I think that you have learnt sufficiently that the Christians do rightly in abstaining from the general silliness and deceit and fussiness and pride of the Jews. But do not suppose that you can learn from man the mystery of the Christians' own religion.

Explanation of How Christians Live as Sojourners in the World

5

1. For the distinction between Christians and other men, is neither in country nor language nor customs. 2. For they do not dwell in cities in some place of their own, nor do they use any strange variety of dialect, nor practice an extraordinary kind of life. 3. This teaching of theirs has not been discovered by the intellect or thought of busy men, nor are they the advocates of any human doctrine as some men are. 4. Yet while living in Greek and barbarian cities, according as each obtained his lot, and following the local customs, both in clothing and food and in the rest of life, they show forth the wonderful and confessedly strange character of the constitution of their own citizenship. 5. They dwell in their own fatherlands, but as if sojourners in them; they share all things as citizens, but they suffer all things as strangers. Every foreign country is their fatherland, and every fatherland is a foreign country. 6. They marry as all men, they bear children, but they do not expose their offspring. 7. They offer free hospitality, they but guard their purity. 8. Their lot is cast in the flesh, but they do not live after the flesh. 9. They pass their time upon the earth, but they have their citizenship in heaven. 10. They obey the appointed laws, and they surpass the laws in their own lives. 11. They love all men and are persecuted by all men. 12. They are unknown, and they are condemned. They are put to death, and they gain life. 13. They are poor and make many rich; they lack all things and have all things in abundance. 14. They are dishonored, and are glorified in their dishonor, they are maligned and are justified. 15. They are abused and give blessing; they are insulted and render honor. 16. When they do good, they are punished as evildoers, when they are punished, they rejoice as men who receive life. 17. They are warred upon by the Jews as foreigners, and they are persecuted by the Greeks, and those who hate them cannot state the cause of their enmity.

6

1. To put it shortly, what the soul is to the body, that is what Christians are to the world. 2. The soul is spread through all members of the body, and Christians throughout the cities of the world. 3. The soul dwells in the body but is not of the body, and Christians dwell in the world but are not of the world. 4. The soul is invisible and is guarded in a visible body, and Christians are recognized when they are in the world, but their religion remains invisible. 5. The flesh hates the soul and wages war upon it, though it has suffered no evil, because it is prevented from gratifying its pleasures, and the world hates the Christians though it has suffered no evil, because they are opposed to its pleasures. 6. The soul loves its limbs and the flesh which hates it, and Christians love those that hate them. 7. The soul has been shut up in the body, but itself sustains the body; and Christians are confined in the world as in a prison, but themselves sustain the world. 8. The soul dwells immortal in a mortal tabernacle, and Christians sojourn among corruptible things, waiting for the incorruptibility that is in heaven. 9. The soul, when ill-treated in food and drink becomes better, and Christians when persecuted day by day increase more. 10. God has appointed them to so great a post, and it is not right for them to decline it.

On How Christians Were Entrusted with the Truth by God's Beloved Child

7

1. For it is not, as I said, an earthly discovery that was given to them, nor do they take such pains to guard some mortal invention, nor have they been entrusted with the dispensation of human mysteries. 2. But in truth, the Almighty and all-creating and invisible God himself founded among men the truth from heaven, and the holy and incomprehensible word, and established it in their hearts, not, as one might suppose, by sending some minister to men, or an angel, or ruler, or one of those who direct earthly things, or one of those who are entrusted with the dispensations in heaven. Instead [by sending] the very Artificer and Creator of the universe himself, by whom he made the heavens, by whom he enclosed the sea in its own bounds, whose mysteries all the elements guard faithfully; from whom the sun received the measure of the courses of the day, to whose command the moon is obedient to give light by night, whom the stars obey, following the course of the moon,

by whom all things were ordered, and ordained, and placed in subjection, the heavens and the things in the heavens, the earth and the things in the earth, the sea and the things in the sea, fire, air, abyss, the things in the heights, the things in the depths, the things between them him he sent to them. 3. Yes, but did he send him, as a man might suppose, in sovereignty and fear and terror? 4. Not so, but in gentleness and meekness, as a king sending a son, he sent him as King, he sent him as God, he sent him as Man to men, he was saving and persuading when he sent him, not compelling, for compulsion is not an attribute of God. 5. When he sent him, he was calling, not pursuing; when he sent him, he was loving, not judging. 6. For he will send him as judge, and who shall endure his coming?[2] ...they are thrown to wild beasts that they may deny the Lord, and are not overcome? 8. Do you not see that the more of them are punished, the more that others multiply? 9. These things do not seem to be the works of man; these things are a miracle of God; these things are the proofs of his coming.

8

1. For before he came, what man had any knowledge at all of what God is? 2. Or do you accept the vain and foolish statements of those pretentious philosophers, of whom some said that God is fire (they give the name of God to that to which they shall go) and some water, and some one of the other elements which were created by God. 3. And yet if any of these arguments is acceptable it would be possible for each one of the other created things to be declared God. 4. Now these things are the miracle mongering and deceit of the magicians; 5. but of men there is none who has either seen him or known him, but he himself manifested himself. 6. Now he manifested himself through faith, by which alone it is given to see God. 7. For God the Master and Creator of the universe, who made all things and arranged them in order, was not only kind to man but also long-suffering. 8. Indeed, he was ever so and is and will be, kindly and good and true and free from wrath, and he alone is good. 9. And having formed a great and unspeakable design, he communicated it to his Child alone. 10. And so long as he kept it in a mystery and guarded his wise counsel, he seemed to neglect us and to be careless; 11. But when he revealed it through his beloved Child, and manifested the things prepared from the beginning, he gave us all things at once, both to share in his benefits and to see and understand, and which of us would ever have expected these things?

---

2 There is a break in the text here.

9

1. Having thus planned everything by himself with his Child, he permitted us up to the former time to be borne along by unruly impulses as we willed, carried away by pleasures and lust. Not at all because he delighted in our sins, but in forbearance; not in approval of the time of iniquity which was then, but fashioning the time of righteousness which is now, that we, who at that time were proved by our own deeds to be unworthy of life, may now be granted it by the goodness of God, and that when we had made it plain that it was impossible for us by ourselves to enter into the kingdom of God, we might be made able by the power of God. 2. But when our iniquity was fulfilled and it had become fully manifest, that its reward of punishment and death waited for it, and the time came which God had appointed to manifest henceforth his kindness and power (O the excellence of the kindness and the love of God!) he did not hate us nor reject us nor remember us for evil, but was long-suffering, endured us, himself in pity took our sin, himself gave his own Son as ransom for us, the Holy for the wicked, the innocent for guilty, the just for the unjust, the incorruptible for the corruptible, the immortal for the mortal. 3. For what else could cover our sins but his righteousness? 4. In whom was it possible for us, in our wickedness and impiety, to be made just, except in the Son of God alone? 5. O the sweet exchange! O the inscrutable creation! O the unexpected benefits, that the wickedness of many should be concealed in the one righteous, and the righteousness of the one should make righteous many wicked! 6. Having convinced us then of the inability of our nature to attain life in time past, and now having shown the Savior who is able to save, even where it was impossible, it was his will for both reasons that we should believe on his goodness, and regard him as nurse, father, teacher, counsellor, physician, mind, light, honor, glory, strength, life, and to have no care for clothing and food.

On the Imitation of God

10

1. If you also desire this faith, and first receive complete knowledge of the Father.[3]... 2. For God loved human beings, for whose sake he made the world, to whom he subjected all things which are in the earth, to whom he gave reason, to whom he gave mind, on whom alone he enjoined that they should

---

3 There is a break in the text here.

look upward to him, whom he made in his own image, to whom he sent his only-begotten Son, to whom he promised the kingdom in heaven, and he will give it to those who loved him. 3. And when you have this full knowledge, with what joy do think you will be filled, or how greatly will you love him who thus first loved you? 4. But by your love you will imitate the example of his goodness. And do not wonder that it is possible for man to be the imitator of God; it is possible when he wills this. 5. For happiness consists not in domination over neighbors, nor in wishing to have more than the weak, nor in wealth and power to compel those who are poorer, nor can anyone be an imitator of God in doing these things, but these things are outside his majesty. 6. But whoever takes up the burden of his neighbor, and wishes to help another, who is worse off in that in which he is the stronger, and by ministering to those in need the things which he has received and holds from God becomes a god to those who receive them, this man is an imitator of God. 7. Then, though your lot be placed on earth you will see that God lives in heaven, then you will begin to speak of the mysteries of God, then you will both love and admire those who are being punished because they will not deny God, then you will condemn the deceit and error of the world, when you know what is the true life of heaven, when you despise the apparent death of this world, when you fear the death which is real, which is kept for those that shall be condemned to the everlasting fire, which will punish up to the end those that were delivered to it. 8. Then you will marvel at those who endure for the sake of righteousness the fire that is for a season, and you will count them blessed when you know that other fire.

Knowledge and Teaching from the Word [4]

11

1. My speech is not strange, nor my inquiry unreasonable, but as a disciple of apostles I am becoming a teacher of the heathen. I administer worthily that which has been handed down to those who are becoming disciples of the truth. 2. For whoever has been properly taught and has become a lover of the word does not seek to learn plainly the things which have been clearly shown by the word to disciples, to whom the Word appeared and revealed them, speaking boldly, not being perceived by the unbelieving, but relating them to disciples, who were held by him to be faithful and gained knowledge

---

4 Chapters 11–12 appear to be from a different text that was added to the manuscript at some point during its transmission.

of the mysteries of the Father? 3. And for his sake he sent the Word to appear to the world, who was dishonored by the chosen people, was preached by apostles, was believed by the heathen. 4. He was from the beginning, and appeared new, and was proved to be old, and is ever young, as he is born in the hearts of the saints. 5. He is the eternal one, who today is accounted a Son, through whom the church is enriched, and grace is unfolded and multiplied among the saints, who confers understanding, manifests mysteries, announces seasons, rejoices in the faithful, is given to them that seek, that is, to those by whom the pledges of faith are not broken, nor the decrees of the fathers transgressed. 6. Then is the fear of the law sung, and the grace of the prophets known, the faith of the gospels is established, and the tradition of apostles is guarded, and the grace of the church exults. 7. And if you do not grieve this grace you will understand what the Word says through the agents of his choice, when he will. 8. For in all things which we were moved by the will of him who commands us to speak with pain, we become sharers with you through love of the things revealed to us.

12

1. If you consider and listen with zeal to these truths, you will know what things God bestows on those that love him rightly, who become a paradise of delight, raising up in themselves a fertile tree with all manner of fruits, and are adorned with diverse fruits. 2. For in this garden has been planted "the tree of knowledge and the tree of life" (Gen 2:9), but the tree of knowledge does not kill, but disobedience kills. 3. For that which was written is quite plain, that God in the beginning planted "A tree of knowledge and a tree of life in the midst of Paradise" (Gen 2:9), and he showed that life is through knowledge. But those who did not use it in purity were in the beginning deprived of it by the deceit of the serpent; 4. for neither is there life without knowledge, nor sound knowledge without true life; therefore both are planted together. 5. And when the apostle saw the force of this, he blamed the knowledge which is exercised apart from the truth of the injunction which leads to life and said: "Knowledge puffs up, but love edifies" (1 Cor 8:1). 6. For he who thinks that he knows anything without knowledge that is true and testified to by life, he does not know but is deceived by the serpent, not loving life. But he who has full knowledge with fear and seeks after life plants in hope, looking for fruit. 7. Let your heart be knowledge, and your life the true and comprehended word. 8. And if you bear the tree of this and pluck its fruit you will always enjoy that which is desired by God, which the serpent does

not touch, and deceit does not infect, and Eve is not corrupted but a virgin is trusted, 9. and salvation is set forth, and apostles are given understanding, and the Passover of the Lord advances, and the seasons are brought together, and are harmonized with the world, and the Word teaches the saints and rejoices, and through it the Father is glorified; to whom be glory forever. Amen.

The Apology of Quadratus

Context
Author: Quadratus
Provenance: Possibly Athens
Date: c. AD 117–120 or c. 124–125[1]

Eusebius of Caesarea on Quadratus (*Ecclesiastical History* 4.3)

1. After Trajan had reigned for nineteen and a half years, Aelius Hadrian became his successor as the next emperor. Quadratus addressed a discourse to him that contained an apology for our religion because certain wicked men had attempted to trouble the Christians. The work is still in the hands of a great many of the brothers and sisters, and also in our own, and it provides clear proofs of Quadratus' understanding and of his apostolic orthodoxy.

2. Quadratus himself reveals the early date at which he lived in the following words:

> But our savior's works were always present, since they were true. Those who were healed, and those who were raised from the dead—they were seen not only when they were being healed and when they were raised, but were also always present, not only while the savior was sojourning but also after he departed. They existed for a sufficient time so that some of them made it to our time.

---

1 See Paul Foster, "The Apology of Quadratus," in *The Writings of the Apostolic Fathers*, 54–55.

12

The Fragments of Papias

Context
Author: Papias
Provenance: Hierapolis
Date: c. AD 110–130[1]

Fragment 3[2]

1. Five books of Papias still exist, and they bear the title the *Expositions of the Sayings of the Lord*. Irenaeus mentions that these are the only works written by him, indicating this with the following words: "These things are attested by Papias, an ancient man who was a hearer of John and a companion of Polycarp, in his fourth book. For five books have been written by him." These are the words of Irenaeus. 2. But Papias himself in the preface to his writings does not say that he was a hearer and eyewitness of the holy apostles; instead, he shows by the words that he uses that he received the doctrines of the faith from those who were their friends.

3. He says: "But I will not hesitate to write down for you, along with my interpretations, whatever things I have carefully learned from the elders and carefully remembered, guaranteeing their truth. Unlike most people, I did not take pleasure in those that have a lot to say but in those that teach the truth; not in those that present strange commandments but in those that deliver the commandments that are given by the Lord to the faith and that spring

---

[1] See Charles E. Hill, "The Fragments of Papias," in *The Writings of the Apostolic Fathers*, 42–43.

[2] Eusebius, *Ecclesiastical History* 3.39.

from the truth itself. 4. If then, anyone came who had been a follower of the elders, I questioned him about the words of the elders—what Andrew or Peter said, or what was said by Philip, or by Thomas, or by James, or by John, or by Matthew, or by any other of the disciples of the Lord, and what things Aristion and the presbyter John, the disciples of the Lord, say. For I did not think that what was to be gotten from the books would profit me as much as what came from the living and abiding voice."

5. It is worthwhile observing here that the name John is twice mentioned by him. The first one he mentions in connection with Peter and James and Matthew and the rest of the apostles, clearly meaning the evangelist; but the other John he mentions after an interval, and places him among others outside of the number of the apostles, putting Aristion before him, and he distinctly calls him a presbyter. 6. This shows that the statement of those is true, who say that there were two persons in Asia that bore the same name, and that there were two tombs in Ephesus, each of which, even to the present day, is called John's. It is important to notice this. For it is probable that it was the second, if one is not willing to admit that it was the first that saw the Revelation, which is ascribed by name to John.

7. And Papias, of whom we are now speaking, confesses that he received the words of the apostles from those that followed them, but says that he was himself a hearer of Aristion and the presbyter John. At least he mentions them frequently by name and gives their traditions in his writings. These things we hope, have not been uselessly adduced by us. 8. But it is fitting to add to the words of Papias which have been quoted above other passages from his works, in which he relates some other wonderful events that he claims to have received from tradition. 9. That Philip the apostle dwelt at Hierapolis with his daughters has been already stated. But it must be noted here that Papias, their contemporary, says that he heard a wonderful tale from the daughters of Philip. For he relates that in his time one rose from the dead. And he tells another wonderful story of Justus, surnamed Barsabbas: that he drank a deadly poison, and yet, by the grace of the Lord, suffered no harm. 10. The Book of Acts records that the holy apostles after the ascension of the Savior put forward this Justus, together with Matthias, and prayed that one might be chosen in place of the traitor Judas, to fill up their number. The account is as follows: "And they put forward two, Joseph, called Barsabbas, who was surnamed Justus, and Matthias; and they prayed and said..." (Acts 1:23).

11. The same writer gives other accounts that he says came to him through unwritten tradition, certain strange parables and teachings of the Savior, and some other more mythical things. 12. To these belong his statement that there

will be a period of some thousand years after the resurrection of the dead, and that the kingdom of Christ will be set up in material form on this very earth. I suppose he got these ideas through a misunderstanding of the apostolic accounts, not perceiving that the things said by them were spoken mystically in figures. 13. For he appears to have been of very limited understanding, as one can see from his writings. It was due to him that so many of the church writers after him adopted a similar opinion, giving their support because of the antiquity of the man; as for instance Irenaeus and anyone else that may have proclaimed similar views. 14. Papias also gives in his own work other accounts of the words of the Lord on the authority of Aristion, who was mentioned above, and traditions as handed down by the presbyter John; we refer those to anyone who is fond of learning. But now we must add to his words that we have already quoted the tradition that he gives about Mark, the author of the gospel.

15. "This the presbyter also said: Mark, having become the interpreter of Peter, wrote down accurately, though not in order, everything he remembered of the things said or done by Christ. For he neither heard the Lord nor followed him, but afterward, as I said, he followed Peter, who adapted his teaching to the needs of his hearers, but with no intention of giving a connected account of the Lord's sayings, so that Mark committed no error while he wrote things as he remembered them. For he was careful of one thing: not to omit any of the things which he had heard, and not to state any of them falsely." These things are related by Papias about Mark.

16. But about Matthew he writes as follows: "So then Matthew wrote the oracles in the Hebrew language, and everyone interpreted them as he was able." And the same writer uses testimonies from the first Epistle of John and from that of Peter likewise. And he relates another story of a woman, who was accused of many sins before the Lord, which is contained in the Gospel according to the Hebrews. These things we have thought it necessary to observe in addition to what has been already stated.

Fragment 14[3]

[Irenaeus:] The elders who saw John, the disciple of the Lord, remembered that they had heard from him how the Lord taught about those times and said: "The days will come in which vines will grow, each having ten thousand branches, and in each branch there will be ten thousand twigs, and in each true twig there will be ten thousand shoots, and in every one of the shoots

---
[3] Irenaeus, *Against Heresies* 5.33.

there will be ten thousand clusters, and on every one of the clusters there will be ten thousand grapes, and every grape when pressed will give twenty five measures of wine. And when any one of the saints grasps a cluster, another will cry out, 'I am a better cluster, take me; bless the Lord through me.' In the same way, [he said] that a grain of wheat would produce ten thousand ears, and that every ear would have ten thousand grains, and every grain would yield ten pounds of clear, pure, fine flour; and that apples, and seeds, and grass would produce in similar proportions; and that all animals, feeding then only on the productions of the earth, would become peaceful and harmonious and be in perfect subjection to humanity." Testimony about these things can be found in the writing by Papias, an ancient man, who was a hearer of John and a friend of Polycarp, in his fourth book (for five books were composed by him), and he added the following: "Now these things are credible to believers. And Judas the traitor," he says, "not believing, and asking, 'How will such growth be accomplished by the Lord?' the Lord said, '[Those who reach these times], they will see.'"

The Apology of Aristides

Context
Author: Aristides[1]
Provenance: Athens
Date: AD 124/125 or 131/132 [2]

Opening Address to Emperor Hadrian; on God

1

I, O king, in the providence of God came into the world; and when I had considered the heaven and the earth, the sun and the moon and the rest, I marveled at their orderly arrangement. And when I saw that the universe and all that is within it is moved by necessity, I perceived that the mover and controller is God. For everything that causes motion is stronger than that which

---

[1] The version included here is the Greek preserved in the Greek novel, *Barlaam and Josaphat* (chapter 27). Any critical research on Aristides must consider both the Greek and the Syriac versions. The Greek version was found rather remarkably by J. Armitage Robinson around 1890. Robinson had recently reviewed the proof-sheets of the Syriac translation, when he happened to read through the Latin version of Barlaam and Josaphat, wherein he recognized some phrasing that sounded remarkably similar to what he had read in the Syriac proof-sheets. Robinson admits "it was with some impatience" that he waited to return to Cambridge, where he was able to compare the works. He realized that the Greek Barlaam and Josaphat contained nearly all of the Apology of Aristides. For this account, along with the Syriac translation, see J. Rendel Harris and J. Armitage Robinson, *The Apology of Aristides on behalf of the Christians* (Cambridge University Press, 1893).

[2] For the date of 124/125, see Robert M. Grant, *Greek Apologists of the Second Century* (Westminster Press, 1988), 35–37; for 131/132 see Alessandro Galimberti, "Hadrian, Eleusis, and the Beginning of Christian Apologetics" in *Hadrian and the Christians*, ed. Marco Rizzi (Walter de Gruyter, 2010), 80–83.

is moved, and that which controls is stronger than that which is controlled. The self-same being, then, who first established and now controls the universe—this one I affirm to be God, who is without beginning and without end, immortal and self-sufficient, above all passions and infirmities, above anger and forgetfulness and ignorance and the rest. Through him also all things subsist. He does not require sacrifice and libation nor anything that appears to the senses; but all people stand in need of him.

Three Kinds of Worshippers: Pagans, Jews, and Christians

2

Having thus spoken about God as far as I am able to speak of him, let us next proceed to discuss human beings so that we may see who participates in the truth and who in error. For it is clear to us, O king, that there are three classes of people in this world: these being the worshippers of the gods acknowledged among you, and Jews, and Christians. Further they who pay homage to many gods are themselves divided into three classes, namely, Chaldeans, Greeks, and Egyptians; for these have been guides and preceptors to the rest of the nations in the service and worship of these many-titled deities.

On Pagan Worship: The Chaldeans Worship in Error

3

Let us see then which of them participate in truth and which of them in error. The Chaldeans, then, not knowing God, went astray after the elements and began to worship the creation more than their Creator. And of these they formed certain shapes and styled them a representation of the heaven and the earth and the sea, of the sun too and the moon and the other primal bodies or luminaries. And they shut them up together in shrines and worship them, calling them gods, even though they must guard them securely because they fear they should be stolen by robbers. And they did not perceive that anything which acts as guard is greater than that which is guarded, and that he who makes is greater than that which is made. For if their gods are unfit to look after their own safety, how will they bestow protection upon others? The Chaldeans, therefore, have wandered into a great error by adoring lifeless and good-for-nothing images. And it occurs to me as surprising, O king, how it is that their so-called philosophers have quite failed to observe that the elements themselves are perishable. And if the elements are perishable and subject to necessity, how are they gods? And if the elements are not gods, how do the images made in their honor come to be gods?

4

Let us proceed then, O king, to the elements themselves that we may show that they are not gods but perishable and mutable, produced out of that which did not exist at the command of the true God, who is indestructible and immutable and invisible; yet God sees all things and as he wills, modifies and changes things. What then shall I say concerning the elements? They err who believe that the sky is a god. For we see that it revolves and moves by necessity and is compacted of many parts, being thence called the ordered universe. Now the universe is the construction of some designer; and that which has been constructed has a beginning and an end. And the sky with its luminaries moves by necessity. For the stars are carried along in array at fixed intervals from sign to sign, and, some setting, others rising, they traverse their courses in due season to mark off summers and winters, as it has been appointed for them by God; and obeying the inevitable necessity of their nature they transgress not their proper limits, keeping company with the heavenly order. Therefore, it is clear that the sky is not a god but rather a work of God. They erred also who believed the earth to be a goddess. For we see that it is despitefully used and tyrannized over by men, and it is furrowed and kneaded and becomes of no account. For, if it is burned with fire, it becomes devoid of life; for nothing will grow from the ashes. Besides, an excess of rain falls on it, it dissolves away, both it and its fruits. Moreover, it is trodden under foot of men and the other creatures; it is dyed with the blood of the murdered; it is dug open and filled with dead bodies and becomes a tomb for corpses. In light of all this, it is inadmissible that the earth is a goddess but rather it is a work of God for the use of men.

5

They also erred who believed the water to be a god. For it, too, has been made for the use of men, and it is controlled by them; it is defiled and destroyed and suffers change on being boiled and dyed with colors; and it is congealed by the frost, and polluted with blood, and is introduced for the washing of all unclean things. Therefore, it is impossible that water should be a god, but it is a work of God.

They also err who believe that fire is a god. For fire was made for the use of men, and it is controlled by them, being carried about from place to place for boiling and roasting all kinds of meat, and even for (the burning of) dead bodies. Moreover, it is extinguished in many ways, being quenched through man's agency. So, it cannot be allowed that fire is a god, but it is a work of God.

They also err who think the blowing of the winds is a goddess. For it is clear that it is under the dominion of another; and for the sake of man it has been designed by God for the transport of ships and the conveyance of grain and for man's other wants. It rises too and falls at the bidding of God, from which it is concluded that the blowing of the winds is not a goddess but only a work of God.

6

They also err who believe the sun to be a god. For we see that it moves by necessity and revolves and passes from sign to sign, setting and rising to give warmth to plants and tender shoots for the use of man. Besides it has its part in common with the rest of the stars, and it is much smaller than the sky; it suffers eclipse of its light and is not the subject of its own laws. Wherefore it is concluded that the sun is not a god, but only a work of God. They also err who believe that the moon is a goddess. For we see that it moves by necessity and revolves and passes from sign to sign, setting and rising for the benefit of men; and it is less than the sun and waxes and wanes and has eclipses. Wherefore it is concluded that the moon is not a goddess but a work of God.

7

They also err who believe that man is a god. For we see that he is moved by necessity, and is made to grow up, and becomes old even though he wishes he would not. And at one time he is joyous; at another he is grieved when he lacks food and drink and clothing. And we see that he is subject to anger and jealousy and desire and change of purpose and has many infirmities. He is destroyed too in many ways by means of the elements and animals, and by ever-assailing death. It cannot be admitted, then, that man is a god, but only a work of God.

Great therefore is the error into which the Chaldeans wandered, following their own desires. For they reverence the perishable elements and lifeless images, and do not perceive that they themselves make these things to be gods.

On Pagan Worship: The Greeks Worship in Error

8

Let us proceed then to the Greeks, that we may see whether they have any discernment concerning God. The Greeks, indeed, though they call themselves wise proved more deluded than the Chaldeans in alleging that many gods have come into being, some of them male, some female, practiced masters in every passion and every variety of folly. And the Greeks themselves represented them to be adulterers and murderers, wrathful and envious and passionate, slayers of fathers and brothers, thieves and robbers, crippled and limping, workers in magic, and victims of frenzy. Some of them died (as their account goes), and some were struck by thunderbolts, and became slaves to men, and were fugitives, and they mourned and lamented, and changed themselves into animals for wicked and shameful ends.

Therefore, O king, they are ridiculous and absurd and impious tales that the Greeks have introduced, giving the name of gods to those who are not gods, to suit their unholy desires, in order that, having them as patrons of vice, they might commit adultery and robbery and do murder and other shocking deeds. For if their gods did such deeds why should not they also do them? So, from these misguided practices it has been the lot of mankind to have frequent wars and slaughters and bitter captivities.

9

But, further, if we discuss their gods individually, you will see how great the absurdity is; for instance, how Kronos is brought forward by them as a god above all, and they sacrifice their own children to him. And he had many sons by Rhea, and in his madness devoured his own offspring. And they say that Zeus cut off his members and cast them into the sea, where Aphrodite is said in fable to be engendered. Zeus, then, having bound his own father, cast him into Tartarus. You see the error and brutality that they advance against their god? Is it possible, then, that a god should be manacled and mutilated? What absurdity! Who with any wit would ever say so?

Next Zeus is introduced, and they say that he was king of their gods, and that he changed himself into animals that he might debauch mortal women. For they allege that he transformed himself into a bull for Europe, and into gold for Danae, and into a swan for Leda, and into a satyr for Antiope, and into a thunderbolt for Semele. Then by these there were many children,

Dionysus and Zethus and Amphion and Herakles and Apollo and Artemis and Perseus, Kastor and Helenes and Polydeukes and Minos and Rhadamanthys and Sarpedon, and the nine daughters whom they called the Muses. Then too they bring forward statements about the matter of Ganymedes.

Hence it happened, O king, to mankind to imitate all these things and to become adulterous men and lascivious women, and to be workers of other terrible iniquities, through the imitation of their god. Now how is it possible that a god should be an adulterer or an obscene person or a parricide?

10

Along with him, too, they bring forward one Hephaistos as a god, and they say that he is lame and wields a hammer and tongs, working as a smith for his living. Is he then badly off? But it cannot be admitted that a god should be a cripple, and besides be dependent on mankind.

Then they bring forward Hermes as a god, representing him to be lustful, and a thief, and covetous, and a magician (and maimed) and an interpreter of language. But it cannot be admitted that such a one is a god.

They also bring forward Asklepios as a god, who is a doctor and prepares drugs and compounds plasters for the sake of making a living. For he was badly off. And afterwards he was struck, they say, with a thunderbolt by Zeus on account of Tyndareos, son of Lacedaimon; and so was killed. Now if Asklepios, in spite of his divinity, could not help himself when struck by lightning, how will he come to the rescue of others?

Again, Ares is represented as a god, fond of strife and given to jealousy, and a lover of animals and other such things. And at last, while corrupting Aphrodite, he was bound by the youthful Eros and by Hephaistos. How then was he a god who was subject to desire, and a warrior, and a prisoner and an adulterer?

They also allege that Dionysus is a god, who holds nightly revels and teaches drunkenness, and carries off the neighbors' wives, and goes mad and takes to flight. And at last, he was put to death by the Titans. If then Dionysus could not save himself when he was being killed, and besides used to be mad, and drunk with wine, and a fugitive, how should he be a god?

They also allege that Herakles got drunk and went mad and cut the throats of his own children, then he was consumed by fire and so died. Now how should he be a god, who was drunk and a slayer of children and burned to death? Or how will he come to the help of others, when he was unable to help himself?

11

They represent Apollo also as a jealous god, and besides as the master of the bow and quiver, and sometimes of the lyre and flute, and as divining to men for pay? Can he then be very badly off? But it cannot be admitted that a god should be in want, and jealous, and a harping minstrel.

They represent Artemis also as his sister, who is a huntress and has a bow with a quiver; and she roams alone upon the hills with the dogs to hunt the stag or the wild boar. How then should such a woman, who hunts and roams with her dogs, be a divine being?

Even Aphrodite herself they affirm to be a goddess, who is adulterous. For at one time she had Ares as a paramour, and at another time Anchises and again Adonis, whose death she also laments, feeling the want of her lover. And they say that she even went down to Hades to purchase back Adonis from Persephone. Did you ever see, O king, greater folly than this, to bring forward as a goddess one who is adulterous and given to weeping and wailing?

And they represent that Adonis is a hunter god, who came to a violent end, being wounded by a wild boar and having no power to help himself in his distress. How then will one who is adulterous, and a hunter, and mortal give himself any concern for mankind?

All this and much more of a similar nature, and even far more disgraceful and offensive details, have the Greeks narrated, O king, concerning their gods—details which it is not proper either to state or for a moment to remember. And hence mankind, taking an impulse from their gods, practiced all lawlessness and brutality and impiety, polluting both earth and air by their awful deeds.

On Pagan Worship: The Egyptians Worship in Error

12

The Egyptians, again, being more stupid and witless than these, have gone further astray than all the nations. For they were not content with the objects of worship of the Chaldeans and the Greeks, but in addition to these brought forward also brute creatures as gods, both land and water animals, and plants and herbs; and they were defiled with all madness and brutality more deeply than all the nations on the earth.

For originally they worshipped Isis, who had Osiris as brother and husband. He was slain by his own brother Typhon; and therefore Isis with Horos her son fled for refuge to Byblus in Syria, mourning for Osiris with bitter lamentation, until Horos grew up and killed Typhon. So that neither did Isis have power to help her own brother and husband; nor could Osiris defend himself when he was being killed by Typhon; nor did Typhon, the slayer of his brother, when he was perishing at the hands of Horos and Isis, find means to rescue himself from death. And though they were revealed in their true character by such mishaps, they were believed to be very gods by the simple Egyptians, who were not satisfied even with these or the other deities of the nations; instead, they brought forward also brute creatures as gods. For some of them worshipped the sheep, and some the goat; another tribe worshipped the bull and the pig; others again, the raven and the hawk, and the vulture and the eagle; and others the crocodile; and some the cat and the dog, and the wolf and the ape, and the dragon and the asp; and others the onion and the garlic and thorns and other created things. And the poor creatures do not perceive about all these that they are utterly helpless. For though they see their gods eaten by men of other tribes, and burnt as offerings, and slain as victims, and moldering in decay, they have not perceived that they are not gods.

Further Errors with the Pagans' Worship

13

So the Egyptians and the Chaldeans and the Greeks made a great error in bringing forward such beings as gods, and in making images of them, and in deifying dumb and senseless idols. And I wonder how they saw their gods sawn out and hacked and docked by the workmen, and besides aging with time and falling to pieces, and being cast from metal, and yet did not discern concerning them that they were not gods. For when they have no power to see to their own safety, how will they take care of men?

But further, the poets and philosophers among the Chaldeans and the Greeks and the Egyptians, while they desired by their poems and writings to magnify the gods of their countries, rather revealed their shame, and laid it bare before all men. For if the body of man while consisting of many parts does not cast off any of its own members, but preserving an unbroken unity in all its members, is harmonious with itself, how shall variance and discord be so great in the nature of God? For if there had been a unity of nature among the gods, then one god ought not to have pursued or slain or injured another. And if the gods were pursued by gods, and slain, and kidnapped and struck with lightning by them, then there is no longer any unity of nature, but divided counsels, all mischievous. So that not one of them is a god. It is clear then, O king, that all their discourse on the nature of the gods is an error.

But how did the wise and erudite men of the Greeks not observe that inasmuch as they make laws for themselves, they are judged by their own laws? For if the laws are righteous, their gods are altogether unrighteous, as they have committed transgressions of laws, in slaying one another, and practicing sorceries, and adultery and thefts and intercourse with males. If they were right in doing these things, then the laws are unrighteous, being framed contrary to the gods. Whereas in fact, the laws are good and just, commending what is good and forbidding what is bad. But the deeds of their gods are contrary to law. Their gods, therefore, are lawbreakers, and all liable to the punishment of death; and they are impious men who introduce such gods. For if the stories about them are mythical, the gods are nothing more than mere names; and if the stories are founded on nature, still they who did and suffered these things are no longer gods; and if the stories are allegorical, they are myths and nothing more.

It has been shown then, O king, that all these polytheistic objects of worship are the works of error and perdition. For it is not right to give the name of gods to beings that can be seen but cannot see; but one ought to revere the invisible and all-seeing and all-creating God.

On the Error of Jewish Worship

14

Let us proceed then, O king, to the Jews also, that we may see what truth there is in their view of God. For they were descendants of Abraham and Isaac and Jacob, and they migrated to Egypt. And from there God brought them forth with a mighty hand and an uplifted arm through Moses, their lawgiver; and by many wonders and signs he made known his power to them. But even they proved stubborn and ungrateful, and often served the idols of the nations, and put to death the prophets and just men who were sent to them. Then when the Son of God was pleased to come upon the earth, they received him with cruel violence and betrayed him into the hands of Pilate the Roman governor; and paying no respect to his good deeds and the countless miracles he worked among them, they demanded a sentence of death by the cross. And they perished by their own transgression; for to this day they worship the one God Almighty, but not according to knowledge. For they deny that Christ is the Son of God; and they are much like the heathen, even though they may seem to make some approach to the truth from which they have removed themselves. So much for the Jews.

On Christian Worship and Living

15

Now the Christians trace their origin from the Lord Jesus Christ. And he is acknowledged by the Holy Spirit to be the son of the Most High God, who came down from heaven for the salvation of men. And being born of a pure virgin, unbegotten and immaculate, he assumed flesh and revealed himself among men that he might recall them to himself from their wandering after many gods. And having accomplished his wonderful dispensation, by a voluntary choice he tasted death on the cross, fulfilling a grand dispensation. And after three days he came to life again and ascended into heaven. And if you would read, O king, you may judge the glory of his presence from the holy Scripture, which is called the gospel among themselves. He had twelve disciples, who after his ascension to heaven went forth into the provinces of the whole world and declared his greatness. As for instance, one of them traversed the countries about us, proclaiming the doctrine of the truth. From this it is that they who still observe the righteousness enjoined by their preaching are called Christians.

And these are they who more than all the nations on the earth have found the truth. For they know God, the Creator and Fashioner of all things through the only-begotten Son and the Holy Spirit; and they worship no other God other than him. They have the commands of the Lord Jesus Christ himself written upon their hearts; and they observe them, looking forward to the resurrection of the dead and life in the world to come. They do not commit adultery nor fornication, nor bear false witness, nor covet the things of others; they honor father and mother, and they love their neighbors; they judge justly, and they never do to others what they would not wish to happen to themselves; they appeal to those who injure them, trying to win them as friends; they are eager to do good to their enemies; they are gentle and meek; they abstain from all unlawful conversation and from all impurity; they do not despise the widow, nor oppress the orphan; and he that has, gives ungrudgingly to support one who is in need. If they see a stranger, they take him under their roof, and rejoice over him as over a very brother; for they call themselves brothers and sisters not after the flesh but after the spirit. And they are ready to sacrifice their lives for the sake of Christ; for they observe his commands without swerving, and live holy and just lives, as the Lord God enjoined upon them. And they give thanks to him every hour, for all meat and drink and other blessings.

16

Truly then, this is the way of the truth which leads those who travel therein to the everlasting kingdom promised through Christ in the life to come. And that you may know, O king, that in saying these things I do not speak of things I have made up, if you choose to look into the writings of the Christians, you will find that I state nothing beyond the truth. Rightly then, did your son apprehend, and justly was he taught to serve the living God and to be saved for the age that is destined to come upon us. For great and wonderful are the sayings and deeds of the Christians; for they speak not the words of men but those of God. But the rest of the nations go astray and deceive themselves; for they walk in darkness and bruise themselves like drunken men.

Closing

17

Thus ends, O king, my discourse to you, which has been dictated in my mind by the Truth. Therefore, let your foolish sages cease their idle talk against the Lord; for it is profitable for you to worship God the Creator and to give ear to his incorruptible words, that you may escape from condemnation and punishment, and that you may be found to be heirs of life everlasting.

14

Justin Martyr: The First Apology

Context
Author: Justin Martyr
Provenance: Rome
Date: AD 153 or 155–157[1]

Opening Address

1

To the emperor Titus Aelius Hadrianus Antoninus Pius Augustus Caesar, and to his son Verissimus, the philosopher, and to Lucius, the natural son of Caesar and the adopted son of Pius, a lover of learning, and to the sacred Senate, with the whole People of the Romans. I, Justin, the son of Priscus and grandson of Bacchios, natives of Flavia Neapolis in Palestine, present this address and petition on behalf of those from all nations who are unjustly hated and mistreated, myself being one of them.

On the Charges against Christians

2

Reason directs those who are truly pious and philosophical to honor and

---

1 For AD 155–157, see Robert M. Grant, *Greek Apologists of the Second Century* (Westminster Press, 1988), 52–53; for AD 153, see Denis Minns and Paul Parvis, *Justin, Philosopher and Martyr: Apologies* (Oxford University Press, 2009), 44. There is also debate over whether the two apologies are in fact one. For a detailed discussion of this question, see ibid., 21–28, which also proposes a detailed solution worthy of serious consideration.

love only what is true, and to not follow traditional opinions if these are worthless. For not only does sound reason direct us to refuse the guidance of those who did or taught anything wrong, but it is proper for the lover of truth to choose to do and say what is right, even if death is threatened—he must choose this even before his own life. Since you are called pious and philosophers, guardians of justice and lovers of learning, give heed to everything; and if you are indeed such, it will be manifested. For we have come, not to flatter you by this writing, nor please you by our address, but to beg that you pass judgment after an accurate and searching investigation, not flattered by prejudice or by a desire of pleasing superstitious men, nor induced by irrational impulse or evil rumors which have long been prevalent, to give a decision which will prove to be against yourselves. For as for us, we reckon that no evil can be done to us, unless we are convicted as evildoers or are proved to be wicked men; and you, you can kill, but not hurt us.

3

But lest anyone think that this is an unreasonable and reckless utterance, we demand that the charges against the Christians be investigated. If these are substantiated, they should be punished as they deserve. But if no one can convict us of anything, true reason forbids you, for the sake of a wicked rumor, to wrong blameless men. Instead, reason directs to punish those who bring charges based on passion.[2] And every sober-minded person will declare this to be the only fair and equitable proposal, namely, that the subjects render an unexceptional account of their own life and doctrine; and that, on the other hand, the rulers should give their decision in obedience, not to violence and tyranny, but to piety and philosophy. In this way both rulers and ruled would benefit. For even one of the ancients somewhere said, "Unless both rulers and ruled philosophize, it is impossible to make states blessed" (Plato, *Resp.* 5.1473c–d). It is our task, therefore, to provide to all an opportunity for inspecting our life and teachings, lest, on account of those who are accustomed to being ignorant of our affairs, we should incur the penalty due to them for mental blindness; and it is your business when you hear us to be found, as reason demands, good judges. For if, when you have learned the truth, you do not do what is just, you will be before God without excuse.

---

2 The translation has been amended here to roughly follow Minns and Parvis, *Justin, Philosopher and Martyr*, 84–85.

4

By the mere application of a name, nothing is decided, either good or evil, apart from the actions implied in the name; and indeed, so far at least as one may judge from the name we are accused of, we are most excellent people. But as we do not think it just to beg to be acquitted on account of the name, if we be convicted as evil doers, so, on the other hand, if we be found to have committed no offence, either in the matter of thus naming ourselves, or of our conduct as citizens, it is your part very earnestly to guard against incurring just punishment, by unjustly punishing those who are not convicted. For from a name neither praise nor punishment could reasonably spring, unless something excellent or base in action be proved. And you do not punish those among yourselves who are accused before they are convicted; but in our case you receive the name as proof against us, and this although, so far as the name goes, you ought rather to punish our accusers. For we are accused of being Christians, and to hate what is excellent is unjust. Again, if any of the accused deny the name, and say that he is not a Christian, you acquit him, as having no evidence against him as a wrong doer; but if anyone acknowledges that he is a Christian, you punish him on account of this acknowledgment. Justice requires that you inquire into the life both of him who confesses and of him who denies, that by his deeds it may be apparent what kind of man each is. For as some who have been taught by the Master, Christ, not to deny him, give encouragement to others when they are put to the question, so in all probability do those who lead wicked lives give occasion to those who, without consideration, take upon them to accuse all the Christians of impiety and wickedness. And this also is not right. For of philosophy, too, some assume the name and the garb who do nothing worthy of their profession; and you are well aware that those of the ancients, whose opinions and teachings were quite diverse, are yet all called by the one name of philosophers. And of these some taught atheism; and the poets who have flourished among you raise a laugh out of the uncleanness of Jupiter with his own children. And those who now adopt such instruction are not restrained by you; but, on the contrary, you bestow prizes and honors upon those who euphoniously insult the gods.

5

Why, then, should this be? In our case, who pledge ourselves to do no wickedness, nor to hold these atheistic opinions, you do not examine the charges made against us. But, yielding to unreasoning passion, and to the instigation of evil demons, you punish us without consideration or judgment. For the truth will be spoken; since long ago these evil demons, effecting apparitions of themselves, both defiled women and corrupted boys, and showed such fearful sights to men, that those who did not use their reason in judging of the actions that were done were struck with terror; and being carried away by fear, and not knowing that these were demons, they called them gods, and gave to each the name that each of the demons chose for himself. And when Socrates endeavored, by true reason and examination, to bring these things to light and deliver men from the demons, then the demons themselves, by means of men who rejoiced in iniquity, compassed his death as an atheist and a profane person, on the charge that "he was introducing new divinities"; and in our case they display a similar activity. For not only among the Greeks did reason [Logos] prevail to condemn these things through Socrates, but also among the Barbarians were they condemned by Reason [or the Word, the Logos] himself,[3] who took shape, and became man, and was called Jesus Christ; and in obedience to him, we not only deny that they who did such things as these are gods, but assert that they are wicked and impious demons, whose actions will not bear comparison with those even of men desirous of virtue.

6

Hence are we called atheists. And we confess that we are atheists, so far as gods of this sort are concerned, but not with respect to the most true God, the Father of righteousness and temperance and the other virtues, who is free from all impurity. But both him, and the Son (who came forth from him and taught us these things, and the host of the other good angels who follow and are made like to him), and the prophetic Spirit, we worship and adore, knowing them in reason and truth, and declaring without grudging to everyone who wishes to learn, as we have been taught.

[...]

On Serving God and Caesar

10

But we have received by tradition that God does not need the material offerings which men can give, seeing, indeed, that he himself is the provider of all things. And we have been taught, and are convinced, and do believe,

---

3 The same word used for reason (λόγος) can also mean word/Word,

that he accepts those only who imitate the excellences which reside in him: temperance, and justice, and philanthropy, and as many virtues as are peculiar to a God who is called by no proper name. And we have been taught that he in the beginning did of his goodness, for man's sake, create all things out of unformed matter; and if men by their works show themselves worthy of his design, they are deemed worthy, and so we have received—of reigning in company with him, being delivered from corruption and suffering. For as in the beginning, he created us when we were not, so do we consider that, in like manner, those who choose what is pleasing to him are, on account of their choice, deemed worthy of incorruption and of fellowship with him. For the coming into being at first was not in our own power; and in order that we may follow those things which please him, choosing them by means of the rational faculties he has himself endowed us with, he both persuades us and leads us to faith. And we think it for the advantage of all men that they are not restrained from learning these things but are even urged thereto. For the restraint which human laws could not effect, the Word, inasmuch as he is divine, would have effected, had not the wicked demons, taking as their ally the lust of wickedness which is in every man and which draws variously to all manner of vice, scattered many false and profane accusations, none of which attach to us.

11

And when you hear that we look for a kingdom, you suppose, without making any inquiry, that we speak of a human kingdom; whereas we speak of that which is with God, as appears also from the confession of their faith made by those who are charged with being Christians, though they know that death is the punishment awarded to him who so confesses. For if we looked for a human kingdom, we should also deny our Christ, that we might not be slain; and we should strive to escape detection, that we might obtain what we expect. But since our thoughts are not fixed on the present, we are not concerned when men cut us off; since also death is a debt which must at all events be paid.

12

And more than all other men are we your helpers and allies in promoting peace, seeing that we hold this view, that it is alike impossible for the wicked, the covetous, the conspirator, and for the virtuous, to escape the notice of God, and that each man goes to everlasting punishment or salvation according to the value of his actions. For if all men knew this, no one would choose wickedness even for a little, knowing that he goes to the everlasting punishment of fire; but would by all means restrain himself, and adorn himself with virtue, that he might obtain the good gifts of God and escape the punishments. For those who endeavor to escape detection when they offend on account of the laws and punishments you impose (and they offend, too, under the impression that it is quite possible to escape your detection, since you are but men)—those persons, if they learned and were convinced that nothing, whether actually done or only intended, can escape the knowledge of God, would by all means live decently on account of the penalties threatened, as even you yourselves will admit. But you seem to fear lest all men become righteous, and you no longer have any to punish. Such would be the concern of public executioners, but not of good princes. But, as we before said, we are persuaded that these things are prompted by evil spirits, who demand sacrifices and service even from those who live unreasonably; but as for you, we presume that you who aim at [a reputation for] piety and philosophy will do nothing unreasonable. But if you also, like the foolish, prefer custom to truth, do what you have power to do. But rulers who esteem opinion over truth have as much power as robbers have in a desert. And that you will not succeed is declared by the Word, whom we know to be more kingly and just than any other ruler, after God who begat him. For as all shrink from succeeding to the poverty or sufferings or obscurity of their fathers, so whatever the Word forbids us to choose, the sensible man will not choose. That all these things should come to pass, I say, our teacher foretold, he who is both Son and Apostle of God the Father of all and the Ruler, Jesus Christ; from whom also we have the name of Christians. From which we become more assured of all the things he taught us, since whatever he beforehand foretold should come to pass is seen in fact coming to pass; and this is the work of God, to tell of a thing before it happens, and as it was foretold so to show it happening. It is possible to pause here and add no more, reckoning that we demand what is just and true; but because we are well aware that it is not easy suddenly to change a mind possessed by ignorance, we intend to add a few things, for the sake of persuading those who love the truth, knowing that it is not impossible to put ignorance to flight by presenting the truth.

13

What sober-minded man, then, will not acknowledge that we are not atheists, worshipping as we do the Maker of this universe, and declaring, as we have been taught, that he has no need of streams of blood and libations and incense; whom we praise to the utmost of our power by the exercise of prayer and thanksgiving for all things that we are supplied, as we have been taught that the only honor that is worthy of him is not to consume by fire what he has brought into being for our sustenance, but to use it for ourselves and those who need, and with gratitude to him to offer thanks by invocations and hymns for our creation, and for all the means of health, and for the various qualities of the different kinds of things, and for the changes of the seasons; and to present before him petitions for our existing again in incorruption through faith in him. Our teacher of these things is Jesus Christ, who also was born for this purpose, and was crucified under Pontius Pilate, procurator of Judaea, in the times of Tiberius Caesar; and that we reasonably worship him, having learned that he is the Son of the true God himself, and holding him in the second place, and the prophetic Spirit in the third, we will prove. For they proclaim our madness to consist in this, that we give to a crucified man a place second to the unchangeable and eternal God, the Creator of all; for they do not discern the mystery that is herein, to which, as we make it plain to you, we pray you to give heed.

[...]

17

And everywhere we, more readily than all men, endeavor to pay to those appointed by you the taxes both ordinary and extraordinary, as we have been taught by him; for at that time some came to him and asked him, if one ought to pay tribute to Caesar; and he answered, "Tell me, whose image does the coin bear?" And they said, "Caesar's." And again, he answered them, "Render therefore to Caesar the things that are Caesar's, and to God the things that are God's" (Matt 22:17–21). Therefore, to God alone we render worship, but in other things we gladly serve you, acknowledging you as kings and rulers of men, and praying that with your kingly power you be found to possess also sound judgment. But if you pay no regard to our prayers and frank explanations, we will suffer no loss, since we believe (or rather, indeed, are persuaded) that every man will suffer punishment in eternal fire according to the merit of his deeds, and will render account according to the power he has received from God, as Christ intimated when he said, "To whom God has given more, of him will more be required" (Luke 12:48).

[...]

On the Resurrection and Christ

19

And to any thoughtful person would anything appear more incredible, than, if we were not in the body, and someone were to say that it was possible that from a small drop of human seed bones and sinews and flesh can be formed into a shape such as we see? For let this now be said hypothetically: if you yourselves were not such as you now are, and born of such parents [and causes], and one were to show you human seed and a picture of a man, and were to say with confidence that from such a substance such a being could be produced, would you believe before you saw the actual production? No one will dare to deny [that such a statement would surpass belief]. In the same way, then, you are now incredulous because you have never seen a dead man rise again. But as at first you would not have believed it possible that such persons could be produced from the small drop, and yet now you see them thus produced, so also judge that it is not impossible that the bodies of men, after they have been dissolved, and like seeds resolved into earth, should in God's appointed time rise again and put on incorruption. Those who say that each thing returns to that from which it was produced, and that beyond this not even God himself can do anything, imagine such a power worthy of God that we are unable to conceive it; but this we see clearly, that they would not have believed it possible that they could have become such and produced from such materials, as they now see both themselves and the whole world to be. And that it is better to believe even what is impossible to our own nature and to men, than to be unbelieving like the rest of the world, we have learned. For we know that our Master Jesus Christ said, that "what is impossible with men is possible with God" (Matt 19:26), and, "Fear not them that kill you, and after that can do no more; but fear him who after death is able to cast both soul and body into hell" (Matt 10:28). And hell is a place where those are to be punished who have lived wickedly, and who do not believe that those things which God has taught us by Christ will come to pass.

[...]

21

And when we say also that the Word, who is the first-born of God, was produced without sexual union, and that he, Jesus Christ, our teacher, was crucified and died, and rose again, and ascended into heaven, we propound nothing different from what you believe regarding those whom you esteem sons of Jupiter. For you know how many sons your esteemed writers ascribed to Jupiter: Mercury, the interpreting word and teacher of all; Aesculapius, who, though he was a great physician, was struck by a thunderbolt, and so ascended to heaven; and Bacchus too, after he had been torn limb from limb; and Hercules, when he had committed himself to the flames to escape his toils; and the sons of Leda, and Dioscuri; and Perseus, son of Danae; and Bellerophon, who, though sprung from mortals, rose to heaven on the horse Pegasus. For what will I say of Ariadne, and those who, like her, have been declared to be set among the stars? And what of the emperors who die among yourselves, whom you deem worthy of deification, and on whose behalf you produce someone who swears he has seen the burning Caesar rise to heaven from the funeral pyre? And what kind of deeds are recorded of each of these reputed sons of Jupiter, it is needless to tell those who already know. This only will be said: that they are written for the advantage and encouragement of youthful scholars; for all reckon it an honorable thing to imitate the gods. But far be such a thought concerning the gods from every well-conditioned soul, as to believe that Jupiter himself, the governor and creator of all things, was both a parricide and the son of a parricide, and that being overcome by the love of base and shameful pleasures, he came into Ganymede and into those many women whom he had violated, and that his sons did like actions. But, as we said above, wicked devils perpetrated these things. And we have learned that those only are deified who have lived near to God in holiness and virtue; and we believe that those who live wickedly and do not repent are punished in everlasting fire.

22

Moreover, the Son of God called Jesus, even if only a man by ordinary generation, yet, on account of his wisdom, is worthy to be called the Son of God; for all writers call God the Father of men and gods. And if we assert that the Word of God was born of God in a peculiar manner, different from ordinary generation, let this, as said above, be no extraordinary thing to you, who say that Mercury is the angelic word of God. But if anyone objects that he was crucified, in this also he is on a par with those reputed sons of Jupiter of yours, who suffered as we have now enumerated. For their sufferings at death are recorded to have been not alike, but diverse; so that not even by the peculiarity of his sufferings does he seem to be inferior to them. But, on the contrary, as we promised in the preceding part of this discourse, we will now prove him superior—or rather have already proved him to be so—for the superior is revealed by his actions. And if we even affirm that he was born of a virgin, accept this in common with what you accept of Perseus. And in that we say that he made whole the lame, the paralytic, and those born blind, we seem to say what is very similar to the deeds said to have been done by Aesculapius.

23

And [we wish] that this may now become evident to you: [firstly] that the things we assert are conformity with what has been taught us by Christ, and by the prophets who preceded him, are alone true, and are older than all the writers who have existed; that we claim to be acknowledged, not because we say the same things as these writers said, but because we say true things.[4] [Secondly] that Jesus Christ is the only proper Son who has been begotten by God, being his Word and first-begotten, and power; and, becoming man according to his will, he taught us these things for the conversion and restoration of the human race. [Thirdly] that before he became a man among men, some, influenced by the demons before mentioned, related beforehand, through the instrumentality of the poets, those circumstances as having really happened, which, having fictitiously devised, they narrated, in the same manner as they have caused to be fabricated the scandalous reports against us of infamous and impious actions, of which there is neither witness nor proof...

[...]

On False Christian Teachers Not Being Persecuted

26

After Christ's ascension into heaven, the devils put forward certain men who said that they themselves were gods; and they were not only not persecuted by you, but even deemed worthy of honors. There was a Samaritan, Simon, a native of the village called Gitto, who in the reign of Claudius Caesar, and in your royal city of Rome, did mighty acts of magic by virtue of the art of the devils operating in him. He was considered a god, and as a god was honored by you with a statue, which was erected on the river Tiber between the two bridges, and bore this inscription in the language of Rome: "Simoni Deo

---

4 This section is very awkward in Greek. For an alternative rendering, see Minns and Parvis, *Justin, Philosopher and Martyr*, 139–141.

Sancto," "To Simon the holy God." And almost all the Samaritans, and a few even of other nations, worship him, and acknowledge him as the first god; and a woman, Helena, who went about with him at that time, and had formerly been a prostitute, they say is the first idea generated by him. And a man, Menander, also a Samaritan, of the town Capparetaea, a disciple of Simon, and inspired by devils, we know to have deceived many while he was in Antioch by his magical art. He persuaded those who adhered to him that they should never die, and even now there are some living who hold this opinion of his. And there is Marcion, a man of Pontus, who is even at this day alive, and teaching his disciples to believe in some other god greater than the Creator. And he, by the aid of the devils, has caused many of every nation to speak blasphemies, and to deny that God is the maker of this universe, and to assert that some other being, greater than he, has done greater works. All who take their opinions from these men, are, as we before said, called Christians; just as also those who do not agree with the philosophers in their doctrines, have yet in common with them the name of philosophers given to them. And whether they perpetrate those fabulous and shameful deeds—the upsetting of the lamp, and promiscuous intercourse, and eating human flesh—we know not; but we do know that they are neither persecuted nor put to death by you, at least on account of their opinions. But I have a treatise against all the heresies that have existed already composed, which, if you wish to read it, I will give you.

On Exposing and Abusing Children

27

But as for us, we have been taught that to expose newly born children is the act of wicked men; and this we have been taught lest we should harm anyone and lest we should sin against God, first, because we see that almost all so exposed (not only the girls, but also the males) are brought up to prostitution. And as the ancients are said to have reared herds of oxen, or goats, or sheep, or grazing horses, so now we see you rear children only for this shameful use; and for this pollution a number of females and hermaphrodites, and those who commit unmentionable iniquities, are found in every nation. And you receive the hire of these, and duty and taxes from them, whom you ought to exterminate from your realm. And anyone who uses such persons, besides the godless and infamous and impure intercourse, may possibly be having intercourse with his own child, or relative, or brother. And there are some who prostitute even their own children and wives, and some are openly mutilated for the purpose of sodomy. And they refer these mysteries to the mother of the gods, and along with each of those whom you esteem gods there is painted a serpent, a great symbol and mystery. Indeed, the things which you do openly and with applause, as if the divine light were overturned and extinguished, you accuse us of these things; in truth, this does no harm to us who shrink from doing any such things, but harms only those who do them and bear false witness against us.

On Divine Foreknowledge and Human Choice

28

For among us the prince of the wicked spirits is called the serpent, and Satan, and the devil, as you can learn by looking into our writings. And that he would be sent into the fire with his army, and the men who follow him, and would be punished for an endless duration, Christ foretold. For the reason why God has delayed doing this is his regard for the human race. For he foreknows that some are to be saved by repentance, some even that are perhaps not yet born. In the beginning he made the human race with the power of thought and of choosing the truth and doing right, so that all men are without excuse before God; for they have been born rational and contemplative. And if anyone disbelieves that God cares for these things, he will thereby either insinuate that God does not exist, or he will assert that though he exists he delights in vice, or exists like a stone, and that neither virtue nor vice are anything, but only in the opinion of men these things are reckoned good or evil. And this is the greatest profanity and wickedness.

[...]

On Predictions of Christ: Christ Was Not a Magician

31

There were, then, among the Jews certain men who were prophets of God, through whom the prophetic Spirit published beforehand things that were to come to pass, before they happened. And their prophecies, as they were spoken and when they were uttered, the kings who happened to be reigning among the Jews at the several times carefully preserved in their possession, when they had been arranged in books by the prophets themselves in their own Hebrew language. And when Ptolemy, king of Egypt, formed a library and endeavored to collect the writings of all men, he heard of these prophets and sent to Herod, who was at that time king of the Jews, requesting that the books of the prophets be sent to him. And Herod the king did indeed send them, written, as they were, in the foresaid Hebrew language. And when their contents were found to be unintelligible to the Egyptians, he again sent and requested that men be commissioned to translate them into the Greek language. And when this was done, the books remained with the Egyptians, where they are until now. They are also in the possession of all Jews throughout the world; but they, though they read, do not understand what is said, but count us foes and enemies. And, like yourselves, they kill and punish us whenever they have the power, as you can well believe. For in the Jewish war that lately raged, bar Kokhba, the leader of the revolt of the Jews, gave orders that Christians alone should be led to cruel punishments, unless they would deny Jesus Christ and utter blasphemy. In these books, then, of the prophets we found Jesus our Christ foretold as coming, born of a virgin, growing up to man's estate, and healing every disease and every sickness, and raising the dead, and being hated, and unrecognized, and crucified, and dying, and rising again, and ascending into heaven, and being called the Son of God. We find it also predicted that certain persons should be sent by him into every nation to publish these things, and that rather among the gentiles [than among the Jews] men should believe on him. And he was predicted before he appeared, first 5,000 years before, and again 3,000, then 2,000, then 1,000, and yet again 800; for in the succession of generations prophets after prophets arose.

32

Moses then, who was the first of the prophets, spoke in these very words: "The scepter will not depart from Judah, nor a lawgiver from between his feet, until he come for whom it is reserved; and he will be the desire of the nations, binding his foal to the vine, washing his robe in the blood of the grape" (Gen 49:10). It is up to you to make accurate inquiry and ascertain up to whose time the Jews had a lawgiver and king of their own. Up to the time of Jesus Christ, who taught us, and interpreted the prophecies which were not yet understood, [they had a lawgiver] as was foretold by the holy and divine Spirit of prophecy through Moses, "that a ruler would not fail the Jews until he should come for whom the kingdom was reserved" (Gen 49:10) (for Judah was the forefather of the Jews, from whom also they have their name of Jews). And after he appeared, you began to rule the Jews and gained possession of all their territory. And the prophecy, "He will be the expectation of the nations" (Gen 49:10), signified that there would be some of all nations who should look for him to come again. And this indeed you can see for yourselves and be convinced of by fact. For of all races of men there are some who look for him who was crucified in Judaea, and after whose crucifixion the land was straightway surrendered to you as spoil of war. And the prophecy, "binding his foal to the vine, and washing his robe in the blood of the grape," was a significant symbol of the things that were to happen to Christ and of what he was to do. For the foal of a donkey stood bound to a vine at the entrance of a village, and he ordered his acquaintances to bring it to him then; and when it was brought, he mounted and sat upon it, and entered Jerusalem, where the vast temple of the Jews stood, which afterward was destroyed by you. And after this he was crucified, that the rest of the prophecy might be fulfilled. For this "washing his robe in the blood of the grape" was predictive of the passion he was to endure, cleansing by his blood those who believe on him. For what is called by the Divine Spirit through the prophet "his robe" are those men who believe in him in whom abides the seed of God, the Word. And what is spoken of as "the blood of the grape" signifies that he who should appear would have blood, though not of the seed of man, but of the power of God. And the first power after God the Father and Lord of all is the Word, who is also the Son; and of him we will, in what follows, relate how he took flesh and became man. For as man did not make the blood of the vine, but God, so it was hereby intimated that the blood should not be of human seed, but of divine power, as we have said above. And Isaiah, another prophet, foretelling the same things in other words, spoke this way: "A star will rise out of Jacob, and a flower will spring from the root of Jesse; and his arm will the nations trust" (Isa 11:1). And a star of light has arisen, and a flower has sprung from the root of Jesse—this Christ. For by the power of God he was conceived by a virgin of the seed of Jacob, who was the father of Judah, who, as we have shown, was the father of the Jews. And Jesse was his forefather according to the saying, and he was the son of Jacob and Judah according to lineal descent.

33

And hear again how Isaiah in express words foretold that he should be born of a virgin; for he spoke this way: "Behold, a virgin will conceive and bring forth a son, and they will say for his name, 'God with us'" (Isa 7:14). For things which were incredible and seemed impossible with men, these God predicted by the Spirit of prophecy as about to come to pass, in order that, when they came to pass, there might be no unbelief but faith, because of their prediction. But lest some, not understanding the prophecy now cited, should charge us with the very things we have been ascribing to the poets, who say that Jupiter went into women through lust, let us try to explain the words. This, then, "Behold, a virgin will conceive," signifies that a virgin should conceive without intercourse. For if she had had intercourse with anyone whatsoever, she was no longer a virgin; but the power of God having come upon the virgin overshadowed her, and it caused her while yet a virgin to conceive. And the angel of God who was sent to the same virgin at that time brought her good news, saying, "Behold, you will conceive by the Holy Spirit, and will bear a son, and he will be called the Son of the Highest, and you will name him Jesus; for he will save his people from their sins" (Luke 1:32; Matt 1:21). This is just as they who have recorded all that concerns our Savior Jesus Christ have taught, whom we believed, since by Isaiah also, whom we have now adduced, the Spirit of prophecy declared that he should be born as we intimated before. It is wrong, therefore, to understand the Spirit and the power of God as anything else than the Word, who is also the first-born of God, as the foresaid prophet Moses declared; and it was this which, when it came upon the virgin and overshadowed her, caused her to conceive, not by intercourse, but by power. And the name Jesus in the Hebrew language means Savior in the Greek tongue. Therefore, too, the angel said to the virgin, "you will name him Jesus, for he will save his people from their sins" (Matt 1:21). And that the prophets are inspired by no other than the Divine Word, even you, as I fancy, will grant.

34

And hear what part of earth he was to be born in, as another prophet, Micah, foretold. He spoke this way: "And you, Bethlehem, the land of Judah, are not the least among the princes of Judah; for out of you will come forth a Governor, who will feed my people" (Mic 5:2). Now there is a village in the land of the Jews, about four miles from Jerusalem, in which Jesus Christ was born, as you can ascertain also from the registers of the taxing made under Cyrenius, your first procurator in Judaea.

35

And how Christ, after he was born was to escape the notice of other men until he grew to man's estate, which also came to pass, hear what was foretold regarding this. There are the following predictions: "Unto us a child is born, and unto us a young man is given, and the government will be upon his shoulders" (Isa 9:6), which is significant of the power of the cross, for to it, when he was crucified, he applied his shoulders, as will be more clearly made out in the ensuing discourse. And again, the same prophet Isaiah, being inspired by the prophetic Spirit, said, "I have spread out my hands to a disobedient people, to those who walk in a way that is not good. They now ask of me judgment and dare to draw near to God" (Isa 65:2; 58:2). And again, in other words, through another prophet, he says, "They pierced my hands and my feet, and for my vesture they cast lots" (Ps 22:16). And indeed David, the king and prophet, who uttered these things, suffered none of them. But Jesus Christ stretched forth his hands, being crucified by the Jews speaking against him and denying that he was the Christ. And as the prophet spoke, they tormented him, and set him on the judgment-seat, and said, "judge us." And the expression "They pierced my hands and my feet" was used in reference to the nails of the cross which were fixed in his hands and feet. And after he was crucified, they cast lots for his clothing, and they that crucified him parted it among them. And that these things did happen, you can ascertain from the Acts of Pontius Pilate. And we will cite the prophetic utterances of another prophet, Zephaniah,[5] to the effect that he was foretold expressly as to sit upon the foal of a donkey and to enter Jerusalem. The words are these: "Rejoice greatly, O daughter of Zion; shout, O daughter of Jerusalem: behold, my King comes to you; lowly, and riding upon a donkey, and upon a colt, the foal of a donkey" (Zech 9:9).

36

But when you hear the utterances of the prophets spoken as it were personally, you must not suppose that they are spoken by the inspired themselves, but by the Divine Word who moves them. For sometimes he declares things that are to come to pass in the manner of one who foretells the future; sometimes he speaks as from the person of God the Lord and Father of all; sometimes as from the person of Christ; sometimes as from the person of the people answering the Lord or his Father, just as you can see even in your own writers, one man being the writer of the whole, but introducing the persons who converse. And this the Jews, who possessed the books of the prophets, did not understand, and therefore they did not recognize Christ even when he came,

---

5 Justin meant Zechariah.

but they even hate us who say that he has come and who prove that, as was predicted, he was crucified by them.[6]

On the Prophets Speaking from th Persons of the Father, Son, and Spirit

37

And that this too may be clear to you, the following words were spoken from the person of the Father through Isaiah the prophet: "The ox knows his owner, and the donkey his master's manger; but Israel does not know, and my people have not understood. Woe, sinful nation, a people full of sins, a wicked seed, children that are transgressors; you have forsaken the Lord" (Isa 1:3). And again elsewhere, when the same prophet speaks in like manner from the person of the Father, "What is the house that you will build for me? says the Lord. The heaven is my throne, and the earth is my footstool" (Isa 66:1). And again, in another place, "Your new moons and your sabbaths my soul hates; and the great day of the fast and of ceasing from labor I cannot stand; nor, if you come to be seen by me, will I hear you. Your hands are full of blood; and if you bring fine flour, incense, it is an abomination to me; the fat of lambs and the blood of bulls I do not desire. For who has required this at your hands? But loose every bond of wickedness, tear asunder the tight knots of violent contracts, cover the homeless and naked, give my bread to the hungry" (Isa 1:14; 58:6). You can now perceive what kind of things are taught through the prophets from [the person of] God.

38

And when the Spirit of prophecy speaks from the person of Christ, the utterances are of this sort: "I have spread out my hands to a disobedient people, to those who walk in a way that is not good" (Isa 65:2). And again: "I gave my back to the scourges, and my cheeks to the beatings; I did not turn away my face from the shame of spittings; and the Lord was my helper; therefore, I was not confounded, but I set my face as a firm rock; and I knew that I should not be ashamed, for he is near that justifies me" (Isa 50:6). And again, when he says, "They cast lots upon my vesture, and pierced my hands and my feet. And

---

6 Justin gives additional predictions of Christ in chapters 40–42, 48–52, which have been excluded from this edition for the sake of concision. The prophecies that have been included here are representative of Justin's approach.

I lay down and slept, and rose again, because the Lord sustained me" (Ps 22:18; 3:5). And again, when he says, "They spoke with their lips, they shook their heads, saying 'Let him deliver himself'" (Ps 22:7). And that all these things happened to Christ at the hands of the Jews, you can ascertain. For when he was crucified, they did shoot out their lips and shake their heads, saying, "Let him who raised the dead save himself" (cf. Matt 27:39).

39

And when the Spirit of prophecy speaks as predicting things that are to come to pass, he speaks in this way: "For out of Zion will go forth the law, and the word of the Lord from Jerusalem. And he will judge among the nations and will rebuke many people; and they will beat their swords into ploughshares, and their spears into pruning-hooks; nation will not lift up sword against nation, neither will they learn war anymore" (Isa 2:3). And that it happened in this manner, we can convince you. For from Jerusalem there went out into the world, men, twelve in number, and these illiterate, of no ability in speaking; but by the power of God they proclaimed to every race of men that they were sent by Christ to teach to all the word of God; and now we who formerly used to murder one another not only refrain from warring against our enemies, but also, that we may not lie nor deceive our examiners, willingly die confessing Christ. For that saying, "The tongue has sworn, but the mind is unsworn" (Euripides, *Hippolytus* 608), might be imitated by us in this matter. But if the soldiers enrolled by you, and who have taken the military oath, prefer their allegiance to their own life, and parents, and country, and all kindred, though you can offer them nothing incorruptible, it would be ridiculous if we, who earnestly long for incorruption, should not endure all things in order to obtain what we desire from him who is able to grant it.

[...]

Further Remarks on Divine Foreknowledge and Human Choice

43

But lest some suppose, from what has been said by us, that we say that whatever happens, happens by a fatal necessity, because it is foretold as known beforehand, this too we explain. We have learned from the prophets, and we hold it to be true, that punishments, and chastisements, and good rewards, are rendered according to the merit of each man's actions. Since if it is not so, and instead all things happen by fate, nothing at all is in our own power. For if it be fated that this man, e.g., be good, and this other evil, neither is the former meritorious nor the latter to be blamed. And again, unless humans have the power of avoiding evil and choosing good by free choice, they are not accountable for their actions, of whatever kind they be. But that it is by free choice they both walk uprightly and stumble, we thus demonstrate. We see the same man making a transition to opposite things. Now, if it had been fated that he was to be either good or bad, he could never have been capable of both the opposites, nor of so many transitions. But if this was the case, then not even would some be good and others bad, since we thus make fate the cause of evil, and exhibit her as acting in opposition to herself; or that which has been already stated would seem to be true, that neither virtue nor vice is anything, but that things are only reckoned good or evil by opinion; which, as the true word shows, is the greatest impiety and wickedness. But this we assert is inevitable fate, that they who choose the good have worthy rewards, and they who choose the opposite have their merited awards. For not like other things, as trees and quadrupeds, which cannot act by choice, did God make man; for neither would man be worthy of reward or praise if he did not himself choose the good, but were created for this end; nor, if he were evil, would he be worthy of punishment, not being evil of himself, but being able to be nothing else than what he was made.

[...]

Concluding Thoughts on Predications of Christ

53

Though we could bring forward many other prophecies, we forbear, judging these sufficient for the persuasion of those who have ears to hear and understand. And considering also that those persons are able to see that we do not make mere assertions without being able to produce proof, like those fables that are told of the so-called sons of Jupiter. For why should we have believed that a crucified man is the first-born of the unbegotten God, and himself will pass judgment on the whole human race, unless we had found testimonies about him published before he came and was born as man, and unless we saw that things had happened accordingly? We have seen the devastation of the land of the Jews, and men of every race persuaded by his teaching through the apostles, and rejecting their old habits, in which, being deceived, they had their conversation. Indeed, we see ourselves too, and know that the

Christians from among the gentiles are both more numerous and more true than those from among the Jews and Samaritans. For all the other human races are called gentiles by the Spirit of prophecy; but the Jewish and Samaritan races are called the tribe of Israel and the house of Jacob. And the prophecy in which it was predicted that there should be more believers from the gentiles than from the Jews and Samaritans, we will produce. It ran thus: "Rejoice, O barren, you that does not bear; break forth and shout, you that does not travail, because many more are the children of the desolate than of her that has a husband" (Isa 54:1). For all the gentiles were "desolate" of the true God, serving the works of their hands; but the Jews and Samaritans, having the word of God delivered to them by the prophets, and always expecting the Christ, did not recognize him when he came, except a few, of whom the Spirit of prophecy by Isaiah had predicted that they should be saved. He spoke as from their person: "If the Lord had not left us a seed, we should have been as Sodom and Gomorrah" (Isa 1:9). For Sodom and Gomorrah are related by Moses to have been cities of ungodly men, which God burned with fire and brimstone, and overthrew, no one of their inhabitants being saved except a certain stranger, a Chaldean by birth, whose name was Lot, with whom also his daughters were rescued. And those who care may yet see their whole country desolate, and burned, and remaining barren. And to show how those from among the gentiles were foretold as more true and more believing, we will cite what was said by Isaiah the prophet, for he spoke as follows: "Israel is uncircumcised in heart, but the gentiles are uncircumcised in the flesh" (Jer 9:26).[7] So many things therefore, as these, when they are seen with the eye, are enough to produce conviction and belief in those who embrace the truth, and are not bigoted in their opinions, nor are governed by their passions.

On the Influence of Demons

54

But those who hand down the myths that the poets have made, provide no proof to the youths who learn them; and we proceed to demonstrate that they have been uttered by the influence of the wicked demons, to deceive and lead astray the human race. For having heard it proclaimed through the prophets that the Christ was to come, and that the ungodly among men were to be punished by fire, they put forward many to be called sons of Jupiter, under the impression that they would be able to produce in men the idea that

---

7 This is a reference from Jeremiah not Isaiah.

the things said about Christ were mere marvelous tales, like the things said by the poets. And these things were said both among the Greeks and among all nations where the demons heard the prophets foretelling that Christ would especially be believed in; but that when they heard what was said by the prophets they did not accurately understand it but imitated what was said of our Christ, like men who are in error, we will make plain. The prophet Moses was, as we have already said, older than all writers; and by him, as we have also said before, it was predicted in this way: "There will not fail a prince from Judah, nor a lawgiver from between his feet, until he comes for whom it is reserved; and he will be the desire of the gentiles, binding his foal to the vine, washing his robe in the blood of the grape" (Gen 49:10). The devils, accordingly, when they heard these prophetic words, said that Bacchus was the son of Jupiter, and gave out that he was the discoverer of the vine, and they counted the donkey among his mysteries; and they taught that, having been torn in pieces, he ascended into heaven. And because in the prophecy of Moses it had not been expressly indicated whether he who was to come was the Son of God, and whether he would, riding on the foal, remain on earth or ascend into heaven, and because the name of "foal" could mean either the foal of a donkey or the foal of a horse, they, not knowing whether he who was foretold would bring the foal of a donkey or of a horse as the sign of his coming, nor whether he was the Son of God, as we said above, or of man, gave out that Bellerophon, a man born of man, himself ascended to heaven on his horse Pegasus. And when they heard it said by the other prophet Isaiah, that he should be born of a virgin, and by his own means ascend into heaven, they pretended that Perseus was spoken of. And when they knew what was said, as has been cited above, in the prophecies written long ago, "Strong as a giant to run his course" (Ps 19:5), they said that Hercules was strong and had journeyed over the whole earth. And when, again, they learned that it had been foretold that he should heal every sickness and raise the dead, they produced Aesculapius.

55

But in no instance, not even in any of those called sons of Jupiter, did they imitate the being crucified; for it was not understood by them, all the things said of it having been put symbolically. And this, as the prophet foretold, is the greatest symbol of his power and role; and it is also proven by the things that fall under our observation. For consider all the things in the world, whether without this form they could be administered or have any community. For the sea is not traversed without being put to flight by the ship's secure sail; and the earth is not ploughed without a plough; diggers and mechanics do not perform their work except with tools which have this shape. And the human form differs from that of the irrational animals in nothing else than in its being erect and having the hands extended, and having on the face extending from the forehead what is called the nose, through which there is respiration for the living creature; and this shows no other form than that of the cross. And so it was said by the prophet, "The breath before our face is the Lord Christ" (Lam 4:20 LXX). And the power of this form is shown by your own symbols on what are called "vexilla" [banners] and trophies, with which all your state possessions are made, using these as the insignia of your power and government, even though you do so unwittingly. And with this form you consecrate the images of your emperors when they die, and you name them gods by inscriptions. Since, therefore, we have urged you both by reason and by an evident form, and to the utmost of our ability, we know that now we are blameless even though you disbelieve; for our part is done and finished.

56

But the evil spirits were not satisfied with saying, before Christ's appearance, that those who were said to be sons of Jupiter were born of him; but after he had appeared, and been born among men, and when they learned how he had been foretold by the prophets, and knew that he should be believed in and looked for by every nation, they again, as was said above, put forward other men, the Samaritans Simon and Menander, who did many mighty works by magic, and deceived many, and still keep them deceived. For even among yourselves, as we said before, Simon was in the royal city Rome in the reign of Claudius Caesar, and so greatly astonished the sacred senate and people of the Romans, that he was considered a god, and honored, like the others whom you honor as gods, with a statue. Therefore, we pray that the sacred senate and your people may, along with yourselves, be arbiters of this our memorial, in order that if anyone is entangled by that man's doctrines, he may learn the truth, and so be able to escape error; and as for the statue, if you please, destroy it.

57

Nor can the devils persuade men that there will be no conflagration for the punishment of the wicked; as they were unable to effect that Christ should be hidden after he came. But this only can they effect: that they who live irrationally, and were brought up licentiously in wicked customs, and are prejudiced in their own opinions, should kill and hate us; these persons we not only do not hate, but, as is proved, pity and endeavor to lead to repentance. For we do not fear death, since it is acknowledged that we must surely die; and there is nothing new, but all things continue the same in this administration of things; and if satiety overtakes those who enjoy even one year of these things, they ought to give heed to our doctrines, that they may live eternally free both from suffering and from want. But if they believe that there is nothing after death, but declare that those who die pass into insensibility, then they become our benefactors when they set us free from sufferings and necessities of this life, and prove themselves to be wicked, and inhuman, and bigoted. For they kill us with no intention of delivering us, but they cut us off that we may be deprived of life and pleasure.

58

And, as we said before, the devils put forward Marcion of Pontus, who is even now teaching men to deny that God is the maker of all things in heaven and on earth, and that the Christ predicted by the prophets is his Son, and preaches another god besides the Creator of all, and likewise another son. And many have believed this man, as if he alone knew the truth, and they laugh at us, though they have no proof of what they say, but they are carried away irrationally as lambs by a wolf, and they become the prey of atheistical doctrines and of devils. For they who are called devils attempt nothing else than to seduce men from God who made them, and from Christ his first-begotten; and those who are unable to raise themselves above the earth they have nailed, and do now nail, to things earthly, and to the works of their own hands; but those who devote themselves to the contemplation of things divine, they secretly beat back; and if they do not have a wise sober-mindedness, and a pure and passionless life, they drive them into godlessness.

[...]

On Baptism, the Eucharist, and Weekly Worship Gatherings

61

I will also relate how we dedicated ourselves to God when we had been made new through Christ; lest, if we omit this, we seem to be unfair in the explanation we are making. As many as are persuaded and believe that what we teach and say is true, and undertake to be able to live accordingly, these people are instructed to pray and to entreat God with fasting for the remission of their sins that are past, we praying and fasting with them. Then they are brought by us where there is water, and they are regenerated in the same manner in which we were ourselves regenerated. For, in the name of God, the Father and Lord of the universe, and of our Savior Jesus Christ, and of the Holy Spirit, they then receive the washing with water. For Christ also said, "Unless you are born again, you will not enter into the kingdom of heaven" (John 3:5). Now, it is obvious to all that it is impossible for those who have been born to enter again into their mothers' wombs. And how those who have sinned and repent will escape their sins is declared by Isaiah the prophet, as I wrote above. He speaks in this way: "Wash yourselves and make yourselves clean; put away the evil of your doings from your souls; learn to do right; defend the fatherless and plead for the widow; and come and let us reason together, says the Lord. And though your sins be as scarlet, I will make them white like wool; and though they be as crimson, I will make them white as snow. But if you refuse and rebel, the sword will devour you; for the mouth of the Lord has spoken it" (Isa 1:16–20).

And we have learned the reason for this [rite] from the apostles. Since at our birth we were born without our own knowledge or choice, by our parents coming together, and we were brought up in bad habits and wicked training; in order that we may not remain the children of necessity and of ignorance, but may become the children of choice and knowledge, and may obtain in the water the remission of sins formerly committed, there is pronounced over him who chooses to be born again and has repented of his sins, the name of God the Father and Lord of the universe; he who leads to the laver the person that is to be washed calls God by this name alone. For no one can utter the name of the ineffable God; and if anyone dares to say that there is a name, he raves with a hopeless madness. And this washing is called illumination because they who learn these things are illuminated in their understandings. And in the name of Jesus Christ, who was crucified under Pontius Pilate, and in the name of the Holy Spirit, who through the prophets foretold all things about Jesus, he who is illuminated is washed.

62

And the devils, indeed, having heard this washing proclaimed by the prophet, instigated those who enter their temples, and are about to approach them with libations and burnt offerings, also to sprinkle themselves; and they cause them also to wash themselves entirely, as they depart [from the sacrifice], before they enter into the shrines in which their images are set. And the command, too, given by the priests to those who enter and worship in the temples, that they take off their shoes, the devils, learning what happened to the above-mentioned prophet Moses, have given in imitation of these things. For at that juncture, when Moses was ordered to go down into Egypt and lead out the people of the Israelites who were there, and while he was tending the flocks of his maternal uncle in the land of Arabia, our Christ conversed with him under the appearance of fire from a bush, and said, "Take off your shoes, and draw near and hear" (cf. Exod 3:5). And he, when he had taken off his shoes and drawn near, heard that he was to go down into Egypt and lead out the people of the Israelites there; and he received mighty power from Christ, who spoke to him in the appearance of fire, and he went down and led out the people, having done great and marvelous things; which, if you desire to know, you will learn accurately from his writings.

63

And all the Jews even now teach that the nameless God spoke to Moses; where the Spirit of prophecy, accusing them by Isaiah the prophet mentioned above, said "The ox knows his owner, and the donkey his master's manger; but Israel does not know me, and my people do not understand" (Isa 1:3). And Jesus the Christ, because the Jews did not know what the Father was, and what the Son, in like manner accused them; and he said, "No one knows the Father, but the Son; nor the Son, but the Father, and those to whom the Son reveals him" (Matt 11:27). Now the Word of God is his Son, as we have said before. And he is called Angel and Apostle; for he declares whatever we ought to know, and he is sent forth to declare whatever is revealed; as our Lord himself says, "He that hears me, hears him that sent me" (Luke 10:16). From the writings of Moses also this will be manifest; for thus it is written in them, "And the Angel of God spoke to Moses, in a flame of fire out of the bush, and said, 'I am who I am, the God of Abraham, the God of Isaac, the God of Jacob, the God of your fathers; go down into Egypt, and bring forth my people'" (Exod 3:6). And if you wish to learn what follows, you can do so from the same writings; for it is impossible to relate the whole here. But so much is written for the sake of proving that Jesus the Christ is the Son of God and his Apostle, being in times of old the Word, and appearing sometimes in the form of fire, and sometimes in the likeness of angels; but now, by the will of God, having become man for the human race, he endured all the sufferings that the devils instigated the senseless Jews to inflict upon him; who, though they have it expressly affirmed in the writings of Moses, "And the angel of God spoke to Moses in a flame of fire in a bush, and said, 'I am who I am, the God of Abraham, and the God of Isaac, and the God of Jacob,'" yet maintain that he who said this was the Father and Creator of the universe. Therefore, also the Spirit of prophecy rebukes them and says, "Israel does not know me; my people have not understood me" (Isa 1:3). And again, Jesus, as we have already shown, while he was with them, said, "No one knows the Father, but the Son; nor the Son but the Father, and those to whom the Son will reveal him" (Matt 11:27). The Jews, accordingly, being throughout of opinion that it was the Father of the universe who spoke to Moses, though he who spoke to him was indeed the Son of God, who is called both Angel and Apostle, are justly charged, both by the Spirit of prophecy and by Christ himself, with knowing neither the Father nor the Son. For they who affirm that the Son is the Father, are proved neither to have become acquainted with the Father nor to know that the Father of the universe has a Son; who also, being the first-begotten Word of God, is even God. And in times of old he appeared in the shape of fire and in the likeness of an angel to Moses and to the other prophets; but now in the times of your reign, having, as we before said, become man by a virgin, according to the counsel of the Father, for the salvation of those who believe in him, he endured both to be despised and to suffer, that by dying and rising again he might conquer death. And that which was said out of the bush to Moses, "I am who I am, the God of Abraham, and the God of Isaac, and the God of Jacob, and the God of your fathers" (Exod 3:6), this signified that they, even though dead, are yet in existence, and are men belonging to Christ himself. For they were the first of all men to busy themselves in the search after God; Abraham being the father of Isaac, and Isaac of Jacob, as Moses wrote.

[...]

65

But we, after we have thus washed him who has been convinced and has assented to our teaching, bring him to the place where those who are called brothers and sisters are assembled, in order that we may offer hearty prayers in common for ourselves and for the baptized person, and for all others in every place, that we may be counted worthy, now that we have learned the truth, and that by our works we may be found good citizens and keepers of the commandments, so that we may be saved with an everlasting salvation. Having concluded the prayers, we salute one another with a kiss. There is then brought to the president of the brothers and sisters bread and a cup of wine mixed with water; and he taking them, gives praise and glory to the Father of the universe, through the name of the Son and of the Holy Spirit, and offers thanks at considerable length for our being counted worthy to receive these things at his hands. And when he has concluded the prayers and thanksgivings, all the people present express their assent by saying Amen. In Hebrew, this word "Amen" means "so be it." And when the president has given thanks, and all the people have expressed their assent, those who are called by us deacons give to each of those present to partake of the bread and wine mixed with water over which the thanksgiving was pronounced, and to those who are absent they carry away a portion.

66

And this food is called among us the Eucharist, of which no one is allowed to partake but the man who believes that the things which we teach are true, and who has been washed with the washing that is for the remission of sins and for regeneration, and who is so living as Christ has enjoined. For we do not receive these as common bread and common drink, but in like manner as Jesus Christ our Savior, having been made flesh by the Word of God, had both flesh and blood for our salvation, so likewise have we been taught that the food which is blessed by the prayer of his word, and from which our blood and flesh by transmutation are nourished, is the flesh and blood of that Jesus who was made flesh. For the apostles, in the memoirs composed by them, which are called Gospels, have thus delivered to us what was enjoined upon them; that Jesus took bread, and when he had given thanks, said, "Do this in remembrance of me, this is my body" (Luke 22:19), and that, after the same manner, having taken the cup and given thanks, he said, "This is my blood"; and gave it to them alone. The wicked devils have imitated this in the mysteries of Mithras, commanding the same thing to be done. For, that bread and a cup of water are placed with certain incantations in the mystic rites of one who is being initiated, you either know or can learn.

67

And we afterwards continually remind each other of these things. And the wealthy among us help the needy; and we always keep together; and for all the things that we are given, we bless the Maker of all through his Son Jesus Christ, and through the Holy Spirit. And on the day called Sunday, all who live in cities or in the country gather together in one place, and the memoirs of the apostles or the writings of the prophets are read, as long as time permits; then, when the reader has ceased, the president verbally instructs and exhorts to the imitation of these good things. Then we all rise together and pray, and, as we said before, when our prayer has ended, bread and wine and water are brought, and the president in like manner offers prayers and thanksgivings, according to his ability, and the people assent, saying Amen. And then [the elements] over which thanks have been given are distributed to and partaken by each person, and to those who are absent a portion is sent by the deacons. And they who are well to do and willing, give what each thinks fit; and what is collected is deposited with the president. The president brings aid to the orphans, and widows, and those who, through sickness or any other cause, are in need, and to those who are in bonds, and to the strangers sojourning among us; in short, the president takes care of all who are in need. But Sunday is the day on which we all hold our common assembly, because it is the first day on which God, having made a change in the darkness and matter, made the world; and Jesus Christ our Savior on the same day rose from the dead. For he was crucified on the day before that of Saturn [Saturday]; and on the day after that of Saturn, which is the day of the Sun [Sunday], having appeared to his apostles and disciples, he taught them these things, which we have submitted to you also for your consideration.

Closing

68

And if these things seem to you to be reasonable and true, honor them. But if they seem nonsensical, despise them as nonsense, and do not decree death against those who have done no wrong, as you would against enemies. For we forewarn you, that you will not escape the coming judgment of God, if you continue in your injustice; and we ourselves will invite you to do that which is pleasing to God. And though from the letter of the greatest and most illustrious Emperor Hadrian, your father, we could demand that you order judgment to be given as we have desired, we have instead made this appeal and explanation, not on the ground of Hadrian's decision, but because we know that what we ask is just. And we have subjoined the copy of Hadrian's epistle, that you may know that we are speaking truly about this. And the following is the copy:

Epistle of Emperor Hadrian to Roman Senator Gaius Minicius Fundanus on Behalf of Christians[8]

I have received the letter addressed to me by your predecessor Serenius Granianus, a most illustrious man; and this communication I am unwilling to pass over in silence, lest innocent persons be disturbed, and informers be given opportunity to practice villainy. Accordingly, if the inhabitants of your province will so far sustain this petition of theirs as to accuse the Christians in some court of law, I do not prohibit them from doing so. But I will not allow them to make use of mere complaints and outcries. For it is far more just, if anyone desires to make an accusation, that you give judgment upon it. If, therefore, anyone makes the accusation and provides proof that the accused persons do anything contrary to the laws, you are to adjudge punishments in proportion to the offences. And this, by Hercules, you will give special heed to, that if any man brings an accusation against any of these persons purely based on his own calumny, you will award to him more severe punishments in proportion to his wickedness.

---

8 Justin attached this rescript to his apology. It is included in this edition as source of insight into the relationship between the empire and Christianity in the second century.

Justin Martyr: The Second Apology

Context
Author: Justin Martyr
Provenance: Rome
Date: c. AD 153–165[1]

Address: On the Persecution of Christians

1

Romans, the things that have recently happened in your city under Urbicus,[2] and the things that are likewise being unreasonably done everywhere by the governors, have compelled me to frame this composition for your sakes, who are men of like passions, and brothers and sisters, though you know it not, and though you are unwilling to acknowledge it on account of your glorying in what you esteem dignities. For everywhere, whoever is corrected by father, or neighbor, or child, or friend, or brother, or husband, or wife for a fault, for being hard to move, for loving pleasure and being hard to urge to what is right (except those who have been persuaded that the unjust and intemperate will be punished in eternal fire, but that the virtuous and those

---

[1] It is possible that parts of the Second Apology are various notes that Justin wrote up to his death (AD 165). "Justin, we think, kept tinkering with his original apology, adapting it and perhaps expanding it. And he would have kept notes—perhaps a notebook—of materials excised and resources that could be deployed in street-corner or bathhouse debate—precisely the sort of debate described in the Second Apology itself..." (Denis Minns and Paul Parvis, *Justin, Philosopher and Martyr: Apologies* [Oxford University Press, 2009], 27).

[2] At the time, Quintus Lollius Urbicus was the Prefect of Rome.

who lived like Christ will dwell with God in a state that is free from suffering—we mean, those who have become Christians)...[3]

...and the evil demons, who hate us, and who keep such men as these subject to themselves, and serving them in the capacity of judges, incite them, as rulers actuated by evil spirits, to put us to death. But that the cause of all that has taken place under Urbicus may become quite plain to you, I will relate what has been done.

2

A certain woman lived with an intemperate husband; she herself, too, having formerly been intemperate. But when she came to the knowledge of the teachings of Christ, she became sober-minded, and she endeavored to persuade her husband likewise to be temperate, citing the teaching of Christ, and assuring him that there will be punishment in eternal fire inflicted upon those who do not live temperately and in conformity with right reason. But he, continuing in the same excesses, alienated his wife from him by his actions. For she, considering it wicked to live any longer as a wife with a husband who sought in every way means of indulging in pleasure contrary to the law of nature, and in violation of what is right, wished to be divorced from him. And when she was persuaded by her friends, who advised her still to continue with him in the idea that some time or other her husband might give hope of amendment, she did violence to her own feeling and remained with him. But when her husband had gone into Alexandria and was reported to be conducting himself worse than ever, she—that she might not, by continuing in matrimonial connection with him, and by sharing his table and his bed, become a partaker also in his wickedness and impieties—gave him what you call a bill of divorce, and she was separated from him. But this noble husband of hers—while he ought to have been rejoicing that those actions that formerly she unhesitatingly committed with the servants and hirelings, when she delighted in drunkenness and every vice, she had now given up, and he ought to have desired that he too should give up the same—when she had gone from him without his desire, he brought an accusation against her, affirming that she was a Christian. And she presented a paper to you, the emperor, requesting that first she be permitted to arrange her affairs, and afterwards to make her defense against the accusation, when her affairs were set in order. And this you granted. And her former husband, since he was now no longer able to prosecute her, directed his assaults

---

3 There is a missing line in the manuscript.

against a man, Ptolemaeus, whom Urbicus punished, and who had been her teacher in the Christian doctrines. And he did this in the following way. He persuaded a centurion—who had cast Ptolemaeus into prison, and who was friendly to himself—to take Ptolemaeus and interrogate him on this sole point: whether he was a Christian. And Ptolemaeus, being a lover of truth, and not of a deceitful or false disposition, when he confessed himself to be a Christian, was bound by the centurion and for a long time punished in the prison. And, at last, when the man came to Urbicus, he was asked this one question only: whether he was a Christian. And again, being conscious of his duty, and the nobility of it through the teaching of Christ, he confessed his discipleship in the divine virtue. For he who denies anything either denies it because he condemns the thing itself, or he shrinks from confession because he is conscious of his own unworthiness or alienation from it, neither of which cases is that of the true Christian. And when Urbicus ordered him to be led away to punishment, one Lucius, who was also himself a Christian, seeing the unreasonable judgment that had thus been given, said to Urbicus: "What is the basis of this judgment? Why have you punished this man, not as an adulterer, nor fornicator, nor murderer, nor thief, nor robber, nor convicted of any crime at all, but who has only confessed that he is called by the name of Christian? This judgment of yours, O Urbicus, does not suit the Emperor Pius, nor the philosopher, the son of Caesar, nor the sacred senate." And he said nothing else in answer to Lucius than this: "You also seem to me to be such a one." And when Lucius answered, "Most certainly I am," he again ordered him also to be led away. And he professed his thanks, knowing that he was delivered from such wicked rulers and was going to the Father and King of the heavens. And still a third having come forward, was condemned to be punished.

3

I too, therefore, expect to be plotted against and fixed to the stake by some of those I have named, or perhaps by Crescens,[4] that lover of bravado and boasting; for the man is not worthy of the name of philosopher who publicly bears witness against us in matters which he does not understand, saying that the Christians are atheists and impious, and doing so to win favor with the deluded mob, and to please them. For if he assails us without having read the

---

4 Crescens was probably a Cynic philosopher (see the end of this section), although it also possible he was a Stoic (see Runar M. Thorsteinsson, "Justin's Debate with Crescens the Stoic," *Zeitschrift für antikes Christentum* 17, no. 3 [2013]: 451–478). Eusebius credits Crescens with bringing about Justin's martyrdom (Eusebius, *Ecclesiastical History* 4.16).

teachings of Christ, he is thoroughly depraved and far worse than the illiterate, who often refrain from discussing or bearing false witness about matters they do not understand. Or, if he has read them and does not understand the majesty that is in them, or, understanding it, acts thus that he may not be suspected of being such [a Christian], he is far worse and thoroughly depraved, being conquered by illiberal and unreasonable opinion and fear. For I would have you to know that I proposed to him certain questions on this subject and interrogated him, and I found most convincingly that he, in truth, knows nothing. And to prove that I speak the truth, I am ready, if these disputations have not been reported to you, to conduct them again in your presence. And this would be an act worthy of a prince. But if my questions and his answers have been made known to you, you are already aware that he is acquainted with none of our matters; or, if he is acquainted with them, but, through fear of those who might hear him, does not dare to speak out, like Socrates, he proves himself, as I said before, no philosopher but an opinionated man; at least he does not regard that Socratic and most admirable saying: "But a man must in no way be honored before the truth" (Plato, *Republic* 10.595c). But it is impossible for a Cynic, who makes indifference his end, to know any good but indifference.

On Why Christians Do Not Commit Suicide to Rush to Heaven

4

But lest someone say to us, "Go then all of you and kill yourselves, and pass even now to God, and do not trouble us," I will tell you why we do not so, but why, when examined, we fearlessly confess. We have been taught that God did not make the world aimlessly but made it for the sake of the human race; and we have before stated that he takes pleasure in those who imitate his properties, and he is displeased with those that embrace what is worthless either in word or deed. If then, we all kill ourselves, we will become the cause, as far as in us lies, why no one should be born, or instructed in the divine doctrines, or even why the human race should not exist; and we will, if we so act, be ourselves acting in opposition to the will of God. But when we are examined, we make no denial, because we are not conscious of any evil, but we count it impious not to speak the truth in all things, which also we know is pleasing to God, and because we are also now very desirous to deliver you from an unjust prejudice [against Christians].

On the Fall and Influence of Angels

5

But if this idea takes possession of someone—that if we acknowledge God as our helper, we should not, as we say, be oppressed and persecuted by the wicked—this, too, I will solve. God, when he had made the whole world, and subjected earthly things to man, and arranged the heavenly elements for the increase of fruits and rotation of the seasons, and appointed this divine law—for these things also he evidently made for man—committed the care of men and of all things under heaven to angels whom he appointed over them. But the angels transgressed this appointment, and they were captivated by love of women, and they begat children who are those that are called demons. And besides, they afterwards subdued the human race to themselves, partly by magical writings, and partly by fears and the punishments they occasioned, and partly by teaching them to offer sacrifices, and incense, and libations, of which things they stood in need after they were enslaved by lustful passions; and among men they sowed murders, wars, adulteries, intemperate deeds, and all wickedness. Therefore, also the poets and mythologists, not knowing that it was the angels and those demons who had been begotten by them that did these things to men, and women, and cities, and nations, which they related, ascribed them to god himself, and to those who were accounted to be his very offspring, and to the offspring of those who were called his brothers, Neptune and Pluto, and to the children again of these their offspring. For whatever name each of the angels had given to himself and his children, by that name they called them.

[...]

On God Preserving the World on Account of Christians

7

Therefore, God delays causing the confusion and destruction of the whole world, by which the wicked angels and demons and men will cease to exist, because of the seed of the Christians, who know that they are the cause of preservation in nature. Since, if it were not so, it would not have been possible for you to do these things and to be impelled by evil spirits. But the fire of judgment would descend and utterly dissolve all things, even as formerly the flood left no one but him only with his family who is by us called Noah, and by you Deucalion, from whom again such vast numbers have sprung, some of them evil and others good. For so we say that there will be the conflagration, but not as the Stoics, according to their doctrine of all things being changed into one another, which seems most degrading. But neither do we affirm that it is by fate that men do what they do or suffer what they suffer, but that each man by free choice acts rightly or sins; and that it is by the influence of the wicked demons that earnest men, such as Socrates and the like, suffer persecution and are in bonds, while Sardanapalus, Epicurus, and the like, seem to be blessed in abundance and glory. The Stoics, not observing this, maintained that all things take place according to the necessity of fate. But since God in the beginning made the race of angels and men with free-will, they will justly suffer in eternal fire the punishment of whatever sins they have committed. And this is the nature of all that is made: to be capable of vice and virtue. For neither would any of them be praiseworthy unless there were power to turn to both [virtue and vice]. And this also is shown by those men everywhere who have made laws and philosophized according to right reason, by their prescribing to do some things and refrain from others. Even the Stoic philosophers, in their doctrine of morals, steadily honor the same things, so that it is evident that they are not very felicitous in what they say about principles and incorporeal things. For if they say that human actions come to pass by fate, they will maintain either that God is nothing else than the things which are ever turning, and altering, and dissolving into the same things, and will appear to have had a comprehension only of things that are destructible, and to have looked on God himself as emerging both in part and in whole in every wickedness; or that neither vice nor virtue is anything; which is contrary to every sound idea, reason, and sense.

[...]

On the Word in Socrates

10

Our doctrines, then, appear to be greater than all human teaching; this is because Christ, who appeared for our sakes, became the whole rational being, both body, and reason, and soul. For whatever either lawgivers or philosophers uttered well, they elaborated by finding and contemplating some part of the Word. But since they did not know the whole of the Word, which is Christ, they often contradicted themselves. And those who by human birth were more ancient than Christ, when they attempted to consider and prove things by reason, were brought before the tribunals as impious persons and busybodies. And Socrates, who was more zealous in this direction than all of them, was accused of the very same crimes as ourselves. For they said that he was introducing new divinities and did not consider those to be gods whom the state recognized. But he cast out from the state both Homer and the rest of the poets, and he taught men to reject the wicked demons and those who did the things that the poets related. And he exhorted them to become acquainted with the God who was to them unknown, by means of the investigation of reason, saying, "That it is neither easy to find the Father and Maker of all, nor, having found him, is it safe to declare him to all" (cf. Plato, *Timaeus* 28c). But these things our Christ did through his own power. For no one trusted in Socrates so as to die for this doctrine, but in Christ, who was partially known even by Socrates (for he was and is the Word who is in every man, and who foretold the things that were to come to pass both through the prophets and in his own person when he was made of like passions, and taught these things), not only philosophers and scholars believed, but also artisans and people entirely uneducated, despising both glory, and fear, and death; [these things happened] since he is a power of the ineffable Father and not the mere instrument of human reason.

On the Debt of Death

11

But neither should we be put to death, nor would wicked men and devils be more powerful than we, were not death a debt due by every man that is born. Therefore, we give thanks when we pay this debt. And we judge it right and opportune to tell here, for the sake of Crescens and those who rave as he does, what is related by Xenophon. Hercules, says Xenophon, coming to a place where three ways met, found Virtue and Vice, who appeared to him in the form of women: Vice, in a luxurious dress, and with a seductive expression rendered blooming by such ornaments, and her eyes of a quickly melting tenderness, said to Hercules that if he would follow her, she would always enable him to pass his life in pleasure and adorned with the most graceful ornaments, such as were then upon her own person; and Virtue, who was of squalid look and dress, said, "If you obey me, you will adorn yourself not with ornament nor beauty that passes away and perishes, but with everlasting and precious graces." And we are persuaded that everyone who flees those things that seem to be good, and follows hard after what are reckoned difficult and strange, enters into blessedness. For Vice, when by imitation of what is incorruptible (for what is really incorruptible she neither has nor can produce) she has thrown around her own actions, as a disguise, the properties of virtue, and qualities that are really excellent, leads captive earthly-minded men, attaching to Virtue her own evil properties. But those who understood the excellences that belong to that which is real, are also uncorrupt in virtue. And this every sensible person ought to think both of Christians and of the athletes, and of those who did what the poets relate of the so-called gods, concluding as much from our contempt of death, even when it could be escaped.

[...]

13

When I discovered how the evil spirits had disguised divine doctrines of the Christians in order to turn aside others from joining them, I laughed at those who framed these falsehoods, and at the disguise itself, and at popular opinion. And I confess that I both boast and with all my strength strive to be found a Christian, not because the teachings of Plato are different from those of Christ, but because they are not in all respects similar, as neither are those of the others: Stoics, and poets, and historians. For each man spoke well in proportion to the share he had of the spermatic word (cf. James 1:21), seeing what was related to it. But they who contradict themselves on the more important points appear not to have possessed the heavenly wisdom and the knowledge that cannot be spoken against. Whatever things were rightly said among all men, these are the property of us Christians. For next to God, we worship and love the Word who is from the unbegotten and ineffable God, since he became man for our sakes, that becoming a partaker of our sufferings, he might also bring us healing. For all the writers were able to see realities darkly through the sowing of the implanted word that was in them. For the seed and imitation imparted according to capacity is one thing, and quite another is the thing itself, of which there is the participation and imitation according to the grace that is from him.

[...]

16

Justin Martyr: The Dialogue with Trypho

Context
Author: Justin Martyr
Provenance: Ephesus or Caesarea[1]
Date: Possibly 155–165[2]

Introduction; On Justin's Studies in Philosophy, his Conversion, and the Soul

1

One morning, while Justin was walking along the gymnasium porticos, a certain man named Trypho, with others in his company, met him.[3]

TRYPHO: Greetings, philosopher!

---

[1] The *Dialogue with Trypho* is a discussion or debate between Justin and a Jew named Trypho and some of Trypho's friends. For a recent summary of the questions surrounding the work's context, content, and the ongoing divisions within Christianity over the question of Torah observance, see Andrew Radde-Gallwitz, "Justin Martyr and the Golden Calf: Ethnic Argumentation in the New Israel," in *Golden Calf Traditions in Early Judaism, Christianity, and Islam*, ed. Eric F. Mason and Edmondo F. Lupieri (Brill, 2018), 227–237.

[2] Justin refers to his *First Apology* in chapter 120: "…I gave no thought to any of my people, that is, the Samaritans, when I wrote an address to Caesar, but stated that they were wrong to trust Simon the magician…." The text contains no clues about the latest time it may have been written, therefore it could have been written any time up to Justin's death (AD 165).

[3] The Greek for *The Dialogue with Trypho* is in prose; however, the prose is arranged in such a way that Justin and Trypho's discussion is interrupted with frequent interjections identifying the speakers, which disrupts the dialogue's flow and readability. The editor of this edition has arranged *The Dialogue with Trypho* as an actual dialogue, using names to indicate the speaker and omitting unnecessary narration. Paragraphs without names represent narration.

And immediately after saying this, Trypho turned around and walked along with Justin. The man's friends likewise followed him.

JUSTIN: What is so important?

TRYPHO: I was instructed by Corinthus the Socratic in Argos, that I should not despise or treat with indifference those who array themselves in the philosopher's robe but to show them all kindness, and to associate with them, as perhaps some benefit might spring from the discussion either to some such man or to myself. Further, it is good for both if either the one or the other is benefited. On this account, therefore, whenever I see any one in such clothes, I gladly approach him; and now, for the same reason, I have approached you; and these persons accompany me in hopes of hearing for themselves something profitable from you.

JUSTIN: But who are you, most excellent man?

TRYPHO: I am called Trypho, and I am a Hebrew of the circumcision. Having escaped from the recent war there,[4] I am spending my days in Greece, mainly at Corinth.

JUSTIN: And how would you benefit from philosophy as much as from your own lawgiver and the prophets?

TRYPHO: Why not? Do not the philosophers turn every discourse to the topic of God? And do not questions continually arise to them about his unity and providence? Is not this truly the duty of philosophy, to investigate the Deity?

JUSTIN: Certainly, so we too have believed. But most people have not thought about this, whether there be one or more gods, and whether they have a regard for each one of us or not, as if this knowledge contributed nothing to our happiness. No, they moreover attempt to persuade us that God takes care of the universe with its genera and species, but not of me and you, and each individually, since otherwise we would surely not need to pray to him night and day. But it is not difficult to understand the upshot of this; for fearlessness and license in speaking result in persons who maintain these opinions. They do and say whatever they choose, neither dreading punishment nor hoping for any benefit from God. For how could they? They affirm that the same things will always happen and, further, that you and I will again live in like manner, having become neither better men nor worse. But there are some others who, having supposed the soul to be immortal and immaterial, believe that though they have committed evil they will not suffer punishment (for the immaterial is insensible), and that the soul, in consequence of its immortality, needs nothing from God.

---

4 The war Trypho refers to is the Bar Kokhba revolt, also known as the Third Roman-Jewish War (AD 132–136).

TRYPHO: Tell us your opinion of these matters, and what idea you hold about God, and what your philosophy is.

2

JUSTIN: I will tell you what seems to me; for philosophy is, in fact, the greatest possession and most honorable before God, to whom it leads us and alone commends us; and these are truly holy men who have bestowed attention on philosophy. What philosophy is, however, and the reason why it has been sent down to men, have escaped the observation of most; for there would be neither Platonists, nor Stoics, nor Peripatetics, nor Theoretics, nor Pythagoreans, if this knowledge was common. I wish to tell you why philosophy has become many-headed. It has happened that those who first handled philosophy, and who were therefore esteemed illustrious men, were succeeded by those who made no investigations about truth but only admired the perseverance and self-discipline of the former, as well as the novelty of the doctrines; and each thought that what he had learned from his teacher was the truth. Then, moreover, those latter persons handed down to their successors such things, and others similar to them; and this system was called by the name of him who was styled the father of the doctrine. Being at first desirous of personally conversing with one of these men, I surrendered myself to a certain Stoic; and having spent a considerable amount of time with him, when I had not acquired any further knowledge of God (for he did not know himself, and said such instruction was unnecessary), I left him and took myself to another, who was called a Peripatetic, who fancied himself as shrewd. And this man, after having entertained me for the first few days, requested me to settle the fee, in order that our interaction might not be unprofitable. Him, too, for this reason I abandoned, believing him to be no philosopher at all. But when my soul was eagerly desirous to hear the peculiar and choice philosophy, I came to a very celebrated Pythagorean—a man who thought much of his own wisdom. And then, when I had an interview with him, willing to become his hearer and disciple, he said, 'What then? Are you acquainted with music, astronomy, and geometry? Do you expect to perceive any of those things which lead to a happy life, if you have not been first informed on those points that wean the soul away from sensible objects and render it fit for objects that appertain to the mind, so that it can contemplate that which is honorable in its essence and that which is good in its essence?' Having commended many of these branches of learning, and telling me that they were necessary, he dismissed me when I confessed to him my ignorance. Accordingly, I took it rather impatiently, as was to be expected when I failed in my hope, the more so because I deemed that the man had some knowledge; but reflecting again on the amount of time that I would have had to spend on those branches of learning, I was not able to endure any further procrastination. In my helpless condition it occurred to me to have a meeting with the Platonists, for their fame was great. From then on, I spent as much of my time as possible with one who had lately settled in our city—a wise man, holding a high position among the Platonists—and I progressed and made the greatest improvements daily. And the perception of immaterial things quite overpowered me, and the contemplation of ideas furnished my mind with wings, so that in a little while I supposed that I had become wise; and such was my stupidity, I expected soon to look upon God, for this is the end of Plato's philosophy.

3

JUSTIN: And while I was thus disposed, when I wished to be filled with great quietness and to shun the path of men, I used to go into a certain field not far from the sea. And when I was near that spot one day, and thinking I was alone, a certain old man, by no means contemptible in appearance, exhibiting meek and venerable manners, followed me at a little distance. And when I turned around to him, having halted, I fixed my eyes rather keenly on him.

OLD MAN: Do you know me?

JUSTIN: No.

OLD MAN: Why, then, do you look at me like that?

JUSTIN: I am astonished, because you have happened to be in my company in the same place; for I had not expected to see anyone here.

OLD MAN: I am concerned about some of my household. They have gone away from me; and therefore, I have come to personally search for them, hoping, perhaps, that they will make their appearance somewhere. But why are you here?

JUSTIN: I delight in such walks, where my attention is not distracted and my thoughts go uninterrupted; and such places are most fit for philology.[5]

OLD MAN: Are you, then, a philologian but no lover of deeds or of truth? And do you not aim at being a practical man so much as being a sophist?

JUSTIN: What greater work could one accomplish than this: to show the reason that governs all, and having laid hold of it, and being mounted upon it, to look down on the errors of others and their pursuits? But without philosophy and right reason, prudence would not be present to anyone. Therefore, it is necessary for every man to philosophize and to regard this as the

---

5 Here philology means the love of argumentation, reasoning, or learned conversation.

greatest and most honorable work. But other things are only of second-rate or third-rate importance, though, indeed, if they be made to depend on philosophy, they are of moderate value, and worthy of acceptance. But deprived of it, and not accompanying it, they are vulgar and coarse to those who pursue them.

OLD MAN: Does philosophy, then, make happiness?

JUSTIN: Certainly, and it alone.

OLD MAN: What, then, is philosophy? And what is happiness? Please tell me, unless something hinders you from saying.

JUSTIN: Philosophy, then, is the knowledge of that which really exists, and a clear perception of the truth; and happiness is the reward of such knowledge and wisdom.

OLD MAN: But what do you call God?

JUSTIN: That which always maintains the same nature, and in the same manner, and is the cause of all other things—that, indeed, is God.

OLD MAN: Is not knowledge a term common to different matters? For in arts of all kinds, he who knows any one of them is called a skillful man in the art of generalship, or of ruling, or of healing equally. But in divine and human affairs it is not so. Is there a knowledge that brings understanding of human and divine things, and then a thorough acquaintance with the divinity and the righteousness of them?

JUSTIN: Certainly.

OLD MAN: What, then? Is it in the same way we know man and God, as we know music, and arithmetic, and astronomy, or any other similar branch?

JUSTIN: By no means.

OLD MAN: You have not answered me correctly, then, for some [branches of knowledge] come to us by learning, or by some employment, while of others we have knowledge by sight. Now, if one were to tell you that there exists in India an animal with a nature unlike all others but of such and such a kind, multiform and various, you would not know it before you saw it; and neither would you be competent to give any account of it, unless you should hear from one who had seen it.

JUSTIN: Certainly not.

OLD MAN: How then should the philosophers judge correctly about God or speak any truth, when they have no knowledge of him, having neither seen him at any time nor heard him?

JUSTIN: But, father, the Deity cannot be seen merely by the eyes as other living beings can. The Deity is discernible to the mind alone, as Plato says, and I believe him.

4

OLD MAN: Is there then, such and so great power in our mind? Or can a man not perceive [what exists] by the senses? Will the mind of man see God at any time, if it is not instructed by the Holy Spirit?

JUSTIN: Plato indeed says that the mind's eye is of such a nature, and has been given for this end, that we may see that very Being when the mind is pure itself, who is the cause of all discerned by the mind, having no color, no form, no greatness—nothing, indeed, which the bodily eye looks upon. But it is something of this sort, he goes on to say, that is beyond all essence, unutterable and inexplicable, but alone honorable and good, coming suddenly into souls well-dispositioned, on account of their affinity to and desire of seeing him.

OLD MAN: What affinity, then, is there between us and God? Is the soul also divine and immortal and a part of that very regal mind? And even as that sees God, so also is it attainable by us to conceive of the Deity in our mind, and thence to become happy?

JUSTIN: Certainly.

OLD MAN: And do all the souls of all living beings comprehend him? Or are the souls of men of one kind and the souls of horses and of donkeys of another kind?

JUSTIN: No; the souls which are in all are similar.

OLD MAN: Then, will horses and donkeys see, or have they seen at some time or other, God?

JUSTIN: No; men will not, except for those who will live justly, purified by righteousness, and by every other virtue.

OLD MAN: It is not, therefore, on account of his affinity, that a man sees God, nor because he has a mind, but because he is temperate and righteous?

JUSTIN: Yes, and because he has that by which he perceives God.

OLD MAN: What then? Do goats or sheep injure anyone?

JUSTIN: No one in any respect.

OLD MAN: Therefore, these animals will see [God] according to your account.

JUSTIN: No; for their body being of such a nature, is an obstacle to them.

OLD MAN: If these animals could assume speech, be well assured that they would with greater reason ridicule our body; but let us now dismiss this subject, and let it be conceded to you as you say. Tell me, however, this: Does the soul see [God] while it is in the body or after it has been removed from the body?

JUSTIN: While it is in the human body, it is possible for it to attain to this by means of the mind; but especially when it has been set free from the body, and being apart by itself, it gets possession of that which it was accustomed to continually and wholly love.

OLD MAN: Does the soul remember [the sight of God] when it is again in the body?

JUSTIN: It does not appear to me so.

OLD MAN: What, then, is the advantage to those who have seen [God]? Or if one who has seen [God] cannot remember this, what more does he have than the one who has not seen?

JUSTIN: I cannot tell.

OLD MAN: And what do those suffer who are judged to be unworthy of this spectacle?

JUSTIN: They are imprisoned in the bodies of certain wild beasts, and this is their punishment.

OLD MAN: Do they know, then, that it is for this reason they are in such forms, and that they have committed some sin?

JUSTIN: I do not think so.

OLD MAN: Then it seems that these reap no advantage from their punishment; moreover, I would say that they are not punished unless they are conscious of the punishment.

JUSTIN: No indeed.

OLD MAN: Therefore, souls neither see God nor transmigrate into other bodies; for they would know that they are punished in this way, and they would be afraid to commit even the most trivial sin afterwards. But that they can perceive that God exists, and that righteousness and piety are honorable, I also quite agree with you.

JUSTIN: You are right.

5

OLD MAN: These philosophers know nothing, then, about these things; for they cannot tell what a soul is.

JUSTIN: It does not appear so.

OLD MAN: Nor ought it to be called immortal; for if it is immortal, it is plainly unbegotten.

JUSTIN: It is both unbegotten and immortal, according to some who are styled Platonists.

OLD MAN: Do you say that the world is also unbegotten?

JUSTIN: Some say so. I do not, however, agree with them.

OLD MAN: You are right; for what reason has one for supposing that a body so solid, possessing resistance, composite, changeable, decaying, and renewed every day, has not arisen from some cause? But if the world is begotten, souls also are necessarily begotten; and perhaps at one time they were not in existence, for they were made on account of men and other living creatures, if you will say that they have been begotten wholly apart, and not along with their respective bodies.

JUSTIN: This seems to be correct.

OLD MAN: They are not, then, immortal?

JUSTIN: No; since the world has appeared to us to be begotten.

OLD MAN: But I do not say, indeed, that all souls die; for truly that would be a piece of good fortune to the evil. What then? The souls of the pious remain in a better place, while those of the unjust and wicked are in a worse place, waiting for the time of judgment. Thus, some that have appeared worthy of God never die; but others are punished so long as God wills them to exist and to be punished.

JUSTIN: Is what you say, then, of a like nature with that which Plato in *Timaeus* hints about the world, when he says that it is indeed subject to decay, inasmuch as it has been created, but that it will neither be dissolved nor meet with the fate of death on account of the will of God? Does it seem to you the very same can be said of the soul and generally of all things? For those things that exist after God, or will at any time exist, these have the nature of decay and are such as may be blotted out and cease to exist; for God alone is unbegotten and incorruptible, and therefore he is God, but all other things after him are created and corruptible. For this reason, souls both die and are punished: since, if they were unbegotten, they would neither sin, nor be filled with folly, nor be cowardly, and again ferocious; nor would they willingly transform into swine, and serpents, and dogs; and it would not indeed be just to compel them, if they were unbegotten. For that which is unbegotten is similar to, equal to, and the same with that which is unbegotten; and neither in power nor in honor should the one be preferred to the other, and hence there are not many things which are unbegotten; for if there were some difference between them, you would not discover the cause of the difference, though you searched for it; but after letting the mind ever wander to infinity, you would at length, wearied out, take your stand on one Unbegotten, and say that this is the cause of all. Did such escape the observation of Plato and Pythagoras, those wise men, who have been as a wall and fortress of philosophy to us?

6

OLD MAN: It makes no difference to me whether Plato or Pythagoras, or, in short, any other man held such opinions. For the truth is so; and you would perceive it from this. The soul assuredly is or has life. If, then, it is life, it would cause something else, and not itself, to live, even as motion would move something else than itself. Now, that the soul lives, no one would deny. But if it lives, it lives not as being life, but as the partaker of life; but that which partakes of anything is different from the thing it partakes. Now the soul partakes of life, since God wills it to live. Thus, then, it will not partake [of life] when God does not will it to live. For to live is not its attribute, as it is God's; but as a man does not live always, and the soul is not forever conjoined with the body, since, whenever this harmony must be broken up, the soul leaves the body, and the man exists no longer; even so, whenever the soul must cease to exist, the spirit of life is removed from it, and there is no more soul, but it goes back to the place from where it was taken.

7

JUSTIN: Should anyone, then, employ a teacher? Or where can anyone be helped, if not even in the teachers there is truth?

OLD MAN: There existed, long before this time, certain men more ancient than all those who are esteemed philosophers, both righteous and beloved by God, who spoke by the Divine Spirit, and foretold events that would take place, and which are now taking place. They are called prophets. These alone both saw and announced the truth to men, neither revering nor fearing any man, not influenced by a desire for glory, but speaking those things alone which they saw and which they heard, being filled with the Holy Spirit. Their writings are still extant, and he who has read them is very much helped in his knowledge of the beginning and end of things, and of those matters which the philosopher ought to know, provided he has believed them. For they did not use proofs in their treatises, seeing that they were witnesses to the truth above all proofs, and worthy of belief; and those events which have happened, and those which are happening, compel you to assent to the utterances made by them, although, indeed, they were entitled to credit on account of the miracles which they performed, since they both glorified the Creator, the God and Father of all things, and proclaimed his Son, the Christ [sent] by him: which, indeed, the false prophets, who are filled with the lying unclean spirit, neither have done nor do, but venture to work certain wonderful deeds for the purpose of astonishing men, and glorify the spirits and demons of error. But pray that, above all things, the gates of light may be opened to you; for these things cannot be perceived or understood by all, but only by the man to whom God and his Christ have imparted wisdom.

8

JUSTIN TO TRYPHO: When he had spoken these and many other things, which there is no time for mentioning at present, he went away, bidding me attend to them; and I have not seen him since. But straightway a flame was kindled in my soul; and a love of the prophets, and of those men who are friends of Christ, possessed me; and while considering his words in my mind, I found this philosophy alone to be safe and profitable. Thus, and for this reason, I am a philosopher. Moreover, I wish that all persons, making a resolution similar to my own, do not keep themselves away from the words of the Savior. For these words possess an incredible power in themselves, and they are sufficient to inspire those who turn aside from the path of righteousness with awe; while the sweetest rest is afforded to those who make a diligent practice of them. If then, you have any concern for yourself, and if you are eagerly looking for salvation, and if you believe in God, you may—since you are not indifferent to the matter —become acquainted with the Christ of God, and, after being initiated, live a happy life.

When Justin had said this, Trypho's friends laughed; but Trypho smiled.

TRYPHO: I approve of your other remarks and admire the eagerness with which you study divine things; but it was better for you to abide in the philosophy of Plato, or of some other man, cultivating endurance, self-control, and moderation, rather than be deceived by false words, and follow the opinions of men of no reputation. For if you remain in that mode of philosophy and live blamelessly, a hope of a better destiny is left to you; but when you have forsaken God, and reposed confidence in man, what safety still awaits you? If then, you are willing to listen to me (for I have already considered you a friend), first be circumcised, then observe what ordinances have been enacted with respect to the Sabbath, and the feasts, and the new moons of God. And, in a word, do all things that have been written in the Law, and then perhaps you will obtain mercy from God. But Christ—if he has indeed been born and exists anywhere—is unknown, and does not even know himself, and he has no power until Elijah comes to anoint him and make him manifest to all. And you, having accepted a groundless report, invent a Christ for yourselves and for his sake are foolishly perishing.

[...]

On Why Christians Do Not Observe the Law

10

JUSTIN: Is there any other matter, my friends, in which we are blamed, than this: that we live not after the Law, and are not circumcised in the flesh as your forefathers were, and do not observe Sabbaths as you do? Are our lives and customs also slandered among you? And I ask this: have you also believed that we eat men; and that after the feast, having extinguished the lights, we engage in promiscuous concubinage? Or do you condemn us in this alone, that we adhere to such tenets, and believe in an opinion, untrue, as you think?

TRYPHO: This is what we are amazed at. But those things about which the crowds speak are not worthy of belief; for they are most repugnant to human nature. Moreover, I am aware that your precepts in the so-called Gospel are so wonderful and so great, that I suspect no one can keep them, for I have carefully read them. But this is what we are most at a loss about: that you, professing to be pious, and supposing yourselves better than others, are not in any way from them, and do not alter your mode of living from the nations, in that you observe no festivals or Sabbaths, and do not have the rite of circumcision. And further, resting your hopes on a man that was crucified, you yet expect to obtain some good thing from God, while you do not obey his commandments. Have you not read that the soul not circumcised on the eighth day will be cut off from his people? And this has been ordained for strangers and for slaves equally. But you, despising this covenant rashly, reject the consequent duties and attempt to persuade yourselves that you know God, when, however, you perform none of those things which they who fear God do. If, therefore, you can defend yourself on these points, and make it clear in what way you hope for anything whatsoever, even though you do not observe the Law, this we would very gladly hear from you, and we will make other similar investigations."

11

JUSTIN: There will be no other God, O Trypho, nor was there from eternity any other existing, other than he who made and disposed all this universe. Nor do we think that there is one God for us and another for you, but that he alone is God who led your fathers out from Egypt with a strong hand and a high arm. Nor have we trusted in any other (for there is no other), but in him in whom you also have trusted, the God of Abraham, and of Isaac, and of Jacob.

But we do not trust through Moses or through the Law; for then we would do the same as yourselves. I have read that there will be a final law, and a covenant, the greatest of all, which it is now incumbent on all men to observe, as many as are seeking after the inheritance of God. For the Law promulgated on Horeb is now old, and it belongs to yourselves alone; but this is for all universally. Now, law placed against law has abrogated that which is before it, and a covenant which comes after in like manner has put an end to the previous one. And an eternal and final law—namely, Christ —has been given to us, and the covenant is trustworthy, after which there will be no law, no commandment, no ordinance. Have you not read this which Isaiah says: "Hear me; hear me, my people; and, you kings, give ear to me: for a Law will go forth from me, and my judgment will be for a light to the nations. My righteousness approaches swiftly, and my salvation will go forth, and nations will trust in my arm" (Isa 51:4–5 LXX)? And by Jeremiah, concerning this same new covenant, he speaks in this way: "Behold, the days will come, says the Lord, when I will make a new covenant with the house of Israel and with the house of Judah; not according to the covenant that I made with their fathers, in the day that I took them by the hand to bring them out of the land of Egypt" (Jer 31:31–32). If, therefore, God proclaimed a new covenant that was to be instituted, and this as a light of the nations, we see and are persuaded that men approach God, leaving their idols and other unrighteousness, through the name of him who was crucified, Jesus Christ, and they abide by their confession even to death, and maintain devotion. Moreover, by the works and by the attendant miracles, it is possible for all to understand that he is the new Law, and the new covenant, and the expectation of those who out of every people wait for the good things of God. For the true spiritual Israel, and descendants of Judah, Jacob, Isaac, and Abraham (who in uncircumcision was approved of and blessed by God on account of his faith, and called the father of many nations), are we who have been led to God through this crucified Christ, as will be demonstrated while we proceed.

12

Justin also referred to another passage, in which Isaiah exclaims: "Hear my words, and your soul will live; and I will make an everlasting covenant with you, the sure mercies of David. Behold, I have given him for a witness to the people; nations that do not know you, will call on you; peoples who do not know you, will escape to you, because of your God, the Holy One of Israel; for he has glorified you" (Isa 55:3–5 LXX).

JUSTIN: This same Law you have despised, and his new holy covenant you have slighted; and now you neither receive it nor repent of your evil deeds. "For your ears are closed, your eyes are blinded, and the heart is hardened," Jeremiah has cried;[6] yet not even then do you listen. The lawgiver is present, yet you do not see him; the gospel is preached to the poor; the blind see; yet you do not understand. You now need a second circumcision, though you glory greatly in the flesh. The new law requires you to keep a perpetual Sabbath, and you, because you are idle for one day, suppose you are pious, not discerning why this has been commanded of you. And if you eat unleavened bread, you say the will of God has been fulfilled. The Lord our God does not take pleasure in such observances. If there is any perjured person or a thief among you, let him cease to be so; if any adulterer, let him repent; then he has kept the sweet and true sabbaths of God. If anyone has impure hands, let him wash and be pure.

[...]

On the Typological Interpretation of the Mosaic Law

40

JUSTIN: The mystery of the lamb that God directed to be sacrificed as the Passover was a type of Christ; it is with his blood, in proportion to their faith in him, that Christians anoint their houses (that is, themselves, who believe in him). For you can understand that the creation that God created—namely, Adam—was a house for the spirit that proceeded from God. And that this injunction was temporary, I will prove in what follows. God does not permit the lamb of the Passover to be sacrificed in any other place than where his name was named; knowing that the days will come, after the suffering of Christ, when even the place in Jerusalem will be given over to your enemies, and all the offerings, in short, will cease; and the lamb that was commanded to be wholly roasted was a symbol of the suffering of the cross, which Christ would undergo. For the lamb, which is roasted, is roasted and dressed up in the form of the cross. For one spit is transfixed right through from the lower parts up to the head, and one across the back, to which are attached the legs of the lamb. And the two goats, which were ordered to be offered during the fast, of which one was sent away as the scapegoat, and the other sacrificed, were similarly declarative of the two

---

6 A reference to Isaiah 6:10 rather than Jeremiah.

appearances of Christ. The first, in which the elders of your people and the priests, having laid hands on him and put him to death, sent him away as the scapegoat; and his second appearance, because in the same place in Jerusalem you will recognize him whom you have dishonored, and who was an offering for all sinners willing to repent, and keeping the fast which Isaiah speaks of, "loosening the terms of the violent contracts" (Isa 58:6), and keeping the other precepts, likewise enumerated by him, and which I have quoted (which those believing in Jesus also do). And further, you are aware that the offering of the two goats, which were directed to be sacrificed at the fast, was not permitted to take place similarly anywhere else, but only in Jerusalem.

41

JUSTIN: And the offering of fine flour, sirs, which was prescribed to be presented on behalf of those purified from leprosy, was a type of the bread of the Eucharist, the celebration of which our Lord Jesus Christ prescribed in remembrance of the suffering that he endured on behalf of those who are purified in soul from all iniquity, in order that we may at the same time thank God for having created the world, with all things therein, for the sake of man, and for delivering us from the evil that we were in, and for utterly overthrowing principalities and powers by the one who suffered according to his will. Hence God speaks by the mouth of Malachi, one of the twelve prophets, as I said before, about the sacrifices at that time presented by you: "I have no pleasure in you, says the Lord; and I will not accept your sacrifices at your hands; for, from the rising of the sun to the setting of the same, my name has been glorified among the gentiles, and in every place incense is offered to my name, and a pure offering; for my name is great among the gentiles, says the Lord; but you profane it" (Mal 1:10–12). He then speaks of those gentiles, namely us, who in every place offer sacrifices to him (namely, the bread and cup of the Eucharist), affirming both that we glorify his name and that you profane it. The command of circumcision, which called for boys to be circumcised on the eight day, was a type of the true circumcision, by which we are circumcised from deceit and iniquity through him who rose from the dead on the first day after the Sabbath, our Lord Jesus Christ. For the first day after the Sabbath, remaining the first of all the days, is called the eighth according to the number of all the days of the cycle, and yet it remains the first.

[...]

On Righteousness and the Law Before and After Christ

45

TRYPHO: I do not mean to interrupt these matters, which you say must be investigated, but I have an urgent question, which I hope you will let me ask first.

JUSTIN: Ask whatever you please, as it occurs to you; and I will endeavor, after questions and answers, to resume and complete the discourse.

TRYPHO: Tell me, will those who lived according to the Law given by Moses, live in the same manner with Jacob, Enoch, and Noah, in the resurrection of the dead, or not?

JUSTIN: When I quoted, sir, the words spoken by Ezekiel, that "even if Noah and Daniel and Jacob were to plead on behalf of sons and daughters, the request would not be granted them" (Ezek 14:20), but that each one will be saved by his own righteousness, I also said that those who regulated their lives by the Law of Moses would in like manner be saved. For the Law of Moses contains things that are naturally good, and pious, and righteous, and were prescribed to be done by those who obey it, and it also contains things that were appointed to be performed because of the hardness of the people's hearts; both were recorded and done by those who were under the Law. Since those who did what is universally, naturally, and eternally good are pleasing to God, they will be saved through this Christ in the resurrection equally with those righteous men who were before them, namely Noah, and Enoch, and Jacob, and whoever else there be, along with those who have known this Christ, Son of God, who was before the morning star and the moon, and submitted to become incarnate, and be born of this virgin of the family of David, in order that, by this dispensation, the serpent that sinned from the beginning, and the angels like him, may be destroyed, and that death may be scorned and brought to an end at the second coming of the Christ himself for those who believe in him and live acceptably. At that time some will be sent to be punished unceasingly into judgment and condemnation of fire, but others will exist in freedom from suffering, from corruption, and from grief, and in immortality.

46

TRYPHO: But if some, even now, wish to live in the observance of the institutions given by Moses, and yet believe in this Jesus who was crucified, recognizing him to be the Christ of God, and that it is given to him to be absolute

Judge of all, and that his is the everlasting kingdom, can they also be saved?

JUSTIN: Let us consider that also together; is it possible for someone to now observe all the Mosaic institutions?

TRYPHO: No; for we know that, as you said, it is not possible anywhere to sacrifice the lamb of the Passover, or to offer the goats ordered for the fast, or, in short, to make all the other offerings.

JUSTIN: Tell me then yourself, I pray, some things that can be observed; for you will be persuaded that, though a man does not keep or has not performed the eternal decrees, he may assuredly be saved.

TRYPHO: It is possible to keep the Sabbath, to be circumcised, to observe months, and to be washed if you touch anything prohibited by Moses or after sexual intercourse.

JUSTIN: Do you think that Abraham, Isaac, Jacob, Noah, and Job, and all the rest before or after them equally righteous, also Sarah the wife of Abraham, Rebekah the wife of Isaac, Rachel the wife of Jacob, and Leah, and all the rest of them, until the mother of Moses the faithful servant, who observed none of these [statutes], will be saved?

TRYPHO: Were not Abraham and his descendants circumcised?

JUSTIN: I know that Abraham and his descendants were circumcised. The reason why circumcision was given to them I stated at length in what has gone before. And if what has been said does not convince you, let us again search into the matter. But you are aware that, up to Moses, no one in fact who was righteous observed any of these rites at all of which we are talking, or received one commandment to observe, except that of circumcision, which began from Abraham.

TRYPHO: We know it, and we admit that they are saved.

JUSTIN: You perceive that God by Moses laid all such ordinances upon you on account of the hardness of your people's hearts, in order that, by the large number of them, you might keep God continually, and in every action, before your eyes, and never begin to act unjustly or impiously. For he directed you to place around you [a fringe] of purple dye (Num 15:38), in order that you might not forget God; and he commanded you to wear a phylactery (Deut 6:6), certain characters, which indeed we consider holy, being engraved on very thin parchment; and by these means stirring you up to retain a constant remembrance of God; at the same time, however, convincing you, that in your hearts you have not even a faint remembrance of God's worship. Yet not even so were you dissuaded from idolatry; for in the times of Elijah, when [God] recounted the number of those who had not bowed the knee to Baal, he said the number was seven thousand (1 Kgs 19:18); and in Isaiah he rebukes you for having sacrificed your children to idols. But we, because we refuse to sacrifice to those to whom we were in times of old accustomed to sacrifice, undergo extreme penalties, and rejoice in death—believing that God will raise us up by his Christ and will make us incorruptible, and undisturbed, and immortal; and we know that the ordinances imposed because of the hardness of your people's hearts, contribute nothing to the performance of righteousness and of piety.

47

TRYPHO: But if someone, knowing that this is so, after he recognizes that this man is Christ, and has believed in and obeys him, wishes, however, to observe these [institutions], will he be saved?

JUSTIN: In my opinion, Trypho, such a one will be saved, if he does not strive in every way to persuade other men—I mean those gentiles who have been cut off[7] from error by Christ—to observe the same things as himself, telling them that they will not be saved unless they do so. This you did yourself at the commencement of the discourse, when you declared that I would not be saved unless I observe these institutions.

TRYPHO: Why then have you said, "In my opinion, such a one will be saved," unless there are some who affirm that such will not be saved?

JUSTIN: There are such people, Trypho. And these people do not venture to have any interaction with or to extend hospitality to such persons; but I do not agree with them. But if some, through weak-mindedness, wish to observe the institutions given by Moses, from which they expect some virtue, but which we believe were appointed by reason of the hardness of the people's hearts, along with their hope in this Christ, and [wish to perform] the eternal and natural acts of righteousness and piety, yet choose to live with the Christians and the faithful, as I said before, not inducing them either to be circumcised like themselves, or to keep the Sabbath, or to observe any other such ceremonies, then I hold that we ought to join ourselves to such and associate with them in all things as kinsmen and brothers and sisters. But if, Trypho, some of your race, who say they believe in this Christ, compel those gentiles who believe in this Christ to live in all respects according to the Law given by Moses, or choose not to associate so intimately with them, I in like manner do not approve of them. But I believe that even those, who have been persuaded by them to observe the legal dispensation along with their confession of God in Christ, will probably be saved. But I also hold, further, that any people who

---

7 Literally, "circumcised from wandering"

have confessed and known this man to be Christ, yet who have gone back for some reason to the legal dispensation, and have denied that this man is Christ, and have not repented before death, will by no means be saved. Further, I hold that those of the seed of Abraham who live according to the Law, and do not believe in this Christ before death, will likewise not be saved, and especially those who have anathematized and do anathematize in the synagogues this very Christ and everything by which they might obtain salvation and escape the vengeance of fire. For the goodness and the loving-kindness of God, and his boundless riches, hold righteous and sinless the man who, as Ezekiel tells us, repents of sins and reckons sinful, unrighteous, and impious the man who falls away from piety and righteousness to unrighteousness and ungodliness (Ezek 33:11–20). Therefore, our Lord Jesus Christ also said, "In whatsoever things I will take you, in these I will judge you."[8]

[...]

On the Existence of the Word before Creation

61

JUSTIN: I will give you another testimony, my friends, from the Scriptures, that God begat before all creatures a Beginning, [who was] a certain rational power [proceeding] from himself, who is called by the Holy Spirit, now the Glory of the Lord, now the Son, again Wisdom, again an Angel, then God, and then Lord and Word; and on another occasion he calls himself Captain, when he appeared in human form to Joshua the son of Nun. For he can be called by all those names, since he ministers to the Father's will and since he was begotten of the Father by an act of will; just as we see happening among ourselves; for when we give out some word, we beget the word; yet not by abscission, so as to lessen the word [that remains] in us, when we give it out; and just as we see also happening in the case of a fire, which is not lessened when it has kindled [another] but remains the same; and that which has been kindled by it likewise appears to exist by itself, not diminishing that from which it was kindled. The Word of Wisdom, who is himself this God begotten of the Father of all things, and Word, and Wisdom, and Power, and the Glory of the Begetter, will bear evidence to me, when he speaks by Solomon the following: "If I will declare to you what happens daily, I will call to mind events from everlasting, and review them. The Lord made me the beginning of his ways for his works.

---

8 Source unknown. This saying is also quoted by Clement of Alexandria, *Salvation of the Rich* 40.2.

From everlasting he established me in the beginning, before he had made the earth, and before he had made the deeps, before the springs of the waters had issued forth, before the mountains had been established. Before all the hills, he begets me. God made the country, and the desert, and the highest inhabited places under the sky. When he made ready the heavens, I was along with him, and when he set up his throne on the winds; when he made the high clouds strong, and the springs of the deep safe, when he made the foundations of the earth, I was with him, arranging. I was that in which he rejoiced; daily and at all times I delighted in his countenance because he delighted in the finishing of the habitable world, and he delighted in the sons of men. Now, therefore, O son, hear me. Blessed is the man who will listen to me, and the mortal who will keep my ways, watching daily at my doors, observing the posts of my ingoings. For my outgoings are the outgoings of life, and my will has been prepared by the Lord. But they who sin against me, trespass against their own souls; and they who hate me love death" (Prov 8:21–36).

62

JUSTIN: And the same sentiment was expressed, my friends, by the word of God by Moses, when it indicated to us, with regard to him whom it has pointed out, that God speaks in the creation of man with the very same design, in the following words: "Let us make man after our image and likeness. And let them have dominion over the fish of the sea, and over the fowl of the heaven, and over the cattle, and over all the earth, and over all the creeping things that creep on the earth. And God created man: after the image of God, he created him; male and female, he created them. And God blessed them and said, 'Increase and multiply, and fill the earth, and have power over it'" (Gen 1:26, 28). And that you may not change the [force of the] words just quoted, and repeat what your teachers assert—either that God said to himself, "Let us make," just as we, when about to do something, oftentimes say to ourselves, "Let us make"; or that God spoke to the elements, namely, the earth and other similar substances of which we believe man was formed, "Let us make,"—I will quote again the words narrated by Moses himself, from which we can indisputably learn that [God] conversed with someone who was numerically distinct from himself, and also a rational being. These are the words: "And God said, 'Behold, Adam has become as one of us, to know good and evil'" (Gen 3:22). In saying, therefore, "as one of us," [Moses] has declared that [there is a certain] number of persons associated with one another, and that they are at least two. For I would not say that the dogma of that heresy which is said to be among you is true, or that the teachers of it can prove that [God] spoke to angels, or that the human frame was the workmanship of angels. But this Offspring, which was truly brought forth from the Father, was with the Father before all the creatures, and the Father communed with him; even as the Scripture by Solomon has made clear, that he whom Solomon calls Wisdom, was begotten as a Beginning before all his creatures and as Offspring by God, who has also declared this same thing in the revelation made by Joshua the son of Nun. Listen, therefore, to the following from the book of Joshua, that what I say may become clear to you; it is this: "And it came to pass, when Joshua was near Jericho, he lifted up his eyes and saw a man standing over against him. And Joshua approached him and said, 'Are you for us or for our adversaries?' And he said to him, 'I am Captain of the Lord's host; I have now come.' And Joshua fell on his face on the ground, and he said to him, 'Lord, what do you command your servant?' And the Lord's Captain said to Joshua, 'Take off your shoes, for the place where you are standing is holy ground.' And Jericho was shut up and fortified, and no one went out of it. And the Lord said to Joshua, 'Behold, I give into your hand Jericho, and its king, [and] its mighty men'" (Josh 5:13–6:2).

[...]

On the Reign of a Thousand Years

80

TRYPHO: I remarked to you sir, that you are very anxious to be safe in all respects, since you cling to the Scriptures. But tell me, do you really admit that this place, Jerusalem, will be rebuilt; and do you expect your people to be gathered together, and made joyful with Christ and the patriarchs, and the prophets, both the men of our nation, and other proselytes who joined them before your Christ came? Or have you given way, and admitted this in order to have the appearance of winning against us in the controversies?"

JUSTIN: I am not so miserable a fellow, Trypho, as to say one thing and think another. I admitted to you previously that I and many others are of this opinion, and we [believe] that such will take place, as you assuredly are aware; but, on the other hand, I signified to you that many who belong to the pure and pious faith, and are true Christians, think otherwise. Moreover, I pointed out to you that some who are called Christians, but are godless, impious heretics, teach doctrines that are in every way blasphemous, atheistical, and foolish. But that you may know that I do not say this before you alone, I will draw up a statement, so far as I can, of all the arguments that have passed between us, in which I will record myself as admitting the very same things that I admit to you. For I choose to follow not men or men's doctrines, but God and the doctrines [delivered] by him. For if you have fallen in with some who are called Christians but who do not admit this [truth], and venture to blaspheme the God of Abraham, and the God of Isaac, and the God of Jacob, who say there is no resurrection of the dead, and that their souls, when they die, are taken to heaven—do not imagine that they are Christians, even as one, if he would rightly consider it, would not admit that the Sadducees, or similar sects of Genistae, Meristae, Galileans, Hellenists, Pharisees, Baptists, are Jews (do not hear me impatiently when I tell you what I think), but are [only] called Jews and children of Abraham, worshipping God with the lips, as God himself declared, but the heart was far from him. But I and others, who are right-minded Christians on all points, are assured that there will be a resurrection of the dead, and a thousand years in Jerusalem, which will then be built, adorned, and enlarged, as the prophets Ezekiel and Isaiah and others declare.

81

JUSTIN: For Isaiah spoke thus about this space of a thousand years: "For the heaven will be new, and the earth will be new, and the former will not be remembered or come into their heart; but they will find joy and gladness in it, which things I create. For, behold, I make Jerusalem as rejoicing, and my people as joy; and I will rejoice over Jerusalem, and be glad over my people. And the voice of weeping or crying will no longer be heard in her. And there will no longer bethere a person of immature years or an old man who will not fulfill his days. For the young man will be a hundred years old; but the sinner who dies a hundred years old, he will be accursed. And they will build houses and will themselves inhabit them; and they will plant vines and will themselves eat the produce of them and drink the wine. They will not build, and others inhabit; they will not plant, and others eat. For according to the days of the tree of life will be the days of my people; the works of their toil will abound. My elect will not toil fruitlessly, or beget children to be cursed; for they will be a seed righteous and blessed by the Lord, and their offspring with them. And it will come to pass that before they call, I will hear; while they are still speaking, I will say, 'What is it?' Then will the wolves and the lambs feed together, and the lion will eat straw like the ox; but the serpent [will eat] earth as bread. They will not hurt or maltreat each other on the holy mountain, says the Lord" (Isa 65:17–25). Now we have understood that the expression used among these words, "According to the days of the tree [of life] will be the days of my people; the works of their toil will abound" obscurely predicts a thousand years. For as Adam was told that in the day he ate of the tree he would die, we know that he did not complete a thousand years. We have perceived, moreover, that the expression, "The day of the Lord is as a thousand years" (Ps 90:4; 2 Pet 3:8), is connected with this subject. And further, there was a certain man with us, whose name was John, one of the apostles of Christ, who prophesied, by a revelation that was made to him, that those who believed in our Christ would dwell a thousand years in Jerusalem (cf. Rev 20:4–5), and that thereafter the general, and, in short, the eternal resurrection and judgment of all men would likewise take place. Just as our Lord also said, "They will neither marry nor be given in marriage, but will be equal to the angels, the children of the God of the resurrection" (Luke 20:35–36).

82

JUSTIN: For the prophetic gifts remain with us, even to the present time. And therefore you should understand that [the gifts] formerly among your nation have been transferred to us. And just as there were false prophets contemporaneous with your holy prophets, so are there now many false teachers amongst us, of whom our Lord forewarned us to beware. So, we are in no respect deficient, since we know that he foreknew all that would happen to us after his resurrection from the dead and ascension to heaven. For he said we would be put to death, and hated for his name's sake, and that many false prophets and false Christs would appear in his name and deceive many; and so it has happened. For many have taught godless, blasphemous, and unholy doctrines, forging them in his name; and many even now are teaching things that proceed from the unclean spirit of the devil and which were put into their hearts. Therefore, we are most anxious that you be persuaded not to be misled by such persons, since we know that everyone who can speak the truth and yet does not speak it, will be judged by God, as God testified by Ezekiel when he said, "I have made you a watchman to the house of Judah. If the sinner sins, and you warn him not, he himself will die in his sin; but I will hold you accountable for his blood. But if you warn him, you shall be innocent" (Ezek 3:17–19). And on this account, we are, through fear, very earnest in desiring to converse [with men] according to the Scriptures, but not for the sake of money, glory, or pleasure. For no man can convict us of any of these [vices]. We no longer wish to live like the rulers of your people, whom God reproaches when he says, "Your rulers are companions of thieves, lovers of bribes, followers of the rewards" (Isa 1:23). Now, if you know of certain people amongst us who are of this sort, do not on their account blaspheme the Scriptures and Christ, and do not assiduously strive to give falsified interpretations.

[...]

On Christ's Reception of the Holy Spirit

88

JUSTIN: Now, it is possible to see amongst us women and men who possess gifts of the Spirit of God. It was prophesied that the powers enumerated by Isaiah would come upon him [i.e. Jesus] (cf. Isa 11:1–3), not because he needed power but because these would not continue after him. And let this be a proof to you, namely, what I told you was done by the Magi from Arabia, who as soon as the child was born came to worship him, for even at his birth he was in possession of his power. And as he grew up like all other men, by using the fitting means, he assigned its own [requirements] to each development, and was sustained by all kinds of nourishment, and waited for thirty years, more or less, until John appeared before him as the herald of his approach, and preceded him in the way of baptism, as I have already shown. And then, when Jesus had gone to the river Jordan, where John was baptizing, and when he had stepped into the water, a fire was kindled in the Jordan. And when he came out of the water, the Holy Spirit lighted on him like a dove, as the apostles of this very Christ of ours wrote. Now, we know that he did not go to the river because he stood in need of baptism or of the descent of the Spirit like a dove, just like he submitted to be born and to be crucified not because he needed these things but for the sake of the human race, which from Adam had fallen under the power of death and the guile of the serpent, and each one of which had committed personal transgression. For God, wishing both angels and men, who were endowed with free-will, and had at their own disposal the ability to do whatever he had strengthened each to do, made them so, that if they chose the things acceptable to himself, he would keep them free from death and from punishment; but that if they did evil, he would punish each as he sees fit. For it was not his entrance into Jerusalem sitting on a donkey, which we have showed was prophesied, that empowered him to be Christ, but it furnished men with a proof that he is the Christ; just as it was necessary in the time of John for men to have a proof, so that they might know who the Christ is. For when John remained by the Jordan and preached the baptism of repentance, wearing only a leather girdle and clothes made of camels' hair, eating nothing but locusts and wild honey, men supposed him to be Christ. But he cried to them, "I am not the Christ, but the voice of one crying; for he that is greater than I will come, whose shoes I am not worthy to untie" (Mark 1:7). And when Jesus came to the Jordan, he was considered to be the son of Joseph the carpenter; and he appeared without comeliness, as the Scriptures declared; and he was deemed a carpenter (for he was in the habit of working as a carpenter when among men, making ploughs and yokes, by which he taught the symbols of righteousness and an active life); but then the Holy Spirit, and for man's sake, as I formerly stated, lighted on him in the form of a dove, and there came at the same instant from the heavens a voice, which was uttered also by David when he spoke, personating Christ, what the Father would say to him: "You are my Son; this day I have begotten you" (Ps 2:7); [the Father] saying that his generation would take place for men at the time when they would become acquainted with him: "You are my Son; this day I have begotten you."

[…]

On Righteousness and the Curse

93

JUSTIN: [God] sets before every race of mankind that which is always and universally just, as well as all righteousness. Every race knows that adultery, fornication, homicide, and such like are sinful. Though they all commit such practices, they do not escape from the knowledge that they act unrighteously whenever they so do, with the exception of those who are possessed with an unclean spirit, and who have been debased by education, by wicked customs, by sinful institutions, and who have lost (or rather quenched and put away) their natural ideas. For we may see that such persons are unwilling to submit to the same things that they inflict upon others, and that they reproach each other with hostile consciences for the acts that they perpetrate. And therefore, I think that our Lord and Savior Jesus Christ spoke well when he summed up all righteousness and piety in two commandments. They are these: "You shall love the Lord your God with all your heart, and with all your strength, and your neighbor as yourself" (Matt 22:37). For the man who loves

God with all the heart, and with all the strength, being filled with a God-fearing mind, will revere no other god; and since God wishes it, he will revere that angel who is beloved by the same Lord and God. And the man who loves his neighbor as himself will wish for him the same good things that he wishes for himself, and no man will wish evil things for himself. Accordingly, he who loves his neighbor will pray and labor that his neighbor may possess the same benefits as himself. Now, nothing else is a neighbor to man than that similarly-affectioned and reasonable being—that is, the race called man. Therefore, since all righteousness is divided into two branches, namely, in so far as it regards God and men, Scripture says that whoever loves the Lord God with all his heart and all his strength, and love his neighbor as himself, would be truly a righteous man. But you were never shown to be possessed of friendship or love either toward God, or toward the prophets, or toward yourselves. Instead, as is evident, you are forever found to be idolaters and murderers of righteous men, so that you laid hands even on Christ himself. To this very day you abide in your wickedness, loathing those who prove that this man who was crucified by you is the Christ. Indeed, more than this, you suppose that he was crucified as hostile to and cursed by God, which supposition is the product of your most irrational mind. For though you have the means of understanding that this man is Christ from the signs given by Moses, you will not do this. Rather, in addition, fancying that we can have no arguments, you put whatever question comes into your minds, while you yourselves are at a loss for arguments whenever you meet with some firmly established Christian.

94

JUSTIN: For tell me, was it not God who commanded by Moses that no image or likeness of anything that was in heaven above or which was on the earth should be made, and yet who caused the brazen serpent to be made by Moses in the wilderness and set it up for a sign by which those bitten by serpents were saved? Yet he is free from unrighteousness. For by this, as I previously remarked, he proclaimed the mystery, by which he declared that he would break the power of the serpent that caused the transgression of Adam, and [would bring] to them that believe on him by this sign (that is, him who was to be crucified) salvation from the fangs of the serpent, which are wicked deeds, idolatries, and other unrighteous acts. Unless the matter is understood in this way, give me a reason why Moses set up the brazen serpent for a sign, and bade those that were bitten to gaze at it, and the wounded were healed;

and this, too, when he had himself commanded that no likeness of anything whatsoever should be made.

A COMPANION OF TRYPHO: You have spoken truly. We cannot give a reason. For I have frequently interrogated the teachers about this matter, and none of them gave me a reason. Therefore, continue what you are speaking; for we are paying attention while you unfold the mystery, on account of which the doctrines of the prophets are falsely slandered.

JUSTIN: Just as God commanded the sign to be made by the brazen serpent and yet he is blameless, even so, though a curse lies in the law against persons who are crucified, yet no curse lies on the Christ of God, by whom all that have committed things worthy of a curse are saved (Gal 3:13).

95

JUSTIN: For the whole human race will be found to be under a curse. For it is written in the Law of Moses, "Cursed is everyone that does not uphold all the things written in the book of the Law by doing them" (Deut 27:26). And no one has accurately done all, nor will you venture to deny this; but some more and some less than others have observed the ordinances enjoined. But if those who are under this law appear to be under a curse for not having observed all the requirements, how much more will all the nations appear to be under a curse who practice idolatry, who seduce youths, and commit other crimes? If then, the Father of all wished for his Christ to take upon himself the curses of all for the whole human family, knowing that, after he had been crucified and was dead, he would raise him up, why do you argue about him, who submitted to suffer these things according to the Father's will, as if he were accursed? Why do you not express great regret about your actions? For although his Father caused him to suffer these things on behalf of the human family, you did not commit the deed as in obedience to the will of God. For you did not practice piety when you killed the prophets. And let none of you say, "If his Father wished him to suffer this, in order that by his stripes the human race might be healed, we have done no wrong." However, if you repent of your sins, and recognize him to be Christ, and observe his commandments, then you may assert this; for, as I have said before, remission of sins will be yours. But if you curse him and them that believe in him, and, when you have the power, put them to death, how is it possible that retribution will not be made against you, as of unrighteous and sinful men, altogether hard-hearted and without understanding, because you laid your hands on him?

[...]

On Identifying Prophecies about Christ in the Scriptures

114

JUSTIN: The Holy Spirit sometimes caused something that was a type of the future to be done clearly; but sometimes he uttered words about what was to take place, as if it was then taking place, or had taken place, and unless those who read perceive this art, they will not be able to follow the words of the prophets as they ought. For example's sake, I will repeat some prophetic passages, so that you may understand what I say. When he speaks by Isaiah, "He was led as a sheep to the slaughter, and like a lamb before the shearer" (Isa 53:7), he speaks as if the suffering had already taken place. And when he says again, "I have stretched out my hands to a disobedient and gainsaying people" (Isa 65:2), and when he says, "Lord, who has believed our report?" (Isa 53:1)—the words are spoken as if announcing events that had already come to pass. For I have shown that Christ is oftentimes called a stone in parable, and in figurative speech Jacob and Israel. And again, when he says, "I will behold the heavens, the works of my fingers" (Ps 8:3), unless I understand his method of using words, I will not understand intelligently. Instead I will understand like your teachers, who suppose that the Father of all, the unbegotten God, has hands and feet, and fingers, and a soul, like a composite being; and they for this reason teach that it was the Father himself who appeared to Abraham and to Jacob. Blessed therefore are we who have been circumcised the second time with knives of stone. For your first circumcision was and is performed by iron instruments, for you remain hard-hearted; but our circumcision, which is the second, having been instituted after yours, circumcises us from idolatry and from absolutely every kind of wickedness by sharp stones, that is, by the words from the apostles of the cornerstone cut out without hands. And our hearts are thus circumcised from evil, so that we are happy to die for the name of the good Rock, which causes living water to burst forth for the hearts of those who by him have loved the Father of all, and which gives the water of life to those who desire to drink it. But you do not comprehend me when I speak these things; for you have not understood what it has been prophesied that Christ would do, and you do not believe us who draw your attention to what has been written. For Jeremiah cries: "Woe unto you! You have forsaken the living fountain and have dug for yourselves broken cisterns that can hold no water. Shall there be a wilderness where Mount Zion is, because I gave Jerusalem a bill of divorce in your sight?" (Jer 2:13).

[...]

On Christians as the Children of Abraham, the True Israel, and Children of God

119

JUSTIN: Would you suppose, sirs, that we could ever have understood these matters in the Scriptures if we had not received grace to discern them by the will of him whose pleasure it was? This is so that the saying of Moses might come to pass, "They provoked me with strange [gods], they provoked me to anger with their abominations. They sacrificed to demons whom they knew not; new gods that came newly up, whom their fathers knew not. You have forsaken the God that begat you and forgotten the God that brought you up. And the Lord saw, and was jealous, and was provoked to anger by reason of the rage of his sons and daughters; and he said, 'I will turn my face away from them, and I will show what will come on them at the last; for it is a very contrary generation, children in whom there is no faith. They have moved me to jealousy with that which is not God, they have provoked me to anger with their idols; and I will move them to jealousy with that which is not a nation, I will provoke them to anger with a foolish people. For a fire is kindled from my anger, and it will burn to hades. It will consume the earth and her increase and set on fire the foundations of the mountains; I will heap mischief on them'" (Deut 32:16–23). And after that Righteous One was put to death, we flourished as another people, and shot forth as new and prosperous corn; as the prophets said, "And many nations will join themselves to the Lord in that day as a people; and they will dwell in the midst of all the earth" (Zech 2:11). But we are not only a people, but also a holy people, as we have shown already. "And they will call them the holy people, redeemed by the Lord" (Isa 62:12). Therefore, we are not a people to be despised, nor a barbarous race, nor such as the Carian and Phrygian nations; but God has even chosen us, and he has become manifest to those who had previously not sought after him. "Behold, I am God," he says, "to the nation that did not call on my name" (Isa 65:1). For this is the nation that God in the times of old promised to Abraham, when he declared that he would make him a father of many nations; not meaning, however, the Arabians, or Egyptians, or Idumaeans, since Ishmael became the father of a mighty nation, and so did Esau; and there is now a great number of Ammonites. Noah, moreover, was the father of Abraham, and in fact of all men; and others were the ancestors of others. What larger measure of grace, then, did Christ bestow on Abraham? This, namely, that he called him with his voice, telling him to leave the land where he dwelt. And he has called all of us by that voice, and we have left already the way of living in which we used to spend our days, passing our time in evil after the fashions of the other inhabitants of the earth. And along with Abraham we will inherit the holy land, when we will receive the inheritance for an endless eternity, being children of Abraham through the same faith. For as he believed the voice of God, and it was counted to him as righteousness, in like manner we, having believed God's voice spoken by the apostles of Christ, and promulgated to us by the prophets, have renounced even to death all the things of the world. Accordingly, he promises to him a nation of similar faith, God-fearing, righteous, and delighting the Father; but it is not you, "in whom there is no faith" (Deut 32:20).

[...]

123

JUSTIN: As, therefore, all these latter prophecies refer to Christ and the nations, you should believe that the former refer to him and them in like manner. For the proselytes have no need of a covenant, if, since there is one and the same Law imposed on all that are circumcised, the Scripture speaks about them in this way: "And the stranger will also be joined with them and will be joined to the house of Jacob" (Isa 14:1). The proselyte, who is circumcised so that he may have access to the people, becomes like one of themselves; but we who have been deemed worthy to be called a people remain Gentiles because we have not been circumcised. It is ridiculous for you to imagine that the eyes of the proselytes are to be opened while your own are not, and that they will be enlightened while you are blind and deaf. And it will be still more ridiculous for you if you say that the Law has been given to the nations, but you have not known it. For you would have stood in awe of God's wrath and would not have been lawless, wandering sons; being much afraid of hearing God say about you: "Children in whom there is no faith. And who are blind, but my servants? And deaf, but they that rule over them? And the servants of God have been made blind. You see often, but you have not observed; your ears have been opened, and you have not heard" (Deut 32:20; Isa 42:19). Is God's commendation of you honorable? And is God's testimony proper for his servants? You are not ashamed though you often hear these words. You do not tremble at God's threats, for you are a foolish and hard-hearted people. "Therefore, behold, I will proceed to remove this people," says the Lord; "and I will remove them, and destroy the wisdom of the wise, and hide the understanding of the prudent" (Isa 29:14). Deservedly too; for you are neither wise nor prudent but crafty and unscrupulous; wise only to do evil, but utterly incompetent to know the hidden counsel of God, or the faithful covenant of the Lord, or to find out the everlasting paths. "Therefore, says the Lord, I will raise up to Israel and to Judah the seed of men and the seed of beasts" (Jer 31:27). And by Isaiah he speaks thus about another Israel: "In that day will there be a third Israel among the Assyrians and the Egyptians, blessed in the land that the Lord of Sabaoth has blessed, saying, blessed will my people in Egypt and in Assyria be, and Israel will be my inheritance" (Isa 19:24). Since then, God blesses this people, and calls them Israel, and declares them to be his inheritance, how is it that you do not repent of the deception you practice on yourselves, as if you alone were the [true] Israel, and do not repent of loathing the people whom God has blessed? For when he speaks to Jerusalem and its surrounding area, he thus adds: "And I will beget men upon you, even my people Israel; and they will take possession of you, and you will be a possession to them; and you will no longer be childless by them" (Ezek 36:12).

TRYPHO: Are you saying that you are Israel? And that God speaks such things of you?

JUSTIN: If we had not entered into a lengthy discussion on these topics, I might have doubted whether you ask this question in ignorance; but since we have brought the matter to a conclusion by demonstration and with your assent, I do not believe that you are ignorant of what I have just said, or desire again mere contention, but that you are urging me to exhibit the same proof to these men. Again in Isaiah, if you have ears to hear it, God, speaking of Christ in parable, calls him Jacob and Israel. He speaks thus: "Jacob is my servant, I will uphold him; Israel is my elect, I will put my Spirit upon him, and he will bring forth judgment to the gentiles. He will not strive nor cry; neither will anyone hear his voice in the street. A bruised reed he will not break, and smoking flax he will not quench; but he will bring forth judgment to truth; he will shine and will not be broken until he has set judgment on the earth. And in his name will the gentiles trust" (Isa 42:1–4). Therefore, as from the one man, Jacob, who was surnamed Israel, all your nation has been called Jacob and Israel; so we from Christ, who begat us to God, like Jacob, and Israel, and Judah, and Joseph, and David, are called and are the true sons of God and keep the commandments of Christ.

124

When Justin saw that they were upset because he said that Christians are the sons of God, he anticipated their questioning.

JUSTIN: Listen, sirs, how the Holy Spirit speaks of this people, saying that they are all sons of the Highest and how this very Christ will be present in their assembly, rendering judgment to all men. The words are spoken by David, and they are, according to your version of them, thus: "God stands in the congregation of gods; he judges among the gods. How long do you judge unjustly, and accept the persons of the wicked? Judge for the orphan and the poor; do justice to the humble and needy. Deliver the needy; save the poor out of the hand of the wicked. They do not know; nor have they understood. They walk in darkness. All the foundations of the earth will be shaken. I said, 'You are gods, and are all children of the Most High. But you die like men, and you fall like one of the princes.' Arise, O God! Judge the earth, for you shall inherit all nations" (Ps 82). But it is written in the version of the seventy,[9] "Behold, you die like men, and you fall like one of the princes," in order to highlight the disobedience of men—I mean of Adam and Eve—and the fall of one of the princes, that is, of him who was called the serpent, who fell with a great overthrow because he deceived Eve. But as my discourse is not intended to touch on this point, but is intended to prove to you that the Holy Spirit reproaches men because they were made like God, free from suffering and death, provided that they kept his commandments, and were deemed deserving of the name of his sons, and yet they, becoming like Adam and Eve, work out death for themselves—let the interpretation of the Psalm be held just as you wish, yet thereby it is demonstrated that all men are deemed worthy of becoming "gods" and of having power to become sons of the Highest, and that all men will be each by themselves judged and condemned like Adam and Eve. Now I have proved at length that Christ is called God.

[...]

On Christ's Divinity and the Word as Begotten of the Father

126

JUSTIN: But if you knew, Trypho, who he is that is called at one time the Angel of great counsel, and a Man by Ezekiel, and like the Son of man by Daniel, and a Child by Isaiah, and Christ and God to be worshipped by David, and Christ and a Stone by many, and Wisdom by Solomon, and Joseph and Judah and a Star by Moses, and the East by Zechariah, and the Suffering One and Jacob and Israel by Isaiah again, and a Rod, and Flower, and Cornerstone, and Son of God, you would not have blasphemed him who has now come, and been

---

9 That is, the Septuagint (LXX).

born, and suffered, and ascended to heaven, and who will also come again, and then your twelve tribes will mourn. For if you had understood what has been written by the prophets, you would not have denied that he was God, Son of the only, unbegotten, unutterable God. For Moses says somewhere in Exodus the following: "The Lord spoke to Moses and said to him, 'I am the Lord, and I appeared to Abraham, to Isaac, and to Jacob, being their God; and my name I revealed not to them, and I established my covenant with them'" (Exod 6:2). And again, he says, "A man wrestled with Jacob" (Gen 32:24), and he asserts it was God. Jacob said about that, "I have seen God face to face, and my life is preserved" (Gen 32:30). And it is recorded that he called the place where he wrestled with him, appeared to and blessed him, the Face of God (Peniel). And Moses says that God also appeared to Abraham near the oak in Mamre, when he was sitting at the door of his tent at midday. Then he goes on to say: "And he lifted up his eyes and looked, and behold, three men stood before him; and when he saw them, he ran to meet them" (Gen 18:2). After a little while, one of them promises a son to Abraham: "Why did Sarah laugh, saying, 'Will I really bear a child, now that I am old?' Is anything impossible with God? At the time appointed I will return, according to the time of life, and Sarah will have a son. And they went away from Abraham" (Gen 18:13). Again, he speaks of them this way: "And the men rose up from there and looked toward Sodom" (Gen 18:16). Then to Abraham he who was and is again speaks: "I will not hide from Abraham, my servant, what I intend to do" (Gen 18:17). I have demonstrated from the writings of Moses that he who is described as God appeared to Abraham, to Isaac, and to Jacob, and the other patriarchs, was appointed under the authority of the Father and Lord, and ministers to his will. And so, when the people desired to eat flesh, and Moses had lost faith in him, who also there is called the Angel, and who promised that God would give them to satiety, he who is both God and the Angel, sent by the Father, is described as saying and doing these things. For the Scripture says: "And the Lord said to Moses, 'Will the Lord's hand not be sufficient? You will know now whether my word will conceal you or not'" (Num 11:23). And again, in other words, it says: "But the Lord spoke to me: 'You will not cross over the Jordan.' The Lord your God, who goes before your face, he will cut off the nations" (Deut 31:2).

127

JUSTIN: These and other such sayings are recorded by the lawgiver and by the prophets, and I suppose that I have stated sufficiently that wherever God says, "God went up from Abraham" (Gen 18:22), or, "The Lord spoke to Moses" (Exod 6:29), and "The Lord came down to behold the tower that the sons of men had built" (Gen 11:5), or when "God shut Noah into the ark" (Gen 7:16), you must not imagine that the unbegotten God himself came down or went up from any place. For the ineffable Father and Lord of all neither has come to any place, nor walks, nor sleeps, nor rises; but he remains in his own place, wherever that is, quick to behold and quick to hear, having neither eyes nor ears, but being of indescribable might. He sees all things, and knows all things, and none of us escapes his observation; and he is not moved or confined to a spot in the whole world, for he existed before the world was made. How, then, could he talk with any one, or be seen by any one, or appear on the smallest portion of the earth, when the people at Sinai were not able to look even on the glory of him who was sent from him; and Moses himself could not enter into the tabernacle that he had erected when it was filled with the glory of God; and the priest could not endure to stand before the temple when Solomon conveyed the ark into the house in Jerusalem that he had built for it? Therefore, neither Abraham, nor Isaac, nor Jacob, nor any other man, saw the Father and ineffable Lord of all, and also of Christ, but [saw] him who was according to his will his Son, being God, and the Angel because he ministered to his will; whom also it pleased him to be born man by the Virgin; who also was fire when he conversed with Moses from the bush. Since, unless we comprehend the Scriptures in this way, it must follow that the Father and Lord of all had not been in heaven when what Moses wrote took place: "And the Lord rained on Sodom and Gomorrah fire and brimstone from the Lord out of heaven" (Gen 19:24); and again, when it is said by David: "Lift up your gates, you rulers; and be lifted up, you everlasting gates; and the King of glory will enter" (Ps 24:7), and again, when he says: "The Lord says to my Lord: 'Sit at my right hand until I make your enemies your footstool'" (Ps 110:1).

128

JUSTIN: And that Christ is Lord, and God the Son of God, and appeared formerly in power as Man, and Angel, and in the glory of fire as at the bush, and also was manifested at the judgment executed on Sodom, has been demonstrated fully by what has been said.

Then Justin repeated all that he had previously quoted from Exodus, about the vision in the bush, and the naming of Joshua (Jesus), and continued:

JUSTIN: And do not suppose, sirs, that I am speaking superfluously when I repeat these words frequently. I do this because I know that some wish to anticipate these remarks and to say that the power sent from the Father of all—which appeared to Moses, or to Abraham, or to Jacob, is called an Angel because he came to men (for by him the commands of the Father have been proclaimed to men)—is called Glory because he appears in a vision sometimes that cannot be borne, is called a Man and a human being because he appears arrayed in such forms as the Father pleases, and they call him the Word because he carries tidings from the Father to men. But they teach that this power is indivisible and inseparable from the Father, just as they say that the light of the sun on earth is indivisible and inseparable from the sun in the heavens, as when it sinks, the light sinks along with it, so the Father, when he chooses, they say, causes his power to spring forth, and when he chooses, he makes it return to himself. In this way, they teach, he made the angels. But it is proved that there are angels who always exist and are never reduced to the form out of which they sprang. And that this power, which the prophetic word calls God, as has been also amply demonstrated, and Angel, is not numbered [as different] in name only like the light of the sun, but is indeed something numerically distinct, I have discussed briefly in what has gone before. I did this when I asserted that this power was begotten from the Father by his power and will, but not by abscission, as if the essence of the Father were divided, as all other things partitioned and divided are not the same after as before they were divided. As an example of this, I took the case of fires kindled from a fire: the kindled fires are distinct from the original fire, and yet, even though the original fire can kindle many fires from itself, it is by no means made less [by kindling other fires] but remains the same.

[...]

On Jacob's Marriages as Types for Judaism and the Church

134

JUSTIN: If then, the teaching of the prophets and of God moves you, it is better for you to follow God than your imprudent and blind masters, who even until this time permit each man to have four or five wives. And if anyone sees a beautiful woman and desires to have her, they quote the doings of Jacob [called] Israel, and of the other patriarchs, and maintain that it is not wrong to do such things because they are miserably ignorant in this matter. For, as I before said, certain dispensations of weighty mysteries were accomplished in each act of this sort. For in the marriages of Jacob I will mention what dispensation and prophecy were accomplished, in order that you may thereby know that your teachers never looked at the divine motive that prompted each act, but only at the groveling and corrupting passions. Attend therefore to what I say. The marriages of Jacob were types of that which Christ was about to accomplish. For it was not lawful for Jacob to marry two sisters at once. And he served Laban for [one of] the daughters; and being deceived in [the obtaining of] the younger, he again served seven years. Now Leah is your people and synagogue, but Rachel is our church. And for these, and for the servants in both, Christ even now serves. For while Noah gave to the two sons the seed of the third as servants, now on the other hand Christ has come to restore both the free sons and the servants amongst them, conferring the same honor on all of them who keep his commandments, even as the children of the free women and the children of the bond women born to Jacob were all sons and equal in dignity. And it was foretold what each should be according to rank and according to foreknowledge. Jacob served Laban for speckled and many-spotted sheep; and Christ served, even to the slavery of the cross, for the various and many-formed races of mankind, acquiring them by the blood and mystery of the cross. Leah was weak-eyed, for the eyes of your souls are excessively weak. Rachel stole the gods of Laban and has hidden them to this day; and we have lost our paternal and material gods. Jacob was hated for all time by his brother; and we now, and our Lord himself, are hated by you and by all men, though we are brothers by nature. Jacob was called Israel; and Israel has been demonstrated to be the Christ, who is, and is called, Jesus.

135

JUSTIN: And when Scripture says, "I am the Lord God, the Holy One of Israel, who has made known Israel your King" (Isa 43:15), will you not understand that truly Christ is the everlasting King? For you are aware that Jacob, the son of Isaac, was never a king. And therefore, Scripture again, explaining to us, says what king is meant by Jacob and Israel: "Jacob is my Servant; I will uphold him. And Israel is my Elect; my soul will receive him. I have given him my Spirit, and he will bring forth judgment to the gentiles. He will not cry aloud, and his voice will not be heard outside. The bruised reed he will not break, and the smoking flax he will not quench, until he will bring forth judgment to victory. He will shine, and he will not be broken until he set judgment on the earth. And in his name will the gentiles trust" (Isa 42:1–4). Then is it Jacob the patriarch in whom the gentiles and yourselves will trust? Or is it not Christ? As, therefore, Christ is the Israel and the Jacob, even so we, who have been quarried out from the side of Christ, are the true Israelite race. But let us attend rather to the very word: "And I will bring forth," he says, "the seed out of Jacob, and out of Judah; and it will inherit my holy mountain; and my Elect and my servants will possess the inheritance and will dwell there; and there will be folds of flocks in the thicket, and the valley of Achor will be a resting-place of cattle for the people who have sought me. But as for you, who forsake me, and forget my holy mountain, and prepare a table for demons, and fill a mixed drink for the demons, I will give you to the sword. You will all fall by slaughter; for I called you, and you did not answer, and you did evil before me, and you chose the things I did not desire" (Isa 65:9–12). Such are the words of Scripture; understand, therefore, that the seed of Jacob now referred to is something else, and not, as may be supposed, spoken of your people. For it is not possible for the seed of Jacob to leave an entrance for the descendants of Jacob, or for [God] to have accepted the very same persons whom he had reproached with unfitness for the inheritance and to promise it to them again. But as the prophet says, "And now, O house of Jacob, come and let us walk in the light of the Lord; for he has sent away his people, the house of Jacob, because their land was full, as at the beginning, of soothsayers and divinations" (Isa 2:5), even so it is necessary for us here to observe that there are two seeds of Judah, and two races, as there are two houses of Jacob: the one begotten by flesh and blood, the other by faith and the Spirit.

[…]

On Noah as a Type of Christ

138

JUSTIN: You know, then, sirs, that God has said in Isaiah to Jerusalem: "I saved you in the flood of Noah" (cf. Isa 54:9). By this, God meant that the mystery of saved men appeared in the flood. For righteous Noah, along with the other mortals at the flood, that is, with his own wife, his three sons and their wives, being eight in number, were a symbol of the eighth day, which was the day Christ appeared when he rose from the dead, forever the first in power. For Christ, being the first-born of every creature, became again the chief of another race regenerated by himself through water, and faith, and wood, containing the mystery of the cross—just as Noah was saved by wood when he rode over the waters with his household. Accordingly, when the prophet says, "I saved you in the times of Noah," as I have already remarked, he addresses the people who are equally faithful to God and possess the same signs. For when Moses had the rod in his hands, he led your nation through the sea.

And you believe that this was spoken to your nation only or to the land. But the whole earth, as the Scripture says, was inundated, and the water rose in height fifteen cubits above all the mountains, so that it is evident this was not spoken to the land but to the people who obeyed him—the people for whom he had also before prepared a resting-place in Jerusalem, as was previously demonstrated by all the symbols of the flood (I mean, that by water, faith, and wood, those who are prepared beforehand, and who repent of the sins that they have committed, will escape from the impending judgment of God).

139

JUSTIN: For another mystery was accomplished and predicted in the days of Noah, of which you are not aware. It is this: in the blessings that Noah blessed his two sons, and in the curse pronounced on his son's son. For the Spirit of prophecy would not curse the son that had been blessed by God along with [his brothers]. But since the punishment of the sin would cling to all the descendants of the son that mocked at his father's nakedness, he made the curse originate with his son. Now, in what he said, he foretold that the descendants of Shem would keep in retention the property and dwellings of Canaan, and again that the descendants of Japheth would take possession of the property of which Shem's descendants had dispossessed Canaan's descendants, and spoil the descendants of Shem, even as they plundered the sons of Canaan. And listen to the way in which it has so come to pass. For you, who have derived your lineage from Shem, invaded the territory of the sons of Canaan by the will of God; and you possessed it. And it is manifest that the sons of Japheth, having invaded you in turn by the judgment of God, have taken your land from you and have possessed it. Thus, it is written: "And Noah awoke from the wine and knew what his younger son had done to him; and he said, 'Cursed be Canaan, the servant; he will be a servant to his brothers and sisters.' And he said, 'Blessed be the Lord God of Shem; and Canaan will be his servant. May the Lord enlarge Japheth and let him dwell in the houses of Shem; and let Canaan be his servant'" (Gen 9:24–27). Accordingly, as two peoples were blessed (those from Shem, and those from Japheth), and as the offspring of Shem were decreed first to possess the dwellings of Canaan, and the offspring of Japheth were predicted as in turn receiving the same possessions, and to the two peoples there was the one people of Canaan handed over for servants—so, Christ has come according to the power given to him from the Almighty Father; and Christ, summoning men to friendship, and blessing, and repentance, and dwelling together, has promised, as has already been proved, that there will be a future possession for all the saints in this same land. And hence all men everywhere, whether bond or free, who believe in Christ and recognize the truth in his own words and those of his prophets, know that they will be with him in that land, and inherit everlasting and incorruptible good.

[...]

On Free Will in Humans and Angels

141

JUSTIN: But so that you may not have a pretext for saying that Christ must have been crucified, and that those who transgressed must have been among your nation, and that the matter could not have been otherwise, I said briefly by anticipation, that God, wishing men and angels to follow his will, resolved to create them free to do righteousness. He let them possess reason so that they may know by whom they are created, and through whom they, not existing formerly, do now exist; and he gave them a law so that they should be judged by him if they do anything contrary to right reason. And we, men and angels, will be convicted of having acted sinfully, unless we repent beforehand. But if the word of God foretells that some angels and men will be certainly punished, it did so because it foreknew that they would be unchangeably [wicked], but not because God had created them so. All who wish for mercy from God can obtain it, if they repent. And the Scripture foretells that they will be blessed, saying, "Blessed is the man to whom the Lord does not impute sin" (Ps 32:2); that is, having repented of his sins, so that he may receive remission of them from God. And this is not as you deceive yourselves and some others who resemble you in this, who say, that even though they be sinners, but know God, the Lord will not impute sin to them. As proof of this, we have the fall of David, which happened through his boasting, but was forgiven when he so mourned and wept, as it is written. But if even to such a man [as David], no remission was granted before repentance, and only when this great king, and anointed one, and prophet, mourned and conducted himself so, how can the impure and utterly abandoned, if they do not weep and mourn and repent, entertain the hope that the Lord will not impute to them sin? And this fall of David, in the matter of Uriah's wife, proves, sirs, that the patriarchs had many wives, not to commit fornication, but that a certain dispensation and all mysteries might be accomplished by them; since, if it was allowable to take any wife, or as many wives as one chooses and how he chooses, which the men of your nation do over all the earth, wherever they sojourn, or wherever they have been sent, taking women under the name of marriage, much more would David have been permitted to do this.[10]

Conclusion

142

TRYPHO: You see that it was not intentionally that we came to discuss these points. And I confess that I have been particularly pleased with the discussion; and I think that these men are of quite the same opinion as myself. For we have found more than we expected, and more than it was possible to have expected. And if we could do this more frequently, we should be much helped in the searching of the Scriptures themselves. But since you are on the eve of departure, and expect daily to set sail, do not hesitate to remember us as friends when you are gone.

JUSTIN: For my part, if I had remained, I would have wished to do the same thing daily. But now, since I expect, with God's will and aid, to set sail, I exhort you to give all diligence in this very great struggle for your own salvation, and to be earnest in setting a higher value on the Christ of the Almighty God than on your own teachers.

After this they left Trypho, wishing him safety on his voyage and from every misfortune. And Justin, praying for them, said:

JUSTIN: I can wish no better thing for you, sirs, than this, that, recognizing in this way that intelligence is given to every man, you may be of the same opinion as we are, and believe that Jesus is the Christ of God.

---

10 The narrative includes the following line, which indicates its addressee (a certain Marcus Pompeius): "When I had said this, dearest Marcus Pompeius, I came to an end."

Tatian the Syrian: Address to the Greeks

Context
Author: Tatian
Provenance: Rome[1]
Date: 158–160

On Civil Obedience and the Worship of God Alone

4

Why, men of Greece, do you want to bring the civil powers violently against us? And, if I am not disposed to comply with certain practices of some of them, is that a sufficient reason for me to be abhorred as a vile miscreant? Does the sovereign [emperor] order the payment of tribute? I am ready to render it. Does my master command me to act as a bondsman and to serve? I acknowledge my service. Man is to be honored as a fellow man; God alone is to be feared—God who is not visible to human eyes nor can be comprehended. I will only refuse to obey [the empire] if I am commanded to deny God. If that happens, I will rather die than show myself false and ungrateful. Our God did not begin to exist in time. He alone is without beginning, and he himself is the beginning of all things. God is a Spirit (John 4:24), not pervading matter, but the Maker of material spirits and of the forms that are in matter. He is invisible, intangible, being himself the Father of both sensible and invisible

---

1 See Emily J. Hunt, *Christianity in the Second Century: The Case of Tatian* (Routledge, 2003), 1–3 for the work's provenance and Tatian's biography. The monograph also seeks to locate Tatian within various second century "streams" of the Christian faith.

things. We know him from his creation, and we apprehend his invisible power by his works (Rom 1:20). I refuse to adore any workmanship that he has made for our sakes. The sun and moon were made for us; how, then, can I adore my own servants? How can I speak of sticks and stones as gods? For the spirit that pervades matter is inferior to the more divine Spirit; and this spirit, being on the level of matter,[2] is not to be honored equally with the perfect God. Nor should even the ineffable God be presented with gifts; for he who needs nothing is not to be misrepresented by us as though he were needy. But I will set forth our views more distinctly.

On the Logos and the Creation of the World

5

God was in the beginning; and the beginning, we have been taught, is the power of the Word. For the Lord of the universe, who is himself the necessary ground of all being, was alone, inasmuch as no creature was yet in existence. But, inasmuch as he was all power, himself the necessary ground of things visible and invisible, all things were [established] through the powerful Word. The Word himself also, who was in [God], subsists. And by his simple will the Word springs forth; and the Word, not coming forth in vain, becomes the first-begotten work of the Father. We know the Word to be the beginning of the world. But he came into being by participation, not by abscission; for what is cut off is separated from the original substance, but that which comes by participation, making its choice of function, does not render him deficient from whom it is taken. For just as from one torch many fires are lighted, but the light of the first torch is not lessened by the kindling of many torches, so also the Word coming forth from the power of the Father does not deprive the begetter of the power of rational speech.[3] I myself, for instance, talk, and you hear; yet, certainly, I who converse do not become destitute of speech by the transmission of speech,[4] but by the utterance of my voice I endeavor to reduce to order the unarranged matter in your minds. And as the Word, begotten in the beginning, begat in turn our world, having first created for himself the necessary matter, so also I, in imitation of the Word, being begotten again, and having become possessed of the truth, am trying to reduce to order the confused matter which is kindred with myself. For matter is not, like God,

---
2 Following Molly Whittaker, *Tatian: Oratio ad Graecos and Fragments* (Oxford University Press, 1982), 9.
3 This phrase follows ibid., 11.
4 The word for "speech" is λόγος, the same Greek word translated as "Word."

without beginning, nor, as having no beginning, is of equal power with God. It is begotten and not produced by any other being, but brought into existence by the Framer of all things alone.

On the Resurrection

6

And on this account, we believe that there will be a resurrection of bodies after the consummation of all things. It will not be as the Stoics affirm (according to the return of certain cycles, the same things being produced and destroyed for no useful purpose), but it will be a resurrection once for all, when our periods of existence are completed, and in consequence solely of the constitution of things under which men alone live, for the purpose of passing judgment upon them. This sentence is not passed by Minos or Rhadamanthus, before whose death not a single soul, according to the mythic tales, was judged; instead, the Creator, God himself, becomes the arbiter. And, although you regard us as mere triflers and babblers, it does not trouble us, since we have faith in this doctrine. For just as before I was born, I did not know who I was and only existed in the potentiality of fleshly matter, but being born, after a former state of nothingness, I have obtained through my birth a certainty of my existence. In the same way, having been born, and through death existing no longer, and seen no longer, I will exist again, just as before I was not, but was afterward born. Even if all traces of my flesh are destroyed by fire and the world receives the vaporized matter, or they are dispersed through rivers and seas, or they are torn in pieces by wild beasts, I am preserved in the storehouses of a wealthy Lord. And, although the poor and the godless do not know what is stored up, the Sovereign God, when he pleases, will restore the substance that is visible to him alone to its pristine condition.

On the Creation and Fall of Human Beings

7

For the heavenly Word, made spirit from the Spirit and Word from the power of the Word,[5] in imitation of the Father who begat him, made man an image of immortality, so that, as incorruption is with God, in like manner, man, sharing in a part of God, might have the immortal principle also. The Word,

---

5 Following ibid., 13.

too, before the creation of men, was the Framer of angels. And each of these two orders of creatures was made free to act as it pleased, not having the nature of good, which again is with God alone, but is brought to perfection in men through their freedom of choice, in order that the bad man may be justly punished, having become depraved through his own fault, but the just man be deservedly praised for his virtuous deeds, since in the exercise of his free choice he refrained from transgressing the will of God. Such is the constitution of things in reference to angels and men. And the power of the Word, having in itself a faculty to foresee future events, not as fated, but as taking place by the choice of free agents, foretold from time to time the issues of things to come; it also became a forbidder of wickedness by means of prohibitions, and the praiser of those who remained good. And, when men attached themselves to one who was more subtle than the rest, having regard to his being the first-born (Gen 3:1), and declared him to be God, though he was resisting the Law of God, then the power of the Word excluded the beginner of the folly and his adherents from all fellowship with himself. And so, he who was made in the likeness of God, since the more powerful spirit was separated from him, became mortal. But that first-begotten one through his transgression and ignorance became a demon; and they who imitated him, that is his illusions, became a host of demons, and through their freedom of choice they have been given up to their own infatuation.

[...]

On the Question of the Soul's Immortality

13

The soul is not in itself immortal, O Greeks, but mortal. Yet it is possible for it not to die. If it does not know the truth, it dies and is dissolved with the body. When this happens, it rises again at the end of the world with the body, receiving death by punishment in immortality. But, if it acquires the knowledge of God, it does not die, although for a time it will be dissolved. In itself there is darkness, and there is nothing luminous in it. And this is the meaning of the saying, "The darkness did not overcome the light" (John 1:5). For the soul does not preserve the spirit, but is preserved by it, and the light overcomes the darkness. The Word, in truth, is the light of God, but the ignorant soul is darkness. On this account, if it continues alone, it tends downward toward matter and dies with the flesh; but, if it enters into union with the Divine Spirit, it is no longer helpless, but it ascends to the regions to which the Spirit guides it; for the dwelling-place of the Spirit is above, but the origin of the soul is from beneath. Now, in the beginning the Spirit was a constant companion of the soul, but the Spirit left it because it was not willing to follow. Yet, the soul, retaining as it were a spark of its power though unable by reason of the separation to discern the perfect, while seeking for God it fashioned to itself in its wandering many gods, following the sophistries of the demons. But the Spirit of God is not with all, but, taking up its abode with those who live justly, and intimately combining with the soul [of these persons], by prophecies it announced hidden things to other souls. And the souls that are obedient to wisdom have attracted to themselves the kindred Spirit; but the disobedient, rejecting the minister of the suffering God, have shown themselves to be fighters against God rather than his worshippers.

On Demons

14

And such are you also, O Greeks. You are profuse in words, but with minds strangely warped; and you acknowledge the dominion of many rather than the rule of the one [God], accustoming yourselves to follow demons as if they were mighty. For, as the inhuman robber is accustomed to overpowering those like himself by daring; so the demons, going to great lengths in wickedness, have utterly deceived the souls among you which are left to themselves by ignorance and false appearances. These beings do not indeed die easily, for they do not partake of flesh; but while living they practice the ways of death and die themselves as often as they teach their followers to sin. Therefore, what is now their chief distinction, that they do not die like men, they will retain when about to suffer punishment: they will not partake of everlasting life nor receive it instead of death in a blessed immortality. And as we [humans], to whom it now easily happens to die, afterward receive either immortality with enjoyment or immortality with pain, so the demons, who abuse the present life for the purposes of wrongdoing, dying continually even while they live, will hereafter have the same immortality, like that which they had during the time they lived, but the nature of this immortality will be like that of the men who voluntarily performed what the demons prescribed to them during their lifetime. And [compared to the demons] do not fewer kinds of sin break out among men because of the brevity of their lives? Are not the transgressions of the demons more abundant because of their boundless existence?

On Union with God

15

But further, it is now right for us to seek what we once had but have lost: to unite the soul with the Holy Spirit and to strive after union with God. The human soul consists of many parts and is not simple; it is composite, so as to manifest itself through the body. For neither could it ever appear by itself without the body, nor does the flesh rise again without the soul. Man is not, as the croaking philosophers say, merely a rational animal, capable of understanding and knowledge; for, according to them, even irrational creatures appear possessed of understanding and knowledge. But man alone is the image and likeness of God; and I mean by man, not one who performs actions similar to those of animals, but one who has advanced far beyond mere humanity—to God himself. This question we have discussed more minutely in the treatise concerning animals.[6] But the principal point to be spoken of now is this: what is intended by the image and likeness of God. That which cannot be compared is no other than abstract Being; but that which is compared is no other than that which is like. The perfect God is without flesh; but man is flesh. The bond of the flesh is the soul; that which encloses the soul is the flesh. Such is the nature of man's constitution; and, if it be like a temple, God is pleased to dwell in it by the Spirit, his representative. But, if it be not such a habitation, man excels the wild beasts in articulate language only—in other respects his manner of life is like theirs, as one who is not a likeness of God. But none of the demons possess flesh; their structure is spiritual, like that of fire or air. And only by those whom the Spirit of God dwells in and fortifies are the bodies of the demons easily seen, not at all by others—I mean those who possess only soul; for the inferior has not the ability to apprehend the superior. On this account the nature of the demons has no place for repentance; for they are the reflection of matter and of wickedness. But matter desired to exercise lordship over the soul; and according to their free-will these gave laws of death to men; but men, after the loss of immortality, have conquered death by submitting to death in faith. And by repentance a call has been given to them, according to the word that says, "Since they were made a little lower than the angels" (Ps 8:5). And, for everyone who has been conquered, it is possible again to conquer, if he rejects the condition that brings death. And what that is, may be easily seen by men who long for immortality.

[...]

---

[6] Tatian's treatise on animals does not survive.

On Tatian's Conversion

29

Therefore, having seen these things, and moreover also having been admitted to the mysteries, and having everywhere examined the religious rites performed by the effeminate and the pathic, and having found among the Romans their Latiarian Jupiter delighting in human gore and the blood of slaughtered men, and Artemis not far from the great city sanctioning acts of the same kind, and one demon here and another there instigating to the perpetration of evil—retiring by myself, I sought how I might be able to discover the truth. And, while I was giving my most earnest attention to the matter, I happened to meet with certain barbaric writings, too old to be compared with the opinions of the Greeks, and too divine to be compared with their errors; and I was led to put faith in these by the unpretentious manner of the language, the inartificial character of the writers, the foreknowledge displayed of future events, the excellent quality of the precepts, and the declaration of the government of the universe as centered in one Being. And, my soul being taught of God, I discerned that the former class of writings lead to condemnation, but that these put an end to the slavery that is in the world and rescue us from a multiplicity of rulers and ten thousand tyrants, while they give us, not indeed what we had not before received, but what we had received but were prevented by error from retaining.

[...]

On Christian Philosophy as More Ancient than Greek Philosophy

31

But now it seems proper for me to demonstrate that our philosophy is older than the systems of the Greeks. Moses and Homer will be our limits, each of them being of great antiquity; the one being the oldest of poets and historians, and the other the founder of all barbarian wisdom. Let us, then, institute a comparison between them; and we will find that our doctrines are older, not only than those of the Greeks but than the invention of letters. And I will not bring forward witnesses from among ourselves, but rather have recourse to Greeks. To do the former would be foolish because it would not be allowed by you; but the other will surprise you, when, by contending against you

with your own weapons, I adduce arguments of which you had no suspicion.[7]
[...]

40.

Therefore, from what has been said, it is evident that Moses was older than the ancient heroes, wars, and demons. And we ought rather to believe him, who stands before them in terms of time, than the Greeks, who, without being aware of it, drew his doctrines as from a fountain. For many of the sophists among them, stimulated by curiosity, endeavored to adulterate whatever they learned from Moses and from those who have philosophized like him, first that they might be considered as having something of their own, and secondly, that covering up by a certain rhetorical artifice anything they did not understand, they might misrepresent the truth as if it were a fable. But what the learned among the Greeks have said concerning our polity and the history of our laws, and how many and what kind of men have written of these things, will be shown in the treatise against those who have discoursed of divine things.

[...]

Conclusion

42

These things, O Greeks, I Tatian, a disciple of the barbarian's philosophy, have composed for you. I was born in the land of the Assyrians, having been first instructed in your doctrines, and afterwards in those which I now undertake to proclaim. Now, knowing who God is and what his work is, I present myself to you prepared for an examination of my doctrines, while I adhere immovably to the mode of life that is according to God.

---

  7 In chapters 32–39, Tatian presents a timeline of persons and events that is intended to show that Moses preceded Homer. On this theme, see Arthur J. Droge, *Homer or Moses? Early Christian Interpretations of the History of Culture* (J.C.B. Mohr [Paul Siebeck], 1989).

18

ATHENAGORAS OF ATHENS: EMBASSY FOR THE CHRISTIANS

Context
Author: Athenagoras
Provenance: Athens[1]
Date: AD 177–180

To the Emperors Marcus Aurelius Antoninus and Lucius Aurelius Commodus, conquerors of Armenia and Sarmatia, and more than all, philosophers.

On the Mistreatment of Christians

1

In your empire, greatest of sovereigns, different nations have different customs and laws; and no one is hindered by law or fear of punishment from following his ancestral usages, however ridiculous these may be. A citizen of Ilium calls Hector a god, and pays divine honors to Helen, taking her for Adrasteia. The Lacedaemonian venerates Agamemnon as Zeus, and Phylonoe the daughter of Tyndarus; and the man of Tenedos worships Tennes. The Athenian sacrifices to Erechtheus as Poseidon. The Athenians also perform religious rites and celebrate mysteries in honor of Agraulus and Pandrosus, women who were deemed guilty of impiety for opening the box. In short, among every nation and people, men offer whatever sacrifices and celebrate whatever mysteries they please. The Egyptians reckon among their gods even

---

[1] See David Rankin, *Athenagoras: Philosopher and Theologian* (Ashgate, 2009), 23–25 for the work's provenance and an introduction to Athenagoras' thought.

cats, and crocodiles, and serpents, and asps, and dogs. And both you and the laws give permission to all of these, deeming, on the one hand, that to believe in no god at all is impious and wicked, and on the other, that it is necessary for each man to worship the gods he prefers, in order that through fear of the deity, men may be kept from wrongdoing. But do not be like the multitude that is led astray by hearsay. Why is a mere name repulsive to you? Names are not deserving of hatred; an unjust action is what calls for penalty and punishment. And accordingly, with admiration of your mildness and gentleness, and your peaceful and benevolent disposition toward every man, individuals live in the possession of equal rights; and the cities, according to their rank, share in equal honor; and the whole empire, under your intelligent sway, enjoys profound peace. But you have not cared in the same way for us who are called Christians. Although we commit no wrong (the sequel to this discourse will show that we, of all men, are most piously and righteously disposed toward the Deity and toward your government), you allow us to be harassed, plundered, and persecuted; the multitude makes war upon us for our name alone. We venture, therefore, to lay a statement of our case before you, and you will learn from this discourse that we suffer unjustly and contrary to all law and reason. We ask you to bestow some consideration upon us also, that at last we may cease to be slaughtered at the instigation of false accusers. For the fine imposed by our persecutors does not aim merely at our property, nor their insults at our reputation, nor the damage they do us at any other of our greater interests. These we hold in contempt, though to the generality they appear matters of great importance; for we have learned not only not to return blow for blow, nor to take to court those who plunder and rob us, but, to those who strike us on one side of the face, to offer the other side also, and, to those who take away our coat, to give also our cloak. But, when we have surrendered our property, they plot against our very bodies and souls, pouring upon us wholesale charges of crimes of which we are guiltless even in thought, but which belong to these idle talkers themselves, and to the whole tribe of those who are like them.

2

If, indeed, anyone can convict us of a crime, be it small or great, we do not ask to be excused from punishment, but are prepared to undergo the sharpest and most merciless inflictions. But if the accusation relates merely to our name—and it is undeniable, that up to the present time the stories told about us rest on nothing more than the common undiscriminating popular talk, nor has any Christian been convicted of a crime—it will befit you, illustrious and benevolent and most learned sovereigns, to remove by law this malicious treatment, so that, just as throughout the world both individuals and cities partake of your beneficence, we also may feel grateful to you, celebrating that we are no longer the victims of false accusation. For it does not comport with your justice that others, when charged with crimes, should not be punished until they are convicted, but that in our case the name we bear should have more force than the evidence produced at the trial, when the judges, instead of inquiring whether the person arraigned has committed any crime, vents their insults on the name, as if that were itself a crime. But no name in and of itself is reckoned either good or bad; names appear bad or good according to whether the actions underlying them are bad or good. You, however, have yourselves a clear understanding of this, since you are well instructed in philosophy and all learning. For this reason, too, those who are brought before you for trial, though they may be arraigned on the gravest charges, have no fear, because they know that you will inquire respecting their previous life and not be influenced by names if they mean nothing, nor by the charges contained in the indictments if they should be false. They accept with equal satisfaction, as regards its fairness, the sentence, whether of condemnation or acquittal. What, therefore, is conceded as the common right of all, we claim for ourselves, that we shall not be hated and punished because we are called Christians (for what has the name to do with our being bad men?). Instead, we should be tried on any charges that may be brought against us, and either be released on our disproving them, or punished if convicted of a crime—not tried for the name (for no Christian is a bad man unless he falsely professes our doctrines) but for the wrong that has been done. This is how we see the philosophers judged. Prior to the trial, one is not deemed by the judge either good or bad on account of his science or art. If he is found guilty of wickedness, he is punished, without thereby affixing any stigma on philosophy (for he is a bad man for not cultivating philosophy in a lawful manner, but science is blameless). If he refutes the false charges, he is acquitted. Let this equal justice, then, be done to us. Let the life of the accused persons be investigated, but let the name stand free from all imputation. I must at the outset of my defense entreat you, illustrious emperors, to listen to me impartially. Do not be carried away by the common irrational talk and prejudge the case. Instead, apply your desire of knowledge and love of truth to the examination of our doctrine also. Thus, while you on your part will not err through ignorance, we also, by disproving the charges arising out of the undiscerning rumor of the multitude, will cease to be assailed.

3

Three things are alleged against us: atheism, Thyestean feasts,[2] and Oedipodean intercourse.[3] But if these charges are true, spare no class: proceed at once against our crimes; destroy us, root and branch, with our wives and children, if any Christian is found to live like the brutes. And yet even the brutes do not touch the flesh of their own kind; they select mates by the law of nature, and only at the regular season—not from simple wantonness; they also recognize those from whom they receive benefits. If anyone, therefore, is more savage than the brutes, what punishment shall be deemed adequate to such offences? But, if these things are only idle tales and empty slanders, originating in the fact that virtue is opposed by its very nature to vice, and that opposites war against one another by a divine law (and you are yourselves witnesses that no such iniquities are committed by us, for you forbid information to be laid against us), it remains for you to make inquiry concerning our life, our opinions, our loyalty and obedience to you and your house and government, and thus at length to grant to us the same rights (we ask nothing more) as to those who persecute us. For we will then conquer them, unhesitatingly surrendering, as we now do, our very lives for the truth's sake.

4

As regards, first of all, the allegation that we are atheists (for I will meet the charges one by one, so that we may not be ridiculed for having no answer to give to those who make them), it was with good reason that the Athenians judged Diagoras guilty of atheism. Diogoras not only divulged the Orphic doctrine, and published the mysteries of Eleusis and of the Cabiri, and chopped up the wooden statue of Hercules to boil his turnips, but he openly declared that there was no God at all. But to us, who distinguish God from matter, and teach that matter is one thing and God another, and that they are separated by a wide interval (for the Deity is uncreated and eternal, to be beheld by the understanding and reason alone, while matter is created and perishable), is it not absurd to accuse us of atheism? If our views were like those of Diagoras while we have such incentives for piety (such as established order, the universal harmony, the magnitude, the color, the form, and the arrangement of the world), there would be good reason for our reputation of impiety to be charged against us, and there would be cause for our being thus

---

[2] A reference to cannibalism.
[3] A reference to incest.

harassed. But, since our doctrine acknowledges one God, the Maker of this universe, who is himself uncreated (for that which is does not come to be, but that which is not) but has made all things by the Word that is from him, we are treated unreasonably in both respects, in that we are both defamed and persecuted.

[...]

Against the Charge of Atheism: The Testimony of the Prophets

9

If we satisfied ourselves with advancing such considerations as these, some people might still view our doctrines as merely human. But, since the voices of the prophets confirm our arguments (for I think that you also, with your great zeal for knowledge, and your great attainments in learning, cannot be ignorant of the writings either of Moses or of Isaiah and Jeremiah, and the other prophets, who, lifted in ecstasy above the natural operations of their minds by the impulses of the Divine Spirit, uttered the things with which they were inspired, the Spirit making use of them as a flute-player breathes into a flute), what, then, do these men say? "The Lord is our God; no other can be compared with him" (Isa 41:4). And again: "I am God, the first and the last, and besides me there is no God" (Isa 44:6). In like manner: "Before me there was no other God, and after me there shall be none; I am God, and there is none besides me" (Isa 43:10–11). And as to his greatness: "Heaven is my throne, and the earth is my footstool; what house will you build for me, or where is my resting place?" (Isa 66:1). But I leave it to you, when you meet with the books themselves, to examine carefully the prophecies contained in them, that you may on fitting grounds defend us from the abuse cast upon us.

Against the Charge of Atheism: Christians Worship Father, Son, and Holy Spirit

10

That we are not atheists, therefore, seeing that we acknowledge one God, uncreated, eternal, invisible, impassible, incomprehensible, infinite, who is apprehended only by the understanding and the reason, who is encompassed by light, and beauty, and spirit, and power ineffable, by whom the universe has been created through his Word, and set in order, and is kept in being—I have sufficiently demonstrated. [I say "his" Word], for we also acknowledge a Son of God. Do not let anyone think it ridiculous that God should have a Son. For though the poets, in their fictions, represent the gods as no better than men, our mode of thinking is not the same as theirs, concerning either God the Father or the Son. But the Son of God is the Word of the Father, in idea and in operation; for after the pattern of him and by him were all things made, the Father and the Son being one. And the Son being in the Father, and the Father in the Son, in oneness and power of spirit, the understanding and reason of the Father is the Son of God. But if, in your surpassing intelligence, it occurs to you to inquire what is meant by the Son, I will state briefly that he is the first product of the Father, not as having been brought into existence (for from the beginning, God, who is the eternal mind, had the Word in himself, being from eternity rational), but inasmuch as he came forth to be the idea and energizing power of all material things, which lay like a nature without attributes, and an inactive earth, the heavier particles being mixed up with the lighter. The prophetic Spirit also agrees with our statements. "The Lord," it says, "made me, the beginning of his ways for his works" (Prov 8:22). The Holy Spirit himself also, which operates in the prophets, we assert to be an effluence of God, flowing from him and returning back again, like a beam of the sun. Who, then, would not be astonished to hear men who speak of God the Father, and of God the Son, and of the Holy Spirit, and who declare both their power in union and their distinction in order, called atheists? Nor is our teaching in what relates to the divine nature confined to these points; but we recognize also a multitude of angels and ministers (Heb 1:14), whom God the Maker and Framer of the world distributed and appointed to their various posts by his Word, to occupy themselves about the elements, and the heavens, and the world, and the things in it, and the good ordering of them all.

The Moral Teaching of the Christians Repels the Charge Brought Against Them

11

Do not be surprised if I go into the details of our doctrine. It is so that you may not be carried away by the popular and irrational opinion but may have the truth clearly before you. The opinions we adhere to are not human but uttered and taught by God; and by presenting them to you, we will be able to persuade you not to think of us as atheists. What, then, are the teachings in which we are brought up? "I say to you, love your enemies; bless those who curse you; pray for those who persecute you; that you may be the sons of your Father who is in heaven, who causes his sun to rise on the evil and the good, and sends rain on the just and the unjust" (Matt 5:44–45). Allow me here to lift up my voice boldly, in a loud and audible outcry, pleading as I do before philosophic princes. For who of those that reduce syllogisms, and clear up ambiguities, and explain etymologies, or of those who teach homonyms and synonyms, and predicaments and axioms, and what is the subject and what the predicate, and who promise their disciples by these and such like instructions to make them happy—who of them have so purged their souls as, instead of hating their enemies, to love them; and, instead of speaking ill of those who have reviled them (to abstain from which is of itself an evidence of forbearance), to bless them; and to pray for those who plot against their lives? On the contrary, they never cease with evil intent to search out skillfully the secrets of their art, and are ever bent on working some ill, making the art of words and not the exhibition of deeds their business and profession. But among us you will find uneducated persons, and artisans, and old women, who, if they are unable in words to prove the benefit of our doctrine, instead by their deeds exhibit the benefit arising from their persuasion of its truth. They do not rehearse speeches but exhibit good works. When struck, they do not strike back; when robbed, they do not go to court. They give to those that ask of them, and they love their neighbors as themselves.

Further Arguments Against the Accusation of Atheism

12

Unless we believed that a God presides over the human race, should we have any reason to purge ourselves from evil? Most certainly not. But, because we are persuaded that we will give an account of everything in the present life to God, who made us and the world, we adopt a temperate and benevolent and generally despised method of life, believing that we will suffer no such great evil here, even should our lives be taken from us, compared with what we will there receive for our meek and benevolent and moderate life from the great Judge. Plato indeed has said that Minos and Rhadamanthus will judge and punish the wicked; but we say that, even if a man be Minos or Rhadamanthus himself, or their father, even he will not escape the judgment of God. Are, then, those who consider life to be comprised in this, "Let us eat and drink, for tomorrow we die" (Isa 22:13), and who regard death as a deep sleep and forgetfulness ("sleep and death, twin brothers"),[4] to be regarded as pious? Especially while there are men who consider the present life of very small worth indeed, and who are conducted to the future life by this one thing alone, that they know God and his Word, what is the oneness of the Son with the Father, what is the communion of the Father with the Son, what is the Spirit, what is the unity of these three, the Spirit, the Son, the Father, and their distinction in unity; and who know that the life for which we look is far better than can be described in words, provided we arrive at it pure from all wrong-doing; who, moreover, carry our benevolence to such an extent that we love not merely those who are our friends ("for if you love them," he says, "that love you, and lend to them that lend to you, what reward will you have?" [Matt 5:46])— shall we, I say, when such is our character, and when we live such a life as this, that we may escape condemnation at last, not be regarded as pious? These, however, are only small matters taken from great, and a few things from many, that we may not further trespass on your patience; for those who test honey and whey, judge by a small quantity whether the whole is good.

[...]

Christians Worship God Alone

15

But grant that they acknowledge the same.[5] What then? Because the multitude, who cannot distinguish between matter and God, or see how great is the interval that lies between them, pray to idols made of matter, are we therefore, who do distinguish and separate the uncreated and the created, that which is and that which is not, that which is apprehended by the understanding and that which is perceived by the senses, and who give the fitting name to each of them—are we to come and worship images? If, indeed, matter and God are the same, two names for one thing, then certainly, in not regarding sticks and stones, gold and silver, as gods, we are guilty of impiety. But if they are at the greatest possible remove from one another—as far apart as the artist and the materials of his art—why are we called to account? For as is the potter and the clay (matter being the clay, and the artist the potter),

---

4 Homer, *Iliad*, 16.672.

5 In chapters 13–14, Athenagoras defended Christians' refusal to offer sacrifices and to worship the pagan gods by arguing that God does not require sacrifices (chapter 13) and that the pagans are contradictory in their worship because they have many different gods and cannot agree on which gods to pray to and believe in (chapter 14).

so is God (the Framer of the world) and matter, which is subservient to him for the purposes of his art. But as the clay cannot become vessels of itself without art, so neither did matter, which is capable of taking all forms, receive distinction and shape and order apart from God the Framer. And as we do not hold the pottery of more worth than him who made it, nor the vessels of glass and gold than him who crafted them; but if there is anything about them elegant in art we praise the artificer, and it is he who reaps the glory of the vessels. The same is true of matter and God—the glory and honor of the orderly arrangement of the world rightly belongs not to matter but to God, the Framer of matter. So that, if we were to regard the various forms of matter as gods, we should seem to be without any sense of the true God, because we should be putting the things that are dissoluble and perishable on a level with that which is eternal.

16

The world is, without doubt, beautiful. It excels in its size and in the arrangement of things in the elliptic and around the pole, and for its spherical shape.[6] Yet it is not this, but its Artificer, that we must worship. For when any of your subjects come to you, their rulers and lords, they do not neglect to address themselves to the magnificence of your palace and pay their homage to you, from whom they will obtain whatever they need. If they happen to come upon the royal residence, they bestow a passing glance of admiration on its beautiful structure, but it is to you yourselves that they show honor, as being "all in all." You sovereigns, indeed, rear and adorn your palaces for yourselves; but the world was not created because God needed it; for God is himself everything to himself—light unapproachable, a perfect world, spirit, power, reason. If, therefore, the world is an instrument in tune, and moving in well-measured time, I adore the Being who produced its harmony and tune, and who strikes its notes—not the instrument. For at the musical contests the judges do not pass by the lute players and crown the lutes. Whether, then, as Plato says, the world is a product of divine art, I admire its beauty, and adore the Artificer; or whether it be his essence and body, as the Peripatetics affirm, we do not neglect to adore God, who is the cause of the motion of the body, and descend to the poor and weak elements, adoring in the impassible air (as they term it), passible matter; or, if anyone considers the various parts of the world to be powers of God, we do not approach and give homage to the powers, but their Maker and Lord. I do not ask of matter what it has not to

---

6 Following the translation from David Rankin, *Athenagoras*, 125.

give, nor passing God by do I pay homage to the elements, which can do nothing more than what they were bidden. For, although they are beautiful to look upon, by reason of the art of their Framer, they still only have the nature of matter. And to this view Plato also bears testimony; "for," he said, "that which is called heaven and earth has received many blessings from the Father, but yet it partakes of body; hence it cannot possibly be free from change."[7] If, therefore, while I admire the heavens and the elements in respect of their art, I do not worship them as gods, knowing that the law of dissolution is upon them, how can I call those objects gods which I know were made by men? Attend, I beg, to a few words on this subject.

[...]

On the Source of the Pagan Gods' Power

23

You may say, however, since you excel all men in understanding, "If those whom we make statues of are not gods, then how does it happen that some of the idols manifest power? For it is not likely that images destitute of life and motion can of themselves do anything without a mover. That in various places, cities, and nations, certain effects are brought about in the name of idols, we are far from denying. Nevertheless, however, if some have received benefit, and others, on the contrary, suffered harm, we will not deem those to be gods who have produced the effects in either case. But I have made careful inquiry into both why it is that you think the idols to have this power and who they are that, usurping the idols' names, produce the effects. It is necessary for me, however, in attempting to show who they are that produce the effects ascribed to the idols, and that they are not gods, to have recourse to some witnesses from among the philosophers. First Thales, as those who have accurately examined his opinions report, divides [superior beings] into God, demons, and heroes. God he recognizes as the Intelligence of the world; by demons he understands beings possessed of soul; and by heroes the separated souls of men, the good being the good souls, and the bad the worthless. Plato again, while withholding his assent on other points, also divides [superior beings] into the uncreated God and those produced by the uncreated One for the adornment of heaven, the planets, and the fixed stars, and into demons; about these demons, while he does not think he is fit to speak himself, he thinks that they who have spoken about them should be listened

---

7 Plato, *The Statesman*, 269d.

to. "To speak concerning the other demons, and to know their origin, is beyond our powers; but we ought to believe those who have spoken before, the descendants of gods, as they say—and surely they must be well acquainted with their own ancestors. It is impossible, therefore, to disbelieve the sons of gods, even though they speak without probable or convincing proofs; but as they profess to tell of their own family affairs, we are bound, in accordance with custom, to believe them. In this way, then, let us hold and speak as they do about the origin of the gods themselves. From Earth and Heaven were born Oceanus and Tethys; and of these Phorcus, Kronos, and Rhea, and the rest; and of Kronos and Rhea, Zeus, Hera, and all the others, who, we know, are all called their brothers; besides other descendants again of these."[8] Did, then, he who had contemplated the eternal Intelligence and God (who is apprehended by reason) and declared his attributes (his real existence, the simplicity of his nature, the good that flows forth from him that is truth, and discoursed of primal power, and how "all things are about the King of all, and all things exist for his sake, and he is the cause of all"; and about two and three, that he is "the second moving about the seconds, and the third about the thirds";[9]), did this man think that to learn the truth concerning those, who are said to have been produced from sensible things, namely earth and heaven, was a task transcending his powers? It is not to be believed for a moment. But because he thought it impossible to believe that gods beget and are brought forth, since everything that begins to be is followed by an end, and (for this is much more difficult) to change the views of the multitude, who receive the fables without examination, it was on this account that he declared it to be beyond his powers to know and to speak concerning the origin of the other demons, since he was unable either to admit or teach that gods were begotten. And as regards that saying of his, "The great sovereign in heaven, Zeus, driving a winged chariot, advances first, ordering and managing all things, and there follow him a host of gods and demons;"[10] this does not refer to Zeus, who is said to have sprung from Kronos; for here the name is given to the Maker of the universe. This is shown by Plato himself; not being able to designate him by another title that should be suitable, he availed himself of the popular name, not as peculiar to God, but for distinctness, because it is not possible to discourse about God to all men as fully as one might; and he adds at the same time the epithet "Great," so as to distinguish the heavenly from the earthly, the uncreated from the created, who is younger than heaven

---

8 Plato, *Timaeus* 40d–e.
9 Plato, *Letters* 2.312e.
10 Plato, *Phaedra* 246e.

and earth, and younger than the Cretans, who stole him away, that he might not be killed by his father.

24

What need is there, in speaking to you who have searched into every department of knowledge, to mention the poets, or to examine opinions of another kind? Let it suffice to say this much. If the poets and philosophers did not acknowledge that there is one God, and concerning these gods were not of various opinions, some that they are demons, others that they are matter, and others that they once were men—if this was not the case, there might be some reason for our being harassed as we are. This is because we employ language that makes a distinction between God and matter, and the natures of the two. For, we do not only acknowledge a God, and a Son his Word, and a Holy Spirit, united in essence (the Father, the Son, the Spirit, because the Son is the Intelligence, Reason, Wisdom of the Father, and the Spirit an effluence, as light from fire). We also acknowledge the existence of other powers that exercise dominion over matter, and by means of it, and one in particular, which is hostile to God. Of course, it is not that anything is really opposed to God, like strife to friendship, according to Empedocles, and night to day, according to the appearing and disappearing of the stars. For even if anything had placed itself in opposition to God, it would have ceased to exist, its structure being destroyed by the power and might of God. But, there is one that is opposed to the good that is in God (this good belongs of necessity to him, and co-exists with him, as color with body, without which it has no existence, not as being part of it, but as an attendant property co-existing with it, united and blended, just as it is natural for fire to be yellow and the ether dark blue): the spirit which is over matter, who was created by God, just as the other angels were created by him, and entrusted with the control of matter and the forms of matter. For this is the office of the angels: to exercise providence for God over the things created and ordered by him, so that God may have the universal and general providence of the whole, while the particular parts are provided for by the angels appointed over them. Just as with men, who have freedom of choice as to both virtue and vice (for you would not either honor the good or punish the bad, unless vice and virtue were in their own power; and some are diligent in the matters entrusted to them by you, and others faithless), so is it among the angels. Some, free agents, you will observe, such as those who were created by God, continued in those things for which God had made and over which he had ordained them; but some outraged both the constitution of their nature and the government entrusted to them: namely, this ruler of matter and its various forms, and others of those who were placed about this first firmament (you know that we say nothing without witnesses, but state the things which have been declared by the prophets); these fell into impure love of virgins and were subjugated by the flesh, and he became negligent and wicked in the management of the things entrusted to him. Of these lovers of virgins, therefore, were begotten those who are called giants. And if something has been said by the poets, too, about the giants, do not be surprised at this: worldly wisdom and divine differ as much from each other as truth and plausibility: the one is of heaven and the other of earth. And indeed, according to the prince of matter, "We know we often speak lies that look like truths."[11]

25

These angels, then, who have fallen from heaven, and haunt the air and the earth, and are no longer able to rise to heavenly things, and the souls of the giants, which are the demons who wander about the world, perform similar actions. The demons do according to the natures they have received; the angels do according to the appetites they have indulged. But the prince of matter, as may be seen merely from what transpires, exercises a control and management contrary to the good that is in God.

> *Often this anxious thought has crossed my mind:*
> *Whether it is chance or deity that rules*
> *The small affairs of men; against hope*
> *As well as justice, it drives to exile some*
> *Stripped of all means of life, while others still*
> *Continue to enjoy prosperity.*[12]

Prosperity and adversity, contrary to hope and justice, made it impossible for Euripides to say to whom belongs the administration of earthly affairs, which is of such a kind that one might say of it:

> *How then, while seeing these things, can we say*
> *There is a race of gods, or yield to laws?*[13]

---

11 Hesiod, *Theogony* 27.
12 Euripides, *Fragment* 901 (Nauck).
13 Euripides, *Fragment* 99.

The same thing led Aristotle to say that the things below the heaven are not under the care of Providence, although the eternal providence of God concerns itself equally with us below:

The earth, let willingness move her or not,
Must produce herbs, and thus sustain my flocks.[14]

And that Providence addresses itself to the deserving individually, according to truth and not according to opinion; and all other things, according to the general constitution of nature, are provided for by the law of reason. But because the demoniac movements and operations proceeding from the adverse spirit produce these disorderly attacks, and moreover move men, some in one way and some in another, as individuals and as nations, separately and in common, in accordance with the tendency of matter on the one hand, and of the affinity for divine things on the other, from within and from without—some who are of no small reputation have therefore thought that this universe is constituted without any definite order, and is driven here and there by an irrational chance. But they do not understand that of those things which belong to the constitution of the whole world, there is nothing out of order or neglected, but that each one of them has been produced by reason, and that, therefore, they do not transgress the order prescribed to them; and that man himself, too, so far as he that made him is concerned, is well ordered, both by his original nature, which has one common character for all, and by the constitution of his body, which does not transgress the law imposed upon it, and by the termination of his life, which remains equal and common to all alike; but that, according to the character peculiar to himself and the operation of the ruling prince and of the demons his followers, he is impelled and moved in this direction or in that, notwithstanding that all possess in common the same rationality in themselves.

26

They who draw men to idols, then, are the abovementioned demons, who are eager for the blood of the sacrifices, and lick them; but the gods that please the multitude, and whose names are given to the images, were men, as may be learned from their history. And that it is the demons who act under their names, is proved by the nature of their operations. For some castrate, as Rhea; others wound and slaughter, as Artemis; the Tauric goddess puts all strangers

---

[14] Euripides, *Cyclops* 332.

to death. I pass over those who lacerate with knives and scourges of bones, and I will not attempt to describe all the kinds of demons; for it is not the part of a god to incite to things against nature.

> But when a demon plots against a man,
> He first inflicts some injury upon his mind.[15]

But God, being perfectly good, is eternally doing good. That, moreover, those who exert the power are not the same as those to whom the statues are erected, very strong evidence is provided by Troy and Parium. Troy has statues of Neryllinus, a man of our own times; and Parium has statues of Alexander and Proteus (both the sepulcher and the statue of Alexander are still in the forum). The other statues of Neryllinus, then, are a public ornament, if indeed a city can be adorned by such objects as these; but one of them is supposed to utter oracles and to heal the sick, and on this account the Trojans offer sacrifices to this statue, and overlay it with gold, and hang chaplets upon it. But of the statues of Alexander and Proteus (the latter, you are aware, threw himself into the fire near Olympia), that of Proteus is likewise said to utter oracles; and to that of Alexander—"Wretched Paris, though in form so fair, slave for women"[16]—sacrifices are offered and festivals are held at the public cost, as to a god who can hear. Is it, then, Neryllinus, and Proteus, and Alexander who exert these energies in connection with the statues, or is it the nature of the matter itself? But the matter is brass. And what can brass do of itself, which may be made again into a different form, as Amasis treated the footpan, as told by Herodotus? And Neryllinus, and Proteus, and Alexander, what good are they to the sick? For the image now effects nothing more than it did when Neryllinus was alive and sick.

[...]

The Difference Between Christian and Pagan Sexual Behavior

33

Therefore, having the hope of eternal life, we despise the things of this life, even the pleasures of the soul. Each man thinks of his wife, whom he married according to the laws laid down by us, only for the purpose of having children. For as the farmer, throwing seed onto the ground, awaits the harvest

---

15 Euripides, *Fragments* 455.
16 Homer, *Iliad* 3.39.

and does not sow more upon it [while he waits for it to grow], so to us the procreation of children is the measure of our indulgence in the appetite. Indeed, you would find many among us, both men and women, growing old unmarried, in hope of living in closer communion with God. But if remaining in virginity and in the state of the eunuch brings one nearer to God, while the indulgence of carnal thoughts and desires leads one away from him, in those cases in which we shun the thoughts, much more do we reject the deeds. For we bestow our attention, not on the study of words, but on the exhibition and teaching of actions—that a person should either remain as he was born or be content with one marriage, for a second marriage is only a specious adultery. "For whoever divorces his wife," he said, "and marries another, commits adultery" (Matt 19:9); he does not permit a man to either divorce a woman whose virginity he has taken or to marry again. For he who separates himself from his first wife, even if she has died, is a cloaked adulterer; this man resists the hand of God, because in the beginning God made one man and one woman, and this man dissolves the strictest union of flesh with flesh, which was designed for the intercourse of the race.

34

But though such is our character (Oh! why should I speak of things unfit to be uttered?), the things said of us are an example of the proverb, "The harlot reproves the chaste."[17] For those who have set up a market for fornication and established infamous houses for the young for every kind of vile pleasure—who do not abstain even from males, males with males committing shocking abominations, especially violating the noblest and loveliest bodies in all sorts of ways, so dishonoring the fair workmanship of God (for beauty on earth is not self-made, but sent by the hand and will of God)—these men, I say, revile us for the very things which they are conscious of themselves, and ascribe to their own gods, boasting of them as noble deeds, and worthy of the gods. These adulterers and pederasts defame the eunuchs and the once-married (while they themselves live like fishes, for these gulp down whatever falls in their way, and the stronger chases the weaker; and, in fact, this is to feed upon human flesh, to do violence in contravention of the very laws that you and your ancestors, with due care for all that is fair and right, have enacted), so that not even the governors of the provinces sent by you suffice for the hearing of the complaints against [the Christians], to whom it is not lawful, when they are struck, not to offer themselves for more blows (cf. Matt 5:39), nor

---

17 Source unknown.

when defamed not to bless; for it is not enough to be just (and justice is to return like for like), but it is incumbent on us to be good and patient of evil.

Christians are Innocent of Cannibalism and Murder

35

What man of sound mind, therefore, will affirm, while such is our character, that we are murderers? For we cannot eat human flesh until we have killed someone. The former charge, therefore, being false, if anyone should ask them regarding the second, whether they have seen what they assert, not one of them would be so barefaced as to say that he had. And yet we have slaves, some more and some fewer, by whom we could not help being seen; but even of these, not one has been found to invent even such things against us. For when they know that we cannot endure even to see a man put to death, though justly; who of them can accuse us of murder or cannibalism? Who does not reckon among the things of greatest interest the contests of gladiators and wild beasts, especially those which are given by you? But we, deeming that to see a man put to death is much the same as killing him, have renounced such spectacles. How, then, when we do not even look on [killings], lest we should contract guilt and pollution, can we put people to death? And when we say that those women who use drugs to bring on abortion commit murder and will have to give an account to God for the abortion, on what principle should we commit murder? For it does not belong to the same person to regard the very fetus in the womb as a created being and therefore an object of God's care, and when it has passed into life, to kill it; and not to expose an infant, because those who expose them are chargeable with child-murder, and on the other hand, when it has been reared to destroy it. But we are in all things always alike and the same, submitting ourselves to reason, and not ruling over it.

[...]

Theophilus of Antioch: Apology to Autolycus

Context
Author: Theophilus
Provenance: Possibly Antioch[1]
Date: AD 180–192

Book 1

Opening

1

A fluent tongue and an elegant style can inspire pleasure and vain praise, to the delight of wretched men who have been corrupted in their minds. The lover of truth, however, does not give heed to ornamented speeches but examines the real matter of the speech, what it is, and what kind it is. Since, then, my friend, you have assailed me with empty words, boasting of your gods of wood and stone, hammered and cast, carved and graven, which neither see nor hear (for they are idols and the works of men's hands); and since, besides, you call me a Christian, as if this were a damning name to bear, I, for my part, avow that I am a Christian, and bear this name beloved of God, hoping to be serviceable to God. For it is not the case, as you suppose, that the

---

[1] Autocyclus was a pagan friend of Theophilus. For a reconstruction of Theophilus' biography and views, see Rick Rogers, *Theophilus of Antioch: The Life and Thought of a Second-Century Bishop* (Lexington Books, 2000). Rogers notes that we cannot be certain that Theophilus was a resident of Antioch (ibid., 7). The *Apology to Autolycus* is comprised of three books, which infamously contain no references to the person and life of Jesus.

name of God is hard to bear; but possibly you entertain this opinion of God, because you are yourself yet unserviceable to him.

On God and the Apprehension of God

2

If you say, "Show me your God," I would reply, "Show me yourself, and I will show you my God." Show, then, that the eyes of your soul are capable of seeing, and the ears of your heart able to hear. Just as those who look with the eyes of the body perceive earthly objects and what concerns this life (and they discriminate at the same time between things that differ, whether light or darkness, white or black, deformed or beautiful, well-proportioned and symmetrical or disproportioned and awkward, or monstrous or mutilated; and as in like manner also, by the sense of hearing, we discriminate either sharp, or deep, or sweet sounds), so too, the same holds true regarding the eyes of the soul and the ears of the heart—it is by them we are able to behold God. For God is seen by those who are enabled to see him when they have the eyes of their soul opened. For, all have eyes, but in some they are covered, and do not see the light of the sun. Yet, it does not follow that if the blind cannot see, then the light of the sun does not shine; let the blind blame themselves and their own eyes. So also, you, O man, have the eyes of your soul covered by your sins and evil deeds. As a burnished mirror, so ought man to have his soul pure. When there is rust on the mirror, it is not possible for a man's face to be seen in the mirror; so also, when there is sin in a man, such a man cannot behold God. Therefore, show me yourself, that you are not an adulterer, or a fornicator, or a thief, or a robber, or a stealer; that you do not corrupt boys; that you are not insolent, or a slanderer, or passionate, or envious, or proud, or supercilious; that you are not a brawler, or covetous, or disobedient to parents; and that you do not sell your children—for God is not manifest to those who do these things, unless they have first cleansed themselves from all impurity. All these things, then, involve you in darkness. Just as when a filmy covering on the eyes prevents one from beholding the light of the sun, so also do iniquities, man, involve you in darkness, so that you cannot see God.

3

You will say, then, to me, "You, who see God: explain to me the appearance of God." Hear, O man. The appearance of God is ineffable, indescribable, and cannot be seen by eyes of flesh. For he is in glory incomprehensible, in greatness unfathomable, in height inconceivable, in power incomparable, in wisdom unrivalled, in goodness inimitable, in kindness unutterable. For if I say he is Light, I name but his own work; if I call him Word, I name but his sovereignty; if I call him Mind, I speak but of his wisdom; if I say he is Spirit, I speak of his breath; if I call him Wisdom, I speak of his offspring; if I call him Strength, I speak of his sway; if I call him Power, I am mentioning his activity; if I call him Providence, I but mention his goodness; if I call him Kingdom, I but mention his glory; if I call him Lord, I mention his being judge; if I call him Judge, I speak of him as being just; if I call him Father, I speak of all things as being from him; if I call him Fire, I but mention his anger. You will say, then, to me, "Is God angry?" Yes, he is angry with those who act wickedly, but he is good, and kind, and merciful, to those who love and fear him; for he is a corrector of the godly, and father of the righteous; but he is a judge and punisher of the impious.

4

And he is without beginning, because he is unbegotten; and he is unchangeable, because he is immortal. And he is called God because he placed all things on the security afforded by himself; and because he runs,[2] for "run" means running, and moving, and being active, and nourishing, and foreseeing, and governing, and making all things alive. But he is Lord because he rules over the universe; Father, because he is before all things; Fashioner and Maker, because he is creator and maker of the universe; the Highest, because of his being above all; and Almighty, because he himself rules and embraces all. For the heights of heaven, and the depths of the abysses, and the ends of the earth, are in his hand, and there is no place of his rest. For the heavens are his work, the earth is his creation, the sea is his handiwork; man is his formation and his image; sun, moon, and stars are his elements, made for signs, and seasons, and days, and years, that they may serve and be slaves to man; and all things God has made out of things that were not into things that are, in order that through his works his greatness may be known and understood.

5

For as the soul in man is not seen, being invisible to men, but is perceived

---
2 Gk. θέειν.

through the motion of the body, so God cannot be seen by human eyes; instead, he is beheld and perceived through his providence and works. For, just as any person, when he sees a ship on the sea rigged and in sail and making for the harbor, will no doubt infer that there is a pilot in the ship who is steering it, so, we must perceive that God is the pilot of the whole universe, even though he is not visible to the eyes of the flesh, since he is incomprehensible. For if a man cannot look upon the sun, though it is a very small heavenly body, on account of its exceeding heat and power, will not a mortal man be much more unable to face the glory of God, which is unutterable? As the pomegranate, with the rind containing it, has within it many cells and compartments that are separated by tissues, and has also many seeds dwelling in it, likewise, the whole creation is contained by the spirit of God, and the containing spirit is along with the creation contained by the hand of God. As, therefore, the seed of the pomegranate, dwelling inside, cannot see what is outside the rind, itself being within, neither can man, who along with the whole creation is enclosed by the hand of God, behold God. Then again, an earthly king is believed to exist, even though he is not seen by everyone; for he is recognized by his laws and ordinances, and authorities, and forces, and statues. And are you unwilling to accept that God should be recognized by his works and mighty deeds?

6

Consider, O man, his works: the timely rotation of the seasons; the changes of temperature; the regular march of the stars; the well-ordered course of days and nights, and months, and years; the various beauty of seeds, and plants, and fruits; the diverse species of quadrupeds, birds, reptiles, and fish both of the rivers and of the sea; the instinct implanted in these animals to beget and rear offspring, not for their own profit, but for the use of man; the providence by which God provides nourishment for all flesh; the subjection in which he has ordained that all things serve mankind; the flowing of sweet fountains and unfailing rivers; the seasonable supply of dews, and showers, and rains; the manifold movement of the heavenly bodies, including the morning star rising and heralding the approach of the perfect luminary, and the constellation of Pleiades, and Orion, and Arcturus, and the orbit of the other stars that circle through the heavens, all of which the manifold wisdom of God has called by names of their own. He is God alone who made light out of darkness, and brought forth light from his treasures, and formed the chambers of the south wind, and the treasure-houses of the deep, and the bounds of the seas, and the treasuries of snows and hail-storms, collecting the waters in the storehouses of the deep, and the darkness in his treasures, and bringing forth the sweet, and desirable, and pleasant light out of his treasures. He is the one "who causes the clouds to ascend from the ends of the earth, and who makes lightning for the rain" (Ps 135:7), who sends forth his thunder to terrify, who sends the lightning to warn us of the crash of the thunder (that no soul may faint with the sudden shock), and who so moderates the violence of the lightning as it flashes out of heaven that it does not consume the earth (for, if the lightning were allowed all of its power, it would burn up the earth; and were the thunder allowed all of its power, it would overthrow all the works that are therein).

7

This is my God, the Lord of all, who alone stretched out the heaven and established the breadth of the earth under it, who stirs the deep recesses of the sea and makes its waves roar, who rules its power and stills the tumult of its waves, who founded the earth upon the waters and gave a spirit to nourish it, whose breath gives life to everything, who, if he withdrew his breath, everything would utterly fail. By him you speak, O man; you breathe his breath, yet you do not know him. And this is your condition because of the blindness of your soul and the hardness of your heart. But, if you desire it, you may be healed. Entrust yourself to the Physician, and he will treat the eyes of your soul and of your heart. Who is the Physician? God, who heals and makes alive through his word and wisdom. God by his own word and wisdom made all things; for "by his word were the heavens made, and all the host of them by the breath of his mouth" (Ps 33:6). Most excellent is his wisdom. By his wisdom God founded the earth; and by knowledge he prepared the heavens; and by understanding were the fountains of the great deep broken up, and the clouds poured out their dew. If you perceive these things, O man, living chastely, and holily, and righteously, so you can see God. But above all, let faith and the fear of God rule in your heart, and then you will understand these things. When you will have put off the mortal, and put on incorruption, then you will see God worthily. For God will raise your flesh immortal with your soul; and then, having become immortal, you will see the Immortal, if now you believe in him; and then you shall know that you have spoken unjustly against him.

[...]

On the Name Christian

12

As for your laughing at me and calling me "Christian," you do not know what you are saying. First, because that which is anointed is sweet and serviceable, and far from contemptible. For what ship can be serviceable and seaworthy unless it is anointed first? Or what castle or house is beautiful and serviceable when it has not been anointed? And what man, when he enters this life or into the gymnasium, is not anointed with oil? And what work has either ornament or beauty unless it is anointed and burnished? Then the air and all that is under heaven is in a certain sort anointed by light and spirit; and are you unwilling to be anointed with the oil of God? We are called Christians on this account: because we are anointed with the oil of God.[3]

[...]

Book 2

Absurd Opinions About God

4

Some of the Stoic philosophers say that there is no God at all; or, if there is, they say that he cares for none but himself; and these views mirror the folly of Epicurus and Chrysippus. And others say that all things are produced without external agency, and that the world is uncreated, and that nature is eternal. They have dared to say that there is no providence of God at all, but they maintain that God is only each man's conscience. And others again maintain that the spirit that pervades all things is God. But Plato and those of his school acknowledge indeed that God is uncreated and is the Father and Maker of all things; but then they maintain that matter as well as God is uncreated and that it is coeval with God. But if God is uncreated and matter is uncreated, God is no longer, according to the Platonists, the Creator of all things, nor, so far as their opinions hold, is the monarchy of God established. And further, since God is uncreated, God is also unalterable, so too, if matter were uncreated, it also would be unalterable and equal to God. For,

---

3 On this anointing, see Stuart E. Parsons, *Ancient Apologetic Exegesis: Introducing and Recovering Theophilus's World* (James Clark & Co, 2015), 24–25.

something that is created is mutable and alterable, but something that is uncreated is immutable and unalterable. And what great thing is it if God made the world out of existent materials? For even a human artist, when he gets material from someone, makes of it what he pleases. But the power of God is manifested in this: that out of things that do not exist, he makes whatever he pleases; just as the bestowal of life and motion is the prerogative of no other than God alone. For even man makes an image, but man cannot give reason and breath, or feeling to what he has made. But God has this property in excess of what man can do, in that he makes a work, endowed with reason, life, sensation. As, therefore, in all these respects God is more powerful than man, so also in this: that out of things that do not exist, he creates and has created things that exist, and [he makes] whatever he pleases, as he pleases.

[...]

On Creation

10

And first, [the Prophets] taught us with one consent that God made all things out of nothing. For nothing was coeval with God; but he being his own sphere, and wanting nothing, and existing before the ages, willed to make man by whom he might be known. For man, therefore, he prepared the world. For he that is created is also needy; but he that is uncreated stands in need of nothing. God, then, having his own Word internal within his own inner self,[4] begat him, emitting him along with his own wisdom before all things. He had this Word as a helper in the things that were created by him, and by him he made all things. He is called Beginning because he rules and is Lord of all things fashioned by him. He, then, being Spirit of God, and governing principle, and wisdom, and power of the highest, came down upon the prophets, and through them spoke of the creation of the world and of all other things. For the prophets did not exist when the world came into existence, but there was the wisdom of God which was in him, and his holy Word which was always present with him. Therefore, he speaks thus by the prophet Solomon: "When he prepared the heavens I was there, and when he appointed the foundations of the earth, I was with him, putting things into order" (Prov 8:27 LXX). And Moses, who lived many years before Solomon, or, rather, the Word of God by him as by an instrument, says, "In the beginning God created the heaven and

---

4 Or bowels.

the earth." First, he named the "beginning," and "creation," then he thus introduced God; for not lightly and on slight occasion is it right to name God. For the divine wisdom foreknew that some would trifle and name a multitude of gods that do not exist. In order, therefore, that the living God might be known by his works, and that [it might be known that] by his Word God created the heavens and the earth, and all that is therein, he said, "In the beginning God created the heavens and the earth." Then having spoken of their creation, he explains to us: "And the earth was without form, and void, and darkness was upon the face of the deep; and the Spirit of God moved upon the water." This, sacred Scripture teaches at the outset, to show that matter, from which God made and fashioned the world, was in some manner created, being produced by God.

[…]

15

On the fourth day the luminaries were made. God, possessing foreknowledge, did this because he knew the follies of the vain philosophers; he knew that they were going to say that the things that grow on the earth are produced from the heavenly bodies (so as to exclude God). In order, therefore, that the truth might be obvious, the plants and seeds were produced prior to the heavenly bodies, for what is posterior cannot produce that which is prior. And these contain the pattern and type of a great mystery. For the sun is a type of God, and the moon of man. And as the sun far surpasses the moon in power and glory, so far does God surpass man. And as the sun remains ever full, never becoming less, so does God always abide perfect, being full of all power, and understanding, and wisdom, and immortality, and all good. But the moon, being a type of man, wanes monthly, and in a manner dies; then it is born again, and is crescent, for a pattern of the future resurrection. Likewise, the three days before the luminaries are types of the triad of God,[5] his Word, and his wisdom. And the fourth is the type of man, who needs light, so that there may be God, the Word, wisdom, man. Therefore, also on the fourth day the lights were made. The disposition of the stars, too, contains a type of the arrangement and order of the righteous and pious, and of those who keep

---

5   This is sometimes translated as "Trinity"; however, on this see Rick Rogers, *The Life and Thought of a Second-Century Bishop*, 75–79 and also Rick Rogers, "Theophilus of Antioch," *Expository Times* 120, no. 5 (2009), 221. Rogers argues that "Theophilus is not intending or attempting a Trinitarian formula here as he immediately speaks of a *tetras* (foursome) of 'God, logos, sophia [and] man,' nor elsewhere, as he regularly speaks of pneuma (spirit) as an agent of God independent of both logos and sophia" (ibid.).

the law and commandments of God. For the brilliant and bright stars are an imitation of the prophets, and therefore they remain fixed, not declining, nor passing from place to place. And those which hold the second place in brightness, are types of the people of the righteous. And those, again, which change their position, and flee from place to place, which also are called planets, they too are a type of the men who have wandered from God, abandoning his law and commandments.

16

On the fifth day the living creatures that proceed from the waters were produced, through which also is revealed the manifold wisdom of God in these things; for who could count their multitude and the many various kinds? Moreover, the things proceeding from the waters were blessed by God, so that this also might be a sign of men's being destined to receive repentance and remission of sins, through the water and basin of regeneration—as many as come to the truth, and are born again, and receive blessing from God. But the monsters of the deep and the birds of prey are a likeness of covetous men and transgressors. For as the fish and the birds are of one nature (some indeed abide in their natural state, and do no harm to those weaker than themselves, but keep the law of God, and eat of the seeds of the earth; others of them, again, transgress the law of God, and eat flesh, and injure those weaker than themselves), thus, too, the righteous, keeping the law of God, bite and injure none, but live holily and righteously. But robbers, and murderers, and godless persons are like monsters of the deep, and wild beasts, and birds of prey; for they virtually devour those weaker than themselves. The race, then, of fishes and of creeping things, though partaking of God's blessing, received no specific distinguishing property.

17

And on the sixth day, God having made the quadrupeds, and wild beasts, and the land reptiles, pronounced no blessing upon them, reserving his blessing for man, whom he was about to create on the sixth day. The quadrupeds, too, and wild beasts, were made as a type of some men, who neither know nor worship God, but mind earthly things, and do not repent. For those who turn from their iniquities and live righteously, in spirit fly upwards like birds, and mind the things that are above, and are well-pleasing to the will of God. But those who do not know or worship God, are like birds that have wings but cannot fly or soar to the high things of God. Thus, too, though such persons are called men, yet being pressed down with sins, they focus on groveling and earthly things. And the animals are named wild beasts from their being hunted, not as if they had been made evil or venomous from the beginning (for nothing was made evil by God, but all things good, indeed, very good), but the sin in which man was involved brought evil upon them. For when man transgressed, they also transgressed with him. For just as if the master of the house himself acts rightly, the servants also of necessity conduct themselves well; but if the master sins, the servants also sin with him; so in like manner it came to pass, that in the case of man's sin, he being master, all that was subject to him sinned with him. When, therefore, man again shall have made his way back to his natural condition, and no longer does evil, those also shall be restored to their original gentleness.

18

But as to what relates to the creation of man, man cannot explain his own creation, though the holy Scripture gives a succinct account of it. For when God said, "Let us make man in our image, after our likeness," he first indicates the dignity of man. For God having made all things by his Word, and having reckoned them all mere subordinate works, reckons the creation of man to be the only work worthy of his own hands. Moreover, God is found, as if needing help, to say, "Let us make man in our image, after our likeness." But to no one else than to his own Word and wisdom did he say, "Let us make." And when he had made and blessed man, that man might increase and fill the earth, God put all things under his dominion and at his service; and God appointed from the beginning that man should find nourishment from the fruits of the earth, and from seeds, and herbs, and acorns, having at the same time appointed that the animals should be of habits similar to man's, that they also might eat of all the seeds of the earth.

19

God having thus completed the heavens, and the earth, and the sea, and all that are in them, on the sixth day, rested on the seventh day from all his works that he made. Then holy Scripture gives a summary in these words: "This is the book of the generation of the heavens and the earth, when they were created, in the day that the LORD made the heavens and the earth, and every green thing of the field, before it was made, and every herb of the field before it grew. For God had not caused it to rain upon the earth, and there was not a man to till the ground" (Gen 2:4–5). By this he signifies to us that the whole earth was at that time watered by a divine fountain and had no need for man to till it; but the earth produced all things spontaneously by the command of God, that man might not be wearied by tilling it. But that the creation of man might be made plain, so that there should not seem to be an insoluble problem existing among men, since God had said, "Let us make man"; and since his creation was not yet plainly related, Scripture teaches us, saying: "And a fountain went up out of the earth, and watered the face of the whole earth; and God made man from the dust of the earth, and breathed into his face the breath of life, and man became a living soul" (Gen 2:6–7). Therefore, also by most persons the soul is called immortal. And after the formation of man, God chose for him a region from among the places of the East, excellent for light, brilliant with a very bright atmosphere, [abundant] in the finest plants; and in this he placed man.

[...]

22

Why God Is Said to Have Walked

You will say to me: "You said that God ought not to be contained in a place, and how do you now say that he walked in paradise?" Hear what I say. The God and Father of all cannot be contained, and is not found in a place, for there is no place of his rest; but his Word, through whom he made all things, being his power and his wisdom, assuming the role of the Father and Lord of all, went to the garden in the person of God, and conversed with Adam. For the divine writing itself teaches us that Adam said that he had heard the voice. But what else is this voice but the Word of God, who is also his Son? Not as the poets and writers of myths talk of the sons of gods begotten from intercourse [with women], but as truth expounds, the Word, that always exists, residing within the heart of God. For before anything came into being he had him as a counsellor, being his own mind and thought. But when God wished to make all that he had determined, he begot this Word, uttered, the first-born of all creation, not himself being emptied of the Word, but having begotten the Word, and always conversing with his Word. And hence the holy writings teach us, and all the spirit-bearing men, one of whom, John, says, "In the beginning was the Word, and the Word was with God" (John 1:1), showing that at first God was alone, and the

Word in him. Then he says, "The Word was God; all things came into existence through him; and apart from him not one thing came into existence" (John 1:1, 3). The Word, then, being God, and being naturally produced from God, whenever the Father of the universe wills, he sends him to any place; and the Word, coming, is both heard and seen, being sent by him, and is found in a place.

[...]

On the Fall and Nature of Humanity

25

The tree of knowledge itself was good, and its fruit was good. For it was not the tree, as some think, but the disobedience, which had death in it. For there was nothing else in the fruit than knowledge; but knowledge is good when one uses it correctly. But Adam, being yet an infant in age, was on this account not yet able to receive knowledge worthily. For now, also, when a child is born it is not at once able to eat bread, but is nourished first with milk, and then, with the advancement of years, it advances to solid food. Thus, too, would it have been with Adam; for not as one who grudged him, as some suppose, did God command him not to eat of knowledge. But God wished to test him, whether he was submissive to this commandment. And at the same time, he wished man, infant as he was, to remain for some time longer simple and sincere. For this is holy, not only with God, but also with men, that in simplicity and guileless subjection be yielded to parents. But if it is right that children be subject to parents, how much more to the God and Father of all things? Besides, it is not right for children in infancy to be wise beyond their years; for as one increases in stature at an orderly pace, so also in wisdom. But as when a law has commanded abstinence from anything, and someone has not obeyed, it is obviously not the law that causes punishment but the disobedience and transgression—for a father sometimes enjoins on his own child abstinence from certain things, and when the child does not obey the paternal order, he is flogged and punished on account of the disobedience; and in this case the actions themselves are not the cause of stripes, but the disobedience causes punishment for him who disobeys—so also for the first man, disobedience caused his expulsion from paradise. Not, therefore, as if there were any evil in the tree of knowledge; but from his disobedience did man draw, as from a fountain, labor, pain, grief, and at last fall prey to death.

26

And God showed great kindness to man in this, that he did not let him remain in sin forever; but, as it were, by a kind of banishment, God cast him out of paradise, in order that, having by punishment expiated the sin, within an appointed time, and having been disciplined, man should afterwards be restored. Therefore also, when man had been formed in this world, it is mystically written in Genesis, as if he had been twice placed in paradise (cf. Gen 2:8, 15); so that the one was fulfilled when he was placed there, and the second will be fulfilled after the resurrection and judgment. For just as if a vessel, when on being fashioned it has some flaw, is remolded or remade so that it may become new and whole; so also, this happens to man by death. For somehow or other he is broken up, so that he may rise in the resurrection whole—I mean spotless, and righteous, and immortal. And as to God's calling, and saying, "Where are you, Adam?" (Gen 3:9). God did this, not as if ignorant of this, but, being long-suffering, to give Adam an opportunity for repentance and confession.

27

But someone will say to us, "Was man made by nature mortal?" Certainly not. "Was he, then, immortal?" Neither do we affirm this. But one will say, "Was he, then, nothing?" Not even this hits the mark. He was by nature neither mortal nor immortal. For if God had made him immortal from the beginning, he would have made him God. Again, if God had made him mortal, God would seem to be the cause of his death. Therefore, God made him neither immortal nor mortal, but, as we have said above, capable of both—so that if man should incline to the things of immortality, keeping the commandment of God, he would receive immortality as a reward from God, and should become God; but if, on the other hand, he should turn to the things of death, disobeying God, he should himself be the cause of death to himself. For God made man free, and with power over himself. That, then, which man brought upon himself through carelessness and disobedience, this God now grants to him as a gift through his own philanthropy and pity, when men obey him. For as man, disobeying, drew death upon himself; so, obeying the will of God, he who desires can procure for himself life everlasting. For God has given us a law and holy commandments; and everyone who keeps these can be saved, and, obtaining the resurrection, can inherit incorruption.

[...]

Appendix 1:
Select Readings on Greco-Roman Religion and the Imperial Cult

Cato the Elder on Praying for a Farm [1]

Pray first to Janus and Jupiter with an offering of wine, then speak as follows: "Mars Pater,[2] I pray and implore you to be favorable and kind to me, my house and our household; for this reason I have bidden a suovetaurilia[3] to be driven around my land, ground and farm, that you may prevent, ward off and avert diseases, visible and invisible, dearth and destruction, ruin and storm, and that you permit the crops, corn, vineyards and plantations to grow and flourish, and that you keep safe the shepherds and their sheep, and grant good health and strength to me, my house and our household.

Cicero on Ideal Roman Religious Laws and Practices [4]

MARCUS: Let them approach the gods in purity, let them display piety, let them remove luxury. If anyone behave otherwise, the god himself will enforce the law. Let no one have gods separately, neither new nor foreign, unless they have been recognized publicly; let them worship in private those whose worship has been duly handed down by their ancestors. Let them have sanctuaries in the cities; let them have groves in the country and homes for their

---

1 Cato the Elder, *On Farming* 141 in Mary Beard, John North, and Simon Price, *A Sourcebook*. Vol. 2 of *Religions of Rome* (Cambridge University Press, 1998), 152. This excerpt, written about 160 BC provides an example of Roman prayers and ritual sacrifices made to the gods for divine favor.
   2 Greek for "father."
   3 A ritual sacrifice of a pig, ram, and bull.
   4 Cicero, *On the Laws* 2.19 in James E. G. Zetzel, ed., *Cicero: On the Commonwealth and On the Laws* (Cambridge University Press, 1999), 136. *On the Laws* was likely written about 54–51 BC (ibid., xxvii).

Lares.[5] Let them preserve the rituals of their family and ancestors. Let them worship both those who have always been considered gods of heaven and those whose deeds have placed them in heaven: Hercules, Liber, Aesculapius, Castor, Pollux, Quirinus. Furthermore, as to those praiseworthy qualities on account of which ascent into heaven is granted to humans—Intelligence, Virtue, Piety, Faith—let there be sanctuaries for them, but none for vices. Let them take part in customary rites.

Diodorus Siculus on Two Types of Greco-Roman Gods[6]

About gods, then, the men of ancient times have passed down to later generations two conceptions. For some, they say, are eternal and imperishable, such as sun and moon and the other stars in the sky, and in addition to these, winds and the other things that happen to be of the same nature as these. For each of these has eternal origin and duration. Other gods, they say, were originally earthly humans but through their benefactions to humanity gained immortal honor and glory, such as Heracles, Dionysus, Aristaeus, and the others like them.

Ovid on the Deification of Julius Caesar[7]

Apollo's son came to us from abroad, but Caesar is a god in his own land. The first in war and peace, he rose by wars that closed in triumphs, and by civic deeds to glory quickly won, and even more his offspring's love exalted him as a new and heavenly sign—a brightly flaming star. Of all the achievements of great Julius Caesar, none is more ennobling to his fame than being father of his glorious son.... And, lest that son should come from mortal seed, Julius Caesar must change and be a god....

[Jupiter said to his daughter] "transform his soul, which will be snatched from his doomed body, into a starry light. Do this so that in the future the always god-like Julius may look down upon our Forum and our Capitol from his heavenly residence." Jupiter had hardly pronounced these words, when kindly Venus, although seen by none, stood in the middle of the Senate-house,

---

5 Lares: from Roman religion. Deities believed to offer protection to the area around their statues.

6 Diodorus Siculus, *Library of History* 6.1.2 in Delbert Burkett, *An Introduction to the New Testament and the Origins of Christianity* (Cambridge University Press, 2002), 555. Greek historian Diodorus Siculus completed his massive *Library of History*, chronicling cultures and the history of the world, about 35 BC.

7 Ovid, *Metamorphoses* 15. This Roman poem, written about AD 8, portrays history from the creation of the world up to Julius Caesar's deification.

and caught from the dying limbs and trunk of her own Caesar his departing soul. She did not give it time so that it could dissolve in air, but quickly bore it up toward all the stars of heaven; and on the way, she saw it gleam and blaze, and she set it free. Above the moon it mounted into heaven, leaving behind a long and fiery trail, and as a star it glittered in the sky.

Velleius Paterculus on a Barbarian's Reverence toward Emperor Tiberius[8]

We were encamped on the nearer bank of the river Elbe, while on the farther bank glittered the arms of the enemies' troops, who showed an inclination to flee at every movement and maneuver our vessels. One of the barbarians, advanced in years, tall of stature, and of high rank (to judge by his dress), embarked in a canoe, which was made as per the custom of a hollowed log. Guiding this strange craft, he advanced alone to the middle of the stream and asked permission to land without harm to himself on the bank occupied by our troops, and to see Caesar.[9] Permission was granted. Then he beached his canoe, and, after gazing upon Caesar for a long time in silence, exclaimed: "Our young men are insane, for though they worship you as divine when absent, when you are present, they fear your armies instead of trusting your protection. But I, by your kind permission, Caesar, have today seen the gods of whom I merely used to hear. In my life, I have never hoped for or experienced a happier day." After asking for and receiving permission to touch Caesar's hand, he again entered his canoe, and continued to gaze back upon him until he landed upon his own bank.

---

8 Valleius Paterculus, *Roman History* 2.107, about AD 31.
9 Emperor Tiberius.

Appendix 2:
Select Readings on Persecution and the Early Church

Tacitus: On Nero's Response to the Fire in Rome [1]

[After a fire broke out and destroyed much of Rome,] neither human work nor lavish grants of the emperor nor the means used to appease the gods caused the scandal to abate or dispelled the belief that the fire had been ordered. Therefore to end the rumor, Nero substituted defendants and punished with the most unusual penalties a group of people hated for their shameful deeds, whom the common people called Christians. The author of that name, Christus, had been punished with the death penalty by the procurator Pontius Pilate in the reign of Tiberius. Repressed temporarily, the deadly superstition broke out again not only in Judea, the source of that evil, but also in the City [Rome], where all things atrocious or shameful flow together from everywhere and are celebrated. So first those who confessed were seized, then on their information vast numbers were convicted, not so much on the charge of arson as for hatred of the human race. Mockeries were added to their deaths. Some were covered with the skins of wild animals so that they would be torn to death by dogs. Others were fastened to crosses to be burned, so that where daylight failed they might be lit and used for light at night. Nero had offered his gardens for that spectacle. He also provided a public show in the Circus, where he mixed with the common people in the garb of a chariot-racer or stood in his chariot. Hence, though these people were guilty and deserved the most extreme punishments, pity for them arose, from the feeling that they were being destroyed not for the public good, but for the savagery of one man.

---

1 Tacitus, *Annals* 15.45 in Delbert Burkett, *An Introduction to the New Testament and the Origins of Christianity* (Cambridge University Press, 2002), 610. Tacitus may have not finished writing the *Annals* at the time of his death (about AD 120).

Suetonius: On Emperor Nero and the Punishment of Christians[2]

During [Nero's] reign, many public abuses were severely punished and put down, and many new laws were made. A limit was set to expenditures; the public banquets were confined to a distribution of food; the sale of any kind of cooked food in the taverns was forbidden (excluding beans and vegetables, whereas before every sort of delicacy was available for sale). Punishment was inflicted on the Christians, a group of men given to a new and nefarious superstition. He put an end to the diversions of the chariot drivers, who from immunity of long standing claimed the right of ranging at large and amusing themselves by cheating and robbing the people. The pantomimic actors and their partisans were banished from the city.

Eusebius of Caesarea: On the Martyrdoms of Peter and Paul under Nero[3]

1. When the government of Nero was now firmly established, he began to plunge into unholy pursuits, and he armed himself even against the God of the universe. 2. To describe the greatness of his depravity does not lie within the plan of the present work. As there are many indeed that have recorded his history in most accurate narratives, everyone may at his pleasure learn from them the coarseness of the man's extraordinary madness. Under the influence of this madness, after Nero had destroyed so many people for no reason, he had such bloodlust that he did not spare even his nearest relatives and dearest friends. He destroyed his mother, and his brothers and his wife, with very many others of his own family, and he did so in the same way that he destroyed private and public enemies, with various kinds of deaths. 3. But despite all this, the catalogue of his crimes lacks one crime: he was the first of the emperors who proved to be an enemy of reverence toward God.

4. The Roman Tertullian is a witness to this. He writes as follows: "Examine your records. There you will find that Nero was the first that persecuted this doctrine, particularly then when after subduing all the east, he exercised his cruelty against all in Rome. We glory in having such a man as the leader in our punishment. For whoever knows him can understand that nothing was condemned by Nero unless it was something of great excellence."

---

2 Suetonius, *Twelve Caesars* 6.16.2, written in AD 121.
3 Eusebius, *Ecclesiastical History* 2.25, published about AD 325.

5. Thus publicly announcing himself as the first among God's chief enemies, he went on to slaughter the apostles. It is, therefore, recorded that Paul was beheaded in Rome itself, and that Peter likewise was crucified under Nero. This account of Peter and Paul is substantiated by the fact that their names are preserved in the cemeteries of that place even to the present day. 6. It is also confirmed by Gaius, a member of the church, who arose under Zephyrinus, bishop of Rome. He, in a published disputation with Proclus, the leader of the Phrygian heresy,[4] speaks as follows concerning the places where the sacred corpses of those apostles are laid: 7. "But I can show the trophies of the apostles. For if you will go to the Vatican or to the Ostian way, you will find the trophies of those who laid the foundations of this church."

8. And that they both suffered martyrdom at the same time is stated by Dionysius, bishop of Corinth, in his epistle to the Romans, in the following words: "By your admonition, you have bound together the planting of Peter and of Paul at Rome and Corinth. For both planted and likewise taught us in our Corinth. And they taught together in like manner in Italy, and they suffered martyrdom at the same time." I have quoted these things in order that the truth of the history might be still more confirmed.

Eusebius of Caesarea: On the Jewish War and the Destruction of Jerusalem[5]

1. Josephus again, after relating many things in connection with the calamity that came upon the whole Jewish nation, records, in addition to many other circumstances, that a great many of the most honorable among the Jews were scourged in Jerusalem itself and then crucified by Florus. It happened that he was procurator of Judea when the war began to be kindled, in the twelfth year of Nero.[6]

2. Josephus says that at that time a terrible commotion was stirred up throughout all Syria as a consequence of the revolt of the Jews, and that everywhere the latter were destroyed without mercy, like enemies, by the inhabitants of the cities, "so that one could see cities filled with unburied corpses, and the dead bodies of the aged scattered about with the bodies of infants, and women without even a covering for their nakedness, and the whole province full of indescribable calamities, while the dread of those things that were

---

4 A reference to Montanism, the name given to the heretical late second-century Christian prophetic movement associated with Montanus. It was condemned for promoting new prophecies that were inconsistent with the faith of the apostolic church.

5 Eusebius, *Ecclesiastical History* 2.26.

6 That is, AD 66.

threatened was greater than the sufferings themselves that they anywhere endured." Such is the account of Josephus; and such was the condition of the Jews at that time.

Josephus: On the Romans Entering Jerusalem during the Jewish War [7]

[After the Romans breached the walls of Jerusalem], they went in numbers into the alleys of the city with their swords drawn; they slew those whom they overtook outside. They set fire to the houses where the Jews had fled, burning every soul in them, and destroying many of the rest. When they had entered the houses to plunder them, they found in them entire families dead, and the upper rooms full of dead corpses, that is, of such as died by the famine; they then stood in a horror at this sight, and went out without touching anything. But although they had this commiseration for such as were destroyed in that manner, they did not have the same feelings for those that were still alive. Instead, they slaughtered everyone they met, filling the alleys with dead bodies, and making the whole city run with blood to such a degree indeed that the fire of many of the houses was quenched with blood. And truly it happened that although the killers stopped when evening came, the fire prevailed, burning through the night.

Josephus: On the Romans Destroying Jerusalem during the Jewish War [8]

Now as soon as the army had no more people to slay or to plunder, because there remained none to be the objects of their fury (for they would not have spared any, had there remained any other work to be done), Caesar gave orders that they should now demolish the entire city and temple. But he instructed them to leave standing the greatest towers, namely Phasaelus, and Hippicus, and Mariamne, and also the wall that enclosed the city on the west side. This wall was spared to provide a camp for those who were to stay in garrison. The towers were spared to demonstrate to posterity what kind of city it was and how well fortified it was, which the Roman valor had subdued. But the rest of the wall was so thoroughly laid even with the ground by those that dug it up to the foundation, that there was left nothing to make those that came later believe it had ever been inhabited. This was the end which

---

7   Josephus, *Jewish War* 6.8.5, published about AD 75.
8   Josephus, *Jewish War* 7.1.1.

Jerusalem came to by the madness of those that were for revolution, a city otherwise of great magnificence and of mighty fame among all mankind.

Eusebius of Caesarea: On the First Successors to the Apostles[9]

1. That Paul preached to the gentiles and laid the foundations of the churches "from Jerusalem all the way around to Illyricum" (Rom 15:19), is evident both from his own words and from the account that Luke has given in Acts. 2. And in how many provinces Peter preached Christ and taught the doctrine of the new covenant to those of the circumcision is clear from his own words in his epistle already mentioned as undisputed, in which he writes to the Hebrews of the dispersion in Pontus, Galatia, Cappadocia, Asia, and Bithynia.

3. But the number and the names of those among them that became true and zealous followers of the apostles and were judged worthy to tend the churches founded by them, it is not easy to tell, except those mentioned in the writings of Paul. 4. For he had innumerable fellow-laborers, or "fellow-soldiers," as he called them, and most of them were honored by him with an imperishable memorial, for he gave enduring testimony concerning them in his own epistles. 5. Luke also in Acts speaks of his friends and mentions them by name. 6. Timothy, so it is recorded, was the first to receive the episcopate of the parish in Ephesus, Titus of the churches in Crete.

7. But Luke, who was an Antiochene by birth, a physician by profession, and who was especially intimate with Paul and well acquainted with the rest of the apostles, has left us, in two inspired books, examples of the therapy for souls that he learned from them. One of these books is the Gospel, which he testifies that he wrote as those who were from the beginning eye witnesses and ministers of the word delivered to him, all of whom, as he says, he followed accurately from the first. The other book is the Acts of the Apostles, which he composed not from the accounts of others, but from what he had seen himself. 8. And they say that Paul meant to refer to Luke's Gospel wherever, as if speaking of some gospel of his own, he used the words, "according to my Gospel."

9. As to the rest of his followers, Paul tells us that Crescens was sent to Gaul. Linus, whom he mentions in the Second Epistle to Timothy as his companion at Rome, was Peter's successor in the episcopate of the church there, as has already been shown. 10. Clement also, who was appointed third bishop of the church at Rome, was, as Paul testifies, his co-laborer and fellow-soldier.

---

9 Eusebius, *Ecclesiastical History* 3.4.

11. Besides these, that Areopagite, named Dionysius, who was the first to believe after Paul's address to the Athenians in the Areopagus (as recorded by Luke in Acts) is mentioned by another Dionysius, an ancient writer and pastor of the parish in Corinth, as the first bishop of the church at Athens. 12. But the events connected with the apostolic succession we will relate at the proper time. Meanwhile let us continue the course of our history.

Eusebius of Caesarea: On the Persecution under Domitian[10]

Domitian, having shown great cruelty toward many, and having unjustly put to death no small number of well-born and notable men at Rome, and having without cause exiled and confiscated the property of a great many other illustrious men, finally became a successor of Nero in his hatred and enmity toward God. He was in fact the second that stirred up a persecution against us, although his father Vespasian had undertaken nothing prejudicial to us.

Eusebius of Caesarea: On Other Actions of Domitian[11]

But when this same Domitian had commanded that the descendants of David should be killed, an ancient tradition says that some of the heretics brought accusation against the descendants of Jude (said to have been a brother of the Savior according to the flesh), on the basis that they were of the lineage of David and were related to Christ himself. Hegesippus relates these facts in the following words.

1. "Of the family of the Lord, there were still living the grandchildren of Jude, who is said to have been the Lord's brother according to the flesh. 2. Information was given that they belonged to the family of David, and they were brought to the Emperor Domitian by the Evocatus (for Domitian feared the coming of Christ as Herod also had feared it). And he asked them if they were descendants of David, and they confessed that they were. Then he asked them how much property they had, or how much money they owned. And they both answered that they had only nine thousand denarii, half of which belonged to each of them; 4. and this property did not consist of silver, but of a piece of land which contained only thirty-nine acres, and from which they raised their taxes and supported themselves by their own labor."

5. Then, as evidence of their own labor, they showed their hands, displaying the hardness of their bodies and the callousness produced upon their

---

10 Eusebius, *Ecclesiastical History* 3.17.
11 Eusebius, *Ecclesiastical History* 3.19–20.

hands by continuous toil. 6. And when they were asked about Christ and his kingdom—of what sort it was and where and when it was to appear—they answered that it was not a temporal nor an earthly kingdom, but a heavenly and angelic one, which would appear at the end of the world, when he would come in glory to judge the living and the dead, and to give to all according to their works. 7. Upon hearing this, Domitian did not pass judgment against them. Instead, despising them as insignificant, he let them go and issued a decree to stop the persecution of the church. 8. But when they were released, they ruled the churches because they were witnesses and were also relatives of the Lord. And peace being established, they lived until the time of Trajan. These things are related by Hegesippus.

9. Tertullian also has mentioned Domitian in the following words: "Domitian also, who possessed a share of Nero's cruelty, attempted once to do the same thing that the latter did. But because he had, I suppose, some intelligence, he very soon ceased, and even recalled those whom he had banished."

10. But after Domitian had reigned fifteen years, and Nerva had succeeded to the empire, the Roman Senate, according to the writers that record the history of those days, voted that Domitian's honors should be cancelled, and that those who had been unjustly banished should return to their homes and have their property restored to them. 11. It was at this time that the apostle John returned from his banishment on the island and took up his abode at Ephesus, according to an ancient Christian tradition.

Pliny the Younger: To Emperor Trajan on the Persecution of Christians[12]

I have a rule, master, that I always follow: to refer to you in all of my doubts. For who is more capable of guiding my uncertainty or informing my ignorance? Having never been present at any trials of the Christians, I am unacquainted with the method and limits to be observed either in examining or punishing them. Should any difference be made on account of age—or should there be no distinction between the youngest and the adult? Should repentance lead to a pardon—or if once someone has been a Christian, is recanting meaningless? Should the mere profession of Christianity, albeit without crimes, be punished—or only any crimes associated with the person be punished? In all these points, I am very uncertain.

---

12 Pliny the Younger, *Letters* 10.96. Pliny the Younger, the Roman governor of Bithynia and Pontus, wrote this letter about AD 112.

Meanwhile, the method I have observed toward those who have been denounced to me as Christians is this: I interrogated them, asking whether they were Christians. If they confessed it, I repeated the question twice again, adding the threat of capital punishment. If they still persevered, I ordered them to be executed. For whatever the nature of their creed might be, I could at least feel no doubt that stubbornness and inflexible obstinacy deserved punishment. There were others also possessed with the same infatuation, but being citizens of Rome, I directed them to be transferred to Rome.

These accusations spread (as is usually the case) from the mere fact of the matter being investigated, and several issues came to light. A placard was put up, without any signature, accusing a large number of persons by name. Those who denied they were, or had ever been, Christians, who repeated after me an invocation to the gods, and offered adoration, with wine and frankincense, to your image, which I had ordered to be brought for that purpose, together with those of the gods, and who finally cursed Christ—none of which acts, it is said, those who are really Christians can be forced into performing—these I thought it proper to discharge. Others who were named by that informer at first confessed themselves Christians, and then denied it; true, they had been of that persuasion, but they had quit it, some three years, others many years, and a few as much as twenty-five years ago. They all worshipped your statue and the images of the gods, and cursed Christ.

They affirmed, however, the whole of their guilt or their error was that they were in the habit of meeting on a certain fixed day before it was light, when they sang in alternate verses a hymn to Christ, as to a god. They bound themselves by a solemn oath to avoid wicked deeds and to never commit any fraud, theft or adultery, never to falsify their word, nor deny a trust when they should be called upon to deliver it up. After this, it was their custom to separate and then reassemble to partake of food—but food of an ordinary and innocent kind. Even this practice, however, they had abandoned after the publication of your edict, by which, according to your orders, I had forbidden political associations. I judged it so much the more necessary to extract the real truth, with the assistance of torture, from two female slaves, who were called deaconesses. But I could not discover anything more than depraved and excessive superstition.

I therefore adjourned the proceedings and immediately sought your counsel. For the matter seemed to me well worth referring to you—especially considering the numbers endangered. Persons of all ranks and ages, and of both sexes are, and will be, involved in the prosecution. For this contagious superstition is not confined to the cities only but has spread through the villages and rural districts; it seems possible, however, to halt and fix it. It is certain at least that the temples, which had been almost deserted, are now beginning to be frequented; and the sacred festivals, after a long intermission, are again revived; and there is a general demand for sacrificial animals, which previously for some time had few purchasers. From this it is easy to imagine what multitudes may be reclaimed from this error, if a door be left open to repentance.

Emperor Trajan: A Reply to Pliny the Younger on the Persecution of Christians[13]

The method you have pursued, my dear Pliny, in sifting the cases of those denounced to you as Christians is extremely proper. It is not possible to lay down any general rule that can be applied as the fixed standard in all cases of this nature. No search should be made for these people; when they are denounced and found guilty, they must be punished; with the restriction, however, that if the accused denies that he is a Christian and gives proof that he is not (that is, by adoring our gods), he will be pardoned on the ground of repentance, even though he may have formerly incurred suspicion. Anonymous information provided without the accuser's name must not be admitted in evidence against anyone, as it is introducing a very dangerous precedent, and it is quite out of line with the spirit of our age.

Eusebius of Caesarea: On Clement of Rome and Ignatius of Antioch[14]

1. After Nerva had reigned a little more than a year, he was succeeded by Trajan. It was during the first year of his reign that Abilius, who had ruled the church of Alexandria for thirteen years, was succeeded by Cerdon. 2. He was the third that presided over that church after Annianus, who was the first. At that time Clement still ruled the church of Rome, being also the third that held the episcopate there after Paul and Peter. 3. Linus was the first, and after him came Anencletus.

At this time Ignatius was known as the second bishop of Antioch, Evodius having been the first. Symeon likewise was at that time the second ruler of the church of Jerusalem, the brother of our Savior having been the first.

---

13 Pliny the Younger, *Letters* 10.97.
14 Eusebius, *Ecclesiastical History* 3.21–22.

Eusebius of Caesarea: On the Heresy of the Ebionites [15]

1. The evil demon, however, being unable to tear certain others from their allegiance to the Christ of God, found them susceptible in a different direction, and so he brought them over to his own purposes. The ancients quite properly called these men Ebionites, because they held poor and limited opinions concerning Christ. 2. For they considered him a plain and common man, who was justified only because of his superior virtue, and who was the fruit of the intercourse of a man with Mary. In their opinion, the observance of the ceremonial law was altogether necessary on the basis that they could not be saved by faith in Christ alone and by a corresponding life.

3. There were others, however, besides them, that were of the same name, but avoided the strange and absurd beliefs of the former and did not deny that the Lord was born of a virgin and of the Holy Spirit. But nevertheless, inasmuch as they also refused to acknowledge that he pre-existed, being God, Word, and Wisdom, they turned aside into the impiety of the former, especially when they, like them, endeavored to observe strictly the bodily worship of the law.

4. These men, moreover, thought that it was necessary to reject all the epistles of the apostle, whom they called an apostate from the law; and they used only the so-called Gospel according to the Hebrews and made small account of the rest. 5. The Sabbath and the rest of the discipline of the Jews they observed just like them, but at the same time, like us, they celebrated the Lord's days as a memorial of the resurrection of the Savior. 6. Therefore, because of such a course, they received the name of Ebionites, which signified the poverty of their understanding. For this is the name that the Hebrews call a poor person.

Eusebius of Caesarea: On the Martyrdom of Symeon, Bishop of Jerusalem [16]

1. It is reported that after the age of Nero and Domitian, under the emperor [Trajan] whose times we are now recording, a persecution was stirred up against us in certain cities because of a popular uprising. We understand that in this persecution Symeon, the son of Clopas, who, as we have shown, was the second bishop of the church of Jerusalem, suffered martyrdom. 2. Hegesippus, whose words we have already quoted in various places, is a witness to

---

15 Eusebius, *Ecclesiastical History* 3.27.
16 Eusebius, *Ecclesiastical History* 3.32.

Appendix 2: Select Readings on Persecution and the Early Church

this fact also. Speaking of certain heretics, he adds that Symeon was accused by them at this time; and since it was clear that he was a Christian, he was tortured in various ways for many days, and astonished even the judge himself and his attendants in the highest degree, and finally he suffered a death like that of our Lord. 3. But there is nothing like hearing the historian himself, who writes as follows: "Some of these heretics brought accusation against Symeon, the son of Clopas, on the basis that he was a descendant of David and a Christian; and thus, he suffered martyrdom, at the age of one hundred and twenty years, while Trajan was emperor and Atticus governor." 4. And the same writer says that his accusers also, when the descendants of David were being searched for, were arrested as belonging to that family. And it might be reasonably assumed that Symeon was one of those that saw and heard the Lord, judging from the length of his life, and from the fact that the Gospel makes mention of Mary, the wife of Clopas, who was the father of Symeon, as has been already shown.

5. The same historian says that there were also others, descended from one of the so-called brothers of the Savior, whose name was Judas, who, after they had borne testimony before Domitian, as has been already recorded, on behalf of faith in Christ, lived until the same reign. 6. He writes as follows: "They came, therefore, and took the lead of every church as witnesses and as relatives of the Lord. And profound peace being established in every church, they remained until the reign of the Emperor Trajan, and until the above-mentioned Symeon, son of Clopas, an uncle of the Lord, was informed against by the heretics, and was himself in like manner accused for the same reason before the governor Atticus. And after being tortured for many days, he suffered martyrdom, and all, including even the proconsul, marveled that, at the age of one hundred and twenty years, he could endure so much. And orders were given that he should be crucified."

7. In addition to these things the same man, while recounting the events of that period, records that the church up to that time had remained a pure and uncorrupted virgin, since, if there were any that attempted to corrupt the sound norm of the preaching of salvation, they lay until then concealed in obscure darkness. 8. But when the sacred college of apostles had suffered death in various forms, and the generation of those that had been deemed worthy to hear the inspired wisdom with their own ears had passed away, then the league of godless error took its rise as a result of the folly of heretical teachers, who, because none of the apostles was still living, attempted henceforth, with a bold face, to proclaim, in opposition to the preaching of the truth, the "knowledge which is falsely so called" (1 Tim 6:20).

Eusebius of Caesarea: On Trajan's Decree Forbidding Seeking after Christians[17]

1. At that time, the persecution against us was so great in many places that Plinius Secundus, one of the most noted of governors, being disturbed by the great number of martyrs, communicated with the emperor about the number of those that were put to death for their faith. At the same time, he informed the emperor in his communication that he had not heard of their doing anything profane or contrary to the laws—except that they arose at dawn and sang hymns to Christ as a God—but that they renounced adultery and murder and similar criminal offenses, and they did all things in accordance with the laws.

2. In reply to this, Trajan made the following decree: that the race of Christians should not be sought after, but when found should be punished. On account of this the persecution that had threatened to be a most terrible one was to a certain degree restrained, but there were still left plenty of pretexts for those who wished to do us harm. Sometimes the people or the rulers in various places would lay plots against us, so that, although no great persecutions took place, local persecutions were nevertheless going on in particular provinces, and many of the faithful endured martyrdom in various forms.

3. We have taken our account from the Latin *Apology* of Tertullian, which we mentioned above. The translation runs as follows: "And indeed we have found that search for us has been forbidden. For when Plinius Secundus, the governor of a province, had condemned certain Christians and deprived them of their dignity, he was confounded by their number, and was uncertain what further course to pursue. He therefore communicated with Trajan the emperor, informing him that, aside from their unwillingness to sacrifice, he had found no impiety in them. 4. And he reported this also, that the Christians arose early in the morning and sang hymns to Christ as a God, and for the purpose of preserving their discipline forbade murder, adultery, avarice, robbery, and the like. In reply to this Trajan wrote that the race of Christians should not be sought after, but when found should be punished." Such were the events that took place at that time.

---

17 Ibid., 3.33.

Further Reading

Behr, John. *The Way to Nicaea*. Vol. 1 of *The Formation of Christian Theology*. St. Vladimirs Seminary Press, 2001.
Berding, Kenneth. *The Apostolic Fathers: A Narrative Introduction*. Wipf & Stock, 2017.
Bird, Michael F. and Scott D. Harrow, eds. *The Cambridge Companion to the Apostolic Fathers*. Cambridge University Press, 2021.
Brannan, Rick. *The Apostolic Fathers: A New Translation*. Lexham, 2018.
Brent, Allen. *Ignatius of Antioch: A Martyr Bishop and the Origin of Episcopacy*. T&T Clark, 2007.
Burkett, Delbert. *An Introduction to the New Testament and the Origins of Christianity*. Cambridge University Press, 2002.
Chadwick, Henry. *The Church in Ancient Society: From Galilee to Gregory the Great*. Oxford University Press, 2003.
Ehrman, Bart D. *The Apostolic Fathers*. 2 vols. Loeb Classical Library. Harvard University Press, 2003.
Falls, Thomas B. *St. Justin Martyr: The First Apology, The Second Apology, Dialogue with Trypho, Exhortation to the Greeks, Discourse to the Greeks, The Monarchy of the Rule of God*. Fathers of the Church. Catholic University of America Press, 1948.
Foster, Paul, ed. *The Writings of the Apostolic Fathers*. T&T Clark, 2007.
Grant, Robert M. *An Introduction*. Vol. 1 of *The Apostolic Fathers: A New Translation and Commentary*. Thomas Nelson & Sons, 1964.
Grant, Robert M. *Greek Apologists of the Second Century*. Westminster Press, 1988.
Grundeken, Mark. *Community Building in the Shepherd of Hermas: A Critical Study of Some Key Aspects*. Brill, 2015.
Harris, J. Rendel and J. Armitage Robinson. *The Apology of Aristides on behalf of the Christians*. Cambridge University Press, 1893.
Hartog, Paul. *Polycarp's Epistle to the Philippians and the Martyrdom of Polycarp: Introduction, Text, and Commentary*. Oxford University Press, 2013.
Holmes, Michael W. *The Apostolic Fathers: Greek Texts and English Translations*. 3rd ed. Baker Academic, 2007.

Hunt, Emily J. *Christianity in the Second Century: The Case of Tatian.* Routledge, 2003.
Jefford, Clayton N. *Reading the Apostolic Fathers: A Student's Introduction.* 2nd ed. Baker Academic, 2012.
Jefford, Clayton N. *The Epistle to Diognetus (with the Fragment of Quadratus): Introduction, Text, and Commentary.* Oxford University Press, 2013.
Lookadoo, Jonathon. *The Shepherd of Hermas: A Literary, Historical, and Theological Handbook.* T&T Clark, 2021.
MacDonald, Dennis R. *Two Shipwrecked Gospels: The Logoi of Jesus and Papias's Exposition of Logia about the Lord.* Society of Biblical Literature, 2012.
Milavec, Aaron. *The Didache: Text, Translation, Analysis, and Commentary.* Liturgical Press, 2003.
Minns, Denis and Paul Parvis. *Justin, Philosopher and Martyr: Apologies.* Oxford University Press, 2009.
Mitchell, Margaret M. and Frances M. Young, eds. *Origins to Constantine.* Vol. 1 of *The Cambridge History of Christianity.* Cambridge University Press, 2006.
Parsons, Stuart E. *Ancient Apologetic Exegesis: Introducing and Recovering Theophilus's World.* James Clark & Co, 2015.
Pettersen, Alvyn. *The Second-Century Apologists.* Cascade, 2020.
Rankin, David. *Athenagoras: Philosopher and Theologian.* Ashgate, 2009.
Rizzi, Marco, ed. *Hadrian and the Christians.* Walter de Gruyter, 2010.
Rogers, Rick. *Theophilus of Antioch: The Life and Thought of a Second-Century Bishop.* Lexington, 2000.
Still, Todd D. and David E. Wilhite, eds. *The Apostolic Fathers and Paul.* T&T Clark, 2017.
Tuckett, Christopher. *2 Clement: Introduction, Text, and Commentary.* Oxford University Press, 2012.
Vall, Gregory. *Learning Christ: Ignatius of Antioch & the Mystery of Redemption.* Catholic University of America Press, 2013.
Varner, William. *Second Clement: An Introductory Commentary.* Apostolic Fathers Commentary Series. Cascade, 2020.
Whittaker, Molly. *Tatian: Oratio ad Graecos and Fragments.* Oxford University Press, 1982.
Wilhite, Shawn J. *The Didache: A Commentary.* Apostolic Fathers Commentary Series. Cascade, 2019.

Select Critical Editions

Audet, J.P. *La Didachè. Instructions des Apôtres.* Lecoffre, 1958.
Bardy, G. *Eusèbe de Césarée. Histoire ecclésiastique.* 3 vols. Sources chrétiennes 31, 41, 55. Cerf, 1952–1958.
Bihlmeyer, K. and W. Schneemelcher. *Die apostolischen Väter.* 3rd ed. Mohr, 1970.
Camelot, P.T. *Ignace d'Antioche. Polycarpe de Smyrne. Lettres. Martyre de Polycarpe.* 4th ed. Sources chrétiennes 10. Cerf, 1969.
Goodspeed, E.J. *Die ältesten Apologeten.* Vandenhoeck & Ruprecht, 1915.

Further Reading

Grant, R.M. *Theophilus of Antioch. Ad Autolycum.* Clarendon Press, 1970.
Jaubert, A. *Clément de Rome. Épître aux Corinthiens.* Sources chrétiennes 167. Cerf, 1971.
Kraft, R.A. *Épître de Barnabé.* Sources chrétiennes 172. Cerf, 1971.
Marrou, H. *A Diognète.* 2nd ed. Sources chrétiennes 33. Cerf, 1965.
Musurillo, H. *The Acts of the Christian Martyrs.* Clarendon Press, 1972.
Schoedel, W.R. *Athenagoras. Legatio and De resurrection.* Clarendon Press, 1972.
Whittaker, M. *Die apostolischen Väter I. Der Hirt des Hermas.* 2nd ed. Die griechischen christlichen Schriftsteller 48. Akademie–Verlag, 1967.

Translations Used in this Volume

The lists below show the translations that were used for this volume's selected readings. Texts available in the public domain were revised, with archaic words and grammar updated to reflect contemporary usage. Critical editions and newer translations were also consulted in the revision process where possible. The translation of the Didache is a new translation by Todd A. Scacewater; the translation of the Fragment of Quadratus is a new translation by Kevin Douglas Hill.

1 Clement: Lake
2 Clement: Lake
The Letters of Ignatius: Lake
The Letter of Polycarp to the Philippians: Lake
The Martyrdom of Polycarp: Roberts and Donaldson (ANF 1)
Didache: Scacewater
The Epistle of Barnabas: Roberts and Donaldson (ANF 1)
The Shepherd of Hermas: Lake
The Epistle to Diognetus: Roberts and Donaldson (ANF 1)
The Apology of Quadratus: Hill
The Fragments of Papias: Schaff
The Apology of Aristides: Menzies
The Works of Justin Martyr: Roberts and Donaldson (ANF 1)
Tatian the Syrian, *Address to the Greeks:* Roberts and Donaldson (ANF 2)
Athenagoras of Athens, *Embassy for the Christians:* Roberts and Donaldson (ANF 2)
Theophilus of Antioch, *Apology to Autolycus*: Roberts and Donaldson (ANF 2)
Cato the Elder, *On Farming:* Beard, North, and Price
Cicero, *On the Laws:* Zetzel
Diodorus Siculus, *Library of History:* Burkett
Ovid, *Metamorphoses:* More

Valleius Paterculus, *Roman History:* Shipley
Tacitus, *Annals:* Burkett
Suetonius, *Twelve Caesars:* Rolfe
Pliny the Younger, *Letters:* Melmoth
Eusebius, *Ecclesiastical History:* Schaff
Josephus, *Jewish War:* Whiston

Beard, Mary, John North, and Simon Price. *A Sourcebook.* Vol. 2 of *Religions of Rome.* Cambridge University Press, 1998.

Burkett, Delbert. *An Introduction to the New Testament and the Origins of Christianity.* Cambridge University Press, 2002.

Lake, Kirsopp. *The Apostolic Fathers.* 2 vols. Loeb Classical Library 24, 25. Harvard University Press, 1912–1913.

Melmoth, William. *Pliny Letters in Two Volumes, Volume II.* Macmillan, 1915.

Menzies, Allan. *Recently Discovered Additions to Early Christian Literature.* Vol. 9 of *The Ante-Nicene Fathers.* 1899. Repr., Hendrickson, 1994.

More, Brookes. *Ovid's Metamorphoses.* Cornhill, 1922.

Roberts, Alexander and James Donaldson, eds. *The Apostolic Fathers with Justin Martyr and Irenaeus.* Vol. 1 of *The Ante-Nicene Fathers.* 1885. Repr., Hendrickson, 1994.

Roberts, Alexander and James Donaldson, eds. *Fathers of the Second Century: Hermas, Tatian, Athenagoras, Theophilus, and Clement of Alexandria.* Vol. 2 of *The Ante-Nicene Fathers.* 1885. Repr., Hendrickson, 1994.

Rolfe, J. C. *Suetonius: Lives of the Caesars, Volume II.* Loeb Classical Library 38. Harvard University Press, 1914.

Schaff, Philip, ed. Eusebius: Church History, the Life of Constantine the Great, and Oration in Praise of Constantine. Vol. 1 of *A Select Library of Nicene and Post-Nicene Fathers of the Christian Church*, Series 2. 1890. Repr., Hendrickson, 1994.

Shipley, Frederick W. *Velleius Paterculus: Compendium of Roman History.* Loeb Classical Library 152. Harvard University Press, 1924.

Whiston, William. *The Works of Josephus.* 1895. Repr., Hendrickson 1990.

Zetzel, James E. G. *Cicero: On the Commonwealth and On the Laws.* Cambridge University Press, 1999

Scripture Index

Genesis
1:26	117
1:26	118
1:26	245
1:27	65
1:28	42,
1:28	118
1:28	245
2:4–5	303
2:6–7	303
2:8	305
2:9	169
2:15	305
2:23	30
3:1	270
3:9	305
3:22	245
4:3–8	29
7:16	259
9:24–27	263
11:5	259
12:1–3	32
13:14–16	32
14:14	121
15:5–6	32
15:6	122
17:5	122
18:2	258
18:13	258
18:16	258
18:17	258
18:22	259
18:27	35
19:24	259
25:21–23	122
26:4	42
32:24	258
32:30	258
48:9	122
48:11	122
48:14	122
48:18	122
49:10	201
49:10	202
49:10	209

Exodus
2:14	29
3:5	213
3:6	213
3:6	214
3:11	35
4:10	35
6:2	258
6:29	259
24:18	122
31:18	115
31:18	122
32:7	115
32:7–9	122
32:19	122
32:32	52

33:1	118
33:3	118
34:28	115

Leviticus

16:8	120

Numbers

11:23	258
12:7	35
12:7	47
15:38	242
16:33	51
17	47

Deuteronomy

6:6	242
9:12	52
9:13–14	52
10:6	121
27:26	252
31:2	258
32:8–9	41
32:15	28
32:16–23	254
32:20	255

Joshua

5:13–6:2, 246	

1 Samuel

13:14	36

1 Kings

19:18	242

Job

1:1	35
4:16–5:5	45
5:17–26	53
11:2–3 LXX	41
14:4–5 LXX	35
19:26	40
38:11	37

Psalms

2:7	250
2:7–8	44
3:5	40
3:5	206
8:3	253
8:5	272
12:3–6	34
18:25–26	49
18:44	120
19:1–3	40
19:5	209
22:6–8	35
22:7	206
22:16	117
22:16	118
22:16	204
22:18	118
22:18	206
22:20	117
22:22	119
24:1	52
24:7	259
31:18	34
32:1–2	51
32:2	264
32:10	38
33:6	297
34:11–19	38
34:12	120
37:9	34
37:35–37	34
37:38	34
42:2	119
49:14	51
50:14–15	51
50:16–23	44
51:1–17	36
51:17	51
51:19	115
62:4	34
69:30–32	51
78:36–37	34
82	257
90:4	248
110:1	44

Scripture Index

110:1	259
118:19–20	50
118:22	118
118:24	118
119:20	117
135:7	297
139:7–8	40
141:5	53

Proverbs

1:17	117
1:23–33	54
2:21–22	34
3:12	53
3:34	41
3:34	71
7:3	28
8:21–36	245
8:22	280
8:27 LXX	299
20:27	37

Isaiah

1:2	121
1:3	205
1:3	213
1:3	214
1:9	208
1:10	121
1:11–14 LXX	114
1:14	205
1:16–20	31
1:16–20	212
1:23	249
2:3	206
2:5	262
3:5	28
3:5	29
3:9–10	118
5:21 LXX	116
6:3	43
7:14	202
9:6	204
11:1	202
11:1–3	249
13:22 LXX	39
14:1	255
19:24	256
22:13	282
26:20	50
28:16	118
29:13	34
29:13	60
29:14	255
33:13	120
40:3	121
40:10	43
40:12	123
41:4	279
41:8	31
42:1–4	256
42:1–4	261
42:6–7	123
42:19	255
43:10–11	279
43:15	261
44:6	279
49:6–7	123
49:17	124
50:6	205
50:6–7	117
50:6–7 LXX	117
50:7	118
51:4–5 LXX	238
51:8	117
52:5	65
52:5	78
53:1	253
53:1–12	35
53:5	7
53:5	116
53:7	253
54:1	60
54:1	208
54:9	262
55:3–5 LXX	238
58:2	204
58:6	205
58:6	240
58:9	66
60:17 LXX	47
61:1–2	123

62:12	254	Micah	
65:1	254	5:2	203
65:2	204		
65:2	205	Zechariah	
65:2	253	2:11	254
65:9–12	262	8:17 LXX	114
65:17–25	248	9:9	204
66:1	123	13:7	117
66:1	205	14:5	112
66:1	279		
66:2	33	Malachi	
66:18	67	1:10–12	240
66:24	62		
66:24	67	Matthew	
		1:21	203
Jeremiah		5:7	33
2:13	253	5:39	290
4:3–4	121	5:44–45	281
4:4	120	5:46	282
7:2–3	120	6:9–13	109
7:22–23 LXX	114	6:14–15	33
9:23–24	33	6:24	61
9:26	121	7:1–2	33
9:26	208	7:1–2	90
31:27	256	7:21	61
31:31–32	238	10:16	61
		10:28	61
Lamentations		10:28	196
4:20 LXX	210	10:32	60
		11:27	213
Ezekiel		11:27	214
3:17–19	248	12:50	63
11:19	119	16:24	62
14:14	62	19:9	290
14:20	241	19:26	196
33	31	21:13	65
33:11	31	22:14	116
33:11–20	244	22:17–21	195
36:12	256	22:37	250
37:12	50	26:24	49
		26:41	92
Daniel		27:39	206
7:7–8	115		
7:10	43		
7:24	115		

Scripture Index

Mark
- 1:7 — 250
- 2:17 — 60
- 2:17 — 117

Luke
- 1:32 — 203
- 6:20 — 90
- 6:32 — 65
- 6:35 — 65
- 10:16 — 213
- 12:4–5 — 61
- 12:48 — 195
- 16:10–12 — 63
- 17:2 — 49
- 20:35–36 — 248
- 22:19 — 215

John
- 1:1 — 303
- 1:1 — 304
- 1:3 — 304
- 1:5 — 270
- 3:5 — 212
- 4:24 — 267
- 20:27 — 83

Acts
- 1:23 — 174
- 20:35 — 28
- 21:14 — 98

Romans
- 1:3 — 75
- 1:20 — 268
- 1:32 — 43
- 4:3 — 32
- 4:11 — 122
- 4:17 — 122
- 15:19 — 315

1 Corinthians
- 1:20 — 75
- 2:9 — 43
- 2:9 — 64
- 2:9 — 96

- 3:1–2 — 78
- 8:1 — 169
- 8:1–13 — 10
- 10:19–22 — 10

Galatians
- 3:13 — 252

Ephesians
- 4:26 — 94
- 5:25 — 86

1 Timothy
- 6:20 — 321

Titus
- 3:1 — 28

Hebrews
- 1:5 — 44
- 1:7 — 44
- 1:13 — 44
- 1:14 — 280
- 11:37 — 35
- 12:6 — 53

James
- 1:21 — 226
- 2:23 — 31

2 Peter
- 3:8 — 248

Revelation
- 20:4–5 — 248
- 22:12 — 43

1 Enoch
- 89:56 — 124

Wisdom
- 2:24 — 29
- 12:12 — 40

www.ingramcontent.com/pod-product-compliance
Lightning Source LLC
Chambersburg PA
CBHW050311120526
44592CB00014B/1861